Fidelity with Plausibility

Fidelity with Plausibility

Modest Christologies in the Twentieth Century

Wesley J. Wildman

with a Foreword by

John B. Cobb, Jr.

State University of New York Press

Published by
State University of New York Press

© 1998 State University of New York

For information, address the State University of New York Press,
State University Plaza, Albany, NY 12246

Marketing by Fran Keneston
Production by Bernadine Dawes

Library of Congress Cataloging-in-Publication Data

Wildman, Wesley J., 1961–
    Fidelity with plausibility : modest christologies in the twentieth
century / Wesley J. Wildman : with a foreword by John B. Cobb, Jr.
        p.   cm.
    Includes bibliographical references and index.
    ISBN 0-7914-3595-4 (hc : alk. paper). — ISBN 0-7914-3596-2 (pbk.
    alk. paper)
    1. Jesus Christ—History of doctrines—20th century.   I. Title.
BT198.W464   1998
232'.09'04—dc21   97-43545

1 2 3 4 5 6 7 8 9 10

In honor of

Elizabeth Phoebe

Angelina Matilda

Penelope Persephone

Martha May

A woman of extraordinary grace and courage

Contents

viii

Contents

Supernaturalism and the History of Religions / 82
The Development of Doctrine and the History of Religions / 90

Chapter 3. Christology and the Sciences / 103
The Philosophical Sciences / 104
The Natural Sciences / 117
The Human Sciences / 121
Conclusion / 139

―――――――――――――――――― PART II ――――――――――――――――――
Modest Christology and the Resolution of the Crisis of Plausibility
in Contemporary Christology / 141

Introduction to Part II / 143

Chapter 4. The Absolutist Principle and Modest Christologies / 147
The Origin and Structure of the Absolutist Principle / 148
Absolutist Christology / 158
Modest Christology / 171

Chapter 5. Incarnational and Inspirational Modest Christologies:
Two Case Studies / 191
John Hick: The Logic of Modest Inspirational Christologies / 193
The First Step: The Myth of God Incarnate / 195
The Second Step: Jesus as Inspired / 200
The Third Step: Jesus' Inspiration as Divine Love Incarnate / 211
John Cobb: The Logic of Modest Incarnational Christologies / 217
The First Step: Christ as Principle of Creative Transformation / 221
The Second Step: Identification of Jesus as Christ / 224
The Third Step: Affirming Christian Uniqueness / 231

Chapter 6. Modest Christological Solutions to Internal Challenges / 238
History: Christological Dependence on Knowledge of Jesus / 240
Tradition: Reassessing Christological Development / 260
Metaphysics: The Universal and the Particular / 276
Assessment of These Three Perspectives / 281

Foreword

Reflection about Christ has been central to Christian thinking since the earliest days. This has been equally true in the twentieth century. During this century this reflection has gone through a double shift. First, under the leadership of Karl Barth, a generation of great theologians rejected the historical approach that had been worked out during the nineteenth and early twentieth centuries, reaffirming the Christ of the creeds or of the kerygma. Then, with the decline of neo-orthodoxy, the pendulum swung back to history. In this new situation there is a profusion of Christologies and general confusion in the churches.

This confusion is one reason for the decline of our old-line churches. Many thoughtful believers are clear that they do not want to continue to make assertions about Jesus Christ that are anti-Jewish or sexist, for example, or simply absurdly exaggerated. Many want to avoid, in general, language that appears to belittle the faith of people in other religious communities. Many are attracted by particular images of Christ proposed by feminist and liberationist writers. But this relative clarity about what is to be avoided and attraction to particular images are not accompanied by any coherent understanding of what can or should be affirmed overall about Christ. The resulting vagueness renders the message of the old-line churches uncertain and, therefore, ineffective.

Wesley Wildman undertakes to bring order and clarity to the present situation. He rightly takes Ernst Troeltsch as having posed the basic issues for the twentieth century. It was Troeltsch who showed decisively that historical study could not support the claims to absoluteness or finality for Jesus or for Christian faith. This was recognized more clearly by Barth than by some of those who have continued or renewed the historical approach.

Given the profusion of Christologies, diverse categorizations are possible. Wildman argues persuasively that one distinction is primary. The most fundamental distinction is that between those who assign to Christ an absolute role and those who do not. The absolutist Christologies hold that what happened in Jesus Christ is decisive for the salvation of *all* human beings. In most cases absolutist Christologies go beyond this to depict the Christ event as one of cosmic importance in the relation of God and creatures.

Wildman calls non-absolutist Christologies "modest." They deny that all salvific meaning and power are espressed or embodied in any one historical figure. There is genuinely salvific power in other traditions independent of what happened in Israel and in the Christ event. This does not, of course, deny that Jesus Christ is of great importance in the history of salvation. Some "modest" Christologies argue somewhat immodestly that he is of the greatest importance. It does not mean that Jesus is a "mere" human being. He may be viewed as divine. It means only that those who find salvation in him should be open to recognizing the independent salvific power actually operative in other traditions. What is claimed for Jesus must be correlated with our actual historical knowledge.

Wildman spends much of his time showing the diversity among absolutist Christologies and the diversity among modest ones. Here, too, he offers useful classifications. But the argument throughout is for the primacy of the distinction between absolutist and modest Christologies, even when this distinction separates Christologies that in other ways appear quite similar. In principle, so much hinges on whether the absolutist claim is made, that even when these consequences are not drawn out in particular cases, they remain present.

Wildman does not claim that absolutist doctrines can be demonstrated to be in error. But he does believe that they can be shown to be incongruous with much that we have come to know about human history
and the cosmos. Whereas in the past their positive value may have out-
weighed the problems they caused, today these problems outweigh any
advantages that may be claimed for them. Wildman's appeal is that theologians once-and-for-all repudiate absolutistic claims so that they can work
out the meaning of Jesus Christ in human history and for believers without the baggage that so often renders Christological assertions incredible
and damaging.

An important and surprising claim is that modest Christologies are
more faithful to the actual history of Christological development than are
absolutist ones. Current historical scholarship shows that the earliest
Christologies are not absolutist and explains the trend toward absolutism
in ways that do not support its continuation. Now that our knowledge of
the world renders absolutist claims incredible to most thoughtful people,
it is those theologians who reject them who have the greatest claims to
continuity with the classical tradition.

This book does not work out a Christology. It is, instead, intended as
a prolegomenon to any future Christology. Still, it goes beyond simply arguing that such Christologies should explicitly and unqualifiedly reject absolutism. It also discusses in considerable detail the options that are open
to modest Christologies. In particular it distinguishes between inspiration
Christologies and incarnational Christologies and discusses their strengths
and weaknesses.

A critical problem faced by modest Christologies is what they are to
say about the historical Jesus. Wildman does not believe that the efforts to
avoid all dependence on historical knowledge are successful. On the
other hand, he is acutely sensitive to the failure of our sources to provide
us with dependable historical information and the constantly changing results of scholarship. He finds that most of those writers who have based
Christologies on their reconstruction of distinctive characteristics of the
historical Jesus have claimed too much for their knowledge. Even so, he
sees promise in building on the current state of New Testament research
about Jesus.

Few have surveyed the extant Christological literature so broadly or analyzed it so carefully. Few have described what is needed and what is possible so astutely. Anyone tackling the topic of Christology in the future will do well to take account of the problems and possibilities as Wildman has presented them. We will also look forward to seeing how he himself builds constructively on this initial, critical foundation.

John B. Cobb, Jr.

Preface

Convictions are wonderful and dangerous things. They drive the most noble human achievements, and many of the horrific ones, too. We should celebrate the orientation to life and the steadiness of character produced by convictions. And we should be wary of allowing our convictions to remain unexamined. Such celebration and wariness coexist in the intellectual life, constraining each other. From this symbiosis emerges a fascination with forms of inquiry that are capable of expressing, justifying, correcting, and producing convictions. The imperative to inquire so as to improve and correct convictions does not oblige everyone, but it presents many challenges for those in thrall to it. Not least among these is the fact that inquiry, too, is guided by convictions, and exposing them to the possibility of correction and improvement is even more difficult than doing the same for first-order convictions.

The intricate geography of convictions impresses me greatly. Some seem determined by the cultural or family conditioning of early years, others picked up along the way. Some last for a lifetime, rocklike, while others pass easily into their successors—and these transformations usually depend more on personality and circumstance than on the passion with which convictions are held. These are further reasons to celebrate and be wary, but they are also considerations appropriate to the preface of a book devoted to the task of rationally weighing Christological convictions, to the extent that this is possible: I, too, have my convictions, and they influence what I write here.

One of them is about inquiry. I take it be an opportunistic, even promiscuous, process of attempting to justify, improve, and produce convictions, thought of as fallible hypotheses even when they are of the greatest importance to an individual or society. It is often seat-of-the-pants problem solving. When the goal is to detect the *true*, then correspondence, coherence, pragmatic, and aesthetic criteria all have roles to play. Even deferring to functionally normative traditions has a place in truth seeking of this uncensored sort. And nothing is finally so sacred that it may not, ought not, be questioned; it is our interest in questioning, not our obligation to inquire, that abates in the presence of sacred mystery.

With regard to theology, I interpret its obviously intensive diversity to be necessary in order adequately to apprehend, express, and inquire into that about which theology attempts to speak. Within the range of theological expression, there needs to be some confessional proclamation, some poetic exploration, some evangelical declaration, some community-supporting reflection, some prophetic condemnation, some social analysis, some meditative repose. But there must be truth seeking, too, at least somewhere in the gamut of theological activity, and some truth-seeking inquiry needs to be as systematic as human rationality permits. This is not just for the sake of curiosity; it is also in order to guard against the all too familiar dangers of ideological bias, illusionistic distortion, misplaced concreteness, and excessive reductionism (or, in more theological terms, fanaticism, foolishness, idolatry, and desacralization). Can theology achieve this? To some extent, of course it can. But I see no way to determine how well this can be done in advance of trying, and I want to test the limits of theology's capacities in this regard.

These guiding convictions about inquiry and theology greatly affect the approach taken in this study of twentieth-century Christology. I try hard to attend (though not explicitly in this book) to alternative viewpoints on inquiry and theology, especially when they seem contradictory to my own, so that my convictions do not hover like a curse over the argument of this book. But so far I see no compelling reason to abandon them. In any event, it is as well to identify them at the outset.

There are other convictions at work, too, some of which I will not have noticed, or will not speak of here. I will mention just one of special importance, as it influences the key criterion used to argue that an authentically classical Christology in our time is a modest one. It ought to be introduced biographically, if only to emphasize that provenance of convictions is not the all-determining motivation for holding them, but merely impetus for justifying and improving them.

Some time around Christmas of 1986 I was listening from the back pew to a colleague of mine preach at the Protestant church we both served in Sydney, Australia. My friend was preaching on the incarnation, and his goal was to impress his congregation with the cosmic immensity of this wondrous event. With great rhetorical skill, he gave a profoundly moving account of the magnificence of the cosmos. He spoke of its size in terms of the yielding in leaping orders of magnitude of planets to solar systems to galaxies to clusters of galaxies to the more than one hundred billion galaxies in the visible universe. He spoke of its fifteen-billion-year history since the Big Bang and likened the whole of recorded human history to the tiny last portion of the last page of a large book whose whole extent was the record of cosmic development. He spoke brilliantly, I thought, and then continued with deliberate audacity to say something to the effect that, "And yet, it is here, on this planet, in our history, that the great Creator of this cosmos sent His only-begotten Son to be the unique God-man, to live among us, to reconcile the universe to Himself."

It was at this point that I became viscerally aware of the symbolic character of my position in the last row of the church; my sense of alienation was pronounced, and I felt overwhelmed by the strangeness of the event—so common in Christian churches—unfolding before me. I was not concerned about my flock, who like most liberal Protestant folk were mostly unfazed by the theological ideas that passed through their pulpit. Nor was I worried for my preaching colleague, whose rhetorical flair I greatly admired and whose personal character was genuinely impressive. My alienation was not even self-concerned, for such Christological excess had long seemed to me implausible, without the metaphysical scheme it presupposes being thereby demonstrably impossible.

Rather, it was my evangelical and intellectual instincts that stumbled over my colleague's beautifully contextualized declaration. My overriding impression was of the fantastic impotence of such a message: it could neither *convince* nor even really *inspire*, at least not in the sense of breathing life into most souls. It could not evince a coordinated affirmative response from all of the human faculties because of its comic implausibility by contemporary cultural standards—notwithstanding the apparent result of physical cosmology that a universe of about the size of ours is needed for life as we know it to be possible at all, which is a mere detail incapable of easing the problem. This Christological point of view forces the hiding of intellectual reservations from spiritual assent and the separation of emotional needs for a cosmic *home* from the conviction that sweeping the details of the rest of the cosmos under the Christological rug does not serve to make a *cosmic* home. And yet, there is something to be said about Jesus Christ that is important, and it requires a tradition of testimony, a memorial community, to draw attention to it because it is apt to be lost in the cultural ruckus, with its tendencies to homogenize beautiful differences, to trivialize the spiritual, to neutralize religious offense.

The conviction drawn to my attention in this experience is a criterion for theological adequacy: the balancing of plausibility and fidelity in theological discourse. Plausibility is to be judged by what passes for consensus in as wide an interdisciplinary, cross-cultural domain of intellectual debate as possible. Fidelity is authorized by the necessity of traditions for organizing societies; for making ethical and political judgments; for producing beautiful art, music, and architecture; for preserving ancient wisdom; for checking cultural forces that casually assimilate so as to regulate the potency of religion; for fostering the kind of symbolic engagement with the mystery of life that cultivates souls; for engaging in sustained inquiry; and for orienting ourselves to our world.

This criterion for theological adequacy is widely held in contemporary theology. It is also strongly contested both by those who hold that the gospel can never be subjected to human judgments of plausibility, and by those who think that theology should be thoroughly rational in character. It is a *via media* resisting both extremes and often has been invoked in various formulations to resolve theological debates. This book attempts to apply this middle-of-the-road criterion systematically to the task of weighing the whole range of advantages and disadvantages of two competing classes of Christological visions in the twentieth century. It is important to do this systematically, and with care. After all, it is not so hard to say that my preacher-colleague's absolutist Christological formulation is implausible and unfaithful, nor to carry a few favorably disposed votes with a noisily offered judgment. By contrast, it is genuinely difficult to evaluate that absolutist Christological claim with patient argumentation that tries to comprehend the strengths and weaknesses of alternative formulations.

That difficulty is due, I hope, not to any failure of impartiality on my part, nor to an inability to interpret and apply the *plausibility and fidelity* criterion consistently, but to the fact that Christological reflection is profoundly entangled with many other spheres of human inquiry, both theological and nontheological. This makes the weighing of evidence difficult, but that is the task that needs to be completed in order to evaluate Christological absolutism and Christological modesty. This is also necessary for expressing a systematic argument (as against a colorful opinion or fragments of an argument) in favor of the result of that evaluation, namely, that Christological modesty meets the plausibility and fidelity test.

This brings me to the last conviction that I will mention here. It is the one formed in the process of writing this book, and justified by the argument it contains: Whereas Christological modesty meets the plausibility and fidelity criterion, absolutist Christologies violate it—both parts of it at once. These Christologies are the contemporary holdover of an absolutist hermeneutical distortion in Christology that attained normative status in most theological circles on the coattails of the classical Christology. It is not, however, an essential component of classical Christology itself; indeed, the opposite is the case: classical Christology must be free of absolutist hermeneutical distortions. Christological modesty in a variety of possible forms, therefore, should be affirmed in our time as the authentically classical Christological position. And the virtue of this conclusion? It allows many individually pressing, superficially independent problems in contemporary Christology to be solved or eased in plausible, faithful ways.

Acknowledgments

I am grateful to the people who have helped me along the way in the writing of this book. Claude Welch, Van Harvey, Durwood Foster, and Robert Russell supervised the doctoral research that produced a rapidly abandoned dissertation and was the initial phase of the work on this book. Claude and Bob in particular have been wonderful mentors, patient and supportive, finding many ways to help me. Many of my doctoral colleagues at the Graduate Theological Union, especially Kate McCarthy and Carmichael Peters, and many of my teachers, especially Huston Smith and John Searle, have helped equip me with the theological sensitivity (such as it is) and interdisciplinary awareness (again, such as it is) necessary for a wide-ranging book such as this one.

Robert Neville and Ray Hart at Boston University have been inspirations, and Bob's tangible support of my efforts as a teacher and writer have created the kind of collegial relationship that transforms a good job into a vocational joy. The Boston Theological Society has been for me a means of theological enrichment; Gordon Kaufman, Roger Johnson, and Mark Heim from that group have been especially helpful in this project. A number of friends and colleagues have read parts of the manuscript and made helpful comments: Mike Bone, Susan Only, and Mark Richardson.

xxii

Acknowledgment

I am grateful to my students, not least because they constantly teach their teacher, even when they are unaware of it. My warmest thanks are extended to John Cobb for writing the Foreword and to John Starkey for his superb proofing and comprehensive index. I am also pleased to acknowledge the expertise of the SUNY staff, especially my production editor, Bernadine Dawes.

Finally, there are the intangibles of a rich family and personal life; no author underestimates them, but no one knows how to acknowledge them properly, either. It has been my experience that theological thinking grows with the heart more than with the intellect, and these intangibles are the very stuff of the heart. Lots of groups and individuals come to mind when I think back over the period in which this book was written: the infamous ministers' group of Piedmont, California, especially Sam Lindamood and John Turpin; and friends in Berkeley, Piedmont, New York, and Boston, especially Ken Cheitlin and Gay Lane. I also think of the enormously strong ties to my family, undamaged by half a world of separation, especially Phil and Beth Wildman; and the growing family ties where I live with my beloved Suzanne and two enormously energetic little boys, Samuel and Benjamin.

Grateful acknowledgment for permission to reprint selections is given to the following: Augsburg Fortress, for selections from *Religion in History,* translated by James Luther Adams and Walter F. Bense, copyright © 1991 T & T Clark, Ltd. Augsburg Fortress, for selections from *The Christian Faith* by Ernst Troeltsch, translated by Garrett E. Paul, copyright © 1991. Gerald Duckworth & Co., Ltd., for selections from *Ernst Troeltsch: Writings on Theology and Religion,* edited and translated by Robert Morgan and Michael Pye, copyright © 1977.

Introduction

A Crisis in Contemporary Christology

Throughout the history of Christian theology, when theologians have made Christological statements, virtually all of them have confidently believed them true and thought their confidence justifiable. The kinds of warrants that theologians have relied on to justify their Christological confidence are many and varied, and at one time in the history of theology these various warrants were abundant and mutually supportive. The authority of church teaching, the testimony of Scripture, the witness of piety, the voice of moral insight, and rational understandings of nature, history, anthropology and God furnished the theologian with individually compelling reasons for confidence in traditional Christological assertions. Jointly, these reasons constituted an overwhelmingly persuasive mass of evidence, to the point that Christological debates were usually only about academic details of formulation and exposition; within the circle of theologians, Christology itself was beyond serious doubt.

The crisis in view here is the result of the failure of all of these lines of justification—not just some of them, but *all of them*. Each has come to seem dubious, at best, and irrelevant or demonstrably ineffective, at

1

worst. The resulting crisis has two stages: first, *plausibility declines*; and then *identity fragments* as many sections of what used to pass for the classical Christological consensus seek more plausible and faithful renderings of Jesus Christ and some even repudiate the classical tradition altogether as moribund and the source of the problem.

It is difficult to question the reality of the identity crisis, for there are constant reminders of it in the Christological literature of the modern period. The contention here is that the identity crisis, while influenced by many factors, is precipitated by the crisis of plausibility. The fragmentation of identity is the most recent chapter in an epic saga of failures of warrants, in conjunction with a tragicomedy about an uneasy shifting from limb to limb as theologians judged that one form of justification had collapsed and heavier reliance on some other support was necessary if classical Christological assertions were to be rationally supported—not proved, of course, but merely rendered plausible. Plausibility implies, at least, that there are rational grounds for distinguishing Christological beliefs from fantasy, irrationality, and projective wishing. The danger of the crisis of plausibility—apart from the fragmentation of identity that it provokes—is precisely the loss of such grounds, and so the inability to deflect charges that Christology is fantastic, irrational, or deluded.

The plausibility dimension of this crisis is most apparent where interdisciplinary sensitivities are strong. It is potentially less apparent in the presence of a thorough initiation into the symbolic world of Christianity and the practical working confidence in the Christian view of the world that such initiation brings. It follows that the long-term danger it presents to ecclesial stability and vitality will be recognized more clearly in some church settings than in others and that its relevance and even its reality will be assessed differently among such settings also. The same can be said of other complex challenges to the plausibility of Christian doctrinal loci, such as the understandings of God, church, nature, and history. However, practical confidence of this kind is not enough by itself to deflect concern about this crisis. It calls for sustained critique and *apologia*.

The dramatically increasing dubiousness of the individual warrants for Christology can be sketched here, though with no supporting arguments and no attempt to identify or refute objections. Note that none of the following points constitutes an argument against Christology, at least not without further ado. The crisis in question consists in the undermining of plausibility of warrants for Christology, rather than the collapse of Christology in the face of overwhelming negative arguments. A form of Christo-logical fideism is always an option, albeit an unappealing one to most theologians.

First, the authority of church teaching about Jesus Christ, while helping to form ecclesial identity and establishing a tradition of wisdom to guide Christological inquiry, weakened as a warrant for Christological assertions during the Renaissance and Enlightenment, with some theological traditions slower than others to embrace this. The enthusiasm of Enlightenment mocking of "appeals to authority" now seems premature because many kinds of truth seeking presuppose guiding traditions of wisdom in relation to which hypotheses are formulated and tested. Nevertheless, if traditional testimony justifies at all, it is because of other factors, and not "authority" as such.

Second, though historical criticism has enhanced the Bible's usefulness as a source for knowledge of the person Jesus, it has greatly reduced the Bible's value as a source of justification for Christological doctrine, for at least four reasons. (1) *Authority*: The Bible's authority as such has suffered the same fate as the church's teaching authority. (2) *History*: The use of historical results of any sort as warrant for Christological doctrine has become questionable, either for Karl Barth's reason that the details of Jesus' life are irrelevant to his role as Savior and Lord, or because it is held that Christological claims cannot be tested or supported by any amount of historical research. (3) *Sources*: The sources on which historical reconstructions of Jesus' life are based do not appear to be capable of producing more than a reasonable outline with high probability, leaving a large gap between what most Christology presupposes about the historical Jesus and what history can confirm. (4) *Results*: What Jesus research turns up stands in many cases rather uneasily with traditional Christological affirmations.

Third, traditional testimony deriving from eyewitnesses to the life and passion of Jesus, and mediated by the church (New Testament writings, conciliar decisions, credal affirmations, and church theologians), while offering significant testimony that Jesus was a fascinating and influential personality, has been recognized as a dubious source of support for detailed Christological affirmations. The history of religions and sociology, in particular, have furnished sophisticated explanations of the origins and development of the church's eventual Christological teachings that are quite neutral toward the truth or falsity of the Christological interpretation itself. If the origins of Christology can be convincingly explained without supposing its truth, then justification for Christological assertions will naturally be sought elsewhere than in appeals to traditional testimony.

Fourth, even when appeals to historical research and traditional testimony are confounded, the resurrection of Jesus sometimes still has been used as a source of justification for Christological claims. There are at least two problems with this, however. (1) The theological import of the resurrection is far from obvious, since nontraditional, including heretical and non-Christian, Christological positions have made evidential use of it. (2) The existence of compelling historical and psychological reconstructions of the post-resurrection appearances renders interpretations of the resurrection along traditional lines problematic. Secular historians regard traditional interpretations of the resurrection with suspicion because they are unconvincing, and not just because of a naturalistic bias.

Fifth, it has been common to treat Christian religious experience as a warrant for Christological claims, on the assumption that it is a self-identifying, self-confirming encounter of the Christian soul with the soul of Christ. That is, in the context of a community of believers, the experience contained within itself cognitive content sufficient to identify it as experience of Jesus Christ and conferred conviction about the identity and character of its object upon its subjects. It hardly needs to be pointed out how dubious this interpretation of religious experience is in the light of the study of religions and modern psychology.

Sixth, it has been common also to justify Christological claims by showing how they reasonably may be inferred from a powerful interpretation of nature, of human beings, of history, or of God. Just one example will suffice: anthropocentric understandings of cosmos, evolution, and history naturally suggest Christologies rooted in the implicit Christology of the Prologue to John's Gospel as a reasonable inference. But physical cosmology and evolutionary biology, while powerfully confirming the wonderful character of the human species, do not directly support such anthropocentric understandings, even allowing for the cosmic anthropic principle. For at least the last century, therefore, the Prologue's Christological vision has had to be established somehow differently. The question of whether this can be done at all has been obscured by persistent, unexplained reliance—sometimes explicit, sometimes implicit—on that previously ready-to-hand anthropocentrism.

Seventh, and finally, it has been possible to appeal to the cash value of belief in Christological affirmations as justification for them. This kind of "it works!" argument supposes that the best explanation for the undeniable social, ethical, and transformative efficacy of belief in Jesus Christ is the truth of the church's traditional Christological beliefs. This approach has become problematic for three reasons. (1) The study of religion has produced no shortage of similar examples of efficacy that make no reference, and have no apparent connection, to Jesus Christ. (2) Compelling psychological and sociological interpretations of human groups and the role of convictions within them appear to explain such efficacy without recourse to the assumption of the truth of Christological statements. (3) Sharp ethical critiques of Christianity have demonstrated with more or less success that social disasters from environmental degradation to oppression of women can be traced in part to the impact of Christological beliefs in cultures influenced by Christianity. The claim that believing in Jesus Christ "works" must be far more dialectical than it is in this form of justification of Christological assertions.

It will not do to have Christology standing alone, with fideistic wistfulness, emotional confidence, blind preference, or supposed inexplicable divine command being the only reasons to embrace it. Besides being intellectually objectionable, Christology so conceived would obscure the powerful message of and about Jesus Christ, which I take to be both genuine and needed in our time. In fact, Christology so conceived would represent an abandonment of the classical Christological tradition, which at its best has always been a means to express and preserve the message of the gospel. The crisis here described corresponds, therefore, to a challenge to justify Christology, in spite of the weakening of the plausibility of individual traditional warrants. That this can and must be done is one part of the argument of this book. That it has not been done with optimal effectiveness to date is another.

The Argument of this Book

When ought a problem be called a crisis? *Crisis* is a forbidding word, a word only appropriate for a cluster of problems with an impressive heritage, an intimidating visage, and a long-standing history of resisting solution—a word, in short, for a problem of epic proportions. The *historical* phase of the argument of this book identifies the origins of this crisis, shows how it developed and intensified, estimates its dimensions, and exhibits the reasons for its continued intractability.

That the origins, development, and reality of this crisis need to be emphasized at all may seem paradoxical, if the crisis is as pressing as I say. Indeed, upon reviewing the state of contemporary Christological reflection, the informed onlooker might be forgiven for thinking of it as a disorganized conglomerate of parochial interests that, as far as corporately indicating a general crisis in the foundations of Christology is concerned, cancel each other out. While the identity crisis is obvious, therefore, if there is a plausibility crisis, its manifestations are diverse, and those at work on one manifestation of the problem are in some cases unaware of or uninterested in the connections to other manifestations. Yet the most sinister problems are often the most pervasive and the hardest to identify. The crisis of plausibility must be reckoned with as a key factor in causing the fragmentation of contemporary work in Christology.

The historical interpretation winds throughout the book. Part I is devoted especially to the modern origins and intensification of the crisis, for the understanding of which Ernst Troeltsch is a key figure, though its tentacles extend back well before the time of Troeltsch. Chapter 4 relates this problem to the origins of Christology in the process of analyzing its conceptual structure. Chapters 6 and 7 aim primarily to relate the style of Christology advocated here to many dimensions of the crisis of plausibility, but they also extend the historical case by exhibiting the crisis in many disparate types of Christological reflection in the twentieth century.

Complementing the historical phase of the argument is a *constructive* phase, which also winds throughout the book. It involves describing and defending a "direction of solution" to the crisis of plausibility. The intransigence of the Christological crisis consists in the difficulty of generating a comprehensive solution for it. This lack is highlighted by the proliferation of mutually inconsistent, partially effective theological constructions that represent themselves as solutions to the various superficially unrelated manifestations of this crisis. The constructive phase of the argument presents many aspects of this crisis at once and draws together the various extant, partial solutions, with a view to identifying a core problem, articulating its conceptual structure, and justifying the effectiveness of the proposed line of solution.

The purported feasibility of solutions offered for most conceptual crises is usually dependent on a simplifying distortion of the problem. If the crisis is as the first phase of the argument describes it, it seems *prima facie* unlikely that a relatively simple solution would exist for it. The constructive phase of the argument demonstrates that this reasonable expectation does not hold in this case. In fact, the crisis of plausibility has a straightforward conceptual structure whose core is defined in part as the assertion that the symbol of Jesus Christ is absolutely, uniquely, exhaustively, unsurpassably significant for revelation and salvation. This core principle is called the "absolutist principle," as it necessitates a form of hermeneutical absolutism, distorting the reality to which the Christological symbols refer even while trying to express it. The absolutist principle is discussed indirectly throughout Part I, as it was a great concern in many theological debates in the nineteenth century. It is discussed in detail in chapter 4, and the consequences of its affirmation and repudiation are analyzed throughout Part II.

The existence of an identifiable core to the crisis of plausibility makes its resolution feasible. Since so many attempts have been made in vain to reestablish the plausibility of the various kinds of warrant for Christology, it only makes sense to inquire as to whether a single feature of the many hard-to-warrant Christologies can be held responsible to some degree for the implausibility of each line of justification, and then try to do Christology without that feature. The absolutist principle worsens the prospect for establishing warrants for Christological assertions in every case, as it turns out. Thus, a Christology unburdened by the absolutist principle, whatever other problems it must face, potentially would be able to increase the effectiveness of the various lines of Christological justification whose individual implausibility and collective weakness constitutes the crisis.

The Christological landscape is peppered with claims that Christology without the absolutist principle (under other descriptions) is the *most viable* Christological approach in the contemporary period, though for an enormously wide range of largely independent reasons. This claim to superiority derives partly from the fact that the problem of plausibility is minimized when the absolutist principle is rejected, infusing new life into drained Christological discussions and fostering creative development.

The claim to superiority also derives from the capacity of Christology without the absolutist principle to consolidate contemporary Christological identity around a critical reappropriation of the classical tradition. This is a possibility because the identity crisis in contemporary Christology can be interpreted in part as the result of a praiseworthy protest against a hijacking of the classical Christological tradition by an extremist hermeneutical perspective, which itself attained normative status within the classical tradition, even though it is essentially different from it. Such a reinterpretation of the classical tradition is an alternative to merely uncritically restating it or rejecting it as dangerous and corrupt. Most current Christological positions can reconsider plausibly the question of their identity as "part of the classical tradition" in such terms. The overthrowing of the absolutist principle that occurs when its role is seen to be fundamentally distorting rather than illumining shifts the center of gravity of the classical tradition slightly, so this is very much a reinterpretation rather than an impossible attempt to repristinate some supposedly golden classical era. But there are powerful arguments to the effect that this reinterpretation is as profoundly faithful to the classical tradition as the absolutist principle is distorting of it.

There is an obvious question begged in all this talk of superiority about whether a Christology abandoning the absolutist principle—such a Christology here is called "modest"—would be conceptually feasible. For instance, would it inherit more serious problems than it evaded? Or would it even be a Christology? Another task undertaken here is to commence the argument needed to show that modest Christologies are indeed viable both as solutions to the Christological crisis of plausibility and generally as Christologies. This argument naturally requires actual examples of interesting and viable modest Christologies, so a number of case studies and briefer expositions of modest Christologies have been included, accordingly.

The ideal way to complete this sort of argument is with a constructive Christology, but none is offered here. The assigned task is already a large one, to be sure, but there is another reason for this decision. Modest Christologies come in two varieties, which I take to have comparable plausibility. One is incarnational, but allows for multiple independent historical manifestations of universal principles. The other repudiates the idea of metaphysical incarnation, though perhaps retaining "incarnation" as a metaphor, and speaks of Jesus as an exceptionally inspired religious genius, a person, as Schleiermacher put it, with a powerful God-consciousness. To have advanced a constructive Christology in this work probably would have invited the conclusion that I regarded one of these types as fundamentally more satisfactory than the other. This would have endangered the more important point that there are two rather different kinds of modest Christology that are potentially superior to any Christology conforming itself to the absolutist principle.

A constructive Christological work is planned as a sequel to the present volume. It will elaborate a modest Christology conforming to the conditions for plausibility laid down in the argument of this book and attempt to overcome some of the weaknesses in extant modest Christologies.

Besides the two phases of the main argument just described, this book has two other objectives. First, an attempt is made here to reorient the contemporary Christological debate. There is no shortage of revisionist Christologies at the present time. Most of these Christological investigations and critiques feed into the larger problem of the absolutist principle with various degrees of intensity; this is true, I shall argue, of the concern for the efficacy of Christology in sponsoring healthful social praxis, of the attempt to free Christology of an alleged tendency to sponsor ethical absolutism, of the need to liberate Christological assertions from undue dependence upon historically undecidable information, of the desire to render Christology more consonant with the biblical pictures of Jesus and what must be supposed to have been the case about the development of Christological doctrine, of the demand to render Christology plausible in the light of scientific knowledge of nature and the cosmos, and so on. However, one of the most prominent areas of Christological revisionism focuses on the critique of the idea of metaphysical (as against metaphorical) incarnation. But the heated debates over the intelligibility of the idea of incarnation are not addressed here. In fact, if this work has anything to offer to those debates at all, it is the argument that the Christological fault line runs elsewhere than through the incarnation; the absolutist principle is the key issue, and incarnational Christologies with care can be elaborated without being encumbered by the absolutist principle. The debate over the intelligibility of the incarnation is no more than a clash of metaphysical tastes; most of what is ultimately germane to the deepest Christological questions in that debate can be connected directly to contention over the absolutist principle.

Second, there are rhetorical challenges associated with the argument that extend beyond those described earlier. One set of challenges is connected with avoiding misunderstanding of modest Christologies. So the argument is careful to show that modest Christologies are not necessarily "low" Christologies, that they may not follow a strict "anthropological" schema, that they do not necessarily deny incarnation or resurrection, Trinity, and so on. Another set of challenges involves making sure that the argument of this book is not carelessly identified with extant positions in current Christological debates, such as the critique of the idea of incarnation just mentioned, or the attempt to construct a totalizing theology of religions. Yet another cluster of rhetorical challenges bears on making sure the modest-absolutist distinction to be articulated here is not misconstrued: either as if it were an exhaustive classification (for there are mixed cases), or as if it were especially useful for analyzing individual Christologies (for very different Christologies are found together in the absolutist class, and in the modest class), or as if it were essentially similar to any extant Christological distinction (such as high-low, from above-from below, and so on). A final rhetorical task concerns trying to convince theologians to give sustained attention to modest Christologies. This is undertaken mainly indirectly by exhibiting the value of modest Christologies through the work as a whole. Many glancing remarks through the book have an eye to this rhetorical task, however, and a section of the Conclusion is devoted to arguing that room needs to be made on the current Christological agenda for careful, patient discussion of the virtues and problems of Christological modesty.

The Virtues of Classical Christologies

If the historical argument of this book revolves around the contention that there is a crisis of plausibility in contemporary Christology, the central constructive thesis is that modest Christologies are the ablest representatives of the classical Christological tradition in the contemporary period and for the foreseeable future. This is an audacious assertion, to be sure, but it is far from being one that outstrips the evidence supporting it. The classical Christological tradition is characterized, with some variation, by three great virtues: intellectual vigor, poise, and religious potency (corresponding to truth, beauty, and goodness, respectively). It is according to these criteria that Christology without the absolutist principle must be judged the abler representative of the classical Christological tradition. I will say a word about each of these criteria in closing these introductory remarks.

First, the classical Christological tradition has exhibited pronounced *intellectual vigor*. In practice, this has meant that exponents of the classical tradition have demonstrated the plausibility of Christology in the widest possible context of evaluation. This is the criterion employed in this book for intellectual vigor and the standard by which the comparative intellectual vigor of modest and absolutist Christologies must be judged.

A word needs to be said about the relation between plausibility and truth in this criterion. Only the most wooden adherence to an idea of propositional revelation—one that refuses to examine either its hermeneutical presuppositions or its historical conditions—can regard the truth question in Christology as decisively, permanently settled. For all other positions it is necessary to achieve a holistic coordination of many relevant criteria for truth, acknowledging that different patterns of emphasis among these criteria are adopted by various theological and ecclesial traditions. The judgments necessitated in this situation in all cases will involve questions of fidelity to the gospel and intellectual soundness. Plausibility is an important consideration in *both* because, without it, both evangelical proclamation so as to evoke assent to the good news of and about Jesus Christ and effective articulation and defense of the Christian faith are thwarted.

Clearly, however, canons of plausibility shift with time and context. Thus, the broadest possible historical and intellectual evaluation must be made in assessing plausibility. With even a small amount of historical realism, it is possible to envisage a situation in which plausibility structures mutate to create tension around a formerly unquestioned belief. The increased understanding brought by such historical shifts has proved important for the correction of Christian theology on many occasions in its history; in fact the examples are legion, including the apologists' sanction of Greek philosophy as a context for reflection on Christian faith; the widespread presence in the churches of competing visions of God and the world that prompted doctrinal clarification in church councils; the critical engagement of Neoplatonism by Augustine and of Aristotelian philosophy by Thomas; the dramatic reevaluations of deeply held convictions both in the Reformation and in the Counter-Reformation; the widespread abandonment of an infallibilist view of the Scriptures; the realization that theology may be distorted by the fact that it has been practiced mainly by men; the reconsideration of the status of other religions in and around the Second Vatican Council; and the reemphasis on the importance of relating theology to issues of ecological prudence and social justice. Some of the long-standing assumptions conditioning contemporary interpretations of Christian faith likewise will fall under scrutiny by future generations as new historical situations bring fresh insight. John Henry Cardinal Newman's classical question of whether there is some unchanging essence of Christianity beneath the evident adjustments does not need to be settled for the importance of the criterion of plausibility to be acknowledged.

Second, with regard to *poise*, the classical Christological tradition enjoins its theologians to balance the demand for fidelity to the gospel and the requirement for intellectual soundness in Christological reflection just discussed. On the one hand, without fidelity to the gospel, Christology tends to yield to the apparently universal cultural bias against the essential scandal of any Christology, namely, that God—speaking anthropomorphically and anthropocentrically for now—is concretely and personally concerned for human beings. This scandal of divine concern is deepened in Christology through being particularized in the person and work of Jesus Christ. Cultural wisdom—especially modern secularity—seems ever inclined to flatten out Christological discourse, in order perhaps to tame and confine the paradoxical, disturbing, commanding presence of God in the world. On the other hand, without intellectual soundness, Christology becomes an irrelevant pastime of obscurantist ghetto dwellers whose call to spread the good news is casually betrayed for the sake of self-comfort and the preservation of a dubious identity. In the isolated bliss that results, foolishness is mistaken readily for deep paradox and spiritual wisdom, at least for a while, and Christology helplessly testifies to spiritual timidity and intellectual cowardice.

Christology secures the balance for which the classical tradition calls by insisting both on a Christological critique of contemporary culture and on an intellectual breadth of vision that engages all questions with requisite seriousness. There can be neither capitulation to cultural fads and biases nor faint-hearted withdrawal from cultural insight associated with classical Christology. On the contrary, only through critical dialogue can the ideals of the classical Christological tradition be maintained and the powerful message of the Christian gospel clearly appreciated in each new context. Such poise is exemplified in the work of many theologians throughout the classical tradition, and the modest and absolutist Christologies of today must also be assessed in terms of this criterion.

Third, classical Christologies have always been well endowed with regard to *religious potency*. I am disposed on average to think of so-called "low Christologies"—if that phrase is taken to refer to those Christologies bluntly denying the presence of the divine in Jesus Christ—as religiously insipid, and ecclesially, ethically, spiritually almost useless (which is different from, though not irrelevant to, the judgment that they are false). But there are other ways to sacrifice religious potency in Christology, from settling for the idolatrous comfort of hermeneutical excess to shrinking from the challenge of confronting superficial cultural wisdom. The classical Christological tradition warns us away from these dangers and many others like them.

Regrettably, the means for assessing the religious potency of Christologies are not well developed. In particular, the intellectual resources for making definite connections between the conceptual content of specific doctrines and either the social functioning of ecclesial institutions or the spiritual lives of individual Christians do not exist in the convenient form necessary. Sociologists of religion have made great advances in providing analyses of the social organization and function of ecclesial bodies, and psychologists of religion have likewise taken impressive strides in their interpretation of the human person as a psycho-social-religious creature. Much more work could and must be done in both of these areas. But there is a notable lack of research on the connections between the conceptual details of doctrinal assertions, on the one hand, and social function and religious life, on the other. This is clearly complex terrain, for it involves having to take account of social and ritual practices, the psychological structure of the human person as far as religious beliefs are concerned, the nature of religious symbols, the functioning of the human imagination, and the nuances of theological concepts. Unfortunately, this is precisely the intellectual apparatus needed if the case about the comparative ecclesial and spiritual efficacy of modest and classical Christologies is to be assessed adequately.

It might objected that there has been a great deal of talk by theologians, sociologists, and experts in spirituality on these issues. This is true, but not relevant, for the whole problem has not yet been treated systematically. Taken as a whole, this kind of talk discloses a high level of informality; a failure to make explicit and to examine presuppositions; a lack of awareness of, or inability to specify, the social and psychological principles guiding the claims made; and a welter of conflicting conclusions. While many people have their opinions on these matters—indeed, I will not refrain from stating some of my own in due course—it appears that the conversation has not yet advanced to the stage that precise claims can be made and tested. There are hopeful signs that this territory soon may be more thoroughly explored.[1] But the relative strength of presence in modest and absolutist Christologies of this third mark of the classical Christological tradition will be hard to evaluate with much confidence, so the issue is treated only rarely and in the most general terms. This forces the argument to rely chiefly on the other two marks: intellectual vigor and poise.

Reflections on Ernst Troeltsch
and the Origins of the Crisis of Plausibility
in Contemporary Christology

Introduction to Part I

The aim of Part I is to sketch a crisis of plausibility in twentieth-century Christology through a series of reflections on Christological themes, using Ernst Troeltsch's thought as charcoal and canvas. While the origin of the problem under consideration involves many thinkers, themes, and events, most of its aspects converge with unprecedented intensity in the thought of Ernst Troeltsch. His assumptions about the Christological task expressed in a penetrating way the exquisitely problematic context for Christological reflection that the nineteenth-century had laboriously clarified and bequeathed to the twentieth. This, even more than limitations of competence, accounts for the nearly exclusive focus on European, particularly German, theology in Part I.

The argument of Part I implies that this Christological crisis of plausibility is forced upon the contemporary era by much more than just a few recent developments; over two hundred years of theological reflection have conspired systematically to sharpen the problem and to demand a resolution of it. Part I will also show how Troeltsch's Christological forays hint at an effective resolution of the crisis. The Christological approach advocated in this book emulates Troeltsch's rejection of absolutism, without necessarily imitating his anti-incarnational vision for Christology, his

17

commitment to a naturalistic historicist world view, or his narrowly constrained view of historical study. Part II inks in the details of this case.

As interesting as it would be, a detailed presentation of the Christology of Ernst Troeltsch in relation to the whole of his thought is not
needed here. Such an analysis has been produced recently by Sarah Coakley,[1] and so not even its intrinsic interest is a good reason to attempt
something like the same task in less space. In fact, the procedure to be
adopted submits the historical analysis at every point to the larger goal of
illuminating the crisis of plausibility in twentieth-century Christology. This
is partly because of space constraints and partly because of a choice about
focus. Several methodological consequences follow: the approach to
Troeltsch's thought at times will be directed by different questions than a
purely historical presentation would ask; other nineteenth-century figures—perhaps even unknown to Troeltsch—will be drawn into the picture when their thought helpfully illumines the themes of interest; and
speculative extrapolations of Troeltsch's incomplete Christological offerings will be explored to sharpen insight into the guiding problematic. I
have tried to be careful, however, not to allow these procedures to distort
the historical material.

Most of the conundrums Troeltsch and his contemporaries debated
at the beginning of the twentieth century already had complex histories in
the nineteenth century. These penetrating discussions constitute the intellectual background both to Troeltsch's theological and historical work
and to twentieth-century Christological reflection in general. Several of
these problems had a direct impact on the plausibility of Christology, and
they will be discussed in Part I.

The first of these problems is that of faith and the historical Jesus. It
has two aspects: the challenge of historical access to Jesus of Nazareth and
the question of the relation of faith and historical knowledge. Chapter 1
takes up the problem with special emphasis on the latter. This question of
the relation of faith and historical knowledge achieved sharp focus in
Troeltsch's thought, and the feasibility of his highly original solution crucially depends on his Christological approach.

The impact on Christology of the history of religions is examined in
chapter 2, along with the problem of faith and the development of doctrine. The controversial method of the so-called *religionsgeschichtliche
Schule* was a crucial novel influence on judgments about the plausibility
and fidelity of Christological doctrine at the beginning of the twentieth

century. Troeltsch arguably overreacts in some ways to this challenge, but his anti-absolutist style of Christology commends itself as part of any stable solution.

Chapter 3 explores other fronts of the crisis of Christological plausibility from three overlapping fields of view: the philosophical, natural, and social sciences. Human knowledge by the first two decades of the twentieth century included contributions as diverse as Feuerbach's agnostic projectionist and Freud's developing psychoanalytic readings of Christianity; the application of sociological modes of analysis to religion by Marx, Weber, and Durkheim; the grappling with historical relativism within the philosophy of history; and scientific developments, especially in physics, astronomy, geology, and biology. Troeltsch was at least generally familiar with the problematic, suggestive character of these insights. Each in its own way threw the fundamental problem of justifying Christological assertions into new relief, highlighting facets that tended to remain hidden when the Christological conversation stayed within the pool of the well-established historical and dogmatic spotlights.

Troeltsch's occasional writings, taken together with his somewhat more systematic *Glaubenslehre*, contain a constructive Christology, as fragmentary and inconsistent as it is suggestive. The arguments Troeltsch used to justify his Christology may be thought of, negatively, in three ways. They may be seen as (1) arguments against any kind of Christology, (2) arguments against any kind of Christology making hermeneutically absolute assertions about the significance of the symbol of Jesus Christ, or (3) arguments against any Christology except Troeltsch's nonincarnational variety. Troeltsch appears to have intended these arguments in the second and third senses, but there are two problems with this.

On the one hand, Troeltsch did not distinguish these last two readings of his arguments. He ought to have, however, because the arguments he considers are most effective in the second sense, as aimed against any kind of absolutist Christology, and not especially impressive if thought of in the third sense, as aimed against incarnational Christology. Troeltsch's failure to envision the possibility of an incarnational Christology with the same modest approach to the significance of the Christ symbol as his own nonincarnational offering requires us to be cautious whenever he wields Christological arguments against the incarnation.

On the other hand, Troeltsch's Christological arguments with some justification can be argued to apply in the first sense, as aimed against any kind of Christology. In fact, sometimes Troeltsch himself is argued to have abandoned Christology in the last decade of his life, even though he spent a great deal of energy prior to 1915 on Christological questions. It is essential to be alert, therefore, to the possibility that arguments against absolutist Christology may also function as arguments against all Christology. Though several remarks are made on this point in Part I and elsewhere, showing the possibility of a Christology is more properly the task of a constructive Christology. For the purposes of this work, the possibility of Christology—and theology, too, for that matter—must be assumed.

Troeltsch has little to offer by way of support for my contention that the classical Christological tradition is only circumstantially and not essentially wedded to the absolutist hermeneutical propensity characteristic of some of its interpreters. This shortcoming and his simplistic rejection of incarnation are rather bizarre features of his Christological efforts. However, flaws of this kind neither detract from his penetrating critique of Christological absolutism nor change the fact that he culminates a storm of protest over the habit of hermeneutical absolutism that rumbles through many parts of eighteenth- and nineteenth-century theology.

As a final introductory offering to Part I, a lengthy quote from one of the most important of the Christological fragments in Troeltsch's writings is in order. Troeltsch's positive Christology will be approached from a number of directions in the course of the next three chapters, but, as already explained, expounding it is of secondary interest for my purposes compared with outlining the main characteristics of the Christological problem of plausibility as the nineteenth century shaped it for the twentieth, using Troeltsch as the whetstone for this more general analysis. To give Troeltsch his due, therefore, and to provide the task at hand with a most fitting starting trajectory, it is prudent to allow him to provide a compact overview of his Christology in a translation of his own words:

> For as long as our culture which has in essence arisen around the Mediterranean lasts it is highly improbable that a new religion will emerge which will compare in versatility, profundity and grandeur. Our religious life has probably gained for all time its base and driving force from here. The modern substitutes for Christianity, and the religions of science are strong in criticism but extremely weak in constructive religious power. They often confuse religion with science, art or morality. But whether this culture itself will last forever and extend to the whole

world is a question which no one can answer. It is therefore impossible either to affirm or to deny that Christianity will last forever and community and cult remain bound to the historical personality of Jesus.

Anyone who considers the possibilities of several hundred thousand years of the future of man will be unwilling to say anything about the connection of the future to the present. But this does not devalue the present. What here is true and is life will be preserved or will recur. It will not be made untrue by anything yet to come. We can only maintain and develop the religious powers of the present, certain of doing what is required by the present and of standing within the stream of divine life. Whatever is true, great and profound in our faith today will be so two hundred years hence, even if perhaps in a quite different form. Since we possess these religious powers of the present only in association with the present and reverenced person of Christ, we gather around him unconcerned whether in a hundred years religion will still be nourished on Jesus or will have some other centre. Indefinite future possibilities do not reduce the value of what the present contains in experienced strength and truth. This haunting anxiety of a relativism that plays with big numbers must be driven from our heads. We have resolutely to grasp the divine as it presents itself to us in our time. In our time it presents itself in history and in the connexion of the individual's subjectivity with the substance of an overarching totality of historical life. This in turn receives its most important strength and certainty from the historical person of Jesus. *For us 'God in Christ' can only mean that in Jesus we reverence the highest revelation of God accessible to us and that we make the picture of Jesus the rallying point of all God's testimonies to himself found in our sphere of life.* And we had best abandon altogether reading this meaning into the Christological dogmas of Nicea and Chalcedon (however elastic they may be). There is no need to bring that page of thought into the foreground. There is nothing in it for preaching, devotion and catechism; academic training in theology can also place it in the background. But where the principle idea has to be made clear, one cannot keep silent about it. On the other side it would be good in practical work not to emphasise too much the eternal dependence of millions yet unborn upon the person of Jesus, and instead to bring alive in a practical way how one is oneself bound to him in the present. People who can be happy in their own faith only when they tie all the future millions of years to it know nothing of the real freedom and grandeur of faith.

That is decisive and must determine religious work in the present. It too has therefore an interest in the historical existence of Jesus. If it could not presuppose this, it would have to pioneer totally new paths at least in everything concerning community and cult. But that would mean total dissolution. Thus there is a great deal at stake in the whole question. Only rigorous historical science can in fact bring about a decision. But there is in fact no doubt that this discipline gives us a kernel of facts on which we can base our common interpretation and valuation of Jesus as the embodiment of faith. More than this we do not need if what is at stake is not the church's dogma about Christ but the redeeming truth of the Christian knowledge of God and the gathering of a congregation by which this truth can be carried on and rendered effective.[2]

1

Christology and the Historical Jesus

In 1911, Ernst Troeltsch published in brochure form a version of a lecture that he had delivered at Aarau to a conference for Swiss students. Entitled in translation "The Significance of the Historical Existence of Jesus for Faith," the topic of the discourse was the impact of historical criticism on Christian faith and doctrine.[1] Troeltsch began:

> Christian dogma, as construed by the early church, has finally disintegrated; there is no longer a unitary Christian culture; and historical criticism of the Bible is now a reality. One of the main questions for Christian religious thought today is therefore the effect of historical criticism upon faith in Christ. What can a picture of Jesus subject to and shaped by historical criticism mean for a faith that is by its very nature concerned with the eternal, timeless, unconditioned and supra-historical? When it first formed its religious ideas the primitive Christian community had already taken Jesus out of history and made him Logos and God, the eternal Christ appearing to us in historical form, one who is related in essence to the eternal Godhead and so not unnaturally the object of faith. But historical criticism, grown up in a world no longer dominated by the church, has returned him to history where all is finite and conditioned.

Is it still possible to speak of any inner, essential significance of Jesus for
faith?[2]

These remarks are noteworthy in part because, through allusions to historical criticism, historical relativism, the history of doctrine, the social dimension of Christian doctrine, and the secularization of Christianity's
Western context, Troeltsch indirectly conveys something of his sense of
the way systematic Christian thought should proceed. The remarks are
also colorful and no doubt would have won the immediate attention of
the Swiss students, if they were indeed a part of the original lecture.

There are hints of rhetorically opportunistic exaggeration, such as
when Troeltsch speaks of Christian dogma as having "finally disinte-
grated," or mourns the loss of a "unitary Christian culture," or characterizes the early church as having "taken Jesus out of history." Even with
these excesses, however, Troeltsch's comments accurately convey a sense
of how severe the problems posed by historical criticism for Christian
faith were thought to be at the beginning of the twentieth century. In fact,
in some ways, Troeltsch's point in this quotation is as germane now as it
was then, creating the impression that little advance has been made on
the problematic situation Troeltsch described. Of course, a great deal has
changed, including especially the declining status of the problem of faith
and history in relation to the entire matrix of Christological issues. But the
Christological implications of the tension between faith and history are
still important, and the fundamental terms of the debate have remained
almost unaltered from before Troeltsch's time until now.

The problem of Christian faith and the historical Jesus has two
branches. A basic statement of one branch, the problem of faith's dependence on history, is as follows. The partially self-authenticating and trusting character of Christian faith has *some* relationship with the results and
characteristically skeptical, critical approach of historical critical research,
so how is this relationship to be conceived? Should the assertions about
Jesus Christ made by an intellectually responsible Christian faith be
thought of as fully dependent upon historical research into the life and
person of Jesus for their establishment, as requiring historical research
merely for supplementary support to rule out egregious errors, or as formally independent of historical research? Such Christological assertions
surely do at least *presuppose* something about the historical Jesus, even if
they are not to be thought of as in need of *warranting* by historical re-

search. But the Christian, even in such implicit presupposing, takes a posture that seems to require engaging the results of historical research *on the terms of critical historiography* to precisely the extent that he or she desires to be intellectually responsible. But how can faith be made answerable to historical critical research?

The other branch, the problem of the historical Jesus, is structured by several issues that became problematic under the hand of biblical criticism. The most obvious of these surrounds whether or not the results of life-of-Jesus research are consonant with assertions of Christian faith about Jesus Christ. This issue is closely connected to two others. On the one hand, it has become dubious whether the sources for life-of-Jesus research—no matter what methods are brought to bear on them—are capable of leading to a reliable picture of Jesus' life and character, or even a secure picture with the basic detail needed to offer minimal support to Christological doctrine. On the other hand, the whole history of life-of-Jesus research has sharply raised the question of whether the classical Christology is irretrievably docetic, placing Jesus outside the realm of the truly human. Treating the first of these three issues requires an extensive excursus into the intricate details of Jesus research; the second calls for a survey of the fluctuating decline of confidence in the historical value of the gospel records through the eighteenth and nineteenth centuries; and the third demands an analysis of the argument that Jesus' humanity is essentially marginalized in the classical Christological tradition, a case prosecuted perhaps most famously by Albert Schweitzer in relation to the so-called "two natures" teaching of the Council of Chalcedon (451 CE).

None of the three issues defining the second branch of the problem of faith and history can be dealt with here without moving too far afield from the primary goal of a thematic analysis of the crisis of plausibility in contemporary Christology. Thus, the discussion that follows is confined to understanding the dependence of faith on history in its Christological dimensions, and especially Troeltsch's view of it. For this purpose, it is sufficient to be aware of the connections between the two branches of the problem of faith and history, to remember that the more theological branch—the problem of dependence—is sharpened and really brought into focus by the more historical branch, and to draw in results from the historical paths of inquiry as the discussion of dependence unfolds.

Strategies for Managing Dependence

Troeltsch's attempt to make theological sense of the fact that Christian belief and practice presupposes the historically unverifiable about Jesus of Nazareth has a double context. On the one hand, it is set against the background of his training in the theology of Albrecht Ritschl and his followers. The entire Ritschlian school grappled to various degrees with this problem of dependence, and Troeltsch was imbued with their presuppositions about the problem from his earliest days as a student. On the other hand, Troeltsch's background in sociology, particularly through his friendship with Max Weber, cast the problem of dependence in a light less familiar to Troeltsch's teachers. We begin here, accordingly, with a critical review of the interpretations of this dependence that constituted one part of Troeltsch's framework for approaching the problem. Subsequently, we will consider Troeltsch's positive solution to the problem of dependence conceived both sociologically and theologically.

General Optimism about Managing the Problem

The first and most general point to make is that the nineteenth century presents almost unbroken confidence among theologians that the presupposition in Christian theology and practice of historical facts about Jesus is not an insurmountably difficult state of affairs. This is so in spite of the fact that the late eighteenth-century confidence about the value of the biblical sources for critically assembling a life of Jesus gradually, with notable variations, eroded through the nineteenth century.

The apprehension with which the historical critical method was regarded in many quarters in the eighteenth-century beginnings of the quest for the historical Jesus[3] proved to be justified, both for expected and for unexpected reasons. The obvious fear was that the Bible would rapidly be lost as a supportive resource for faith, either because the results of historical research might not support the assertions of the Christian faith, or because the historical critical method itself might require a partial abandonment of the trusting attitude of faith. But the most intractable problem turned out to be the discovery that the sources are too sparse, vague, and variable, and too burdened with legend, myth, and fiction to allow a precise historical determination of anything beyond the barest outline of Jesus' life and ministry; the situation is far worse with regard to his character and self-understanding. Landmark figures such as Reimarus (1694–1768), Strauss (1808–1874), Weiss (1863–1914), and Schweitzer (1875–1965) produced powerful evidence to support this contention, sometimes as a side effect of their main arguments. The same conclusion is inescapably confirmed (against all recent protest) by the increasing diversity of the results of twentieth-century life of Jesus research: *traditional Christological statements involving historical assertions about Jesus are underdetermined by the available historical data*. There is simply not enough of the right kind of information to ground much reliable knowledge about Jesus, no matter how sophisticated the historical, literary, social and anthropological tools brought to bear on the gospel records.

What then was the source of confidence that dependence of Christian dogmatics and practice on historical assertions about Jesus of Nazareth could be theologically managed? This confidence had five elements that were combined in various ways to produce a variety of "theological management strategies": (1) confidence in the sources, against the growing trend of suspicion toward them; (2) reliance on the biblical pictures of Jesus Christ; (3) reliance on the confirmatory experience of the communion of the Christian with God through Jesus Christ; (4) reliance on the authorizing import of the Christian dogmatic tradition; and (5) espousing a Christology that made fewer historically unverifiable assumptions about the biography of Jesus. The first four of these will be described in turn, deferring the last until after Troeltsch's social psychological analysis of this dependence has been presented.

Invoking History: Harnack

Before the problematic nature of the sources was properly appreciated, historical criticism of the Gospels was enthusiastically greeted by some as an ally for Christian faith. It was received as a means for placing the assertions of faith on a more secure basis, one more compatible with the Enlightenment values of autonomy and suspicion of the supposed arbitrariness of religious authorities. This enthusiastic viewpoint held that careful study of the Gospels would reward hard labor with reliable knowledge about Jesus. A host of "Lives of Jesus" were being produced with the aid of the exciting new historical critical tools. They were premised on confidence that the texts were sufficient for constructing not only the out-

lines of Jesus' life and teaching, but also theological statements about
Jesus' significance and sometimes even detailed biographies and what we
would now call "personality profiles."

This sanguine attitude appears to have been self-perpetuating, in that
the large number of lives of Jesus encouraged even more of them, and almost every bold reading could point to other attempts that were even
bolder. The process of extracting reliable historical knowledge about
Jesus' life and teaching may have become more circuitous for historians
using biblical critical tools in an intellectual culture with an increasingly
naturalistic bias. And the relationship between the critical assumptions of
the historical method and trusting stance of Christian faith remained
problematic. But optimism about actually obtaining historically sound and
theologically useful results remained virtually undisturbed in the early
decades of historical criticism and continued throughout the nineteenth
century in some scholarly circles, in spite of apprehension about the problem that was strengthening at the same time.

Bucking the trend of declining confidence in the historical sources
were a number of optimistic and diligent historians, represented *par excellence* by Adolf von Harnack (1851–1930). Harnack's approach managed the theological problem of faith's dependence on history by means
of an optimistic estimate of what historical research can discover about
Jesus, thereby furnishing for Christology a wealth of relevant information.
In fact, Harnack required from, and found in, the gospel accounts more in
the way of details about Jesus' life and teaching than many historians
thought could be found there, but he made his case powerfully nonetheless. This optimism is especially evident in *What Is Christianity?* a book as
massively influential as it was controversial. In the first half, Harnack identified "the leading features of Jesus' message" and considered this message in relation to certain problems ranging from "the question of
asceticism" to "the Christological question" and "the question of creed."
He then critically examined interpretations of the gospel from several eras
of the history of Christianity in light of his own findings.

All of this was carried off with such simple grace and earnest gravity
that it is no wonder the book was greeted with acclaim by so many believers in the churches and translated so frequently. If nothing else, it was a
fresh presentation of Jesus' message that captured people's imagination
with its natural relevance to the contemporary world and revived the spir-
its of those flagging followers who were saturated with lukewarm presen-

tations of Jesus' person and teaching in the rusty bath, as it seemed, of ecclesial dogma. It was an effective and timely exercise in getting back to ba-
sics, with its ringing affirmation of the infinite value of the human soul to
God and the vitality of the coming kingdom in which love of God and
neighbor hold sway.[4] As Harnack remarked in his preface to the English
translation, "The theologians of every country only half discharge their du-
ties if they think it enough to treat of the gospel in the recondite language
of learning and bury it in scholarly folios."[5] Moreover, Harnack was very
far from presenting a watered down ethic of the higher righteousness of
love, tied to a sentimental affirmation of divine personal concern. For instance, Jesus' purported aggressive critique of worldly goods and attach-
ments is presented quite powerfully, as is his affirmation of this-worldly
pleasures, albeit slightly marred by an inexplicable ranting against asceticism.[6] Very far from being uncritically accommodating, it is partly the *confronting* of his culture and context with the proclamation of Jesus that
made and makes Harnack's book so captivating.

What we see here is an excellent example of the strategy of maximiz-
ing dependence of Christological assertions about Jesus Christ on historical knowledge of the actual Jesus, in conjunction with the assumption that
historical research can unearth enough reliable material about Jesus to
make such a high degree of dependence theologically feasible. The happy
aptness of Harnack's book for many in the churches with weaker than average sympathies for traditional doctrine was an indication of the power
of such a strategy.[7] The question is, of course, whether Harnack's assumptions about the sources for Jesus' life can be adequately justified.

Critics were quick to note the fact that Harnack passed over mostly
silently the emphatic eschatological elements of the New Testament and
the controversies in which the early church became embroiled because of
the delay of the parousia. Harnack acknowledged that Jesus shared in the
apocalyptic mind-set of his day in a general way. But he argued that Jesus
neither allowed it to determine any part of the heart of his ethical, spiritual message, nor drew on apocalyptic, eschatological categories in forming his self-understanding. As a result, Harnack's critics rightly charged
him with reducing the other-worldly character of Jesus' proclamation to
the supernatural affinity of humanity for God and of God for each human
soul, quietly passing over its stranger aspects. Harnack could not have tolerated these omissions had he paid more attention to or felt more sympathy for the perspective of the history of religions.[8] He also oversimplified

the issue of identifying the meaning and actual origin of sayings ascribed to Jesus in the Gospels, which he did through the liberal peppering of his text with phrases such as "His discourses and actions leave no doubt upon this point," and "It is certain, therefore, . . ." and "No one who reads the gospels with an unprejudiced mind, and does not pick his words, can fail to acknowledge that. . . ." These devices were used with rhetorical artfulness and are delightfully elusive to critique because they are pervasive, though this is doubtless due in part to the popular nature of the lectures in which such phrases appear.

In all of these ways, Harnack's confident—perhaps over-confident—mode of interpretation is evident. Other historians, before and especially after Harnack, have been unable to justify such categorical readings.[9] But these criticisms, from one point of view, do not touch the integrity of Harnack's overall interpretation of Jesus Christ and of the Christian religion. Any fair-minded critic would have to grant that Harnack made good on his assumption of the adequacy of the New Testament as a source for information about the historical Jesus to some extent. He offers a historical reconstruction of Jesus' life and teaching that is at least partly viable, in spite of its lack of engagement with the history of religions; much of late twentieth-century North American life-of-Jesus research is far more consonant with Harnack's interpretation, for example, than with the apocalyptic eschatological readings of Weiss and Schweitzer that were to follow Harnack.

Nevertheless, we should push the issue of Harnack's optimistic definiteness a step further. Part of the reason for this definiteness may well have been Harnack's conviction of the importance of the Christian gospel and his confidence in its content. Harnack as historian may have been unduly influenced by such considerations, but it is important to note that *What Is Christianity?* is not simply a work of history. As is well known, it is also and more characteristically *theological*, for at every point Harnack was concerned to present the relevance and liveliness of the Christian gospel for his contemporaries. In the end, this may be the best explanation for Harnack's exhibition of confidence and the most telling evidence for its strategic character: since Harnack needed to recapture historical material in a relevant way for his context, the judicious historical sense of Harnack *qua historian* had to yield to some extent to his evidently intense *theological* interest by becoming more definite than it might otherwise have been. Alternative interpretations of the historical material do make an appearance as steps along the way to the "correct" reading, but Harnack rarely entertained the potential practical and proclamatory significance of *those* alternatives. This would have diluted *his* theological solution, which, however, remains strong by means of a strategic separation of the uncertainty of the historical material from faith's need for more or less unequivocal and relevant access to it.

Invoking the Biblical Pictures of Christ

The increasingly cautious attitude to the sources forced theologians to search for grounds other than detailed biographical knowledge about Jesus for their abiding confidence that dependence of Christology on life-of-Jesus research could be theologically managed. In particular, if Christological assertions referring to Jesus inevitably assume more historically than can be established by historical research, then a different interpretation of historical responsibility must be found. Thus many modern theologians have emphasized the importance of the biblical pictures of Christ (*Bilder Jesu*). These gospel portraits were not in question in the same way as the historical reconstructions of the person who gave rise to them. Though their relevance for Christological construction had to be established, at least that relevance did not depend on the supposition that the Gospels contained a great deal of reliable information about the actual historical figure of Jesus; it was necessary only that the biblical *pictures* of Christ could be understood in the light of the early churches' usage of them. This is a more practical task for historians than the quest for the historical Jesus, though it has its own complexities.

Building relevant connections between Christology and the Gospels' pictures of Jesus seemed to some theologians quite promising as a solution to the problems forced on theology by the quest for the historical Jesus. This quest was not just an extended argument over historical critical details about Jesus' life, though it was certainly that. It was fundamentally a theologically driven enterprise, for the most obvious consequence of life-of-Jesus research was its effect on the theological conception of living faith in Christ of the Christian churches. Did the Christ proclaimed in worship and understood in doctrine correspond to the man of Nazareth, as unearthed by historical research? If this question is answered in the affirmative, is it only because that research is the result of what Schweitzer thought of as each epoch's and each person's tendency to find in the his-

torical Jesus a reflection of itself?[10] Or perhaps a correlation is found because so little is asked of it, the personality, teaching, and biography of
Jesus having been rendered superfluous to the conception of the Christ
of contemporary faith, so that Christian faith in Jesus Christ is made independent of all but the barest facts about Jesus' life?[11] And if no substantial
correspondence can be shown—because of paucity of reliable information or adverse historical findings—is this a great problem for theology or
for the practical life of the churches? Have not the churches from the earliest times made do with inaccurate, sometimes fantastic, usually docetic
images of Jesus of Nazareth?[12] Thus, ought not the emphasis be laid upon
the early churches' kerygma and their pictures of Christ—spelling these
out is, after all, an achievable goal for historical research—rather than
upon the biography of Jesus? Does not the direct encounter with the living Christ as testified to in the biblical pictures of him, and in the worship
and preaching of the church, make irrelevant disputes about the life of
Jesus as well as the dogmatic development of his saving significance?

So it was that the biblical pictures of Jesus were appealed to whole-
heartedly. Relying on the biblical pictures of Jesus Christ to make sense of
the dependence of Christian dogmatics and practice on history, however,
seems to require some additional consideration by which those biblical
pictures could be thought secure from major errors. Thus it was usually
carried off in conjunction with an appeal to the authorizing import either
of religious experience or the Christian tradition, both of which are to be
discussed shortly. Alternatively, historical research was regarded as a way
of keeping in check the possible excesses of faith's appropriation of the
biblical pictures of Jesus Christ, without thereby becoming a foundation
for faith. All of these elements are present in the thought of Albrecht
Ritschl (1822–1889), the grandfather of the tradition Troeltsch inherited.

Ritschl was at some pains to emphasize both the role of historical
knowledge of Jesus and the reality of personal piety in the contemporary
context for faith, and he was not unaware of the basic sources from which
the problem of faith and history developed, including especially David
Friedrich Strauss's *Das Leben Jesu* (1835). He strongly encouraged historical research into the life of Jesus but recognized at the same time that
faith needed no proof from history and indeed was incompatible with
such foreign assurances. Moreover, he was dubious about the possibility
of establishing dogmatics on the basis of historical research, believing in-

stead that it could only take shape in relation to a general idea of Jesus, informed and controlled by the New Testament pictures of him. These pictures constitute the fundamental historical connecting point for dogmatic Christology. This perspective lived on in a related way in the theologies of Kähler and Herrmann and again with variations in the Christologies of Karl Barth, Rudolf Bultmann, and Paul Tillich.

Invoking Immediacy: Kähler, Herrmann, Schweitzer

As different as they were in other ways, Martin Kähler (1835–1912), Wilhelm Herrmann (1846–1922) and Albert Schweitzer (1875–1965) were faced with the dual problem of deficient sources and irreducible dependence of faith on those sources. They all attempted to separate faith and history as much as possible by invoking some external principle that could mediate faith's dependence on history. This, in short, minimizes dependence. Each in his own way appealed to an immediacy of encounter of the Christian with the ever-present spirit of Jesus Christ, witnessed to in the early churches' kerygma and preserved in the New Testament writings. This encounter was seen as an unbreakable bond that transcended (without abrogating) the connection of Christological statements to the historical Jesus.

Schweitzer is well known for arguing that the separation of the Jesus of history from the Christ of faith was the final but *unintended* result of the bold attempt to find out once and for all about the life, teaching, and personality of Jesus. Originally, historical research into the life of Jesus was envisaged as the star witness in the emancipation of true faith in Christ from its dogmatic bondage, for it drove a spectacular wedge between the dogmatic Christ of ecclesiastical tradition and the man of Nazareth about whom those dogmatic claims were supposed to apply. It was discovered, however, that the Jesus of history was a more awkward figure than expected. The emancipatory effort was largely successful, it is true, and responsible dogmatic Christology was forever changed as a result. But the historical Jesus was no more amenable to the theological interests of enlightened modernity than he had been to the ancient dogmatics of ecclesiastical authority. The star witness had turned hostile. Historical criticism had in a very real sense betrayed theology, according to Schweitzer. It had begun by undermining the reliability of the biblical

sources for Christological statements and had finished by returning as historically probable a view of Jesus that was indigestible by traditional Christology.

Thus Schweitzer was led to espouse a more or less unexplained
Christ mysticism that could mediate between the problematic state of
knowledge about the historical Jesus and the reality of the experience of
encounter with Christ in faith. For Schweitzer, it is Christ to whom the believer must give allegiance, and it is Christ who calls the believer to faithful
service in the cause of the kingdom of God, even as Schweitzer understood Christ to have called him to missionary service in Africa. The relation of this Christ to Jesus the man of Nazareth is obscure, however.
Finding a satisfactory interpretation is complicated further by the fact that
this mystical stance can be called "Jesus mysticism" as aptly as "Christ mysticism," on the basis of Schweitzer's way of continually describing the encounter with the mystical Christ in relation to Jesus. For example, in
arguing for the importance of conceiving the Christian faith independently of specific facts about the historical Jesus, Schweitzer wrote:

> We are experiencing what Paul experienced. In the very moment when
> we were coming nearer to the historical Jesus than men had ever come
> before, and were already stretching out our hands to draw Him into our
> own time, we have been obliged to give up the attempt and acknowl-
> edge our failure in that paradoxical saying: "If we have known Christ after
> the flesh yet henceforth know we Him no more." And further we must
> be prepared to find the historical knowledge of the personality and life
> of Jesus will not be a help, but perhaps even an offence to religion.
>
> But the truth is, it is not Jesus as historically known, but Jesus as
> spiritually arisen within men, who is significant for our time and can help
> it. Not the historical Jesus, but the spirit which goes forth from Him and
> in the spirits of men strives for new influence and rule, is that which
> overcomes the world.
>
> . . . The abiding and eternal in Jesus is absolutely independent of
> historical knowledge and can only be understood by contact with His
> spirit which is still at work in the world. In proportion as we have the
> Spirit of Jesus we have the true knowledge of Jesus.[13]

There are so many conventional distinctions (presumably deliber-
ately) confused here that it is not at all clear precisely how Schweitzer envisaged "Jesus," "Christ," "spirit" (or "Spirit"), and Christology as a whole.

The situation is no clearer elsewhere, so it is not possible to attain a completely satisfactory analysis of Schweitzer's Christology. However, invoking the conventional distinction between Christ (as the abiding and eternal in Jesus, and not merely a synonym for Messiah) and Jesus (as the actual earthly Jesus of Nazareth), which Schweitzer did not use in the quotation, it is possible to see that he thought Christ was at least contingently expressed in Jesus. Christ, as the "Spirit of Jesus," is living, capable of entering into intimate contact with human beings, actively at work in the world, and genuinely able to help our time. And this Christ is to be conceived independently of Jesus, in whom it (or perhaps he?) is contingently expressed. Here we see the beginnings of the same strategy that Troeltsch was to explore, though in a different way. Going further with this reading of Schweitzer, however, raises more questions than answers.

What is clearer is that this kind of mystical Christology was for Schweitzer's own life and thought jointly operative with a passionate recognition of and voluntary participation in a fundamental, intuitive ethical stance of reverence for life. It is more in Schweitzer's life than in his thought, however, that the systematic implications of the integration of Christ mysticism with the principle of reverence for life appear, thus leaving many questions open.[14] One of the sharpest is asked by Nils Dahl about the viability of Schweitzer's view as a whole, seeing that his "life-work attests to the power which can lie in a liberal Christianity, but may also raise the question whether it can exist elsewhere than in the shadows of a churchly Christianity. Schweitzer's intensely personal solution could not guide the further work of theology on the problem of the historical Jesus."[15]

The first concern of both Herrmann and Kähler was to do justice to the inviolable character of faith and to defend the right of ordinary Christian believers to hold their faith intelligibly without thereby being at the mercy of the endlessly winding interstices of modern historical research. From one point of view, the certainty of faith made its dependence on tentative historical knowledge unthinkable, in the sense of a category mistake, for these were instances of knowledge of different orders. Yet, in a general way at least, faith was obviously dependent on historical research, if not for its establishment, then at least for its justification and correction, for most expressions of faith in Jesus Christ involved statements that were partly historical in character. Neither was willing to assume that the Bible contained historical information whose accuracy was divinely guaranteed in order to assure a safe source of historical knowledge for theology. Neither possessed Harnack's optimistic sense of what could be obtained in the form of stable historical knowledge from the available sources. And neither was prepared to make appeal to principles of universal, rational religion to secure a foundation for faith that was less subject to the vicissitudes of history. We are fortunate that Herrmann engaged Kähler's solution to the resulting problem, in the process of restating his own with the aid of Kähler's distinction between *Historie* and *Geschichte*.[16]

These two words for history were used more or less interchangeably until Kähler's useful magnification of nuances in 1892 to stipulate a difference of meaning.[17] *Historie* is the domain of critical historians, wherein they ply their craft with as little deference as possible to assumptions drawn from Christian faith, or from any other particular stance, in accordance with the impulse to discover and describe "what happened" so as to win assent from the community of historians. *Geschichte* is history regarded *from a point of view*, in which interpretation from the very outset is knowingly conditioned by one's allegiances—in Kähler's case, one's allegiance to Jesus Christ. Herrmann approved of Kähler's distinction, but they used it differently.

Kähler, in the process of his wholesale attack on life-of-Jesus research, bluntly debunked the purported objectivity and presuppositionlessness of *Historie*—especially *historisch* research into the object of dogmatic concern such as Jesus—as unrealistic.

> Today everyone is on his guard when a dogma is frankly presented as such. But when Christology appears in the form of a "Life of Jesus," there are not many who will perceive the stage manager behind the scenes, manipulating, according to his own dogmatic script, the fascinating spectacle of a colorful biography. . . . Therefore, the dogmatician has the right to set up a warning sign before the allegedly presuppositionless historical (*historisch*) research that ceases to do real research and turns instead to a fanciful reshaping of the data.
>
> . . . How many authors of the "Lives" blithely compose epics and dramas without being aware that this is what they are doing! And because this is done in prose, perhaps even from the pulpit, people think that this is merely a presentation of the historic (*geschichtlich*), biblical picture of Christ. Far from it! What is usually happening is that the image of Jesus is being refracted through the spirit of these gentlemen themselves.[18]

It is profoundly difficult to liberate ourselves from the interests we bring to the historical study of the life of Jesus. This may be seen in an obvious but compelling way by observing that secular historians with no Christian commitment rarely if ever have found in the gospel accounts of Jesus' resurrection reasons to think that a bodily resurrection occurred. It is only among *Christian* historians that we find some who think they see there the kind of evidence that can pass muster with the standards of secular historiography. Is this just a blind coincidence? Of course not; it is a case of historical judgment being influenced by personal, confessional stance, possibly on both sides. Should all historians therefore relinquish their teaching posts and go back to school to learn how to do history properly? Again, of course not. Work in the realm of *Historie* presupposes analogical continuities between the present context of interpretation and the past at every level. As a result, occurrences that are unique, in the sense of not being the analogical precedents of the contemporary historian's experience, are rendered translucent to the searching light of the contemporary historian's method. So there is no *historisch* possibility of comprehending the resurrection of Jesus, or the unique appearance within history of the divine principle of creation.

What warrants the suspension of ordinary historiographical assumptions so that the resurrection, the miracles, or the life of Jesus as a whole may be dealt with positively, and from a Christian point of view? For Kähler, it is the Christian experience of encounter with Christ. Since this element cannot be avoided—and a truly empirical approach might demand that it be *embraced*, conventional historiography notwithstanding—it is better to recognize it explicitly in theological method, according to Kähler. Correspondingly, the primary interest of dogmatic construction should not be in the historical Jesus as such, but in the earliest interpretations of him from a Christian standpoint. After all, contemporary Christian historians themselves inevitably present interpretations of the historical Jesus, and Christologies are precisely that. Historical (*historisch*) tools should be used to reconstruct the historic (*geschichtlich*), biblical Christ, as he is presented in the biblical pictures of him, and dogmatics should be oriented to those pictures.

Kähler anticipated dialectical theology's insistence that it is Jesus' *geschichtlich* significance that has always been and must now be affirmed, whether or not the events that triggered the cascading chain of influences at the origins of Christianity can be reconstructed. Proclamation of the

kerygma of the early churches was therefore for him the starting point for
biblical and systematic theology, as well as for preaching and practical
Christian piety. The obvious result of Kähler's strategy is that dependence
of Christological constructions upon historical details about Jesus' life is
significantly reduced. This is potentially the case whenever the biblical
pictures of Christ are taken to be the appropriate starting point for Christology, though the importance of warranting or correcting or supporting
the pictures of Christ with *historisch* research about Jesus still can be assessed differently. Kähler thought this was less important than Herrmann
did.

Herrmann was less internally consistent but could proceed more adequately than Kähler, precisely because he was more realistic about the
need to know that the historic significance of Jesus was not the result of
delusory desire, mythical power, or social enthusiasm outrunning the
facts.[19] Of course, for both theologians, faith gave immediate assurance of
this fact, for by faith the believer experiences an immediacy of encounter
with the actual Jesus, now risen as Lord. Herrmann insisted that nothing
could interfere with the judgment of faith, and that the living Christ to
which the inner life of the believer is joined is the inner life of the actual
earthly Jesus, as discernible in and through the biblical pictures of him.
But this is not merely a matter of interpretation for Herrmann; it was an
encounter sparked from a generalized but clear impression of Jesus that
could be gained directly from the Gospels and from the kerygma. He did
retain a place for historical (*historisch*) research as a way of ruling out
Christological excesses, but such historical results contributed no more
than basic guidance and correction. The experience of Christ so understood finally determines the value of the results both of historical research
into the life of Jesus and of dogmatic expositions of his significance.[20]

In spite of the fact that both Kähler and Herrmann were committed to
beginning Christology from the historic, biblical pictures of Christ, Herrmann had a higher estimate of the value of *historisch* explication and justification of the cognitive edges of the faith experience—especially for
removing false props from faith and for correcting egregious errors. This
was so much the case that Troeltsch was able to observe in Herrmann an
interesting "struggle between history writing and subjective mysticism."[21]

On the one hand, Kähler could lay hold of the biblical pictures of
Christ in the early churches' kerygma with relative certainty, leaving aside
the antecedent influences for the most part, and then derive a relevant

Christology. The confidence with which those antecedent influences are laid aside, however, smacks of an unjustifiable kind of biblical positivism. Herrmann, on the other hand, dissatisfied with this awkward positivism in Kähler's view, remained committed to the *historisch* task of investigating Jesus' life, *not* in order to produce faith but in order to guide and correct it, even as electrical current is carried in and constrained by wires. The electrical current itself, however, comes not from *historisch* research but from the fellowship of the Christian with the personal life of Jesus, disclosed in the historical (*geschichtlich*) pictures of him in the New Testament. Faith, as Troeltsch put it in speaking of Herrmann, "needs a power supply from history and a foundation outside itself,"[22] but it is Jesus' *geschichtlich* significance rather than *historisch* research that provides this power.

Invoking Tradition: Blondel

French Catholic philosopher Maurice Blondel (1861–1949) presented an alternative approach to those of the Ritschlian tradition we have been considering. Though Blondel's work stands outside the liberal Protestant tradition, he was aware of much of it and was attempting to respond to the same concerns. Blondel's essay on *History and Dogma*[23] affirmed the role of tradition and the believing community in mediating the dependence of faith on history. Thus, he achieved greater social and historical realism than the other views discussed so far, notwithstanding the fact that Ritschl and his successors had lofty views of the church.

Blondel defended the thesis that what he calls "historicism" and "extrinsicism" can be avoided through an appropriate understanding of "tradition." In attacking historicism, Blondel had in mind an apparently skewed interpretation of Alfred Loisy's conception of history,[24] itself a reply in kind to Harnack's *What Is Christianity?* According to Blondel, historicism assumes that historical research is able to light the path from historical occurrences to dogmatic pronouncements unaided and to evoke faith directly out of the content of its own discoveries. On the opposite extreme, extrinsicism factors in history only in an *ad hoc* or extrinsic way as a dispensable source of evidence for already established dogma. Against this extreme view, a reasonably common one among Roman Catholic traditionalists, Blondel insisted on the indispensability of history for faith. And against historicism, which is at best an unfair caricature of Loisy's view, he urged that history had to be mediated by tradition if it were to elicit faith and support dogma, for it was not independently capable of doing so. If faith had to depend upon tradition isolated from history, it would quickly be reduced to an empty shell, with no inner content; if faith had to depend upon history isolated from tradition, the content of faith would be decontextualized and finally unintelligible. Only if tradition and history were united was there hope of passing testimony to the living reality of Christ from generation to generation, and of retaining the historical material in proper relation to that living reality.

Criticism of the Extant Dependence Strategies

Neither Ritschl, Harnack, Schweitzer, Kähler, Herrmann, nor Blondel thought that completely setting aside historical research into the life of Jesus was acceptable, though Kähler's thought had some momentum in that direction as far as *historisch* research into the life of Jesus was concerned. None of them, moreover, thought that faith in Christ could be produced by historical research alone, including Harnack, who was the most optimistic with regard to the historical sources. However, against the unrealistic and polar extreme views that faith was immune from historical research or more or less completely correlative with it, each one of these theologians in his own way and to various degrees thought that faith *had* to relate itself to the probabilistic and shifting results of historical research, that Lessing's famous ugly, broad ditch had to be crossed somehow.

Their solutions were optimism with regard to what historical research could accomplish (Harnack), an optimistic interpretation of the self-authenticating character of the immediacy of encounter with Jesus Christ (Schweitzer), an optimistic view of the authorizing import of this immediacy for the biblical pictures of Jesus Christ (Herrmann and Kähler in their various ways), or an optimistic reading of the stability conferred on the process of transmission of the Christian faith by tradition (Blondel). In all these cases, at least in theory, faith's dependence upon history comes to appear feasible, maintaining belief in Jesus Christ as psychologically possible and the fact of dependence theologically tolerable.

Troeltsch's assessment of this dilemma led him in a number of places to be sharply critical of these strategies for managing the problem of the biblical sources for Christological construction. Thus we turn now to

Troeltsch's critique of his Ritschlian colleagues and teachers, weaving these criticisms in with a discussion of the various proposals. We also will consider what we may infer from Troeltsch's thought by way of critique of Blondel's use of tradition in effect to authorize the reliance of Christian doctrine and practice on the biblical pictures of Christ.

On Ritschl

In *Justification and Reconciliation* (1870–1874), Ritschl spent little time exploring the tension induced in his thought by his double emphasis on historical knowledge of Jesus and personal piety, the problem to which Harnack, Herrmann, and Kähler gave more explicit attention. Ritschl apparently was quite comfortable with his two-pronged solution. Troeltsch thought the result was problematically dualistic, because of "the harsh tension in which Ritschl's picture of Christ stood to the historical critical research which he himself acknowledged,"[25] and he believed that the problem, admitted as a difficult one by Ritschl, "could only be resolved by sheer assertions"[26] in Ritschl's theology. Ritschl, however, evidently was not troubled by the dualism about which Troeltsch complained and would doubtless have thought his own position not dualistic in the least.

Ritschl functioned as the inspiration for Harnack and Herrmann as they sought to grapple with the implications of the double sensitivity they inherited from him toward historical criticism and Christian piety. In passing on this double sensitivity, Ritschl played a vital role in generating awareness of the problem of faith and history and in sparking methods of solution. His thought on this matter functioned as a kind of lattice structure against which the later Ritschlians naturally perceived the problem of faith and history. Troeltsch put the formation of the history of religions method down to the harshness of the bare lattice structure, saying that it was "a natural reaction against the violence of Ritschl's procedure,"[27] thereby indicating indirectly his indebtedness to Ritschl, as well as an often repeated line of criticism.

In the same way, it was the whole character of Ritschl's thought that suggested the Harnackian and Herrmannian strategies for managing the problem of faith and history: Harnack explored Ritschl's emphasis on historical research, and Herrmann made powerful use of Ritschl's stress on the place of the Christian experience of fellowship with Christ. Both of them developed optimistic strategies for managing the dependence of faith on historical research, Harnack in terms of the quality and amount of information that historical research could yield, and Herrmann in terms of the all-important experience of communion with God through Christ. Thus, Ritschl's somewhat under-explicit dual affirmation of historical knowledge and experienced faith helped form the two strategies that dominated the late-nineteenth-century Protestant debate. It is unsurprising therefore that Troeltsch's criticisms of Harnack and Herrmann were elaborated forms of his criticism of Ritschl.

On Harnack

Against Harnack, Troeltsch pointed out that it simply *was not possible* to fulfill his optimistic program—obtaining knowledge about Jesus sufficiently precise and complete to place faith on a secure footing (without, of course, *causing* faith). In fact, Troeltsch charged that Harnack was inclined to "treat those points of history given prominence by religious value-judgments very differently from the rest of history," implying that Harnack's procedure was covertly prejudiced in favor of the results he wanted to obtain.[28] The same criticism was famously made in a more systematic way by Alfred Loisy.[29] Here we see in essence what the twentieth century has played out on a grand scale. Harnack's nonapocalyptic interpretation of Jesus was first challenged and then overwhelmed by Weiss and Schweitzer's apocalyptic treatments, which against considerable resistance eventually gained wide acceptance in Germany and North America in the succeeding decades.[30] And now, with the so-called third quest, the North American consensus of life-of-Jesus researchers is returning to a nonapocalyptic interpretation, actually even less inclined to ascribe apocalyptic instincts to Jesus than Harnack was.[31]

It is not difficult to imagine a systematic Christology accepting a high degree of dependence on historical research in the stable periods between interpretative shifts and rendering the significance of Jesus Christ in intimate connection with the reigning *historisch* reconstruction of his life. But from the point of view of a longer time scale, Christological construction evidently must do justice to the possibility that any of these *historisch* reconstructions might be correct, or else it is forced to solidify around one interpretation, opposing other historical construals for dogmatic reasons. This last position is precisely the one against which the first quest railed so effectively: historical research is not to be dictated to by dogmatics. But then dogmatic Christology must seek to construct itself so that the significance of Jesus Christ can be presented without presupposing anything too specific about the life and teaching of Jesus, lest it be contradicted by a future historical consensus.

The Biblical Pictures of Jesus Christ

Is such an approach the height of intellectual wisdom or the depths of intellectual and religious cowardice? Does not spurning the offer of *historisch* facts to be of concrete, palpable value for opening up the significance of Jesus Christ only result in the adoption of an interpretation of his significance that is immune from historical risk, insipidly secure? It is easy from this point of view to appreciate Harnack's boldness. Perhaps then Christology should shift with the historical tides, giving up its habit of trying to express that about Jesus which is true in all times and all places. But this would be refreshing and frustrating in turns, a roller coaster of intellectual and religious highs and lows. *Some* Christologies, at least, must attempt to present a more stable visage to church and world. It is here that the promise of concentrating on the biblical pictures of Christ becomes so clearly evident. By focusing on the biblical pictures rather than the actual earthly Jesus, perhaps the benefits of rooting a Christology in history (in the sense of *Geschichte*) can be gained without incurring the liabilities of forcing dogmatic statements about Jesus Christ into an impossibly variable relationship with the historians' knowledge of the *historisch* facts about his life. This kind of Christology would have the warm, pulsing reality of historical concreteness, without the disconcerting irritation of having to kowtow to historical details about Jesus that bear substantively on the Christology.

Many theologians in the nineteenth and twentieth centuries have been impressed by the advantages of this approach. But can it be justified? Why would one simply assume that the biblical pictures of Christ were adequate representations of the historical Jesus? Does not the variety among them in and of itself demonstrate beyond doubt that they mislead as much as they enlighten? If the historical Jesus is not the central concern, this approach is understandable, though it might be more consistent to forgo attachment to history altogether and to speak simply of the idea of a savior or a God-man, as Kierkegaard did at one point in urging that the Christian faith depends only on the fact that a human being should have appeared in history of whom the claim was made that he or she was God, or as Kant did in finding in the *idea* of Christ—though not necessarily in the historical person of Jesus—an archetypal representation of ideal humanity. But if the *actual* historical Jesus matters to Christian faith, then it is far from being a negligible point of detail that the biblical pictures of Jesus Christ represent him tendentiously. Kähler is vulnerable to this criticism of over-reliance on the biblical pictures of Christ; Ritschl and Herrmann less so. It seems, then, that depending on the biblical pictures of Jesus for the historical (*geschichtlich*) power supply for a Christology cannot proceed apart from being closely correlated with an energetically pursued quest for the *historisch* Jesus. But what, then, has been gained by centralizing the biblical pictures of Christ in a constructive Christology? Has not the relatively independent stance with regard to *historisch* details been forgone after all?

So it may seem, until the other factor authorizing the biblical pictures of Christ is drawn into the analysis. They can have a special function for Christology because the living fellowship of Christians with Jesus Christ is supposedly in intimate consonance with them, being partly formed by them as well as conferring upon them the judgment of adequacy to the living spirit of Jesus Christ. Protestant Christianity owes the plausibility of this line of reflection most especially to pietism, whose emphasis on experience enfleshed a biblical skeleton. The collapse of that plausibility, still only partially grasped in some contemporary Christian theology, is due to the social psychological analysis both of ordinary and of religious experience. These considerations, by offering convincing examples and analyses of misinterpretation of experiences,[32] show that attempting to confirm the reliability of the biblical pictures of Jesus by appeal to a supposedly self-authenticating "immediacy of encounter with Christ" is really a very dubious way to proceed. Such experiences have an important place in the array of religious phenomena, but their epistemic import needs very cautious assessment.

On Herrmann

Troeltsch criticized Herrmann at this point on numerous occasions, often in conjunction with attacks on Ritschl.[33] Troeltsch urged that the mystical encounter with Jesus Christ is far from completely self-authenticating, as powerful as it can be in many cases, appealing for support to the gloriously inconsistent diversity of pictures of Jesus that spring forth from the encounter, the diversity of the biblical pictures of Christ, and the results of the social psychological study of religion. Having just spoken of the "violence of Ritschl's procedure," and thinking of the social psychological perspective as an essential ingredient of historical criticism, Troeltsch remarked—not entirely free of a ranting tone—that "Herrmann's talk about 'the fact of Christ' which, however, cannot be established like other facts but only seen by faith, is an obscure and mystical expression of the same violence and is almost incomprehensible to people who think historically and critically. The whole position is untenable in the face of historical criticism."[34]

Committing constructive Christology to reliance on the biblical pictures of Christ supported by an appeal to immediacy of encounter with Christ is, therefore, a procedure fraught with difficulties. However, the biblical portraits of Jesus cannot simply be ignored, in some hopelessly romantic (and conceited) expectation that the quest of the historical Jesus is finally discovering the "real" Jesus. Correspondingly, therefore, there must be a place in thinking about the dependence of Christological statements on historical facts for the religious experience Christians call "encounter with Jesus Christ." To Troeltsch it was clear that the quality and content of this encounter also depends upon a community and a context of knowledge, including historical knowledge, so that a greater degree of irreducible dependence of faith in Christ upon knowledge of the history of Jesus had to be admitted.

But how were the roles of religious experience, *historisch* research, appropriation of the *geschichtlich*, biblical pictures of Christ and the community of Christian believers to be coordinated into a theologically viable solution to the problem of faith and history? However this was to be done—and Troeltsch had his own ideas about this—managing this dependence by artificially minimizing it, as Troeltsch believed Harnack and Herrmann did, was simply unrealistic; it did not approach the theoretical problem of dependence in the terms of the problem as it actually existed in practice.

On Blondel

In his affirmation of tradition's role in mediating to the present the living character of the past, Blondel touched on the weak point of the other strategies discussed so far for managing the dependence of faith on history. If Blondel's work had been known to Troeltsch, it is likely that Troeltsch would have thought it a better model of the *actual circumstances* in which faith's dependence on history is found to be feasible than any of the post-Ritschlian strategies. It did not, for instance, artificially minimize the problem of dependence. Rather, it allowed the two sides of the problem to stand in tension, a tension mediated by the community and tradition of the church in practice. This is a major consideration, since the problem of faith and history, thought of as a practical problem for Christian believers, *does in fact* seem to be manageable. It is the *theological rationale* for this more or less successful management of the practical problem that is so elusive.

Troeltsch was of the opinion that the social psychological study of religion held the key to understanding the connection between the manageable practical, and the elusive theological, versions of the problem. Though Blondel explores territory along these lines, Troeltsch could not have accepted Blondel's interpretation of the nature of the Christian tradition because its underlying philosophy of history led to a theory of the development of doctrine with which Troeltsch was in sharp disagreement (we will return to this in the next chapter). Nor did Blondel ever come to grips with the social character of the church, or the way the individual believer's faith relates to the community of which he or she is a part, which were both central features of Troeltsch's view.

Troeltsch on the Dependence of Faith and Dogmatics upon History

Troeltsch's own proposal for managing faith's dependence on history was quite different from the strategies so far mentioned. Each of them intends to give a theologically intelligible account of the way that the dependence of Christian faith on detailed historical information about the historical Jesus *is and ought* to be managed. Any such account must involve both a *description* of how it is that this dependence is *in fact* feasible in practice in the churches, as it seems usually to be, and a *stipulation* of the way that this dependence *ought* to be theoretically managed in principle by theologians who are in the business of constructing Christologies, among other things.

As descriptions, however, these proposals leave a lot to be desired. Though the church sometimes is included as a factor in interpreting this dependence—this is especially obvious in Blondel—there is little or no attention paid to social or psychological analysis of this dependence. Likewise, the actual way Christian believers relate their faith to the results of *historisch* research into the life of Jesus is more or less omitted from the picture. This failure to establish the actual character of the dependence in the life of the Christian churches is a serious defect because church community and cult play a decisive role in helping Christian believers comprehend and handle whatever degree of dependence of faith on history they experience.

As theological stipulations, furthermore, these strategies are also problematic. Stipulated strategies for managing faith's dependence on history are really constructive attempts to construe the practical situation of believer and church so that such dependence as exists can be demonstrated to be theologically justified. Good strategies will permit this justification to be exhibited, whereas poor strategies will not. Such strategies are crucial, but then it is vitally important to construe the practical situation *correctly*. The practical situation of dependence in the life of churches and Christian believers cannot be made to conform to theoretical models of it. Rather, the experience of Christian believers first has to be described with reference to the role of the cult.

Troeltsch's viewpoint implicitly charges all of these strategies with failure both as descriptions and as stipulations for theological construction. His attempt to overcome these weaknesses in a preliminary way is one of the strengths of his own proposal. He believed that, isolated from its historical roots in Jesus, Christianity would inevitably exchange its spiritual distinctiveness for ethical impotence and ecclesial disintegration.[35] This was the basis for his argument that dependence of Christology and Christian faith on history is a virtuous necessity, which is the first point to be taken up in what follows. Subsequently, we shall examine Troeltsch's view of the historical feasibility of dependence, paying particular attention to what he thought was required historically in a Christology and for Christian believers. Given Troeltsch's view of dependence as necessary, it is unsurprising that he never wavered from his insistence that Christological construction had to remain in solid contact with the historical Jesus; furthermore, he thought it could do this in practice. Troeltsch's interpretation of the sociological feasibility of this dependence is the third point to be examined. Finally, these components of Troeltsch's analysis of dependence raise several theological problems, which are taken up last.

Unfortunately, Troeltsch appears somewhat uncertain—even confused in places—when writing on the *solution* to the problem of faith and history, as against the *problem*, about which he wrote clearly, on the whole. He is especially weak on explaining the theological intelligibility of the proposals he does explore, with the result that his creative solution never becomes adequately fleshed out, or even clearly enough stated. Indeed, this part-solution—perhaps this is the best description of it—seems to have been the result of intuition grounded in his familiarity with the social sciences as much as the consequence of any articulated theological convictions. However, he *did have* a creative solution, which consists in combining a Christology of his anti-absolutist sort with a social psychological reading of how to coordinate the available resources (religious experience, historical research, biblical pictures, ecclesial tradition) in a balanced and effective way that does justice to the phenomenology of dependence in cult and believer.

Dependence is Vitally Important

The intuition that led Troeltsch to acknowledge that faith had to depend on historical research to some extent appears to have been his assumption of a social psychological principle that faith in a historical person necessarily involves a generalized belief that certain historical events took place. Otherwise, a slippery slope is established from faith down to wishful thinking, with no sign of anything to block the slide. If *belief that* seems unreliable, because of lack of information or contrary evidence, then *faith in* at best is challenged profoundly, perhaps even undermined. This demanded that faith, even though it be of a different psychological and epistemic order than historical knowledge in the sense of *historisch* facts, could not be completely independent of it. Consider the following quotation:

> Faith is always faith in a concrete thought-content. This thought-content never originates solely from the individual subject. On the contrary, the richer and stronger it is, the more it is the communal work of great epochs of intellectual history and of whole generations, or of outstanding personalities that have profited from these communal achievements.

Faith feels a need to gather up this whole world of ideas in its starting point and to embody it in an archetype, in order always to be able to rectify and revitalize itself. . . . As its requirements increase, its need for support from personalities that supply direction and impetus increases also. Faith therefore depends upon history, but not only for sustenance and information; its own self-understanding depends upon history, and within history upon the embodiment of revelation to which it looks. . . . The Christian faith originated in the historical disclosure of the life of God, and for the sake of clarity and power it must be constantly referred back to this foundation, which is vitally present to the imagination. Even though some individuals may be able to forego this historical referral because they are carried along by the power of the community, the community as a whole cannot forego it if the community is to retain its vital force.[36]

We may wonder at Troeltsch's partial definition of faith as being "in a concrete thought-content" that is not completely internal to the believing subject. But an alternate definition such as faith as ultimate concern (Tillich), while offering a helpfully different perspective on faith, does not materially affect the issue at hand.

Another example is found in the third section of "The Significance of the Historical Existence of Jesus for Faith," entitled "A restatement of the central position of Jesus based on the needs of the religious community," where Troeltsch attacked the view of the aesthete who supposes that the Christian idea should be sufficient for faith, apart from any concrete grounding in historical factuality:

The aesthete expects believers to satisfy their existential hunger on a mythical symbol because he himself never thinks of stilling a real hunger for certainty and conviction but only the unreal needs of the imagination. Someone who really belongs in his heart to the world of Christian experience will never be able to see in the center and head of the congregation, the focal point for all cult and vision of God, a mere myth—no matter how beautiful. For him, God is not an idea or possibility but a holy reality. He will therefore insist upon standing with this symbol of his on the solid ground of real life. It is for him a truly significant fact that a real man thus lived, struggled, believed and conquered, and that from this real life a stream of strength and certainty flows down to him. The symbol is only a real symbol for him in that behind it stands the greatness of a superior and real religious prophet. Not only is God made visible by reference to this; he can also find here support and strength in his own uncertainty, just as elsewhere he needs to hold on to superior personal religious authority, and experiences it in life in many ways. This much is legitimate in Herrmann's talk about 'the fact of Christ'. It is not just that the individual's certainty of salvation can only be gained by becoming certain of Jesus, but rather that the Christian spirit can find no context for supporting and strengthening life without this gathering around Jesus. This in turn must go back to real, vivid life if it is to have inner power and veracity.[37]

And what would be the consequences of failing to provide a firm historical foundation for the Christian faith? In the context of a criticism of biblical scholarship, Troeltsch insisted that "scholarly circles [must] rid themselves of the notion that *everything* in the tradition is unreliable; otherwise the people will eventually cease to trust their own instincts."[38] Elsewhere he was more specific:

Faith cannot escape this admixture of the historical and scientific way of thinking. It must face this and secure the historical basis of its community and cult as far as the historical questions have any significance for these. There is no ducking or ignoring this. The struggle must be fought out and if it were decided against the historicity of Jesus or against any possibility of knowing about him, that would in fact be the beginning of the end of the Christ symbol amongst scientifically educated people. From there doubt and dissolution would soon percolate down to the lower classes, so far as it has not reached there already as a result of the social reforms and anti-ecclesiastical inclinations. It is a mere playing with words to hold on to the Christian principle and yet want to leave the historical questions on one side. That is a practical way out for individuals in difficulties and confusion; it is impossible for a religious and cultic community.[39]

Troeltsch was arguing that faith in Jesus Christ can be sustained only when the historical claims involved in that faith can be held with reasonable confidence; not everything about Jesus' life needs to be known, but neither is radical uncertainty about everything a tenable environment for faith in Jesus Christ. This means that the expressions of Jesus' significance encountered in the biblical pictures of Christ are not sufficient for faith or dogmatic Christology by themselves, for they do not offer the kind of historical confidence Troeltsch thought faith requires. Nor are the biblical pictures as they might be corrected by historical research—in the manner of Herrmann—quite enough, because the need of faith for concrete historical confidence must not be subordinated to faith's need for a presentation of the significance of Jesus Christ such as the biblical pictures offer; the two needs must *both* be met.

To these two needs, as indicated in the first quotation, Troeltsch would also add the need of faith to be in harmony with the intellectual insights of the generation in which it comes to be. The persuasiveness that coherence with convictions about the way the world is brings to a Christology is not unlike that brought to a Christology by the awareness that, in having faith in Jesus, we are trusting one who did certain concrete things in such and such a way, in order to accomplish thus and so. Such coherence is just as psychologically inevitable a need. At this point we enter into Troeltsch's view of the mediating character of theology, for which his more characteristic term was *Kompromiß* (compromise)—a word with positive overtones for him. The psychological untenability of Christology when it is plagued by massive incoherence with cultural assumptions was of great concern to Troeltsch. For now we may focus just on the consequences of Troeltsch's conviction that faith needs a measure of concrete historical assurance.

Dependence is Historically Feasible

What, then, does Christian faith require in the way of a reliable, historical information about Jesus? Troeltsch gave broad indications on this score in a few places. For instance, "It is not a question of individual details but of the factuality of the total historical phenomenon of Jesus and the basic outline of his teaching and his religious personality [that matters]."[40] In the context of an attack on Herrmann, Troeltsch asserted that "for Herrmann's position, any allusion to the dependence of faith on criticism has a powerful, severely shocking impact on the soul. Nevertheless, on closer inspection, we find that the concept loses much of its terror. We do not depend on the thousands of details, but only on the general results of the research."[41]

And again, "It is not a question of individual details but of the factuality of the total historical phenomenon of Jesus and the basic outline of his

teaching and his religious personality. This must be capable of being established by means of historical criticism as historical reality if the 'symbol
of Christ' is to have a firm and strong inner basis in the 'fact' of Jesus."[42]

But how did Troeltsch conceive of what is involved in the "general results" or "basic outline"? This is difficult to say. In his *Glaubenslehre*, he
stated that "the *central* question is whether the apostolic community's
belief in Christ can be traced back to the impact of Jesus and is consistent
with his inner person."[43] More specifically, but with a slightly different emphasis, Troeltsch urged that

> Not all the minor details of historical research in theology are at issue
> here, but the basic facts—the decisive significance of Jesus' personality
> for the origin and formation of faith in Christ, the basic religious and eth-
> ical character of Jesus' teaching and the transformation of his teaching in
> the earliest Christian congregations with their Christ cult. In my opinion
> the decisive chief facts can here be ascertained with certainty despite
> all the questions which remain open. That is sufficient for properly reli-
> gious purposes—the acknowledgment of the historical existence of
> Jesus and the religious interpretation of his teaching. One only needs a
> basic overall picture.[44]

The *Glaubenslehre* offers the clearest presentation of historical requirements of Troeltsch's positive Christology, but it sits uncomfortably
with these other indications. In the paragraph on "The Significance of
Jesus for Faith," Troeltsch argued that historical criticism can assure the
systematic theologian that

> the development of the Christian belief in salvation and in the saving
> death of Christ must be traced back to the impact of the person of Jesus
> himself, i.e., to the resurrection faith and the messianic Christ-cult that
> arose from his impact. The resurrection appearances and the high mes-
> sianic descriptions of Christ, for their part, must be traced back to the ex-
> traordinary impact of his personality. His profoundest impact—his
> religious and ethical proclamation of the value of the soul and the King-
> dom of God in brother-love, as well as his extraordinary consciousness of
> mission and his struggle for a divinely induced world-renewal—all these
> are clearly historical. The only thing that remains questionable is the ex-
> tent to which the image of Jesus in the gospels, and particularly the
> image of Jesus' messianic self-consciousness, was influenced by the com-

munity and its image of Jesus in the Christ-cult. We have not yet achieved clarity about that, and, by the nature of the case, clarity will be difficult to achieve. It will also be difficult to determine how the Christ-cult arose within the community, and how it came to resemble the cults of the mystery religions. . . .

This assured body of facts, however, is sufficient to confirm *religious* faith in its *interpretative* task; we only need clarify what it is that such a religious interpretation of the historical facts can do.[45]

These descriptions of the minimum content of Troeltsch's "reasonable outline" are as clear as he became on the matter, but they are still rather vague. The main problem is that Troeltsch never specified the depth of historical detail required in any case. For example, in relation to the "basic outline of his teaching," is it enough to say that Jesus taught concerning the "kingdom of God"? Or is it also necessary to settle the controverted issue of whether Jesus conceived of that kingdom in primarily imminent apocalyptic terms? And exactly what did Troeltsch mean by Jesus' "religious personality"? It is not at all clear that this can be determined in principle, given the sources; in fact it is quite obvious that much of it simply cannot be. Nor is it clear that that those optimistic enough to attempt such a determination would be able to generate a significant, long-lasting consensus in practice; in fact historians have not been able to do this to date. Furthermore, several quotations lay out the requirements for a reasonable outline with regard to the process by which Jesus was transformed from a religious and ethical teacher and religious genius to the object of worship in the cultic life of the earliest Christian congregations. While this indirectly expresses Troeltsch's inspirational, nonincarnational Christology at this time, it is rather an odd statement of what Christian faith and cult needs to know about Jesus' life and work. It seems, therefore, that Troeltsch himself may have had only the vaguest idea of what he thought a reasonable outline of Jesus' life ought to contain.

As to the issue of whether historians can in practice fulfill the demand for a "basic outline"—whatever that finally means—Troeltsch held a mediating opinion. While willing to give up the older assumption that many details about Jesus' life, character, and teaching could be known, Troeltsch maintained that a general outline could still be obtained with the aid of historical critical methods. In fact, he thought that continued historical research would eventually produce a stable, minimal consensus about the historical Jesus. Even this seems somewhat optimistic, especially in view of developments in Jesus research since Troeltsch's time. Thus, it is not surprising that he offered no significant discussion of whether the New Testament sources are in some sense irretrievably defective for the purposes of establishing such consensus on historical grounds. He did think that the sources were problematic in character. But he was also of the opinion that, if the demands were reasonable, the sources were sufficient to satisfy them.

Troeltsch thought that these demands were in fact reasonable *in the case of a Christology of his inspirational, nonincarnational type*, a Christology that ranges its central themes "around a *personality*, and *not* a dogma or an idea or a moral law or a miraculous community founded by Jesus."[46] This suggests that the reasonable outline is nothing more than the assurance that Jesus was influential, through his teaching and exemplary struggle on behalf of the Kingdom of God, and that he helped to *cause* the eventual reception he received. The formation of the church was not, in other words, an accidental collocation of events, but a direct response to the inspiring impression made by Jesus on those who knew and followed him. But surely Troeltsch's psychological insight about the necessity for dependence of faith on history requires more? Do not faith and cult require concreteness of apprehension in *many aspects* of Jesus' teaching and activity? But if it was not specific, nameable pieces of information that were important to Troeltsch in this regard, what did he think *was* vital?

The suggestion in some of the passages quoted so far that a "mood" of factuality is important is echoed elsewhere in a number of places: "It is impossible to want to withdraw historical facts in general and in principle from scientific criticism. There does remain in this respect a dependence upon scholars and professors, if one wants to put it that way; or better, a dependence upon the general feeling of historical reliability produced by the impression of scientific research."[47]

This is an indication that Troeltsch's criteria for how much history is enough are drawn to no small extent from sociology. That is, his guiding question in determining what historians have to furnish to faith, cult, and dogmatics was not in the first instance What makes theological sense? but What will make Christian belief and healthy cultic life possible in the churches? This constitutes a significant departure from his Ritschlian heritage. It may also explain why Troeltsch never gave a clearer statement of what a reasonable outline entailed. Presumably, Troeltsch envisaged a close correspondence between "the general feeling of historical reliability produced by the impression of scientific research" and the contents of the research itself; an academic cover-up for the sake of the churches would not be feasible because the primary goal of historical research is to expound the truth as nearly as it can be established. So what is to be done when the truth as historical research sees it conflicts (permanently, say) with the conditions necessary for the liveliness of the symbol of Jesus Christ for faith and cult? That would be "the beginning of the end of the Christ symbol amongst scientifically educated people," according to Troeltsch, and thereafter faith and cult would be eroded at every level. Troeltsch could not exclude this kind of outcome in advance, since his view of history—summarized in the concept of *'Historismus'*—allows for radically unanticipated contingencies to impact even the most sacred elements of Christian faith, throwing them into a new light, reenlivening them, rendering them useless, or disclosing them as spent.

Dependence is Sociologically Feasible

With the primacy of sociological over theological considerations for interpreting what constitutes an adequate "basic outline," we come to another aspect of Troeltsch's argument about the feasibility of faith's dependence on history. In this case, Troeltsch's guiding observation was that, no matter how much the theologians may worry about it, the social and psychological demand of cult and believer for dependence of faith on concrete historical facts is a dynamic that rarely gets out of hand. To put Troeltsch's interpretation of this fact in a compact, positive form requires reading between the lines.

Troeltsch intuitively recognized the key to the fact that this dependence is managed successfully in practice: a healthy Christian community, including especially a vital cultic life, was a far more powerful influence than recognized in other solutions to the faith-history problem.[48] Here we see Troeltsch's explanation for the sociological feasibility of dependence coming into view in the form of a cultic "buffer"—to use an image that Troeltsch did not—between the believer and the historian. This is also a sign of his empirical-mindedness, for this does seem, after all, to be how the problem of faith and history is managed in practice. This idea was suggested by Troeltsch in just a few places. In his discussion of faith and history in the *Glaubenslehre*, for instance, he wrote that

> we could say that the relationship of faith to history is simply a matter of psychology, but it is a psychology that is tied to the structure of the community, to the cultus that is so closely identified with the community, to the need for personal support, and, above all, to the concrete content of the faith. A faith without these would ultimately develop into a faith without community or cultus: an utterly individual, personal, and emaciated mysticism, as can be seen all too often in the non-Christian movements of our day.[49]

In addition to an attack on individualism—common in Troeltsch's writings—this passage suggests that the psychological significance of the believer's relation through the community and cult, "the concrete content of the faith," is one of the keys to the problem of faith and history.

A similar theme emerges in "The Significance of the Historical Existence of Jesus for Faith," as a muted overtone quietly gracing a passage in which Troeltsch was struggling to articulate the sense in which Jesus is the living center of the Christian community:

> The decisive point in evaluating the significance of Jesus is therefore not that redemption outside Christianity is impossible, but the need a religious community has for a support, center and symbol of its religious life. The marvel is then that the center and symbol is constituted not in a fixed dogma or an equally fixed moral law but in the picture of a living, many-sided and at the same time elevating and strengthening personality. . . .
>
> Again, this personality does not stand in isolation. There is a rich extension of historical life which can without hesitation be taken into account with it in determining the Christian idea and filling it with living power.[50]

This is a key passage for the issue of the sense in which Jesus is "living," suggesting how important the biblical pictures of Christ are in Troeltsch's rather unstable understanding of this point; but this is not the focus of attention here. Rather, we need to evaluate Troeltsch's speaking of a "picture of a living, many-sided and at the same time elevating and strengthening personality" as the center of the cultic and community life of Christianity. Though this phraseology does call to mind the biblical pictures of Christ, the inescapable impression is left that Troeltsch had in mind a picture created in and through the cultic life itself. This is reinforced by his speaking of the "rich extension of historical life" that can be drawn into the formation of this living picture. The dynamics of cultic life will be taken up in a later chapter. Here it is sufficient to describe—in a kind of midrashic interpolation—the fundamental pattern that Troeltsch appears to have believed characterized the mediation of the tension between believer and historian by community and cultic life.

On the one hand, Christian communities are informed about historical research mostly through their clergy and educated members. Cultic life, however, rarely changes because of information gained in this way. At most, perhaps, a brief line in a sermon or a prayer is different than it might otherwise be, but very little else is altered. Meanwhile, the community fosters what interest there is in historical research—usually present only among a small minority—through other means, such as studies of the Bible or informal discussion among believers.

On the other hand, the individual believer is only partly constrained by the cultic life of his or her community. There is some more or less normative interpretation of the figure of Jesus made available to every believer who participates in the cult's worship (the *picture*), which greatly depends upon the various biblical pictures of Christ, selection among and interpretation of which is determined by the style and emphasis of religious experience that characterizes the community life of individual cultic centers. However, individual believers attach what weight they wish to each particular aspect of that presented interpretation, adding or subtracting whatever elements suit them. Thus the picture is *many-faceted* in two ways: at the level of liturgical, didactic, and homiletic presentation and at the level of individual appropriation. This flexibility between the cult and the imagination of believers is essential for the well-being of the community and for the cultivation of adherents in many different spiritual stages, especially in the "church" type of ecclesial organizations, but also in the "sect" type to a lesser extent.[51]

Perhaps an apt analogy for Troeltsch's view of the cult-mediated relation between historian and believer is the method by which an unmagnetized bar is magnetized slowly by repeatedly rubbing a magnet in one direction along its length. The metal of the bar (the cultic life of the churches) indirectly transfers to its interior—though with considerable resistance—the attractive characteristics of the magnet. Many strokes of the magnet are necessary to create even a small change in the magnetization of the bar, even as a great deal of historical research usually will have little effect upon individual believers. The cult (like the bar) serves both to constrain and to propagate external influences.

The nature of the church as a social reality had been the subject of attention by Friedrich Schleiermacher, both in the *Speeches on Religion* and in his *Glaubenslehre*, and the theme had appeared in other nineteenth-century theologians as well. Troeltsch was intimately familiar with this line of reflection and extended it through his social psychological approach to the problem of faith and history as a complement to his explanation of theological feasibility that relied on his anti-absolutist style of Christology. This mode of thought was also a key factor in Troeltsch's analysis of the malaise of Christian cultic life, for it contributed a sturdy theoretical basis for his attack on what he thought were the negative effects for Christianity and society of the rampant individualism of the modern world.[52] The negative effects of individualism upon Christian community and cult include, as Troeltsch saw, the practical exacerbation of the faith-history problem, for the cultic buffer essential to maintaining parity between the historian and the believer is dissolved when individualism breaks down community life.

Dependence is Theologically Feasible

Why did Troeltsch think that Christology could make do with just the biblical pictures of Jesus Christ and a reasonable outline of his life and teaching? How did Troeltsch expect to escape the typical problem of Christological dependence on history, wherein a Christological assertion implies some historical state of affairs that is beyond the power of historians to verify—in principle or because of inherent limitations in the sources—or perhaps is in their power but not supported by the evidence they actually turn up?

More concretely, does Troeltsch's Christology require or presuppose something about history like a resurrection, miracles, certain discourses, a particular self-understanding on the part of Jesus, specific claims to be Messiah or son of God, a particular intention associated with the events leading to the crucifixion, the moral perfection of his character, the unvarying soundness of his judgment, and so on? These are the areas where

Christology tends to try to sneak over the theological counter historically uncashable checks, relying on the affirmation of Jesus' significance in the biblical pictures of Christ to carry these affirmations of Christological doctrine when the historical evidence gives out or becomes too controversial. Troeltsch's concern was that traditional Christology is a purse full of such dubious historical transactions: all the merchants know to be suspicious of those checks, but they continue to be mindlessly written anyway. Troeltsch believed that the resulting trajectory toward skepticism had to a considerable extent already blighted both church and culture.

This tendency to assume historically what cannot be made good by historical research has been a painful concern for mainline Christology in the twentieth century, and this has resulted in some bold proposals. For example, Barth's presentation of Jesus in his commentary on Romans—and indeed to some extent *Paul's* presentation of Jesus in Romans—presupposes a man whose life and character are formally irrelevant to his role as the one in whom the divine appears incognito. Schubert Ogden's Christology is well known for its attempt to avoid presupposing the unverifiable about Jesus. But these Christologies run aground on Troeltsch's valuable criterion of the psychological and cultic necessity for dependence of faith on historical factuality.

Troeltsch's strategy, by contrast, was *to moderate the Christological assertions* themselves. He staked his Christology on a completely natural world—with religious depth and mystery, to be sure, but a world not blessed with miracles, resurrections, incarnations, humans perfect in character and judgment, supernatural means of salvation, and so on. Troeltsch's Jesus is thus an inspired prophet, whose compelling personal character and spiritual intensity inspired his followers as much as did his message of repentance and love and his expectation of a divine kingdom. Troeltsch emphasized that Jesus *caused* the reception he received in a general way, but accepted that Jesus cannot be supposed to have dictated the way people responded to him in details. Thus Troeltsch was able to affirm the Christ cult as a community celebration of "the possibility of Christian redemption through surrender of the faith and the will, whereby the soul surrenders itself to the God who is revealed in Jesus."[53] This interpretation also enables a deconstruction of traditional understandings of the origins of the Christ cult, by construing its emergence in part as the result of the literalization of poetic language about Jesus to the point that the "revealing and redemptive presence of God in Christ's human personality is then conceived as the *specific indwelling of God in Christ*." The result is the Pauline vision of Jesus Christ as "the Second Adam or the central human being," which gradually intensifies until it becomes "bound up with the concept that Christianity is the absolutely final and everlasting religion, the religion that will gather all human beings unto the end."[54]

Troeltsch believed that his interpretation of Jesus Christ avoided presupposing in Christology what cannot be satisfied by a reasonable *historisch* outline of Jesus' life, on the one hand, and faith's appropriation of the significance and meaning expressed in the biblical pictures of Christ, on the other. Besides being a serious attempt to refrain from presupposing the historically unverifiable about Jesus, Troeltsch also thought that his Christology maintained a healthy level of dependence on the historical Jesus, which his analysis of the nature of faith and cultic life had disclosed as necessary, which his historical judgment had convinced him was achievable, and which that other proponent of an inspirational, nonincarnational Christology, Schweitzer, thought was impossible to secure.

The distinction between Troeltsch's approach and those to which he was opposed is now in the open. It remains to evaluate whether Troeltsch's relinquishing of the absolute, final significance of Jesus Christ achieved a theologically intelligible account of the dependence of faith on history, in terms of both his proposal's ability to satisfy his own self-imposed demands and the adequacy of his proposal to other theological standards.

First, did Troeltsch succeed in his goal of maintaining the dependence of his Christology on history, in the sense of a mood of factuality that tends to support some reasonably general and secure ideas about Jesus? This is one of the self-imposed demands that flows from his analysis of the process of nurturing faith within the Christian cult. His appeal to a reasonable outline of Jesus' life and teaching appears to accomplish this. He needs only the most basic facts: that Jesus was an inspired religious genius, that he called people to follow him, that he taught in parables about the kingdom of God with great power, that he was amazingly determined to give his all for the kingdom of God, and that he helped cause the reception he received, including his transformation within the Christian cult. Most of these basic ideas are granted by most historians of the life and times of Jesus, notwithstanding the problematic character of such questions as the meaning of "kingdom of God." Thus a "mood of factuality" can be established on the few points that Troeltsch deemed vital.

Second, did Troeltsch actually avoid presupposing the historically un-verifiable in his Christology, as he thought he had? Troeltsch did not assert—his Christology did not require it—that Jesus had a particular self-understanding, that Jesus had a specific idea in mind about the meaning of the crucifixion, that Jesus had or did not have specific apocalyptic visions, that he was born of a virgin, that he performed miracles, or that he was resurrected. In fact, Troeltsch was assiduous at every relevant place in the *Glaubenslehre* in phrasing his sentences just in order to avoid being committed to such historical assertions, for all of them lead to extremely complicated historical thickets from which a respectable and stable scholarly consensus has not emerged. Moreover—and this is perhaps the real test—there is nothing in his construal of the reasonable outline of Jesus' life and teaching, nor anything in his assertions about the religious significance and authority of Jesus, that surreptitiously reintroduces the presupposition of these events or others like them. Thus it appears that Troeltsch did not presuppose in his Christology what historical research cannot confirm with high probability and a solid consensus.

Third, is Troeltsch correct that the sociological, historical, and theological feasibility of dependence requires Christology to reject hermeneutically absolutized interpretations of Jesus Christ? Troeltsch was impressed with how difficult it is to avoid presupposing the historically unverifiable in Christologies affirming the revelatory finality, salvific comprehensiveness, and ontological absoluteness of Jesus Christ. Do not such interpretations presuppose a host of interior attitudes, specific intentions, and types of behavior that are in principle out of historical reach? Moreover, Troeltsch showed that *extant strategies* for managing the dependence of faith on historical research fail so long as this hermeneutically absolutized style of Christology is in view. Surely he is correct, then, that his Christological approach reduces the stress associated with being forced by Christology to presuppose the historically unverifiable, while still maintaining the kind of solid dependence of Christology on history required by his social psychological analysis of individual belief and cultic life. But then are these advantages in relation to the problem of faith and history really as desirable as Troeltsch thought? Everything turns here on the soundness of his insufficiently elaborated social psychological analyses of faith and cult. I have tried to show that there is much to commend Troeltsch's arguments and intuitions in this area.

Fourth, did Troeltsch need to be so revolutionary in his Christology in order to secure the advantages he wanted? Though he was correct that Christology without hermeneutical absolutism dramatically improves the prospects for theological justification of dependence, Troeltsch does appear to have overreacted in his narrow judgment about what kinds of Christology enable dependence to be theologically feasible. In particular, he wrote off the elevation of Jesus through the Christ cult as understandable but entirely unjustified. However, it is far from unreasonable to understand God as present in Jesus Christ in some sense, just as it is perfectly plausible to see revelation as occurring in and through creative, projective, even partially delusory interpretations of Jesus Christ. Moreover, nothing would be lost with regard to the problem of dependence of Christology on historical knowledge about Jesus were incarnational insights affirmed, so long as the understanding of incarnation did not lead to the assumption in the resulting Christology of too many more unverifiable historical facts about Jesus of Nazareth. Here, of course, there is a problem. Most incarnational Christologies typically *are* more historically grandiose than Troeltsch's. However, anti-absolutist incarnational Christology can be rendered far less historically presumptuous than hermeneutically absolutized Christology, and to that extent anti-absolutist incarnational Christology could have been condoned by Troeltsch.

Finally, the historical, theological, and social psychological components of Troeltsch's analysis of the problem of faith's, cult's and Christology's dependence on history, when considered together, produce further criterial questions that, by his own standards, Troeltsch ought to have answered. For instance, is it possible that the faith-history problem may one day become *unmanageable*, because historical research overwhelms Christian believers in places where the cultic buffering dynamic is eroded by Western individualism or by some other corrosive force? Since Troeltsch ruled out supernatural governance of ecclesial institutions, and so of the cultic buffering mechanism, is its operation merely a creative contingency, with no theological rationale whatsoever? And what of the theoretical problem of the relationship of the historical Jesus to individual and cultic conceptions of him? Although Troeltsch did indicate the general direction of his Christologically based explanation for the theological feasibility of dependence, he did not adequately relate his position to these questions, which are implicit in the requirement of theological intelligibility.

As for the first two questions, Troeltsch's mature theology seems to have taken the radical line, but ambiguously, and he nowhere spoke to them directly. That is, Troeltsch appears to have thought that the cultic buffering dynamic really could be eroded completely, by the same cultural tides that foster individualism or by something equally destructive, and that its operation is, in any case, a natural contingency for which only a *post facto* theological rationale could be given.

In relation to the third question, it is evident that Troeltsch thought Christology could survive if contact with the historical Jesus was limited to a reasonably reliable outline of his life and teaching rather than a mass of concrete particulars and that he was personally convinced of the reality and efficacy of Jesus Christ within the Christian religious consciousness. But how in Troeltsch's mind were dogmatic statements about Jesus Christ to be connected to the actual person of Jesus (known by historians only in outline), or to the biblical pictures of him (in their variety and partial incompatibility), in such a way as to do justice to the concreteness and vividness with which Jesus Christ was apprehended in the religious life of individual Christians and in the cultic life of the churches? Troeltsch did try out several different ideas for arguing that there was a continuous link from the person of the earthly Jesus to the imaginative picturing of him in cultic life and in individual believers' imaginations. However, they are all incomplete and problematic, and Troeltsch appears never to have been completely satisfied with his creative attempts to answer this question.[55] However, at least while he wrote on Christian doctrine, he appears relatively confident that it could be done.

Troeltsch's fragmentary offerings give out at this point, and we are left to wonder what he might have suggested had he dealt with these theological questions systematically and in detail. But there can be no doubt that Troeltsch's Christological approach, whatever else might be said about it positively or negatively, represents a compelling solution to the problem of the dependence of faith, cult, and Christology on history, a solution whose central pillars are a powerful social-psychological analysis of the phenomenon of dependence, and a Christology that clinched the theological viability of his solution by means of its repudiation of the absolute, universal, exclusive, and unsurpassable salvific and revelatory significance of Jesus Christ. Moreover, if Troeltsch was right—and I have argued that, except for his unnecessary bias against incarnational Christologies, he was—the problem of faith's dependence on history can only ever be satisfactorily solved when Christology politely, gratefully, but decisively disengages itself from the inessential, absolutist hermeneutical habit of the classical Christological tradition and thereby calls forth from that tradition its full potential for powerfully relating Jesus Christ to the modern world.

2
Christology and the History of Religions

At the end of the nineteenth century, it was unusual to regard Christianity as one religious tradition among others, in the sense of approaching both its history and questions of its normativity without dogmatic presuppositions, in the context of the whole history of religions, paying attention to comparable claims to normativity encountered in all traditions in an even-handed way. Of course, awareness of the importance of other religions for understanding Christianity shows up much earlier than Troeltsch—Hegel and Schleiermacher set Christianity within the context of the world religions at the beginning of the nineteenth century, for instance—but such efforts cannot be described as even-handed. Determined approximation to even-handedness is common at the end of the twentieth century, because of the burgeoning field of religious studies. But Troeltsch was known as the theologian of the history-of-religions school just because he wished to bring this approach fully *into Christian systematic theology*. Troeltsch believed that a confessional orientation was axiomatic for theology, but he took it to be the second phase of theological method, to be preceded by an objective description of and accounting for the phenomenon of religion.

The discussion here first treats Troeltsch's theology of the history of religions and then one aspect of the reception of Troeltsch's theological method—the controversy it forced concerning supernaturalism—to see whether the Christological results that he thought followed from the historical and philosophical study of religion can be resisted. Finally, we will consider an application of this method to interpreting the development of Christian doctrine, for the reconception of the Christological tradition occasioned by the history of religions dramatically disrupts that line of justification for Christological assertions which makes appeal to the formation and early development of Christological reflection.

The Theology of the History of Religions

In 1913, the *American Journal of Theology* published a translation of a lecture that Troeltsch had delivered to an audience in the United States in response to the editors' request "to state the meaning of a dogmatics working with the presuppositions and in the spirit of [the history-of-religions school]."[1] As a theological program, Troeltsch stated that the "history of religions school" signifies "recognition of the universally accepted twofold scientific conclusion that human religion exists only in multiple individual forms which develop in very complex relations of mutual contact and influence, and that a decision concerning these forms cannot be made with the old dogmatic expedient of distinguishing between a natural and a supernatural revelation."[2]

Such a dogmatic expedient is impossible when the horizon for reflection is broad enough to encompass the whole variety of religious phenomena, because the Christian distinction between natural and supernatural revelation is contested, or can be appealed to, by adherents of other religious traditions.

How are Christians to deal with the loss of this traditional dogmatic expedient? Troeltsch believed the answer to that question is clear, but acknowledges that it is a challenging one: "Christian theology must approach the religious life of humanity not with a supernaturalist or philosophical apologetic for one's religion, but rather a historical, comparative study of religions. Overwhelmingly difficult as this undertaking may be, and liable as we are to superficial self-deception, this is nevertheless the primary scholarly way in which we have to come to terms with the religious problem today."[3]

The Predogmatic Phase

According to Troeltsch, a Christian theology attentive to the history of religions method has a dogmatic and a predogmatic phase. It is important,
of course, to be alert to the fact that the way Troeltsch used the word *dogmatic* needs careful parsing. The predogmatic phase involves, on the one
hand, the historical explanation of the rise of Christianity from out of its
syncretistic religious environment, paying particular attention to "the
transformation of the gospel into the world-conquering Christ-religion."[4]
On the other hand, it involves the attempt to construct a philosophically
consistent view of the essence and development of religion.

Troeltsch spoke about this second task in terms of the "question of
grounding the validity of Christianity within the stream of the universal
development of the history of religions and over against the entirely analogous claims to validity" found there.[5] Focusing on grounding the validity
of Christianity unnecessarily narrows the conception of the systematic
task for the philosophy of religion, even thought of as oriented to Christian dogmatics. But it is an accurate statement of the motivation that
Troeltsch and many other Christian theologians actually have brought to
such a task. In any event, it is not at all clear that the philosophy of religion is amenable to Troeltsch's envisaged use of it as a preparation for
Christian dogmatics by which the superiority and absoluteness of Christianity can be established, for several reasons.

First, the philosophical study of religions has produced a number of
theories about the origin, function, and significance of religion, and not all
of them are useful for grounding the validity, let alone the absoluteness,
of Christianity. Troeltsch stated that Christian dogmatics must reject "all
purely skeptical, positivistic and illusionistic theories" as incompatible
with the Christian faith. He prescinded from stating his reasons for thinking such a rejection is justified in this article, but dealt with the matter at
length elsewhere.[6] His arguments in those places are forceful and consonant with the main stream of religious studies since his time, which has
regarded religion as an authentic and justifiable human activity, within
limits, and has seen no need to deny the religious relevance even of such
processes as illusion, projection, displacement, and enthusiasm.

Second, and going further, philosophies of religion "that see in religion the revelation of deepest truth,"[7] as Troeltsch put it, while according
a limited validity to Christianity as a matter of methodological assumption,

may not be capable of supporting Troeltsch's desire to establish the absoluteness of Christianity. In *The Absoluteness of Christianity*, Troeltsch himself rejected the prevailing philosophies of religion that were commonly thought in his time to establish this result. The evolutionary apologetic that sees a principle in every religion and Christianity as its highest realization was the object of a sustained attack.[8] Troeltsch argued, in a way that seems obvious now, that the actual history of religions simply does not support the absoluteness of Christianity understood in such a way. And the supernatural apologetic, designed to give the naïve Christian assumption of absoluteness some philosophical backbone, is impossible both because of its ahistorical attitude to religious texts and its refusal to deal fairly with the parallel claims to supernatural authorization within other religious traditions.[9]

What then will Troeltsch advance in the place of these transparent attempts on the part of philosophy of religion to provide an assured basis for a naïve conception of the absoluteness of Christianity? To appreciate his proposal, it is important to notice that Troeltsch in *Absoluteness* actually went further than repudiating the possibility of establishing Christian absoluteness on the basis of the evolutionary apologetic. He suggested that the hypothesis of a common essence or a religious-philosophical principle manifest in all religions is itself dubious. Troeltsch's rejection of "essentialism" in this sense was made on the basis of his view of history as contingent and historical meaning as contextual: "Real history recognizes only individual and temporary structures that are related to their goal strictly in terms of a tendency toward the absolute."[10] This tendency appears in diverse ways that cannot be reduced to a single religious idea; the unity of religious phenomena lies not within history but in the absolutely real beyond it, toward which they tend. This unity may well be increasingly realized in history, but not in such a way that its rational, essential character can be known in advance on the basis of extant historical forms of religion.[11]

"Artificial absoluteness shatters under the impact of real history"[12] because the facts of history do not support the presuppositions of miraculous revelation or of a single great religious idea. However, "study of history that does not stop short with mere facts but seeks out their interconnections will discern in these various claims to absoluteness the contextually appropriate expression of the absoluteness of the goal toward which they are oriented."[13] This shows the ambiguity of the term *essen-*

tialism as applied to the philosophical study of religion.[14] But it also indicates that Troeltsch's philosophy of religion must proceed on the basis of a painstaking comparative analysis of religions and that the absoluteness of Christianity cannot be conceived or demonstrated otherwise. Can such a historical procedure warrant Troeltsch's claim that the historical way of thinking "does not preclude our acknowledging Christianity as the highest religious truth that has relevance for us"? Can such a historical analysis perhaps even positively demonstrate this claim?[15]

Troeltsch's developing answer to this question appears most clearly in the contrast between the first and second editions of *The Absoluteness of Christianity* (1902 and 1912) and his own 1923 review of that book, "The Place of Christianity among the World Religions." The process of development linking his early and late opinions about this issue appears to have been painful for Troeltsch, judging from what appears in some of his writings to be a reluctance to accept what he was coming to believe was true, namely, that Christianity was not absolute, except perhaps for "us" in "European culture." In fact, his indecision or unclarity about this issue produced a massive conceptual fracture in the first edition of *Absoluteness*. As Troeltsch's foreword to the second edition shows, his thought had already substantially clarified by 1912, after the writing of the *Social Teaching* (1911), which was the turning point of his thought in many ways. He did not substantially change the second edition, however, both because of lack of time and because of the value of the first edition of *Absoluteness* as capturing a stage in an ongoing debate.[16] The 1923 essay is clearer in its point of view.

The glaring problem in *Absoluteness* is especially evident in the fourth chapter, "Christianity: Focal Point and Culmination of All Religious Developments." From what has been said so far, we might have expected this chapter title to take the form of a question. In fact, we might even have expected Troeltsch's answer to such a question to be negative, affirming only that each religious tradition possesses culturally relative and historically contextualized absoluteness in virtue of its partial grasping of a transcendent absolute beyond history. Thus, all religious traditions would be conceived in fundamentally the same way, and the possibility of intertraditional norms relevant to assessing final absoluteness would be rejected as historically naïve. This, however, is the view of the 1923 essay and not of *Absoluteness*, though from other writings appearing in the period immediately after *Social Teaching* it appears that Troeltsch may already have reached this conclusion by the time of the 1912 second edition of *Absoluteness*. By contrast, in the fourth chapter of the 1902 edition of *Absoluteness*, Troeltsch answered that it *is* possible to show that Christianity is the highest religion. The flagrant character of the contradiction is astonishing at this end of the twentieth century, but Troeltsch's argument represented at the time a genuine grappling with the problem.

Troeltsch's reasons in 1902 for thinking that a comparative historical analysis of religious traditions can produce such a result were two, and they are not consistent. On the one hand, Troeltsch thought that this kind of absoluteness had to be a matter of personal conviction, "a kind of personal conviction that emerges from comparative observation and absorption in hypothetically adopted values."[17] On the other hand, he gave an analysis—disastrously superficial by late-twentieth-century standards—of the world religions, simply dismissing tribal religions, and concluding that

> among the great religions, Christianity is in actuality the strongest and most concentrated revelation of personalistic religious apprehension. It is even more than that. It occupies a unique position in that it alone has worked out in a radical way the distinction between the higher and lower worlds that is found on every hand. It alone . . . takes empirical reality as actually given and experienced, builds upon it, transforms it, and at length raises it up to a new level . . . Christianity represents the only complete break with the limits and conditions of nature religion.[18]

The key distinction for Troeltsch at this point was between "meditation on Transcendent Being or non-Being" and "redemption through faithful, trusting participation in the person-like character of God, the ground of all life and of all genuine value." But in asserting that "the higher goal and the greater profundity of life are found on the side of personalistic religion,"[19] Troeltsch appears to have replaced the idea of religion in the Enlightenment or in absolute idealism with an equally ahistorical, illegitimately transcultural norm. A similar violation of his own principles is expressed when he said, "An approach based on the historical study of religion shows beyond doubt that Christianity not only occupies a unique position in principle but, more important, that in this unique position it also synthesizes separate tendencies and suggestions into one common goal."[20] Here he was even implying that he wished to revitalize the evolutionary philosophy of religion that he only just finished demolishing.

It is conceivable that such results as Troeltsch reached could be recast as the conclusions of an inquiry that predicted the triumph of Christianity in the drawn out contest of world religions to represent the whole of the human race. Radical pluralists such as John Cobb in our own time do this, though the recasting is extensive. But this was not Troeltsch's aim at all; his concern was with the theoretical absoluteness of Christianity, as this could be established by cross-cultural norms deducible from a comparative historical study of religion.

In the shadow of the emphatic statement that "Christianity must be understood not only as the culmination point but also as the convergence point of all the developmental tendencies that can be discerned in religion,"[21] it is hard to assess the significance of balancing remarks that appear after this historical survey of religion is completed. For example, Troeltsch stated that "it cannot be proved with absolute certainty that Christianity will always remain the final culmination point, that it will never be surpassed."[22] Our confidence that Christianity is the "final" religion therefore is derived from the first reason mentioned above for thinking that Christianity was absolute, namely, personal faith.[23] As Christians, we are borne on the waters of history in a vessel, it seemed to Troeltsch, that is far superior to any other vessel. This superiority may be established using the intellectual precision afforded by the history-of-religions method. But, whereas he began the chapter saying that confidence in this superiority depended on faith, after his analysis of religion he said that faith is needed only to assure us that "absolutely nothing can make a new and higher religion likely for us,"[24] that there never will be any better boats. Apparently the absoluteness of Christianity for the past and present can be established exclusively from history, and without faith, after all.

Such inconsistencies and confusions are clear signs that Troeltsch had misgivings about this position even in 1902. When he returned to revise *Absoluteness* in 1912, it was after his conception of history as an organic set of contingent particularities (the fundamental implication of *Relativismus*) had taken more or less final shape. But his ideas about the place of Christianity among the world religions only achieved completely clear presentation in the 1923 Oxford lecture of that name already mentioned.

The 1923 position can be indicated by a shift away from the construal of "absoluteness for us" that Troeltsch gave this phrase in 1902. Is not "absoluteness for us" either oxymoronic or merely an odd way of saying "important to us"? In the 1902 edition of *Absoluteness*, Troeltsch was inclined to err on the side of apparent self-contradiction, speaking of universal absoluteness for European culture. That is, he believed Christian theology must articulate Christianity's absoluteness, but he could not attach any meaning to "absoluteness" that did not include the universal validity of Christian truth claims. All religions might have a revelation of the absolute beyond history, but Christianity thought of as the culmination and convergence point of all religion necessarily possesses a decisive revelation; what it says about God's personal character and about the human possibility of redemption is superior to related statements made in other religions. To speak of universally applicable claims that are true *of* everyone everywhere, but only true *for* us in Western European culture, is to adopt a position that badly needs explanation, if it is not actually nonsensical.

Troeltsch might have provided an explanation, but he did not do so in *Absoluteness*. For instance, he might have said that Christian truth claims are "relatively true" and, as such, are on equal footing with the relatively true claims made by other religions; they are all approximations to ultimate, mysterious, transcendent truth. Or he might have said with many contemporary philosophers that the concept of 'relative truth' makes no sense[25] and that Christian truth claims are thus wholly true in a common-sense way. In this case, either he vaults Christianity into a superior position by denying that competing claims are wholly true, or he affirms that the world is such that, with regard to religious mysteries, flagrant conflict between absolutely true claims sometimes is possible. Troeltsch would have denied the skeptical or mystical irrationalism of this last option. But in 1902 he was uncomfortably suspended over the chasm separating the first two positions.

This trajectory in Troeltsch's thought was made less ambiguous in "The Place of Christianity." This lecture was delivered after Troeltsch had written the first volume of *Der Historismus und Seine Probleme* (1922) in which he gave sustained attention to the problem of historical relativism and took up the challenge of explaining our conviction of the presence of an absolute within history.[26] Troeltsch there explicated a "relative absoluteness," which corresponds to what aptly has been called a "polymorphous view of truth,"[27] in that he affirmed the absolute normativity of

Christianity for Christians and for European cultures but also allowed that other religions may be normative in completely parallel ways. Therefore, the truth claims in the revelation of Christian and other religions were treated in parallel ways; they are all more or less accurate approximations to the absolutely real. Christian truth claims are absolutely true *for us* only because they are only finally meaningful in the context of European civilization. Cultural and historical locatedness is what brings relativity to truth; propositions are judged true or false against that background. As suggested before, later discussions have discerned philosophical problems in any understanding of truth as relative, but at least Troeltsch had reached the point in 1923 where he could articulate a consistent position.

With this we have the final resting place of Troeltsch's assessment of the predogmatic phase of his theology of the history of religions. It is a viewpoint common even now and represented more consistently by a number of philosophers of religion, including Huston Smith and John Hick in their various ways. It is fittingly expressed in the closing section of the lecture "The Place of Christianity," parts of which are quoted here at length:

> Can we, then, discover no common goal of religion, nothing at all that is absolute, in the objective sense of constituting a common standard for mankind? Instinctive conviction makes us reluctant to admit such a sceptical conclusion, and it will especially be combated on the ground of the reality of the subjective validities which we have discovered. These are not simply illusions or the products of human vanity. They are products of the impulse towards objective truth, and take effect in the practical sphere under constant critical self-purification and effort at self-improvement. . . . This synthesis cannot as yet be already attained in any one of the historical religions, but . . . they all are tending in the same direction, and . . . all seem impelled by an inner force to strive upward towards some unknown final height, where alone the ultimate unity and the final objective validity can lie. . . . But, so far as the human eye can penetrate into the future, it would seem probable that the great revelations to the various civilizations will remain distinct, in spite of a little shifting of their several territories at the fringes, and that the question of their several relative values will never be capable of objective determination, since every proof thereof will presuppose the special characteristics of the civilization in which it arises. . . .

> This is what I wish to say in modification of my former theories. I

hope you feel that I am not speaking in any spirit of scepticism or uncertainty. A truth which, in the first instance, is *a truth for us* does not
cease, because of this, to be very Truth and Life. . . . If each racial group
strives to develop its own highest potentialities, we may hope to come
nearer to one another. This applies to the great world religions, but it
also applies to the various religious denominations, and to individuals in
their intercourse with one another. In our earthly experience the Divine
Life is not One, but Many. But to apprehend the One in the Many constitutes the special character of love.[28]

The Dogmatic Phase

Once this predogmatic foundation is laid, Christian dogmatics proper can
begin. Indeed, it must begin, for the philosophy of religion cannot produce a religious world view. Either it produces skepticism about the possibility of any intellectually and practically serious religious interpretation
of the world, or it offers only a dehistoricized religion based on philosophical principles drawn from the common content of all religions. But
Troeltsch thought that first alternative completely refuted by the actual
history of religions. And, in a telling remark, "The second is an illusion
shattered by the dependence of the religious elements of philosophies on
the great, historical religions, and by the impotence of every form of religion which is purely individualistic and intellectual. Thus we are thrown
back upon history and upon the necessity of constructing out of history a
world of ideas that shall be normative for us. When we have said this,
however, we have recognized the impulse leading to a dogmatics."[29]

It follows that Christian dogmatics in this idiosyncratic sense has a
natural, defensible place within the history-of-religions perspective, and
within the secular university. It is far from being out of date, or of no possible relevance, in a culture for which even religion has become the object
of systematic analysis.

Troeltsch defined the specific major aim of theology as *"the exposition of a normative, Christian world view"*[30] and outlined three tasks for
it. The first task consists in establishing, on the basis of a philosophy of religion, "the fundamental and universal supremacy of Christianity for our
own culture and civilization."[31] This is a direct result of the dogmatic impulse just described and, from the discussion of his shifting philosophy of
religion, it is clear that the sense in which Troeltsch understood this task

of dogmatics also changed over time. The second task consists in specifying the essence of Christianity against the background of both the historical and philosophical predogmatic interests. As we shall see in the examination of the development of doctrine below, for Troeltsch this could not involve an unchanging essence nor one that develops securely on the basis of the assumption of a divine foundation. Rather, it could only be understood contingently and contextually as "the new interpretations and new adaptations corresponding to each new situation, produced by Christianity's historical power."[32] The third task is "the properly dogmatic task," elaborating the essence of Christianity in terms of God, world, humanity, sin, salvation, church and eschatology.[33] With this task, the continuity between Troeltsch's use of the word *dogmatics* and its use in his own tradition is evident.

A dogmatics defined by these three tasks is based on the properly scientific results of the study of religions. Once again, as we have seen, the material content of these results shifted over time in Troeltsch's thinking. What is more important, the reception of these results is not completely scientific in itself because it is conditioned by vivid religious experience, as well as by the practical need to furnish the churches and their clergy with a systematic presentation of the Christian faith for preaching, teaching, and edification.[34] Especially in connection with this need, Troeltsch stated his conviction that "such a dogmatics is unquestionably capable of expressing a definitely earnest, warm, and active religious life."[35] His own *Glaubenslehre*, published from notes of his lectures on dogmatics delivered at the University of Heidelberg in 1912-13, demonstrates this capability. In it, Troeltsch began to carry out the three dogmatic tasks against the background of the historical and philosophical predogmatic interests fostered by the history of religions. But it is far less thoroughgoing in this regard than Troeltsch implied in *The Dogmatics of the History of Religions School* that he would have liked.[36]

Christology

On the history-of-religions approach, as Troeltsch conceived it, no area of Christian doctrine is more profoundly affected than Christology. From his earliest works Troeltsch was preoccupied with the enlargement of the domain of data against which an assessment of the normativity of Jesus Christ had to be made. This especially involved exhibiting the intelligibility and plausibility of the normative status of Jesus Christ *even for Christians* in the broad context of the whole diverse history of human culture and religion, as the first task of the dogmatic phase of a *religionsgeschichtliche Theologie* requires. Troeltsch was also prepared to extend this context to include what was being forced upon the modern mind by physical cosmology: could salvation through Jesus Christ remain normative for Christians in light of the likelihood of alien civilizations on other planets? Further questions confronted Troeltsch. For instance, what was the place of absoluteness in Christianity if Jesus Christ could be at best efficacious and absolute *only for Christians*?

Troeltsch's eventual conclusion about Christology in the face of this complex of problems was two-fold. First, he argued that the history-of-religions approach to early Christianity renders impossible the justification of traditional Christology by appeal to the origins and development of the Christological tradition.[37] In *Absoluteness, Glaubenslehre*, and many of the occasional writings after *Social Teaching*, Troeltsch repeatedly presented the history-of-religions point of view on this development. His characteristic interpretation was that the theology of the developing Christ cult had been imposed on the historical Jesus, who thereby became the beneficiary (or victim) of the process of founder elevation familiar from study of the origins of many religious and other traditions. Troeltsch made this point in numerous ways. For instance, he emphasized the contrast between the supposed status of Christian doctrine as absolute truth and the tentativity of Jesus' preaching, "for whom all ultimate salvation and all ultimate truth were primarily something to be awaited."[38] Or he spoke of the early Christians' identification of Jesus with God—in spite of Jesus' own tendency to retire behind his message—in order to render him an immediate object of faith and in turn to do justice to the actual experience of immediacy that Christians interpreted as fellowship with Christ.[39]

Troeltsch appealed to this same social psychological dynamic in explaining the presence of absolutist hermeneutical tendencies in the classical Christological tradition: such tendencies can ground the sense of naïve absoluteness that some Christians think is required to explain the simple immediacy of their religious experiences. But this is a poor explanation of that sense of immediacy, according to Troeltsch. As religiously valuable as those experiences are, they must not be construed in a naïve way, at least not by theologians. It is vital to press to a deeper analysis with the social psychological tools of the history of religions.[40] This is never for Troeltsch a call for an attack on religious experience as mistakenly directed toward an utterly deluded understanding of Jesus Christ. It is rather for him an attack directed against the absolutist tendencies in the Christological tradition, which he rightly charged tend to be opposed to awarding sophisticated social psychological analyses a key role in the theological understanding of religious experiences.

Second, Troeltsch articulated a positive Christology that interpreted Jesus as a religiously inspired person and emphasized the fact that Jesus still represents the point to which *our* cultural stream must turn ever and again to find the most adequate approach to the divine absolute in which all revelations participate. This Christology changed shape in his various writings.

In the first edition of *Absoluteness*, Troeltsch adopted a position close to Harnack's reading in *What Is Christianity?* He spoke in general terms of "the grandeur, breadth, and freedom of Jesus, whose message remains the highest and greatest that we know," of the "authority of Jesus" that justifies unreserved commitment: "However much the figure of Jesus may be concealed under early Christian apologetics or dogmatic systems based on naïve traditions, it is plainly evident that what constantly radiates from him is the marvelous spontaneity with which he expressed so simply what is highest and most profound, connecting this in the most natural way with the belief that he had been sent by the Father. When the clouds of research have lifted, this final result will remain forever."[41]

In his *Glaubenslehre* Troeltsch was more reserved but not much more specific than this. The underlying theme, however, remains the same: Jesus was a compelling, authoritative person, who proclaimed God's kingdom and revealed God's personal nature with such power that it has remained decisive for Christianity ever since. There is little trace of a doctrine of the person and work of Jesus Christ, the hallmark of traditional Christology. Even his treatment of Jesus Christ under the traditional Protestant rubric of the three offices—prophet, high priest, and king—is merely a series of statements of the traditional understanding coupled with critiques. Troeltsch concluded that section by saying that "whoever cannot share in these certainties will find all such predicates questionable, and will instead be satisfied with the foundational meaning of the *personality* of Jesus as the *revelation* of God, the head of the community, and the effective symbol of saving and healing religious power, for as long as the Christian life-world endures."[42] But what, we insist on knowing, did Troeltsch think was so special about this *personality as revelation*? Only the barest hints are given.

Troeltsch emphasized the kingly office over the other two, in accordance with his view of the importance of the church as the mystic body of Christ, and Christ as its mystic head, or king. He thereby implied that Jesus can be called the living Christ, but every attempt to search out a clear-cut sense in which such a nomenclature can be justified in Troeltsch's theology meets with frustration. He spoke of the "enduring, living capacity of Jesus' personality," but then said that its "impact was thoroughly historical and psychological."[43] Perhaps the safest gloss of Troeltsch's opinion is that Jesus' enduring life is "living" in the sense of the historical transmission of a precious, potent, communal memory.

There remain a few allusions to a mystical presence of Jesus. They are reminiscent of Albert Schweitzer's Jesus mysticism and very nearly as imprecise. However, in one place, it seems that Troeltsch was inclined to see the spirit of Christ as a spiritual principle extending beyond its primary historical realization in Jesus' life. That life was subject to the customary limitations of historical existence.

> But these historical limitations were shattered by his death, which at the same time freed the spirit contained in this manifestation and enabled it to continue as a progressive principle, changing with the times and their needs. . . . The Spirit of Christ has set spirit free, that is the meaning of his death. And since this liberation of the spirit is an act of self-sacrifice and soul-power, it signifies that the Spirit of Christ was set free for love and power by the death of Christ. Hence the Spirit of Christ ensouls the community as its driving force; it is the principle of the continuous extension and deepening of the Christian knowledge of God.[44]

It seems for Troeltsch, then, that the historical transmission of a precious, communal memory can be accorded in his philosophy of history the status of a spiritual principle. As vague as this is, it does settle two issues.

First, the Spirit of Christ, or the ongoing life of Christ, has no meaning or reality apart from its ensouling the Christian community. Not only is there no *revelation* of God through the living Jesus Christ without reception of that revelation, as Tillich was later to put it, but without reception there is no sense in which Jesus Christ can be thought of as having an ongoing life. Second, we are reminded of how rich a view of history Troeltsch possessed. Though supernatural influences were excluded—especially in the form of his frequent criticisms of "excessive supernaturalism," "dualistic supernaturalism," or "dogmatic supernaturalism"[45]—Troeltsch had no objection to supernaturalism in the sense of the divine mystery immanent and active in the historical process. Indeed, his view of God requires some kind of supernaturalism, for God is preeminently a divine *person*, for Troeltsch, simultaneously eternal essence and absolute will.[46] It follows that much that formerly was thought of as "supernatural," such as the ongoing life of Jesus Christ and the process of redemption, has the potential of being reenlivened within history itself in Troeltsch's view of it.

But we must press this historically mediated vision of the spiritual influence of Jesus further. How powerful a conception of historical influence is it? Troeltsch in 1902 thought it possible to "discover in [Jesus'] free spontaneity, which is at the same time the expression of the purest and most concentrated religious power, an indication of the highest revelation of the divine life that *holds sway over us*."[47] But we have seen that in his thought this soon became a simple description of an inevitable consequence of the intimate linkage between European culture and Christianity—Jesus Christ is *de facto* the highest revelation of God for Europeans—rather than a conclusion warranted by diligent research into the history of religions. That is, the Spirit of Christ is one of many parallel historical principles and both its significance and its fate are tied to the setting of European culture. If this culture were to decline, and Troeltsch spoke at times as if this were imminent, then the influence of the Spirit of Christ would decline with it. It is not, therefore, the kind of historical principle that can keep alive a culture and so perpetuate itself out of itself. It contributes to and perishes with its cultural heritage, as far as Troeltsch was concerned. In the final analysis, then, historical principles are contingent, subject to shifting norms, and liable to die, in the manner of symbols. If the symbol of Jesus Christ were to die in this way, then there would be no sense in which Jesus Christ is living, for he has no objective ongoing life.

Moving from Jesus Christ as the mystic, kingly head of the church to the doctrine of Jesus' person, Troeltsch did go so far as to admit that "the secret of Jesus' personality lies not only in the impact that he had, but in how he came to have it."[48] This suggests that a doctrine of the person of

Chapter 2

Jesus Christ is required. But Troeltsch stopped short of actually answering his own implied question. He attacked the traditional metaphysical attempt to answer it in terms of a unity of two natures and weakly added "More recent theology construes this unity, not as incarnation, but as a unity of will."[49] He did not venture to commit himself in regard to this position. We are left with a Christology of an inspirational and nonincarnational type, in which the precise nature of Jesus' inspiration and any insight into its provenance are left unspecified.

Matters are no better in relation to the work of Jesus Christ. Troeltsch clearly identified himself with his interpretation of Abelard's teaching that "the significance of Jesus was not cosmic, but rather lay in his soul-transforming impact"[50]; the need for any supernatural, atoning transaction is repudiated. Troeltsch spoke of God alone as savior and only tolerated the misleading attribution to Jesus of this title because of its importance in Christian piety.[51] Jesus brings about redemption "not as a teacher nor as an example, but as a *personality*: a personality whose religious power and purity, whose knowledge of God and whose proclamation of redemption and the forgiveness of sins creates faith, or completes a faith that is already begun."[52] Once again, the influence of Jesus is transmitted to the present through history, both through the biblical presentations of him and in the community of Christians.

The End of Christology?

Is this, then, the Christology of the *religionsgeschichtliche Schule*? It can be thought of as a rather religiously insipid and cultically useless Christological point of view, compared, say, with just about any of the great Christologies of the classical tradition. It is just this supposed dilution of Christian theology that led Karl Barth to refer to Troeltsch as the "nadir" of liberal Protestantism.[53] There is even a question as to whether Troeltsch himself may have thought that his theology had collapsed.[54]

But would not such a conclusion have been appropriate? When all is said and done, did not the history of religions *destroy Troeltsch's Christology*? By extension, therefore, since the results of the history of religions are relatively secure, has not Christology been permanently, irretrievably undermined? Are not Troeltsch's vociferous denials of this contention, at least until his move to Berlin in 1915, irrelevant to the conclusions that the history of religions presents to Christian theology: the claims of final significance attached to Jesus Christ are paralleled in other religious traditions, the Christ cult errs when it refers to an objectively living Jesus, and the religious experience of Christians is misunderstood if it is thought to be experience of Jesus? Is not the Christ cult founded on an illusion sustained by corporate enthusiasm and the need for absolute assurance, and is not Christian religious experience saturated with projective wishful thinking? Is not Troeltsch's Christology evidence for the contention that a Christology abandoning hermeneutically absolutized renderings of the classical Christological tradition is necessarily a non-Christology? Is not the whole spectrum of Christological options therefore reduced, against all reluctance and denial, to two: either some literally understood, absolutist version of the classical Christology or no Christology? In turn, then, do not the results of the history of religions, with its antipathy toward absolutist Christology so understood, demonstrate beyond reasonable doubt that Christology is finished?

In reply to this barrage of criticism, it is vital to recall the result of Troeltsch's negative argument: he thought that absolutist interpretations of the classical Christological tradition had collapsed under the overwhelming weight of responsibilities incurred when the innocence of ignorance was exchanged for detailed knowledge of the natural world and many cultures and religions. A more modest Christology was the result for Troeltsch and has been the result on many occasions when theologians in the contemporary period have faced the challenge of the history of religious squarely. Therefore, the choice is not between an absolutist Christology and no Christology, but between Troeltsch's modest form of Christology—or something like it—and no Christology. Only an anti-absolutist Christology, Troeltsch rightly argued, has a chance of continuing the classical Christological tradition; the only alternative is the dissolution of Christology altogether.

To resolve *this* question, it avails nothing to pine for the definiteness of the Christological tradition's formerly insufficiently questioned, habitual celebration of the absolute and final revelatory and salvific significance of Jesus Christ, with or without its traditional alliance with a comfortable supernaturalism. It is necessary to press forward to explore more modest Christologies themselves. There are a number of robust and clear Christologies of this more modest type in existence now. That of John Hick is similar to Troeltsch's, in that it rejects a literal interpretation of the absolutist elements in the classical tradition, radically demythologizing the absolutist terminology to protect the possibility of terminological continuity. It is a reminder that Troeltsch's Christological offerings may not be as insipid or useless as they appear from some points of view if only they were presented in a more coordinated way than Troeltsch managed. Those of Raimon Panikkar, John Cobb, and John Macquarrie are quite different from Troeltsch's and are promising in a different way. They try to remain continuous with the classical tradition's affirmation that Jesus Christ was truly divine, truly human, but at the same time they both resist the absolutist, exclusive tendencies plaguing the interpretation of this formula and try to do justice to the social-psychological complexity of the individual and corporate religious experience of Christians.

Christology is not brought to an end by faithful study of the history of religions, but Christology in its literal, exclusive, absolute form is. It is the task of every era to see whether Christian theology can continue to make good on the church's Christological claims about Jesus of Nazareth. In our era, the continuation of the classical Christological tradition must be done with a modest Christology, if it can be done at all.

Supernaturalism and the History of Religions

The Reaction of the Ritschlians

The reception of Troeltsch's theology of the history of religions was understandably stormy, provoking critical responses especially from the older Ritschlians. In Walter Wyman's insightful analysis of this controversy, he observes that "there were two intricately intertwined issues involved: theological method and what might be called 'exclusive supernaturalism.' "[55] Both Julius Kaftan and Ferdinand Kattenbusch, anticipating Karl Barth's stance on the same issue, urged that Christianity was a distinctive phenomenon. Even if historians could study it as they would any religion, theologians certainly could not, on the grounds that "Ritschl and we old Ritschlians see effective in Christianity or in the possibility of preserving *Christian* faith in God a factor which entered from outside, not something that runs latently through the whole history of religions and only becomes fully "clear" in Christianity. . . . We see in Christ a unique and actually supernatural manifestation of God."[56] Thus, at root because of its supernatural distinctiveness, theologians could not do justice to

Christianity by studying it with the same tools and expectations that were appropriate for other religious traditions.

But was this not merely a clash of prejudices? Troeltsch at first glance seems to have been urging simply that, "on the grounds of the 'historical method,' the 'dogmatic' method is illegitimate."[57] Wyman offers a more adequate reading:

> But does the historical method carry with it *naturalistic* presuppositions that exclude any real relation to transcendence from religion? Troeltsch denies that the advocate of the historical method must be committed to that metaphysical position. What he rejects is not the appeal to revelation *per se* by the Ritschlian theologians, but their dualism in claiming that only Christianity rests upon revelation, while all other human religions are human inventions. Such a dualism is untenable special pleading. To treat all religions on the same basis, as analogous formulations, is not to exclude the divine from history, but to see it as everywhere effective: all religions, not just one, rest on revelation.[58]

This, of course, is consistent with Troeltsch's more fully developed position, achieved by the second edition of *Absoluteness* but not incorporated there. In the first edition, Troeltsch himself was guilty of a kind of special pleading, as argued above.

Rejecting Exclusive Supernaturalism

Exclusive supernaturalism involves this kind of special pleading, which Troeltsch called the "supernatural apologetic." At stake in its objection to the theology of the history of religions was an entire way of understanding Christianity and the world. The position of exclusive supernaturalism formerly was more continuous with the whole of life than it is now. In the West, for instance, other religions were often interpreted as not participating in the same kind of supernaturally accorded definitiveness that applied to Christianity. The Bible was variously thought to be a supernaturally guaranteed source of propositional revelation, the result of a supernaturally guaranteed process of development, or one stage along the way of a supernaturally shepherded process of developing doctrine that culminated, as far as Christology was concerned, with Nicea and Chalcedon. Similar positions were held with regard to the teaching of later eras of the Christian tradition, especially in Roman Catholicism. And sin was a prob-

lem whose consequences could be removed from human lives only by supernatural means provided for us by God, and effected through the work
of Jesus Christ, no matter what other traditions had to say about the
human condition.

This indefinitely extendible catalogue of elements of an exclusively
supernatural worldview has become, however, a litany of woe. On the one
hand, the historical, naturalistic consciousness of modernity has undermined the connection of supernaturalist world views of all kinds to the
rest of life. On the other hand, where an impartial supernaturalist world
view survives, as for example in the perennial philosophy, the justification
for awarding prerogatives to one religion over others has become wholly
opaque. The exclusively supernaturalist point of view has degenerated to
the point that now it can be asserted only as a hermetically sealed position. It is, to be sure, a metaphysically possible one, but it has lost almost
all of its plausibility—which is not to say that it commands no popular following—because it must distance itself from the natural consequences of
so many aspects of the contemporary self-understanding.

One way this exclusively supernatural rendering of Christian theology
retains limited plausibility, and a significant popular following, is through
its ability to furnish a direct and naïve account of Christian religious experience, directly and naïvely understood, and thus misunderstood. Another
way is by means of its attacks on the admittedly excessive naturalism and
antireligious bias of modernity, though these attacks are themselves excessive. Despite such scraps of encouragement, the exclusively supernatural Christian religious world view must be maintained in a state of
constant denial. The denial is most strained in the face of the history of religions. Detailed, substantive, personal contact with other religions provides to the imagination no support for according to Christianity
supernatural prerogatives over other religions. The unavoidable conclusion is that, if Christianity is a religion of supernatural, authoritative revelation, then so is every other religion. This, of course, is *precisely* the path
taken by the perennial philosophy, which thereby achieves the one of the
few workable reconceptions of the supernaturalist world view. But, on
this view, supernaturalism comes to refer to the great scale of being and
the reality of the activity of divine and intermediate spiritual powers; there
is no place for supernaturally authorized declarations of the superiority of
one religion over another.

It is refreshing to see the question of Christology put in such direct terms as the liberal Kattenbusch did in the above quotation: "We see in Christ a unique and actually supernatural manifestation of God." In some contemporary theological circles, it seems that openness in regard to such a perspective is frowned upon, even though the theology that results may be entirely consistent with it. It would be better if the supernatural apologetic of exclusive supernaturalism were brought entirely into the open, as most conservative evangelical theology is accustomed to doing. Then this form of resistance to a theology attentive to the history-of-religions method could be seen for what it is: another stage in the systematic retirement of supposedly supernaturally authorized Christian theology from all canons of rational discourse—a withdrawal into a comfortable hermeneutical circle from which even the obvious can be denied without fear of contradiction.

Battling All Supernaturalism

The gross mistake of exclusive supernaturalism does not automatically mar all supernaturalist world views. In fact, I have been proposing the perennial philosophy—with its great chain of being stretching from the Godhead beyond being and not-being, down through the personal God, angels, and other intermediary beings, to creatures such as ourselves, and on down from there—as the leading candidate for a feasible supernaturalist world view, and it has no more tolerance for the absolutist penchant of exclusive naturalism than Troeltsch's religiously vivid, naturalistic, historicist vision of reality. The question remains, however, of whether one of these world views is better attested than the other, and a great deal rides on this point for Christology.

It is important to note that, if the extreme of exclusive supernaturalism must be sidelined in the battle between naturalism and supernaturalism, then so must the extreme of reductionistic naturalism that neither can discern religious depth in nature and history nor can conceive of infinite mystery at the horizon of human being. Between these two extremes lies a hermeneutical war zone from which, supposedly, only one party may emerge victorious: either the dramatic but impartial perennial philosophy (or an equivalent view) or naturalistic religious historicism (or some other form of religious historicism). There are two perspectives on this battle.

On the one hand, supernaturalism of any kind, even its maximally plausible perennial philosophical flag bearer, must face the fact that modern Western cultural insight, for all its dangers and conceits, proffers an enormously powerful group of explanations of the world. It is so fruitful a way of understanding, in fact, that it has made possible societies with hitherto unheard-of complexity and coordination, notwithstanding a host of new and perplexing social and economic problems. It has sponsored scientific enterprises that have produced useful (if dangerous and morally questionable) knowledge at an utterly unprecedented rate. The relative advantage of naturalistic religious historicism is expressed in the inability of supernaturalism to encounter and absorb what is useful and right about this extraordinarily rich view of the world. The most compelling explanation of this is also the most obvious: supernaturalism itself can not compete as an account of the world. It has ceded its historical and intellectual ground to modern historicized, naturalistic consciousness because it was forced to and could not resist.

On the other hand, there can be no question that the impartial supernaturalism of the perennial philosophy accords most closely with most of the world's great wisdom traditions. Moreover, the advent of scientism and the moral questionableness of some of the cultural products of the modern West play into the hands of the perennialist counterattack. And while both sides can claim impressive support in the popular imagination of modern Western societies, there is no question that interest in supernaturalism is on the rise even in secular climates and that it reigns supreme in those cultural and religious traditions that remain closest to nature and least plagued by technologically induced, individualistic alienation.

This indicates the nature of the contention between naturalism and supernaturalism. How is it to be settled? I contend that this cultural and metaphysical debate is far from over. The apologetic bias of exclusive supernaturalism must be rejected, to be sure, and this is accomplished bluntly by any amount of serious attention to the history of religions, as we see in Troeltsch's anti-absolutist Christology. But impartial supernaturalism is much harder to dismiss.

Furthermore, it may finally be difficult to distinguish the most interesting forms of naturalism and supernaturalism. For example, the great chain of being affirmed in perennial philosophy can be interpreted as a naturalistic vision of great mystery in which "higher" levels are helpful psychological projections of conscious creatures such as human beings, or in more traditional fashion with Sankara's Vedanta philosophy as affirming that every level of being "below" that of the unconditioned ultimate is fundamentally unreal. This marks out the familiar weakness of the naturalistic-supernaturalistic distinction: it is vague at the point where it might have been most useful.

Christology and Impartial Supernaturalism

When the supernaturalistic apologetic for Christianity is superseded by a more adequate understanding of the religious mystery of the world, whether through exposure to the concrete reality of other religions, through chiding by impartial supernaturalists, or in some other way, must an anti-absolutist Christology be the result? Indeed no; this is merely the securing of the possibility of a rational theological conversation. But once the history of religions is admitted into the theological purview, it is extremely difficult to maintain the hypothesis that Christianity possesses any decisive finality. Parallel social and psychological processes (such as founder elevation, establishment of cults of worship, and early enthusiastic beliefs about the absolute significance of a religious discovery) are constant reminders that the theologian who wishes to defend the absolute and final revelatory and salvific significance of Jesus Christ must treat other religions in a different way than they wish to treat Christianity or else be reduced to fideistic affirmation of an other-worldly gospel that owes nothing to the traditions that developed, mediated, articulated, and defended it.

Well then, does the anti-absolutist Christology urged upon theologians by the history of religions demand a naturalistic view of the world? Again, no. While there can be no objection to a Christology such as Troeltsch's siding with the naturalistic religious historicist vision, and no possibility of Christological profit from the inexplicable bias of *exclusive* supernaturalism, it would be a mistake to assume that a plausible Christology had to reject *impartial* supernaturalism. Thus, parsing the requirement of Troeltsch's Christology for a rejection of a supernaturalistic view of the world is important.

To that end, note that Troeltsch rejected any understanding of history that is capable of finding in the development of Christian doctrine supernaturally secured testimony to a final, absolute revelatory event in Jesus Christ. This is nothing other than a version of the supernatural apologetic. Troeltsch's Christology also requires the rejection of any metaphysics that postulates *both* a universal mechanism for salvation *and* the ability of a human person—whether God incarnate or not—to fulfill the conditions required to set that redemptive mechanism in motion for everyone and everything in all places at all times. The problem in this case is not with the universal mechanism for salvation as such, but with the idea that it can be triggered for the entire cosmos by a single historical creature, for this makes natural the assignment of absolute, final significance to Jesus Christ, which, in turn, is close to the heart of the implausibility at issue. Neither the religious historicist nor the perennial philosophical world views admit such scenarios.

However, other aspects of a supernaturalistic view of the world are less problematic for Troeltsch's Christology. Though he would have rejected them simply because of his commitment to naturalistic religious historicism, he would not do so for essentially Christological reasons. The ideas of incarnation, healing miracles, nature wonders, and virgin births, for instance, do not necessarily lead to the assumption of absolute finality of revelation and salvation in Jesus Christ. This is because, in general ways, reports of such supposed happenings can be found in other streams of the history of religions, and only the discredited supernaturalistic apologetic attempts to use Christian stories about them to vault Christianity into the religion of absolute, final revelation.

The question of the resurrection of Jesus Christ is the most complex: the absolutizing elements of the thesis of resurrection are undeniable, but a great deal hinges on how the resurrection is understood as to whether Troeltsch *could* have affirmed it without disrupting his Christology. For example, even if the resurrection is construed in bluntly supernaturalist fashion as confirming Jesus' mission and identity as God incarnate, this could well be compatible with an anti-absolutist, supernaturalist Christology; everything would turn on the construal of the term *mission* and the meaning of *incarnation*. Of course, Troeltsch did *not* affirm the resurrection but, again, this was primarily because of the same convictions about the nature of the world that made him diffident about incarnations and miracles and probably only secondarily because of Christological concerns.

The key criterion for the limits of compatibility of Christology and supernaturalism is that the supernaturalistic apologetic must not be invoked. Though Troeltsch thought supernaturalism was a poor hypothesis upon which to base an interpretation of the world, as we have seen, his systematic objection always was directed primarily against the supernaturalistic *apologetic*. Supernaturalism may have been weakened in the encounter with the history of religions, but the supernaturalist apologetic was utterly discredited. Accordingly, Troeltsch should have had no *Christological* objections in principle to the idea of incarnation—no matter how strong his historical and metaphysical objections—so long as *multiple* incarnations or other revelations of universal principles are possible. By rights, therefore, Troeltsch should have admitted the possibility that the twentieth century has sometimes realized: an anti-absolutist, and possibly even supernaturalist, *incarnational* Christology.

The Future of Troeltsch's Theological Approach

Troeltsch's *religionsgeschichtliche Theologie* was a journey into uncharted territory. Not enough distance has been covered even now to tell whether Christian theology can be pursued in this mode in such a way that the Christian movement is effectively served. Nor is it clear exactly how such a theology is to be developed, notwithstanding Troeltsch's prescription for and example of it. The preliminary philosophy of religion is reasonably well understood, of course, though there are challenges of vast proportions yet to be negotiated. By contrast, there are only a few examples of systematic theology carried out in this mode, and the task remains darkly shrouded. Troeltsch's *Glaubenslehre* (1913) is one example, consciously patterned in important respects after the conception of dogmatics of Schleiermacher, who had also attempted to work out a preliminary philosophy of religion. Unfortunately, as noted earlier, Troeltsch's *Glaubenslehre* shows less than the thoroughgoing embedding in the context of other religious traditions that we might have hoped from an example of a *religionsgeschichtliche Theologie*, and there are few explicit signs of grappling with the difficult questions of normativity that are otherwise prominent in Troeltsch's work at this time.

Recently, there have been more and better examples of attempts to pen theologies informed by the history of religions. Some of these, such as Hick's *An Interpretation of Religion*,[59] fall primarily into the category of preliminary philosophy of religion. Others knowingly or unknowingly have been following Troeltsch's prescription for Christian theology more closely.[60] But all of these ventures—now usually carried on under the designation "comparative theology," but better called "comparative-normative theology" to distinguish them from more strictly comparative exercises—still must grapple with a tendency to compromise properly dogmatic interests. And all attempts at a theology attentive to the history of religions at the present time have to fight their way upstream both against the flow of traditional Christian theology and against the inherent difficulties in rendering a theology grounded in philosophical and historical study of religion spiritually and cultically potent.

The Development of Doctrine and the History of Religions

The back of the supernatural apologetic has been broken by the history of religions, with the result that it is not available as a valid form of justification for Christological claims. This presents a severe problem only for those forms of Christology that positively require it, and those advancing hermeneutically absolutized interpretations of Jesus Christ are therefore the most seriously affected. The question to be pursued in more detail here is an application of this result: What is the sense in which an appeal to the process of development of doctrine as justification for Christology must have recourse to the supernatural apologetic? I will argue that the development of doctrine can be a supportive resource for Christology, so long as the supernatural apologetic is *not* permitted to discredit it. That, in turn, is most threatening to hermeneutically extreme absolutist Christologies, for they appear quite arbitrary unless they can appeal to justification in the form of a supernaturally guaranteed process of development of doctrine.

We may begin by noting the dangers of casually dismissing the power of the historical developments that produced the orthodox formulation of the classical Christological tradition (the two-natures doctrine). Troeltsch committed this mistake when he asserted that "the orthodox doctrine of the two natures has been weakened, if not altogether eliminated, by the impact of the historical-psychological viewpoint."[61] This echoed Albert Schweitzer's famous contention that the two-natures doctrine had been unmasked as a fiction by historical criticism. They were both premature, if not simply wrong, because the two-natures doctrine simply had not passed on and certainly did not leap into the grave at their direction. In fact, the opposite occurred, as neoreformation theology shook European and North American Protestantism, and Roman Catholic theology reasserted traditional doctrinal formulations with great energy after the so-called modernist crisis.

In Troeltsch's case as well as Schweitzer's, this error was probably the result of an unreasonably narrow construal of the two-natures doctrine, such that the placement of Jesus firmly within the realm of human life with the aid of historical and social psychological tools was thought sufficient *by itself* to make the attribution to him of a divine nature obviously a mistake induced by an understandably credulous susceptibility to mythic renderings of reality. The inexplicability of this construal as it stands—unless it is for polemical reasons—is heightened by the fact that twentieth-century theology has had few qualms about articulating the two-natures doctrine, newly enhanced by a profounder awareness of the humanity of Jesus. Indeed, some of the most creative examples of the two-natures doctrine have come to light this century, and the forceful placement of Jesus at the crowded crossroads of humanity has been one of the keys to their persuasiveness and ready applicability.

It seems that the classical Christological tradition really has displayed a pronounced capacity for insight and stability. And yet it is incontestable that this tradition is the result of a complex process of development of doctrine in which all of the usual political, social, religious, and psychological factors were present. Accounting for insight and resilience in Christian doctrine understood as a process of historical development was an acute issue in the nineteenth century. How should the changes that had occurred in Christian thought over the centuries, particularly in the period from Jesus to the conciliar pronouncements of the fifth century, be understood so as to justify their normative status for most Christian churches ever since? Two key groups of questions were at stake in this ecclesial struggle for self-understanding. First, is there a determinate, unchanging essence in the Christian church and its proclamation? If so, what sort of a thing is it (a doctrine, an ethical stance, a metaphysical reality, or something else), and when has this essence achieved normative expression (in the person of Jesus, the earliest kerygma, the biblical pictures of Jesus Christ, the credal statements of the early councils, or never)? Second, is the doctrinal generation and development that has in fact occurred appropriate, and how is it to be explained in relation to the apostolic faith and to the question of the essence of Christianity?

Newman, Möhler, Ritschl, Harnack, Loisy, Troeltsch, and others who presented answers to these questions found themselves in a context newly sensitized to the historical particularity of every era and conscious of a *prima facie* diversity in Christian doctrine, ethics, and ecclesial struc-

tures. Even though the dominant concern of these thinkers was to understand the church of the contemporary world in continuous, theologically
intelligible relation to its origins and to its character in previous ages, answers to these questions also have a significant impact on Christological
construction. For instance, if the classical Christological doctrines that received credal expression at the ecumenical councils of the fourth and fifth
centuries are thought to be part of the determinative essence of Christianity, then the duty of a Christology is ever to repristinate or reformulate
those insights. Alternatively, if the essence of Christianity is thought to be
the person of Jesus Christ himself, and the church the Body of Christ,
then the development of the Christological doctrines from the historical
person of Jesus and the early communities of believers may be thought to
be a natural, or even divinely shepherded, process of unfolding ever
deeper meanings that were only implicit in the life and teaching—perhaps
even the self-understanding—of Jesus himself.

The relevance of such considerations for Christology is obvious. If the
development of doctrine is understood to guarantee the validity of the
process that gave rise to the classical Christology of Nicea and Chalcedon,
then the hermeneutically absolutized readings of those conciliar decisions
on which absolutist Christology depends arguably might be assigned normative status also. Of course, there are two steps here. The first has to do
with the process of development itself, and I will dwell on that issue for
the rest of this chapter. The second bears on whether the conciliar pronouncements must necessarily receive the hermeneutically extreme readings they do in absolutist Christology. I will argue that they ought not
necessarily be so read but will defer discussion of this point until chapter
4. The two steps are not entirely independent, however, because rejecting
the idea of supernatural divine guidance of the development of doctrine is
one of the best ways to establish that hermeneutically absolutized readings of classical Christology are arbitrary and excessive.

John Henry Newman's double contribution was to acknowledge a formative role for context in doctrinal development and to affirm the necessary validity of the results of the actual development. However, if the
development of doctrine is not so understood—there are many ways to
do this, and Adolf Harnack is the first to articulate one with systematic
precision—then there may not be the same special validity conferred on
the actual process of Christological development that is our inheritance.
Room would thereby be made for the criticisms of the classical Christolog-

ical tradition that were so important to Harnack's theology. Examination of alternative interpretations of Jesus Christ, perhaps enlarging upon the sometimes muted aspects of the Christological tradition, also would be legitimated. Anti-absolutist Christology of Troeltsch's nonincarnational variety positively requires the kind of critique of the classical tradition that Harnack makes possible. Anti-absolutist Christology of the incarnational sort does not have to question the classical tradition itself, but only the hermeneutically extreme habits that have controlled so much of its interpretation until recent years.

But there is more at stake in this discussion than merely making room for anti-absolutist Christologies. Suppose, going further with Troeltsch and the history-of-religions method, that a mode of analysis of the development of doctrine were to suggest criteria for judging legitimate from illegitimate developments and that these criteria were also relevant to assessing the *content* and not merely the *development* of doctrine. In this case, a particular doctrine itself may be favored by the theory of development. This may sound like a category mistake at first, since a theory of doctrinal development is supposed to explain actual developments of doctrine rather than criticize doctrines themselves. But the criteria applicable to one also can be applicable to the other. This is observable in two examples.

First, the traditional theories of doctrinal development, including Newman's, do not merely explain how, say, the Christology of the Nicea-Constantinopolitan Creed *arose*; they also affirm its *truth* because it was the product of a developing process understood to generate, under certain conditions, true doctrines. Inevitably, the plausibility of that creed's Christological affirmations depend to some extent upon their being authorized by that theory of development.

Second, consider the supposedly more simply descriptive theory of development espoused by the history-of-religions method. Justifying the truth of the products of the developing process is not the apparent goal in this case, but it is one of the results, nonetheless. To explain the development of the classical Christology of Nicea and Chalcedon by means of such social psychological insights as founder elevation and the projective consequences of communal and personal enthusiasm is to undermine any sense in which the process authorizes the results. In particular, absolutist Christology no longer can find any support in appeals to the process of doctrinal development. Therefore, a supposedly neutral mode of explanation of the development of doctrine turns out to be every bit as theologically potent as Newman's theory, only this time it is an anti-absolutist Christology—perhaps like Troeltsch's—that is favored.

If the kind of theory of development of doctrine advocated by Troeltsch can be established on independent grounds, this would impart a significant amount of momentum to any argument for his style of Christology, whether in his nonincarnational, inspirational form, or in the nonabsolutist, incarnational form that often has been advocated since Troeltsch's time. In order to assess the possibility of independently establishing such a theory of the development of doctrine, we will examine the three stages just outlined, exemplifying them with Newman, Harnack, and the history-of-religions method.

John Henry Cardinal Newman

John Henry Newman's evolutionary theory of doctrinal development[62] was expounded in the first work to give sustained attention to the problem of development. That book was probably the most influential and controversial of Newman's writings.[63] Read against the background of the Oxford movement this work is especially interesting. The Tractarians, including Newman before the early 1840s, held a static, almost antiquarian, view of history in which doctrinal developments were explained as clarifications of the apostolic faith.[64] This was understandable. Keble, Pusey, and Newman, being profoundly suspicious of rationalism's elevation of personal judgment to be the primary arbiter of truth, and disturbed by the disintegration of the church to which they thought it led, had advocated in their sermons and tracts what can be described as a romantic turn to tradition and mystery, to antiquity, universality, and catholicity (*quod semper, quod ubique, quod ab omnibus*).[65] The history they sought to recapture tended to be an idealized one and their appeal to it somewhat naïve as a result. Yet the affirmation of continuity with the past was effective in sparking a midcentury Anglo-Catholic revival in England.

The basic instincts of continuity with the past, romantic rebellion against the pretenses of human rationality and practical concern for the church were preserved in Newman's *Essay*, but he abandoned the static view of history that fostered the belief that antiquity could be recaptured in pristine purity as a body of beliefs whose systematic clarification coincides precisely with midnineteenth-century Anglican faith and practice.

The reason for the change was that the historical facts, as they seemed to Newman, simply did not support the principle of clarification: the "apparent variation and growth of doctrine . . . embarrasses us when we would consult history for the true idea of Christianity."[66] For the same reason, the scholastic theory of logical explication was untenable; changes in doctrine were too numerous and varied. The famous *consequence* of Newman's change in thinking was his conversion to Roman Catholicism, for it was the Mother Church rather than the Anglican Communion that now appeared to have the mark of apostolicity in his view. The writing of the first edition of the *Essay*, originally envisaged as a means to test this point, was terminated when Newman reached this conclusion.[67]

The primary constraints on Newman's theory of the development of doctrine were that it should explain the actual history of Christian doctrine adequately and that it should do so without appeal to the concept of continuing revelation, for such an appeal would represent abandonment of the apostolic principle that revelation was complete and once for all in Jesus Christ. His own summary of his hypothesis, which he likened to ideas found less completely developed in the writings of Möhler and De Maistre, and which he thought "has at all times, perhaps, been adopted by theologians,"[68] was as follows:

> that the increase and expansion of the Christian Creed and Ritual, and the variations which have attended the process in the case of individual writers and Churches, are the necessary attendants on any philosophy or polity which takes possession of the intellect and heart, and has had any wide or extended dominion; that, from the nature of the human mind, time is necessary for the full comprehension and perfection of great ideas; and that the highest and most wonderful truths, though communicated to the world once for all by inspired teachers, could not be comprehended all at once by the recipients, but, as being received and transmitted by minds not inspired and through media which were human, have required only the longer time and deeper thought for their full elucidation. This may be called the *Theory of Development of Doctrine*.[69]

The distinction between implicit and explicit knowledge, already present in an Oxford sermon of 1843, is central to Newman's theory. He quoted from the published edition of that sermon:

The mind which is habituated to the thought of God, of Christ, of the Holy Spirit, naturally turns with a devout curiosity to the contemplation of the object of its adoration, and begins to form statements concerning it, before it knows whither, or how far, it will be carried. One proposition necessarily leads to another, and a second to a third; then some limitation is required; and the combination of these opposites occasions some fresh evolutions from the original idea, which indeed can never be said to be entirely exhausted. . . . Creeds and dogmas live in the one idea which they are designed to express, and which alone is substantive; and are necessary, because the human mind cannot reflect upon that idea except piecemeal, cannot use it in its oneness and entireness, or without resolving it into a series of aspects and relations.[70]

The relevant parts of Newman's general epistemology, outlined in chapter 1, "On the Process of Development in Ideas," and applied to Christian doctrine in chapters 2 and 3, make it clear that developments are occasioned and required by changing contexts, for "no sooner do we apprehend than we judge."[71] The result is that the context we bring to our apprehension influences the "series of aspects" into which we resolve the central, substantive, and finally inexhaustible idea. This marks the largest shift from Newman's former adherence to the principle of clarification, which after all is not so incongruous with the statement of the hypothesis of *Essay* quoted above.

Newman was forced by his faithfulness to the historic tradition of Christianity to admit a *role for context* in the determination of the evolving course of doctrinal development. This simple admission became magnified in some quarters after Newman into the more dramatic assertion that context conditions doctrinal developments in such profound ways that recognition of a high degree of contingency must be an essential element of any account of such developments. But the wedge thus jammed in the doorway between the contemporary and apostolic churches was not overly problematical for Newman himself, because he was ready to appeal to the original idea and spiritual reality of Christianity, manifest in its entire tradition, as the controlling influence throughout the process of development, stopping the door from swinging wide open, as it were, and admitting a role for all kinds of influences. Because of this appeal, Newman was able to argue that corrupt developments are distinguishable from genuine ones and advances seven criteria ("notes") for such discriminations.[72] Though there were reservations about these criteria on the part of some theologians, Newman thought they established that the process of doctrinal development was more or less secure from major error. The process of development is ultimately secured for Newman by the infallibility of the pope in matters of faith and morals. Thus, the supernatural apologetic had not been overcome in Newman's thought.

Adolf Von Harnack

Harnack held a different opinion than Newman about the security of the process of doctrinal development. Perhaps Harnack had examined more closely the concrete circumstances of the development of Christian doctrine than Newman, or perhaps he was predisposed to greater suspicion of the supernatural apologetic. In any event, Harnack became aware of the crucial role played by what he called the "acute hellenization" of Christian thought, referring especially to Gnosticism.[73] According to Harnack, the hellenistic, Gnostic context for the first few centuries of the church's life was so powerful that the statements about the central Christian idea inspired by it became dominant to the point of excluding other important insights, eventually resulting, from Harnack's point of view, in the smothering of kerygma by lifeless dogma.

The divergent opinions of Harnack and Newman derive not only from different modes or results of historical inquiry, however, but also from a difference in conception of the essence of Christianity. Newman, in affirming the role of a kaleidoscope of "aspects" for elucidating a living idea, took the essence of Christianity to be a thing assigned solely for the purposes of convenience of expression, because determining the "leading idea" of a "supernatural work" is a task exceeding human capability.[74] However, Harnack, with fitting Protestant suspicion of moves to shore up established doctrine, was more prepared to identify a determinate essence and to find this essence *potentially both illuminated and obscured* in every later doctrinal development. Harnack's summary of Jesus' teaching, and the heart of the gospel, is such

> that it may be grouped under three heads. They are each of such a nature as to contain the whole, and hence it can be exhibited in its entirety under any one of them. *Firstly, the kingdom of God and its coming. Secondly, God the Father and the infinite value of the human soul. Thirdly, the higher righteousness and the commandment of love.* ... [Jesus]

himself stands behind everything that he said. His words speak to us across the centuries with the freshness of the present. It is here that that profound saying is truly verified: "Speak, that I may see thee."[75]

The criticisms of Harnack's formulation of the essence of Christianity are legion, as are the criticisms of his analysis of the New Testament writings and their relation to their context. For the purposes of discerning the distinctive move made in relation to the development of doctrine, however, all that is needed is to notice that Harnack, while doubtless accepting the dynamics of the development of doctrine as Newman expressed them, was less confident that the evolutionary process was assured in general not to take any improper turns. The solidification of the Christian churches around the dogmatic statements of the patristic era was and had continued to be an example of such a dubious, though useful and perhaps inevitable, line of development. Harnack was objecting not so much to the particular doctrines that the church fathers had laid down in their wisdom; after all, the church had to develop in one way or another. Rather, it was the stultifying effect the doctrines had on Christian life and practice about which he was most concerned. This is evident in his conviction that the reformers, while not departing from the patristic doctrines about the Trinity and Jesus Christ, had rediscovered the heart of the gospel in their preaching. Christian doctrine was once again transformed by Jesus Christ into kerygma, the living proclamation of God's kingdom that the earthly Jesus himself had announced.

The very same element of contingency of context that in Newman was monitored carefully, and finally subdued by tradition and papal authority, appears in Harnack as a reaffirmation of the reformers' insight that mistakes can be made, even on a large scale; the heart of the gospel can be coerced by context, disfigured, diluted, and even temporarily lost—just as context can serve as the vehicle for rediscovery of the gospel. There is little question that this gospel heart was itself diluted in Harnack's presentation of it for, as Rudolf Bultmann remarked, "Harnack evidently never experienced such a reaction of shock [to the utter strangeness of the image of primitive Christianity disclosed by the religious-historical school, and] . . . had no 'antennae' for the theology of Karl Barth."[76] There is also little question that Harnack underestimated the in-built self-reforming character of tradition, and that he failed to give due weight to the impossi-

bility of appropriation or rediscovery of the gospel apart from its mediation by Christian tradition, as Alfred Loisy was quick to point out.[77] Nevertheless, Harnack advanced the discussion of the development of doctrine
in a significant way by drawing attention to the fact that the element of
context in the formation and development of doctrine is not as easily controlled as Newman's seven "notes" suggested.

The History-of-Religions School

It was the work of the members of the so-called history-of-religions
school, and especially Troeltsch, that marks the third major development
in late-nineteenth-century discussions of the development of doctrine.[78]
The estimation of the role of context increased at each step. Context was
not just an inevitable contingency in the evolution of doctrine, the condition for the possibility of concrete dogmatic expression, whose deleterious effects had to be controlled either by appeal to tradition or by ever
rediscovering the lively kernel of the gospel beneath the husk of ecclesiastical doctrine. Rather, the continuities of history that Newman and Harnack noticed were *subservient* to context. That is, the social and
intellectual context of a religious community was a determining factor in
the continuities that were discerned within the history of doctrine, the
essences affirmed as the inner referents and meanings of doctrinal expressions, and the criteria for adequacy of explanations given for how present
doctrine is connected in a theologically intelligible way to those essences
or to the doctrines of past eras.

The history-of-religions method, by insisting that every era be studied
on its own terms according to the canons of secular history, helped to re-
move some of the lingering ideality that surrounded Jesus and the early
church.[79] Thus it was that Johannes Weiss was able to see much of the import of the eschatological world view of the New Testament, concluding
that the world of Jesus, and probably even the self-conception of Jesus,
was entirely alien to midnineteenth-century Europe.[80] It is an obvious
methodological procedure, worked out throughout the nineteenth century: temporarily suspend conviction about the religious significance and
spiritual accessibility of Jesus the man, and then, using the same tools that
secular historians apply, see what surfaces as a reliable outline of Jesus
and his world. What turned up for Bousset, Weiss, and later Schweitzer,

however, bore little resemblance to Harnack's Jesus with the sternly simple and uncannily universal message, or to Newman's founder of a saving
religious institution.

What, then, was the essence of Christianity? Did it not depend upon
the situation of the one for whom articulating an essence was important?
Was it not a shifting thing, according to the place and time in which the
gospel is heard and acted on? Was it not a call to war in the crusades and a
call to passive resistance in the Vietnam era; a trumpeting of another
world's supernatural breaking through this earthy veil in the churches
of the Apostle Paul and a naturalistic, miracle-free ethic for seventeenth-
century deists; an affirmation of a gloriously redeeming socioeconomic
structure in medieval Europe, a charge to subvert oppressive hierarchies
in late-twentieth-century Latin America, and an apolitical spiritual message
for Moravian pietism? Was not every era irreducibly unique, substantially
communicable with effort to other times but uncapturable in its essence?
How then could any essence be timeless, and how could there be timeless
criteria for distinguishing between genuine and deviant dogmatic developments? Did not consensus in one way or another determine what doctrinal statements survived and flourished? And was not this consensus
inevitably dependent upon contextual considerations such as world view,
politics, economics, and social structure generally?

Such were the questions that haunted Ernst Troeltsch.[81] In relation to
Christology, against Harnack, he urged that there was not just *one* Jesus
Christ, but many, each one an expression of both the documents testify-
ing to the life and ministry of Jesus Christ and the personal and cultic context within which this testimony is comprehended and applied. Moreover,
according to Troeltsch, there was no longer any *a priori* reason to think
that the patristic Christological doctrines ought to continue to sustain and
nourish the life of the Christian churches, such as there had been with
Newman.

In spite of the use of the image in earlier times, the conception of
doctrinal development had become closely analogous to biological evolution for the first time with Troeltsch: only the fittest of unexpected vari-
ants and natural adaptations survive in an environment requiring
competition for resources, and nothing can *guarantee* the continued existence of any particular species. Troeltsch had no intention of denying
the normativity of scripture or of the person of Jesus in coming to these
conclusions. On the contrary, normativity can be asserted only when his-

tory is conceived of as the contingent flux that Troeltsch affirmed it to be, for norms are *established* and *effective* only insofar as an alternative is conceivable, namely, the failure of a norm to continue to exercise power over the contingencies of the future. The gray-edged field of contingent history and contingent norms, free of supernatural determination, was the context within which Troeltsch eventually was led to find a theory of the development of doctrine and to discover such absoluteness of Christianity as he could. The carefully mapped out playing fields of Newman and Harnack—and older conceptions of the development of doctrine—were laid waste by the contingent realities, vague unpredictability, and creative possibilities of the historical process.

Christology and the Development of Doctrine

With a new conception of the development of doctrine comes a rising tide of support for Troeltsch's style of Christology, or something like it. But let us try to anticipate the natural objection here. Why should this view of the development of doctrine be accepted since there can be no knockdown argument against the supernatural apologetic? Perhaps the problem with Newman's theory of the development of doctrine is merely its lack of resonance with the modern conception of history. But this conception is methodologically biased against the recognition of special divine shepherding in the historical process. More precisely, and with the aid of medieval scholastic terminology, the naturalistic idea of history advocated by the history-of-religions school, in step with the natural sciences, is oriented programmatically to expect sufficient explanations for events, explanations that do not include the possibility of primary divine causation, and to regard references to divine causation in and through ordinary secondary causes as explanatorily redundant.

But is not the methodological bias of the history-of-religions method a good reason for being suspicious of lurking ideological commitments? Indeed, it is. If there is a guiding ideology in some uses of the history-of-religions method, however, it is no more influential or hidden than the ideology that directs the interpretation of the development of doctrine from Newman's point of view. Ideology, here, is secondary to fruitfulness. Which way of understanding history produces the most compelling explanations of the widest possible range of phenomena? Is the assumption of a divinely shepherded process of doctrinal development, in which the implicit richness of Jesus Christ is explicated gradually and assuredly, a good basis for understanding the nature of religious developments of all kinds, Christian as well as non-Christian? Or is a process of creating historical meaning for living religious communities in an *ad hoc* way under the auspices of contingent, consensual norms and inspired by an ongoing encounter with transcendent reality the more workable hypothesis? Deciding for or against supernatural guidance of the development of doctrine thus becomes a choice between two religious views of the world. There are no knock-down proofs for such choices; the decision is a matter of argument and intuition, both of which are formed by exposure to and absorption of a wealth of information, against which various interpretations of history may be tested.

If there is a noticeable correlation between the widest exposure to actual religions and the affirmation of the history of religions' understanding of the development of Christian doctrine, this is a strong argument in favor of that understanding. The earlier part of this chapter argued that the history-of-religions perspective in general, and its implications for the development of Christological doctrines in particular, cannot be effectively resisted without recourse to arbitrariness or artifice. This was certainly Troeltsch's view of the matter, in spite of his recognition that the Christian tradition, too, speaks with authority on the nature of religious experience and the development of doctrine, and the bulk of its self-interpretation very clearly rests on the side of Newman, against the history of religions. But the problem cannot be a matter of which mode of interpretation of developing religious traditions can boast the longest heritage. The salient factor is rather explanatory power, and on this score, the history of religions mode of interpretation is unmatched.

This expresses just how important the history-of-religions perspective is for Troeltsch's Christology, and indeed for any Christology after Troeltsch. The reverse also is true, for the absolutist style of Christology Troeltsch railed against was at odds with the history-of-religions perspective; anti-absolutist continuations of the classical Christological tradition were for Troeltsch and still are the most adequate candidates for resolving the contemporary crisis of Christological plausibility induced by, among other factors, the history of religions.

3
Christology and the Sciences

Troeltsch's Christological explorations were attentive to the perspectives on human life and the world opened up through the nineteenth century by the philosophical, natural, and human sciences. Within the philosophical sciences, Troeltsch was most concerned with the relationship between Christology and the philosophy of history. Among the natural sciences, he was most impressed with astronomy, for it had established the enormous size of the universe and—in conjunction with the discovery of biology that the origin and development of species could be brought under natural laws, laws that presumably applied even-handedly throughout the vast cosmos—posed a severe problem for the plausibility of absolutist renderings of traditional Christological claims. He also reflected on a joint implication of a number of sciences—including archeology, geology, biology, and astronomy—that the earth and its cosmic environment were, to use Troeltsch's description, *immeasurably* old.

In relation to both the philosophical and natural sciences, Troeltsch broke new ground theologically. But nowhere is his theological contribution more formidable than in connection with the human sciences. We have already seen this in the discussion of the *religionsgeschichtliche Schule*, but Troeltsch was also profoundly exercised over the complex relationships among Christology, the human imagination, and the needs of Christian cultic life, which psychology and sociology illuminated with unprecedented vividness. This chapter considers each of these dimensions of the contemporary crisis of Christological plausibility, using Troeltsch's grappling with them as the leading guide.

The Philosophical Sciences

Nourishing the roots of the *religionsgeschichtliche Schule* and the theology to which it gave fruit was a decisive shift in the Western conception of history, as it struggled to come to terms with the problems of historical relativism. This shift was preceded by one at the end of the eighteenth century—expressed differently in the Enlightenment, the philosophy of absolute idealism, and (a little later) positivism—and followed by yet another at the end of the twentieth, in the form of structuralist and poststructuralist approaches to history that usually abandon universal schemes of historical interpretation as vain and misguided. All of these have had a profound impact on conceptions of how a Christology must be constructed if it is to be a plausible and worthy contribution to the great Christological tradition.

The general importance of philosophy of history in the formation of the Christological problem at the beginning of the twentieth century has been made clear in the discussions of the development of doctrine and the history of religions in the last chapter. It remains here to bring out this significance in a more detailed way. A feasible approach is to use Troeltsch's critique of the philosophy of history of G. W. F. Hegel (1770–1831) as a springboard into his own philosophy of history. This is appropriate not merely because of the profound influence of Hegel upon Troeltsch, but also because Troeltsch's philosophy of history is allergic to the very same kind of absolutism in Christology given such powerful support by Hegel's philosophy. Completeness would demand that Auguste Comte (1798–1857) and historical positivism be given their due, but the Christological connections in this case are not as important for understanding Troeltsch.[1]

The Significance of Modern Philosophy of History

That Troeltsch was profoundly influenced by Hegel in his understanding
of history is unsurprising, for the philosophy of history was transformed,
if not strictly created in its modern guise, by the work of the absolute
idealists—Schelling and Hegel in particular. As with most influential
thinkers, even at those times in the nineteenth century when to be called
"Hegelian" may have been a reproach, many of Hegel's insights remained
influential. This transformation in the philosophy of history can be described roughly as the negotiation of a path from *narrative history*, in
which most presuppositions guiding the story line of a historical presentation remain implicit, to *critical history*, in which these presuppositions
are examined openly. This path had to be taken before it was possible to
ask *critically* and *systematically* the questions that had driven the philosophy of history since Augustine's *City of God*: about the meaning of the
entire conglomeration of bare happenings that is history (Was this conglomerate whole purposeful?), about the meaning of historical change
(Did these changes constitute a process of development?), about the
meaning of suffering in history (Did it serve a rational and useful purpose,
or was it merely a painfully irreducible surd?), and about God in history
(Was there an absolute, and could it act or be disclosed in history?).

Absolute idealism's philosophy of history was consistent metahistory
on a macrohistorical scale. Its scientific aim was to provide a definitive
conceptual analysis of the meaning and purpose of history. But it had an
ethical aim also: to orient the present in relation to the currents of cosmic
time. In absolute idealism, the philosophy of history combined scientific
historiography with an existential and intellectual struggle; it was simultaneously an area of scholarly inquiry and an urgent problem to be solved.

Troeltsch understood the philosophy of history in precisely this way.
In his "Moderne Geschichtsphilosophie" (1904),[2] he described the modern philosophy of history from the point of view of its relevance for Christian theology. There he identified the perennial *religious* problems of a
philosophy of history as establishing the position of religion over against
(1) the reductively scientific picture of reality, and (2) other ethical and religious perspectives that are historically rooted. The modern period of the
philosophy of history was inaugurated with the dissolution of the medieval solutions to these problems by "the development of a mechanistic
world-view," on the one hand, and "the development of a homogeneous

view of history that sees all historical events as interconnected, and the growth of a historical criticism that dissolves isolating miracles," on the other.[3] What did Troeltsch think was at stake for religion in the philosophy of history, understood in terms of these two problems? "Both problem areas must be given their due, either by means of a unifying metaphysics or in some other way, if norms of faith and life that have grown up and attained power by virtue of their own inherent strength are to be scientifically grounded and protected against the competition of other norms and against various doubts of a more general nature."[4]

It is doubtful that the Troeltsch of 1923 would have put the matter in quite this way, for there is an air of defensiveness in this quote that does not appear in his later writings. This is due to Troeltsch's belief at the beginning of the century that "theology stands or falls with the possibility of the attainment of universal norms and standards of value."[5] In 1902, as we saw in our examination of *The Absoluteness of Christianity*, Troeltsch thought it was possible to discover universal norms and standards of value *within* history. After *Social Teaching* (1911), by which he was led to his repudiation of this early view through extensive contact with historical details, he became convinced of an alternative to the stark dilemma as he had seen it, namely, the possibility of relative norms. We will approach his idea of relative norms of value by way of an explanation of why Troeltsch was driven to find a solution different from Hegel's to a question that he believed Hegel had posed correctly.

Hegel's Philosophy of History

All big ideas have a historical life, according to Hegel, and these ideas are *realized* in a rational process within history. This process of realization of a concept is a matter of logic for Hegel; for example, the process of religious development under the power of the idea of religion naturally drives toward the next stage of its self-determination, on the basis of its own inner necessary structure, and thence to the next stage, and so on, until the idea itself is realized, if possible. Because big ideas have a history in Hegel's vision, it is possible in principle to infer, for instance, the concept of the 'ideal state' from a historical analysis of forms of the state, or the idea of justice from the history of forms of justice.

More generally, but in an entirely parallel manner, history as a whole is the rational outworking of an idea. This is a remarkable claim, for it entails that the process of history is utterly rational, in spite of the apparent incomprehensibility of so much that happens. Indeed, for Hegel, "reason . . . is *substance* and *infinite power*; it is itself the *infinite material* of all natural and spiritual life, and the *infinite form* which activates this material content."[6] Hegel calls that fundamental idea *"Geist"* (spirit, both divine and human), and he interprets history as a rational process wherein *Geist* attains to self-consciousness through self-expression in an infinitely varied succession of forms. Each one of the historical forms serves to differentiate the immediacy of *Geist* into subject and object, spirit and not-spirit. The experience and recognition of this distinction corresponds to a reunification of the opposites into the self-understanding of *Geist*. More specifically, Hegel envisaged *Geist* as expressing itself in matter, the epitome of rigidity and constraint, and the opposite of the freedom that characterizes spirit. In so doing, *Geist* discovers itself as free, and matter itself is self-consciously recognized as an expression of the essence of *Geist*. It follows that history and spirit are completely correlative in Hegel's understanding of them. So *Geist* attains consciousness and self-consciousness in and through the appearance of these realities in history. As Hegel put it, "Self-consciousness . . . is not merely intuition of the divine, but the self-intuition of God Himself."[7] This entails, in turn, that history is rational and purposeful precisely in so far as *Geist* is.

The concept of 'religion' plays a special role in Hegel's thought, for "Religion is the spirit that relates itself to itself and thus to its essence, to true spirit; it is reconciled with true spirit and finds itself in it."[8] It is the locus, therefore, of the most profound unfolding of *Geist* in history. Positive religion is finite, and "not yet the *idea*, the realization, the actualization of the concept."[9] In the context of the profoundly rational historical process, however, the consummate, absolute religion is revealed: "Spirit's knowing of itself as it is implicitly is the *being-in-and-for-self* of spirit, the consummate, absolute religion in which it is manifest what spirit is, what God is; and this religion is the Christian religion."[10] The supreme moment of self-realization for *Geist*, the decisive climax of the historical process, occurred in the incarnation.[11] There within the concreteness of history *Geist* knows itself as itself when this self-conscious recognition occurs in the conscious life of Jesus. Put differently, reconciliation takes place between the posited opposites of spirit and matter. Freedom is won for matter, and *Geist* is more profoundly self-conscious as a result. History is the forum for the dynamic growth and formation of spirit. Christianity is the

absolute, consummate religion because it testifies to the incarnation in
history and bears within its historical, communal life *Geist* so understood.

Hegel was the last important philosopher to try to use philosophy to
figure out the secret of history. In trying to cut this Gordian knot, of
course, he was also trying to envision himself at the culmination of history, from which "the all" would logically be apparent. It was an attempt,
in a symbolic sense, not just to describe history, but to *end* it. After all,
what is Geist supposed to do after it has penned its own autobiography?
But this attempt to end history can be seen as a form of defiance, a last-
ditch effort to try and make sense *of it all* before the weight of historical
consciousness and its awareness of historical details made utterly impossible the envisagement of grand macro-historical schemes. In fact, it is testimony to the rise of historical consciousness itself, for only the historically
sensitized would feel the sharpness of the problem of the unity of history
in the way that Hegel did, and only the philosopher sensing the specter of
a historical consciousness that produces a mass of indigestible, unintelligible details would so energetically and boldly attempt to end history.
Hegel, therefore, was trying to save history from itself, and the failure of
his last stand is also our problem: how are we supposed to live in a world
in which history can no longer be read as a single grand narrative? How indeed? This archetypally postmodern question was Troeltsch's question
also, and in his grappling with this question he was laboring in the
shadow, and with the legacy, of Hegel.

Troeltsch's Criticism of Hegel

Troeltsch approved of the fact that "the Hegelian school collapsed with
the dissolution of the Hegelian metaphysics; and with the critical displacement of an absolute, rational religion by the recognition of the concrete
character of actual Christianity."[12] This criticism echoes through Troeltsch's writings, and he was often passionate in expressing it. Hegel's philosophy of history defined a purpose for the historical process, a sense of
trajectory and development, an assurance of meaning and moral security.
Troeltsch readily admitted the advantages of this view. For instance, it did
substantial justice to "the metaphysical need of religion for a relationship
to ultimate reality, and it granted a firmer inner necessity to the sequence
and direction of the history of the development of religion."[13] But
Troeltsch thought that, in subjecting the meaning of history to the idea of

the universal absolute, Hegel "sacrificed the particularity and individuality of history and transformed the whole of history into a preliminary stage of the realization of the universal concept; and it contributes nothing to call this concept a concrete one and to distinguish it from universality in the abstract."[14]

Troeltsch advanced a similar criticism in 1913:

> The general picture of a universal investigation in the history of religions has become much clearer and more comprehensive, but for that very reason abounding in difficulties and questions. . . . Under these circumstances, those constructions of the development of religion ventured by Hegel and Schleiermacher appear to us to be completely antiquated exercises of the imagination. Indeed, the very thought of setting forth any one historical religion as complete and final, capable of supplanting all others, seems to us open to serious criticism and doubt.[15]

Again, as a younger scholar in 1897, Troeltsch wrote: "Hegel . . . conformed religion too much to metaphysical monism; above all, he derived the evolution of religion in too doctrinaire and rigid a fashion from the logical necessity of the dialectic idea, thus failing to do justice to the mysterious power of religion and the contingency of its various movements."[16]

Troeltsch's criticism of Hegel almost always was aimed at or around this same point, which really has two related aspects. On the one hand, Troeltsch argued that Hegel's philosophy of history is too remote from the particular, and often painful, details of history, and so readily falsified by them. On the other hand, Troeltsch objected to the subjugation of historical facts to an idea of the historical process.

With regard to the first aspect of Troeltsch's criticism, he did not need to rely upon an *a priori* argument against Hegel's derivation of the history of religions from the logical structure of a preconceived idea established on some other basis than the details of that history. He simply needed to call for the testing of this derivation against the material content of history, and especially the history of religions. When this is done, both the derivations and the ideas they devolve from prove to be arbitrary and inadequate. They may plausibly explain something within the mass of data that has accrued about the religions and history of the world, but they force, trivialize, or overlook much more.

This was the great discovery of Troeltsch in *Social Teaching* (1911), but it had been his intuition all along, as is evident from the presence of this criticism of Hegel as early as 1897, quoted above. It is odd, in view of this, that Troeltsch himself was guilty of egregious errors in this regard, especially in *The Absoluteness of Christianity*, as shown in the last chapter.[17] But Troeltsch's errors were in the analysis of the historical religions. He did remain mostly consistent with his methodological commitment to prioritize historical factuality over philosophical interpretation.

Troeltsch's Conception of History

The second aspect of Troeltsch's criticism of Hegel had a thoroughly programmatic character that derived from Troeltsch's own conception of history. Troeltsch emphasized the *particularity* and *interconnectedness* of all historical events, and the *contingency* and *unpredictability* of all historical processes. To Troeltsch, these were the inescapable conclusions of the nineteenth century's patient and vast work of rewriting the history of the world from almost every perspective, including the cosmic, planetary, cultural-religious, political-economic, religious, and social. There was simply too much variety, too much ambiguity, too much adaptability, and far too much apparent randomness and unpredictability for the historical process to be satisfactorily derivable from an *idea*. Neither the history of religions, nor the history of Christianity, nor the history of Western culture can be written as an evolutionary process under the control of a single idea or historically identifiable essence. Arguments to this effect are common in Troeltsch's writings; in fact it is one of the most prolifically handled themes in all of his writings.[18]

This conception of historical relativism is expressed in Troeltsch's use of the term *Relativismus*. Troeltsch's developed understanding of this term is related closely to his view of history as a whole, for which the general term is *Historismus*. *Relativism* is a slippery term, and *historical relativism* also, as numerous authors have been at pains to point out. Troeltsch used three words for historical relativity: *Relativität*, *Relativierung,* and *Relativismus*. In his earlier writings, *Relativität* and *Relativierung* were applied exchangeably in the sense of the metaphysical affirmation that all historical events are conditioned by their contexts, so that "all historical phenomena are unique, individual configurations."[19] Relativism of values or of knowledge is not *automatically* entailed by this metaphysical thesis. In this earlier stage, *Relativismus* was defined as the additional thesis of epistemological or value relativism proper, which Troeltsch customarily attacked.[20] Later, however, and most frequently overall, *Relativismus* was defined as the metaphysical thesis that formerly was designated by *Relativität* and *Relativierung*. It is this metaphysical thesis to which the use of *relativism* refers here.

The metaphysical thesis of relativism in this sense has epistemic consequences. For instance, it follows that every historical event derives its significance and its power to influence only from its various contexts, and not from the control of any intelligible supernatural force, malevolent or benign, or from any conceivable idea, no matter how elevated from some point of view. However, it does not imply the stronger epistemic thesis that the truth of a proposition itself is dependent upon the context in which it is espoused. This additional thesis was rejected by Troeltsch at first, but conditionally affirmed later in his career.[21] But the key transformation in the philosophy of history—and in Christology—at the beginning of the twentieth century was wrought by the more general metaphysical thesis, and not by the narrower and more dubious conception of relative truth. The definitive expression of this transformation occurred in Europe, with Troeltsch and the advocates of the history-of-religions method. However, it was also expressed in interestingly different ways, more epistemic and practical than historical in emphasis, in the British and American pragmatists—Charles Peirce's synechism, William James's radical pluralism, and John Dewey's sociology of knowledge are the best known examples.

Troeltsch therefore envisaged a view of history that is more attentive to the facts of history and calls for generalizing *from* them, rather than *subjecting* them in advance to a conception of development or reason. In the resulting philosophy of history, Troeltsch proposed a methodological reordering of its component tasks, as compared with Hegel.

The first step is to approach history in its factuality, its irreducible individuality, its unrepeatability. We must begin with historical facts and the smaller meanings they bear, according to Troeltsch, because history is too contingent and variable for us to be sure that our ideas about it will not be overturned at the next moment. Historical meaning and hope, as well as absurdity and despair, are then discovered in history in all of the ordinary ways with which humans are utterly familiar. This does not trivialize the influence of the perspectives we bring to historical interpretation. But the emphasis for Troeltsch is on empirical history and fidelity to actual events as they occurred and meanings as they were discovered.

Only when this perspective is established firmly can we hope hypothetically to weave a deeper, global meaning out of the threads of history. This is the second step in a philosophical interpretation of history for Troeltsch and, though many historians in the twentieth century have forsworn it altogether, Troeltsch remained open to the possibility that such universal patterns of intelligibility might be discernible. Such large-scale interpretation must refrain from the comfortable but self-deceptive activity of specifying the meaning of history in isolation from the facts. The reason this is likely to fail is two-fold. On the one hand, every human being is situated inescapably in a historical context; this limits from the outset the likelihood of producing feasible constructions of the meaning and purpose of the entire historical process. It also assures us that any construction we deduce can say nothing *a priori* against other, unknown constructions of the meaning of history deriving from other cultural-religious contexts. Diligent comparison and analysis is the only rational way to approach disagreements about the true meaning of history, supposing there is such; this Troeltsch urged in *Absoluteness*. On the other hand, it is far from clear that the facts of history can sustain a global interpretation of the kind that Hegel proposed. The only empirical way to proceed is to propose interpretations for the meaning of history as a whole (such as Hegel's) on the basis of detailed appreciation of the facts of history, being scrupulous not to cut short the encounter with facts—that was Hegel's mistake, according to Troeltsch.

Of course, any such proposal about the ultimate meaning and purpose of history itself inevitably will be contingent, on this view. It can never have the assurance of Hegel's deduction from an idea of rational development. Hegel effectively operated with these two components of the philosophy of history in the reverse order of priority, on Troeltsch's analysis. One might say that Hegel could do this only because the full impact of historical relativism had not been appreciated in his time. Alternatively, it is quite reasonable to argue that, with uncanny prescience, Hegel initiated a preemptive strike against the specter of the piling up of endless historical details—the same vision that has led so many thinkers of the twentieth century to abandon macrohistorical speculation.

Does Troeltsch do justice to Hegel in criticizing him? While acknowledging that Hegel wrote at times about divine providence in a tone that smacks of triumphalism, Peter Hodgson vigorously defends Hegel against the charge that the idea dominates the actual in Hegel's thought about history. In fact, Hodgson argues that Hegel's relevance for today derives from his openness to the ambiguity of history and his awareness of its tragic dimensions.

> Hegel was profoundly aware of the presence of evil, passion, self-interest, and violence in human affairs, and he described history in the most dramatic terms as "an altar on which the happiness of nations, the wisdom of states, and the virtue of individuals are slaughtered." . . . In such a state of mind it is very tempting to take refuge in fatalism, viewing history as ultimately absurd. . . . The only alternative to nihilism or complacency is to seek an answer to the question, "To whom, or to what ultimate end have these monstrous sacrifices been made?"
>
> The answer to the question is not to be found by endless reflection on the panorama of sin and suffering. Rather, the latter must be viewed as the means for the realization of a principle or goal that is not given to sense perception but is knowable . . . [by a transcendental deduction as] the absolute or divine idea, God's self-actualizing concept, "the eternal inner life of God," which is at the same time the idea of freedom, the realization of spirit (both divine and human spirit) in history. . . . Thus Hegel was led to the key proposal that there are two principles of history, the first being the *idea*, the divine idea, the idea of freedom, which inwardly impels history toward its end, and the second, human activity or *passion*, which is the historical bearer or instrument of the idea.[22]

Hegel was able to find a way beyond a merely tragic emplotment of history, in the direction of grounding an abstract hope for the present upon the foundational understanding that spirit and freedom are unfolding in history. While this was a major achievement, it is cold comfort to know that freedom is being realized on the macrohistorical level when microhistory is filled with every tragedy from the premature loss of loved ones to the systematic, all-too-human barbarism of cultural genocide. This is a more precise version of Troeltsch's criticism of Hegel. Hodgson expresses it by urging that "the goal of world history lies not merely in the *cognition* of the concept of freedom but in the *realization* of freedom," rightly pointing out that this was "a fact recognized by Hegel's disciples on the left."[23] Hodgson seriously questions both Hegel's uniformly hopeful, if not actually optimistic, emplotment of macrohistory, and his uniformly tragic emplotment of microhistory[24] and concludes that

> history must be emplotted *tragicomically* on both microhistorical and macrohistorical scales. Partial realizations of freedom occur within all the dimensions of history, and long-term trajectories are discernible, but it cannot be claimed that history as such or as a whole is a comic process. It is an ambiguous process, which is to say that it is tragicomic. The final comedy is the divine comedy, not a human comedy. The only unambiguously comic vision of the perfection of freedom lies beyond history with the consummation of all things in God. This is the eschatological significance of the symbol "kingdom of God" or "kingdom of freedom." Yet this symbol also has an innerhistorical significance: the gestalt of the kingdom is a factor within history and has the power to transfigure it.[25]

Hodgson is correct in reminding us that Hegel *was* attuned to concrete historical facts, in spite of the emphasis upon metaphysical construction in the abstract, and that he thought of historical process as "typological rather than dialectical or evolutionary."[26] It is likely, therefore, that Troeltsch misunderstood, or misjudged, the great philosopher at some relevant points. Troeltsch certainly did not so describe Hegel. Nevertheless, even misdirected criticism can be helpful in coming to understand how Troeltsch thought he was applying and correcting Hegel's solution to the problem of philosophy of history in his own systematically less developed, but historically more nuanced, ideas.

Christology and Troeltsch's Philosophy of History

The consequences of Troeltsch's interpretation and critique of Hegel for the absolutist tendency within the classical Christological tradition can now be broached. Though Troeltsch nowhere directly critically engaged Hegel's Christological thought,[27] his criticism of the philosophy of history *underlying* Hegel's Christology is particularly powerful in application to Christology. It combines with his arguments from the development of doctrine and the history of religions to form a trenchant critique of the absolutist hermeneutical habit to which I have been drawing attention.

There is a natural animosity between the view of Jesus Christ in some traditional Christologies and historical relativism, even when defined as the metaphysical thesis of contextuality, individuality, and interconnectedness rather than in any of the more startling epistemic or ethical senses. The bone of contention is the claim that salvation and revelation are final, absolute, and unsurpassable in Jesus Christ, and the reason for the contention is two-fold. On the one hand, the attachment of uniquely definitive significance to the symbol of Jesus Christ bluntly contradicts the insight of Troeltsch's conception of *Relativismus* that meanings emerge only from contextual interconnections and can never escape their contingent nature to achieve an absolute status above the historical flux.

On the other hand, affirming such an absolutist view of the significance of the symbol of Jesus Christ entails positing a solution to the problem of the philosophy of history. Hegel's philosophy brought this entailment out explicitly, but any Christology espousing this kind of view of Jesus Christ at least must imply an interpretation of history that encompasses creation, anthropology, community, evil, ethics, and eschatology, and thus will have to be roughly comparable to Hegel's in scope. All meanings in history must be related intelligibly and uniquely to the significance of the symbol of Jesus Christ. In itself, there is nothing improper about that; even Troeltsch sought such a positive solution. But any such attempt is subject to the questions that Troeltsch leveled against Hegel's philosophy of history: does it explain the facts, and is it held tentatively and experimentally in the way that the metaphysic of history expressed by *Relativismus* required? From Troeltsch's point of view, Hegel's proposal failed on both counts.

Conceivably, it might be possible to defend an absolutist Christology from this attack by holding the absolutist interpretation tentatively, out of respect for the insights of the view of history encapsulated in *Relativismus*. Wolfhart Pannenberg is one advocate of Christological absolutism who has clearly grasped Troeltsch's criticism and counters with precisely this reply. He insists that all theological claims, including assertions of the absolute revelatory and salvific significance of Jesus Christ, must be inescapably fallible *hypotheses*, continually tested in the grueling domain of historical contingencies.[28] From Pannenberg's point of view, we are always in the midst of *anticipating* the consummation of history; accordingly, Christian eschatology demands a double stance of tentativity and tenaciousness with regard to Christology. However, given his criticisms of Hegel, it is likely that Troeltsch would have praised Pannenberg's tentativity as appropriate to our experience of the historical process, while charging him with failure in regard to the demand for plausibility and explanatory power. Nevertheless, because of Pannenberg's epistemology, there can be no question that absolutist Christology achieves its most plausible formulation, with respect to the problem of the philosophy of history, at his hands.

There are many contemporary theologians with no patience even for Pannenberg's tentative form of macrohistorical speculation, let alone Hegel's stridency. Most of these thinkers will gravitate naturally toward a Christology without absolutist characteristics, since this allows them to speak of the significance of Jesus Christ for Christians without committing them to claims about macrohistorical meanings which they believe to be unjustifiable in principle. There is one view, however, for which the collapse of macrohistorical speculation and encompassing grand narratives suggests a way to preserve absolutist Christology. The argument seems never to be *stated* clearly in the theological literature, even when presupposed, and so cannot be attributed to anyone in particular. But it is intrinsically interesting and can be formulated as follows: (1) Christian theological and liturgical tradition testifies to Jesus Christ as the all-determining reality in absolutist fashion; (2) all canons of discourse capable of refuting such an assertion have collapsed; (3) thus Christian theology is rationally *entitled* to continue this testimony; and (4) fidelity to Christian tradition *demands* that this testimony be made.

There are two problems with this argument. First, it is theoretically desperate and hermeneutically over-optimistic to make fidelity to a tradition of testimony the chief justification for an assertion, as if that tradition were univocal, and the path to fidelity brilliantly lit; neither is the case. Second, intersubjective, intertraditional discourse continues even after the widespread belief in the nonviability of macrohistorical speculation and master narratives; such discourse is able to discriminate less adequate from more adequate Christological formulations. Now as always, therefore, Christian theology must concern itself with its entitlement to make assertions. Troeltsch was never close to this kind of irrationalism in theology, even when toward the end of his life he was dubious that anyone could produce a workable macrohistorical interpretation.

The absolutist rendering of the symbol of Jesus Christ—whether in Hegel's definitive, Pannenberg's tenaciously tentative, or the irrationalist-traditionalist way—expresses a principle of purpose, meaning, and development for history as a whole on the basis of a special deposit of revelation and from a relatively small family of historical events. While such a historical vision undeniably has its virtues, Troeltsch's investigations of the history of religions convinced him that such an interpretation was far too narrowly grounded, as we saw in the last chapter. Moreover, its failure to explain adequately more than a small part of human history requires its reevaluation. Even the Christian self-interpretation of its own stream of history faces serious problems, as was evident in our review of Troeltsch's interpretation of the development of doctrine. For these reasons, absolutist Christology must be judged dissonant with our experience of history and historical meaning. Freeing the classical Christological tradition from the distortion of the absolutist hermeneutical habit that plagues it is essential if Christology is to make adequate sense of history in the era after Hegel and Troeltsch.

The Natural Sciences

There is scant material in Troeltsch's writings concerning the cosmic expanse of space-time and its chilling effect on Christology. This is certainly not because Troeltsch thought the point was weak. On the contrary, the vast size and age of the universe and the discovery that the origin and development of religious species such as *Homo sapiens* was a contingent process falling under natural laws had in Troeltsch's judgment the force of an unceremonious refutation of absolutist renderings of the significance of the Christ symbol. In fact, judging from what he *does* say, it is probably because Troeltsch found the argument so compelling and simple to state that he never bothered to elaborate it in great detail.

Troeltsch did not know about the cosmic anthropic principle, which establishes a connection between the possibility of human beings and the size of the universe, among other physical conditions. This fact calls for a more dialectical approach to the problem for Christology of the cosmic expanse of space-time than Troeltsch managed, but his point still has force, especially as he stresses the expanse of time rather than space. I will consider the contemporary version of this problem in a later chapter.

Troeltsch's historical sensitivity led him to believe that religious authenticity and efficaciousness were more widespread than the historical trajectory of influence radiating from Jesus Christ, and that history was larger than the history of a people, or a species, or a planet. Likewise, the principles of the divine Spirit were more subtle and mysterious than could be comprehended in the thought of any number of philosophers. This is a telling factor in Troeltsch's abandonment of Jesus Christ as the unique, definitive expression of the ground of cosmic history, which is the position accorded to Jesus Christ in many Christological views, from the Gospel of John to Hegel and beyond. Whatever is implied about the meaning of history by statements about the significance of Jesus Christ must be interpretable as the perspective of a very recent species in the evolutionary history of a planet whose solar system—whose galaxy!—constitutes a vanishingly small part of the known universe. Even if our very existence implies such dimensions, as the cosmic anthropic principle suggests, interpretations of cosmic history led by anthropocentric readings of our existence and history are desperately, even comically, weak.

This theme began to be stressed in Troeltsch's writings after *The Social Teaching* was completed, as was the case with many of the key shifts in his thought. A typical statement—one of many in Troeltsch's *Glaubenslehre*—appears in the context of a discussion of the problems faced by any presentation of the faith that seeks to take history seriously:

> Theologians all too readily forget the skepticism that overwhelms the modern person who contemplates the immeasurable vastness of time. According to the unanimous opinion of scientists, our planet has existed for three hundred thousand years![29] When confronted with such wild expanses of time, we find it infinitely difficult to think that all eternity is bound up in this historical moment that we call Jesus, and to insist that all of humanity must bind itself to him. This is where we encounter the greatest difficulties with any and all absolutizing of a particular historical moment.
>
>   If we still dare, despite all these serious objections, to maintain a relationship with history, we must do so differently than in the past.[30]

Troeltsch made similar, albeit less pointed, remarks about the immensity of space. For instance, "the whole idea of a world-redeemer has been adversely affected by the impression that the geocentric and anthropocentric view of the world is no longer tenable."[31] Troeltsch's conclusion?

All these impressions have made it impossible to continue to deify Jesus and to assign to him an absolutely central position. But the attempt, associated especially with liberal theology, to transfer to the human Jesus the role of a universal world-redeemer traditionally assigned by the church to Christ, is wholly impossible and fraught with intolerable contradictions.

Yet it is also true, that there is no other way to hold together the Christian community of spirit than through the common confession of Jesus; that it is impossible to keep alive the distinctively Christian idea of God apart from seeing its life-giving embodiment in Jesus; and that all the greatest and most characteristic ideas of Christianity—the idea of a grace that grasps and conquers us, of a certitude available to us, and of a superior power (*Kraft*) that elevates and overcomes us—depend upon a religious appreciation and interpretation of Jesus as divine revelation.[32]

This is a helpfully compact statement of Troeltsch's Christological program: *something can and must be said* about the person of Jesus Christ on the basis of his religious significance, but absolutist renderings of the classical Christological tradition do not say it well enough, because they are in flagrant dissonance with the nature of the cosmos as we have come to know it.

It is not impossible to imagine that the universe gives rise to one such as Jesus Christ whose significance is adequately described only in absolute, universal, unique, and unsurpassable terms. Troeltsch, too, could probably imagine this, despite his rhetorical flourishes about its impossibility.[33] If so, then Troeltsch's problem with absolutist Christologies could not have been the literal impossibility of the presupposed world view. Rather, the problem was that such a universe was no longer believed or wanted by Troeltsch and, if he is right, by the modern West in general. If the universe *were* that way—hundreds of billions of galaxies each with hundreds of billions of solar systems, yet with the culmination of the entire cosmic process occurring (conveniently) on our earth—it would be religiously useless, the cruel trick of a capricious divinity. The nature of the physical cosmos and the historical process thunder a very different message. Thus Troeltsch attacked the absolutism of traditional Christologies by urging its massive implausibility, its cultural irrelevance.

This argument—and many others expounded by Troeltsch—has the logical structure of *undermining a position by attacking a premise es-*

sential to it, or a consequence flowing from it. A complex logical connection links a direct attack on a proposition to the undermining of a position presupposing or entailing the directly attacked proposition. For instance, it may be possible for the Christologies Troeltsch repudiated to shed their dependence upon a premise that formerly guided their expatiation so that attacks upon that now discarded premise have no effect upon the beleaguered Christologies. The impact of Troeltsch's undermining arguments therefore depends not only upon their soundness, but also upon whether the absolutist Christologies he rejected can reformulate themselves effectively to avoid presupposing or entailing the geocentric and anthropocentric attitudes that Troeltsch was attacking.

Troeltsch's commitment to his anti-absolutist Christology turned on his entirely correct belief that no such reformulation is likely. In the case of the cosmic expanse of space-time, the ability of absolutist Christological reflection to reformulate itself for the sake of easing the dissonance it causes is nonexistent. Either it must illegitimately impose a specifically anthropocentric reading on the cosmic anthropic principle, or it must resort to sheer assertions that require the forsaking of explanatory power and relevance to the world as we know it—all out of misguided loyalty to a narrow, anthropocentric interpretation of a time-bound, cosmologically naïve deposit of revelation.

This said, however, it is important also to recognize that here again Troeltsch's theological imagination seems as limited as his cultural understanding was sophisticated. The deification of Jesus is rejected in the last quoted passage along with the assignment to Jesus of an "absolutely central position." But surely a distinction is being trampled underfoot here. As subsequent Christologies have amply demonstrated, it is possible to maintain the incarnation without assigning Jesus an "absolutely central position" in the cosmos. In fact, Jesus the person can be understood as a revelatory exhibition of the Logos of the Prologue to John's gospel—the means of creation of the entire cosmos, as well as its centerpiece and final end—and yet not thereby be assigned an "absolutely central position," so long as the Logos is not thought to be *exhaustively, finally, unsurpassably* manifested in Jesus of Nazareth.

The Human Sciences

Troeltsch led twentieth-century theology into yet another seemingly impenetrable thicket—but an unavoidable one—when he began to take account of sociology and psychology in his reflection upon Christian doctrine. The precedent was their mostly uncontroversial application in historical research, where the insights of these disciplines into individual and corporate humanity had proved essential for gaining a clear understanding of past events and movements. Christian doctrine, however, had remained relatively free of such considerations, because of widespread acceptance of the notion of a definitive revelation that somehow transcended particular human needs and social forces.

After Kant's attempt to formulate the role played by the human subject in all perception and understanding, however, Christian doctrine was destined at some point in the future to leave behind its insulation from psychological considerations. First Schleiermacher, and then, in different ways, Strauss, Feuerbach, Nietzsche, Weber, the history-of-religions school, James, and Freud gave evidence of this inevitability with ever greater sharpness, broadening the problem to include sociological modes of thought in the process. It has since broadened still further with sociobiology and other developments, but the aim here will be to see how this line of development impacted Troeltsch's thought, especially in relation to the plausibility of Christological doctrine. Since Troeltsch wrote extensively on Christianity in the light of sociological modes of thought, we begin there. However, though he did not explore it as systematically, the impact of psychology upon his Christological thought was probably just as great.

The Social Teaching of the Christian Churches

Troeltsch's friendship with sociologist Max Weber was an important influence in raising Troeltsch's awareness of the extent to which Christian institutions and ideas might be conditioned by their various and changing contexts. It has seemed obvious to almost everyone at all times that the churches, along with their doctrines and ethical outlooks, were in fact affected by their social settings and that they in turn were capable of exerting considerable force on those social settings, as was preeminently the case in medieval Catholicism. The issue in Troeltsch's time was rather the character and extent of this two-way influence. For example, even as Weber had demonstrated the intimate connections between Calvinism and capitalism, whereby "Protestant asceticism created for bourgeois capitalism a positive ethic, a soul"[34] that "contains energies which directly further this economic development,"[35] so Troeltsch sought to discern how Calvinism had itself been affected by the rise of capitalist economies.[36] Could developments in Calvinistic doctrine and ethics be understood independently of such factors, as they had always tended to be in histories of ethics and doctrine up to Troeltsch's time? More generally, was pure history of ideas, or of Christian doctrine and ethics, possible any longer? And, more profoundly, "to what extent is Christianity itself an actively productive sociological principle?"[37]

The Social Teaching of the Christian Churches (finished in 1911) was Troeltsch's massive attempt to address these questions. The importance of this work lies partly in the fact that it was unprecedented; Troeltsch himself retrospectively described the driving issues of *Social Teaching* as "extraordinarily difficult questions, about which there had been hardly any useful preparatory work."[38] But it was also important in another way, for Troeltsch's approach to Christian theology was profoundly changed in many respects as a result of the insights he gleaned during his researches. It was this investigation that provided Troeltsch with the detailed knowledge of the history of Christian institutions and ideas necessary for the drawing of his distinctive conclusions about doctrinal development, the history of religions, and the philosophy of history that have already been discussed.

Traces of the impact of *Social Teaching* are discernible in the revisions Troeltsch made to *The Absoluteness of Christianity* (1902[1], 1912[2]) and "What Does 'Essence of Christianity' Mean?" (1903[1], 1913[2]).[39] The example provided here, however, is drawn from changes within *Social Teaching* itself, as the huge work evolved.

At the beginning of *Social Teaching*, Troeltsch was willing in many places to speak of an *independent* fundamental religious and sociological Christian idea that develops in the various social settings of the churches under the guidance and integrity of its own inner spiritual power.[40] This conception of the unfolding of an idea inherently capable of guiding and preserving itself under the contingencies of its development—a clear indication of Hegel's influence on Troeltsch—widened out by the end of *Social Teaching* into the recognition that

> every idea is still faced by brutal facts, and all upward movement is checked and hindered by interior and exterior difficulties. Nowhere does there exist an absolute Christian ethic, which only awaits discovery; all that we can do is to learn to control the world-situation in its successive phases just as the earlier Christian ethic did in its own way. There is also no absolute ethical transformation of material nature or of human nature; all that does exist is a constant wrestling with the problems they raise. Thus the Christian ethics of the present day and of the future will also only be an adjustment to the world-situation, and it will only desire to achieve that which is practically possible.[41]

While acknowledging that interpreting Troeltsch at this point is not completely straightforward, it is fairly safe to say that the concrete contingencies of social situations appeared to him at the end of *Social Teaching* to be more significant conditioning factors, and the intrinsic, inner power of the Christian idea a less significant factor, than he had thought at the outset of his research. It is not that Troeltsch had completely given up by the time *Social Teaching* was finished in 1911 the conviction of a unique and efficacious Christian ethical and spiritual ideal, but only that his estimation of the influence and perhaps even the relevance of this ideal for any particular social setting was revised downwards. In practice, all the resources of the Christian faith do not *determine* the strategy for grappling with social realities but rather simply co-condition the moment in which a creative compromise or adjustment or critique is advanced.

Because of this freedom of development, it is impossible to interpret the trajectories of developing Christian doctrine or institutional life or social teaching as natural or law-like outworkings in changing contexts of an inner essence, on the model of an acorn that is transformed into a vast tree, conditioned by sunlight and soil and water and curious animals, but still recognizably an oak. It is not just the recognition of the unending variety of social contexts that produces this negative conclusion, for this by itself cannot rule out the interpretation of principled organic development, even as an oak is still an oak even when fire scars or nearby trees force the branches in a certain direction in search of adequate light.

Rather, the realization that Christian ideas can be applied creatively in any particular setting in a multitude of ways renders the oak tree analogy desperately inapt—indeed, leads directly to the conclusion that the social teachings and ecclesial doctrines *could have been different*; the oak could have been a eucalyptus.

Harnack tried to account for the admittedly eucalyptus-like appearance of the Christian churches as a contingent but understandable and actually useful deviation from the original oak-tree design, correctable by genetic surgery along the lines of the Protestant reformers, in the light of the historically articulable essence of Christianity. As we saw in our discussion of Troeltsch's view of the development of doctrine, Troeltsch could find no original standard by which later institutional and doctrinal forms could be definitively assessed. Neither a historically defined essence, nor the personality of Jesus, nor the biblical pictures of Jesus Christ, nor the concept of the Spirit of Christ were such *definitive* norms.

The combination of Troeltsch's philosophy of history (*Relativismus*) and his commitment to the history-of-religions method led to his perspective of slowly mutating, contingent norms and lines of development—those just listed, for example—whose overall trajectory usually could be discerned (or constructed) only retrospectively and only extrapolated into the future with great uncertainty. In Christianity, as a matter of contingent fact, these norms and developments continually have been related in a variety of ways to Jesus Christ. But if institutional, ethical, and doctrinal developments were not guided into every new context by a determinate, unchanging essence of any kind—as the genetic material of the acorn guides the growth of the oak—what *were* the criteria for development? For Troeltsch, we saw that what can be called a minimalist kind of solution to the problem of norms for Christian ethics and doctrine was required: it was necessary simultaneously to loosen the ties to origins and to give up the comfortable presumption of supernatural guidance of development, adjusting the estimate of the significance of original impetus and divine guidance from determining forces to contributing factors.

The gap thereby suggested was to be made up with *a combination of social dynamics and psychological needs, creative human construction of meaning and organization, and simple contingencies.* After all, since criteria for development did not derive from some definitive essence, known in advance, they had to be practical, contingent, and variable in character. This is the entry point for social psychological considerations in

Christian theology, as well as for blind chance. In fact, there is no Christian norm that is not affected by social psychological dynamics. Even the criteria of the personality of Jesus, the Bible, and ecclesial tradition have always been interpreted and applied in a range of ways that are inexplicable apart from taking into account social psychological considerations. This is the fundamental result about the norms for Christian ethics and doctrine that emerges from *Social Teaching*.

We have seen how these discoveries of Troeltsch—first made while ranging about in the history of Christian social ethics and the history of religions—affected his thoughts on the history of doctrine, the essence of Christianity, and the philosophy of history. But also propelled into the open were new questions for Christology having to do with the role and meaning of social psychology. Troeltsch tried to face and answer the challenges to Christological plausibility brought by these new questions. Though Troeltsch's specific proposal is problematic, his espousal of a nonabsolutist Christology was the core of his solution, when Christology was in view; this measured response is demanded in our own time. Three examples will illustrate the various dimensions of the impact of a realistic awareness of social psychological realities on the plausibility of Christology.

Christology and the Religious Needs of Christian Communities

In "The Significance of the Historical Existence of Jesus for Faith," Troeltsch asked about the centrality of Jesus Christ to the Christian faith. This is a controversial question to begin with, because, as Troeltsch remarked, "it has no meaning for those who maintain Christ's supra-humanity . . . [nor] for those who see Christianity as a real pardon and liberation of humanity from the curse of sin, suffering and death by means of an act of reconciliation by Christ directed at God."[42] By this rather clumsy observation, Troeltsch meant that the faith of such people so clearly presupposes the historicity and absolute significance of the God-man Jesus that no alternative position is conceivable. Under these circumstances, reflection that entertains an alternative solution would be derailed by the requirement of a pre-determined answer. Troeltsch thought that his concerns were "meaningless" to such people as a result. However, when the presuppositions of Jesus Christ's ontological uniqueness and redemptive indispensability are made objects of inquiry at the behest of what

Troeltsch variously calls "wholehearted historical criticism" or just "modern thought,"[43] three questions suddenly become rather sharp:

1. the historical theological question about how the centrality of Jesus *came to be*;
2. the practical theological question about how the centrality of Jesus is to be *preserved*; and
3. the systematic theological question about why the centrality of Jesus *should* be preserved.

The first and second questions have connected answers. The third question is more complex and needs to be treated separately.

Troeltsch's general answer to the first question was stated without elaboration in the last chapter's discussion of the history of religions. The key social dynamic Troeltsch called upon for his explanation of the emergence of the Christ-cult is the phenomenon of "elevation of the founder." This parallels Troeltsch's answer to the second question. The religious idea of Christianity could never and cannot now survive apart from a concrete, cultic focus on Jesus: "So long as Christianity survives in any form it will always be connected with the central position of Christ in the cult. . . . For social psychological reasons he is indispensable for cult, power, efficacy and expansion, and that should be sufficient to justify the connexion [between the Christian idea and Christ's central position in cult and doctrine]."[44]

The argument for this conclusion turns on the recognition of a sociological principle:[45]

> It is a law of social psychology that individuals with merely parallel thoughts and experiences . . . can never simply co-exist for long without affecting each other and joining forces. Out of the myriad connexions community groups with higher and lower strata are everywhere produced and taken together these need a concrete focus. This law holds for religious life too. Here too, therefore, these kinds of circles emerge with definite hierarchies, firm centres, means of extension and centres of strength from which religious thought can continually renew its power.[46]

Regarding the integrity of this principle (or set of principles) in relation to the wild actualities of the history of religions, Troeltsch adduced an odd mixture of casually stated examples,[47] and then remarked more generally that his conclusion "rests on social-psychological laws which have produced exactly the same phenomena in other religious areas and recur a thousand times over on a smaller scale up to the present. They render utopian the whole idea of a piety that simply springs from every man's heart and nevertheless forms a harmony, that does not need reciprocity and yet remains a living power."[48]

Whether or not Troeltsch overstated his case here is a moot point. Troeltsch definitely went too far, however, when he announced a mere application of this principle in the context of Christianity as if it were a similarly universal law, namely, that this concrete focus or "rallying point" needs to be "presented in a personal and living way in a normative archetype."[49] This is manifestly not the case in the history of religions, even in what Troeltsch called spiritual and ethical religions. There is something to Troeltsch's point, however, at least for some other religions besides Christianity, the most outstanding example being the attitude of reverence, trust, personal allegiance and active emulation taken toward the Buddha in many strands of Mahayana Buddhism, and more strictly toward Gautama in much of Theravada; this is an attitude realized socially as well as individually.

Nothing important hinges on this for Troeltsch, however; his main concern was with the general sociological principle and not the specification of it concerning archetypal personalities. This is merely a momentary lapse into elevating the particularities of Christianity to universal principles applicable to all religions (or even just to Troeltsch's "religions of spirit"), an unfortunate habit of his era that Troeltsch was gradually leaving behind at this time.[50]

By applying a familiar sociological principle to the Christ cult, Troeltsch broke new ground in two ways. First, he suggested a new set of criteria for Christological construction, namely, the practical needs for cohesion, liveliness, and longevity that the cultic dimension of Christianity has; these are needs that must be provided for in a Christology. Second, Troeltsch indicated a constraint on the way constructive Christology can appropriate the reality of religious experience within the Christ cult. Even by speaking of the worshipping life of the churches as a Christ cult appears to have been a deliberate attempt to inject a measure of sociological realism into theological reflection. Christ cults have the same characteristics that the study of religion has discovered in other religious cults. That is, to make the point redundantly, the Christ cult is a cult. A theology that ignores this background and supposes, contrary to fact, that there is some sense in which the Christ-cult is free from typical cultic realities—including the cultivation of enthusiasm, projection, and wishful thinking under a religious description—is simply unrealistic.

Christology and Psychological Needs

Mostly implicit in Troeltsch's argument about the centrality of the Christ figure is his recognition of the role played in the construction of dogmatic statements about Jesus (the first question) and in the development of the Christ-cult (the second question) by the tendency of believers to give voice to what it is about Jesus that is of existential importance to them. Troeltsch's suggestion about a psychological need for humans to be intimately related to an archetypal personality—distinct from the need for community that renders Jesus Christ indispensable in Christian cult and doctrine—is the key to reconstructing his understanding of the process of doctrinal formation. Unfortunately, Troeltsch was not as clear on this point as he was in the case of the need for cultic cohesion.[51] Coakley notes in summarizing Troeltsch that Jesus Christ, considered as an archetypal personality, actually meets "a considerable variety of psychological needs: for vividness, for plasticity, for edification, for concreteness, and above all for one single 'focus' and 'centre' of religious attention."[52] This seems to be consistent with Troeltsch's view on the matter, albeit a clearer statement than he provided.

Though the psychological need for unmediated relation with an archetypal figure is usually expressed in and alongside of the social psychological need for a cultic center of gravity and means of communal cohesion, Troeltsch occasionally separated the two. For instance, in speaking of the resurrection as one factor in the elevation of Jesus from "the revealer of God, into the object of a cult,"[53] Troeltsch drew out psychological rather than social needs: "Historical research has nothing to say about the [Resurrection]. For ourselves, we solve the problem by reference to *the devotion and surrender of the disciples, which convinced them that Jesus lived.*. . . . All these extraordinary circumstances and effects, however, make the process whereby belief in the Messiah came to be transferred to Jesus and underwent subsequent alterations quite understandable."[54]

Elsewhere, with a few exceptions,[55] this theme tends to appear in short but unmistakable remarks, such as the motivation of Christians to obtain a "specific and immediate object of faith"[56] or of the "support, center and symbol" of the Christian community as constituted "in the picture of a living, many-sided and at the same time elevating and strengthening personality," whose "innermost orientation for life" we can adopt and "from it find in full freedom an application which gives shape to our contemporary religious and ethical tasks."[57]

For traditional Christologies, when this psychological dynamic has been recognized—as it often has been—it has seemed to confirm the divine attestation of Jesus, because it can be the occasion for recognizing an apt meeting of human needs for an archetypal figure by God's loving provision of Jesus Christ for precisely that saving purpose. The interpretation placed on the same psychological dynamic can, however, be quite different. These psychological needs are the basis for a plausible explanation as to the provenance of assertions about Jesus' divinity, of legendary accounts of his miraculous ministry, and of beliefs about his absolute, irrevocable significance for revelation and salvation. That is, if the need for social cohesion has maintained the symbol of Jesus Christ at the center of Christian cult and doctrine through the centuries, then the same need in conjunction with these powerful psychological drives accounts for how the symbol of Jesus Christ was elevated into that central position in the first place.

To be clear: the need for social cohesion by itself is not sufficient to explain the *emergence* of Christian cult and doctrine focusing on Jesus. Any gathering of early Christians would have appeared contrived unless their reason for being together were some powerful experience, recognizably similar for each individual. The encounter with Jesus, thought of along the lines of any Christology, would have been a common factor of this sort. But such a common factor may be described differently, according to this argument. An impressive and compelling figure like Jesus—even if the absolutist claims eventually made about him were flatly false—can give rise to a collection of flexible interpretations of him in which individual psychological needs are effectively met. A cultic life can form around the conviction that all the richness of the universe and the majesty of the divine presence is encountered in that figure—who now becomes the cultic center, and very soon an object of worship, readily transformed from Christ the revealer of God to Christ as God.

To flesh out further Troeltsch's position on the emergence of Christian communities and their Christological affirmations, a few examples of Troeltsch's advocacy of this argument are in order. It is important to note, however, that Troeltsch at no point gave a systematic statement of this position; it is only present in brief summaries in a number of his writings. There are many questions left open as a result, especially about the precise nature of the "rallying-point" and the "archetype" dynamics, which are never discussed thoroughly. Nevertheless, the suggestiveness of the remarks is apparent and helpfully increases the specificity of what we can suppose, based on the history of religions perspective, was Troeltsch's reconstruction of Christian origins. For instance, "The dogma concerning Christ which emerged from the Christ cult was only meant to show and give access to the one eternal God in Christ in order to create a new community. It could only establish itself by having its own cult. Regardless of what mythology and mysteries, pagan and gnostic analogies may have contributed, they have only clothed and made comprehensible to ancient consciousness a process which lay in the inner logic of the matter."[58] Again, and more directly, "In the absence of historical critical thinking, Jesus was naturally identified with God *in order that* he might become the immediate object of faith; with critical thinking, the God of Jesus becomes the object of faith, and Jesus is transformed into the historical mediator and revealer.[59]

The question remains whether Troeltsch thought there was anything about the *person* of Jesus that prompted his initial elevation from "historical mediator and revealer" to the definitive locus of the "one eternal God." This last quotation demonstrates a problem encountered reasonably frequently in Troeltsch's writings when interrogating them for an answer to this and similar questions: there is a degree of vagueness that begs for clarification not given in the text. For instance, speaking of Jesus as being "identified with God" is awkward in view of the refusal of mainstream patristic theology to make such an identification without further ado. It may be that Troeltsch had in mind the general member of the Christ cult, or it may be that he would wish to mount an argument that the fathers really did identify Jesus with God; it is not clear which is the case.

Going further, the crucial point is the metaphysical import of designating Jesus Christ as "historical mediator and redeemer." The transformation of Jesus into "historical mediator and revealer" is, as Troeltsch himself argues, a way of speaking about "God's being in Christ,"[60] so it is not at all clear why this is not a kind of identification with God. In the earlier discussion of the Christology of *Glaubenslehre*, we saw that Troeltsch thought that Jesus' personality was central and that God was revealed in and through that personality. This pushes the question of the significance of Jesus closer to his person as such, compared with the emphasis on his function as revealer or savior. But Troeltsch offered his readers little assistance in unpacking this and similar references.

In all, the eschewing of metaphysics while still talking about the significance of the person of Jesus was a Ritschlian characteristic. But Troeltsch's indebtedness to Ritschl notwithstanding, it is likely that Troeltsch was himself not completely clear on what he wished to be committed to by this phrase in relation to the metaphysical status of Jesus. A final answer in relation to Troeltsch's Christology is probably now out of the question, for every proposal depends too much on hint and suggestion drawn from here and there, as his fragmentary Christological writings allow. The *Glaubenslehre* offers the clearest view, but even there the same questions are left open.

One point is less uncertain. Troeltsch definitely *approved* and made positive theological use of such projection as was involved in the establishment of the Christ cult and the doctrines it produced, which projection is involved no matter what view is taken of Jesus Christ.[61] Troeltsch occasionally derided patristic Christology as a mistake-filled fiasco—a strangely intolerant reaction, especially coming from a historian. But insofar as it was not merely the result of political intrigue and deadness of spirit of ecclesial bureaucrats, he would have seen it as a series of errors springing from a fundamentally healthy projective impulse, mistakes that were perhaps inevitable, and maybe even useful rather than harmful from most points of view, including especially the perspective of institutional survival and flourishing.

These views of Troeltsch, present mostly as tantalizing suggestions in his later writings, open up a number of fascinating and critical issues. Here we move toward the third question guiding this presentation, namely, the systematic question about why Christianity *should* survive or remain focused on Jesus Christ. Can Troeltsch consistently maintain his affirmative interpretation of classical Christological doctrines as spiritually and cultically useful, projection-induced doctrinal mistakes? How can what Troeltsch thought of as false or severely misleading statements about Jesus Christ be benign and useful, the result of a natural and healthy social-psychological process? More generally, is not Troeltsch backing himself into a corner by resolutely advocating an anti-absolutist Christology at the same time as passionately seeking to renew the cultic life of the church against disintegration it was suffering from the modern scourge of individualism?[62] After all, absolutism of all sorts has a fine track record for commanding such unity, at least for some sorts of people, and Troeltsch's kind of Christology was and is largely untested in this regard. Moreover, if he is backed into this corner for good reasons—Troeltsch thought paying attention to historical criticism and the outlook of the "modern world" were excellent reasons—then is there any hope for the survival of Christianity in the secular, individualized, fragmented environment of contemporary Western culture? Why *should* Christianity survive? The discussion of this question will be delayed long enough to deal with the third example of the impact of social psychological modes of thought on Christology.

Christology and the Imagination

In simultaneously emphasizing the role of the symbol of Jesus Christ in bringing coherence to the Christian cult, and the need of individual believers to appropriate this symbol as a "specific and immediate object of faith," Troeltsch raised the dual issues of subjectivism and objective reference to the historical Jesus in a new way. Are *any* imaginatively conceived images of Jesus Christ appropriate for individual believers? Can the Christian cult develop unconstrained in random directions? What control if any is exercised by the historical Jesus over the ideas and ideals that are fostered by the Christian cult and lovingly projected onto Jesus in mind-boggling variety by believers of every time and place? These are questions with theological implications both practical and systematic.[63] Their practical significance will be the focus here; that is, the immediate aim is to describe Troeltsch's affirmation of the role of imagination in Christian piety and cultic life.

In this area, once again, the impact of Troeltsch's work on *Social Teaching* is evident, for it left him with an indelible impression of the overwhelming diversity of the Christian tradition's thought about Jesus Christ through the ages. This diversity is present from the beginning, in the very different presentations of Jesus that are preserved for us in the Synoptic Gospels, the Gospel of John and the letters of Paul, and even earlier, as we can construe from the variety of responses to Jesus recorded in the Gospels and the Acts of the Apostles. This diversity remains even in the judgment of recent biblical scholarship about the earliest and most reliable traditions about Jesus. Had Troeltsch been better informed about Christianity as it was developing in many other parts of the world in his own time, his impression of that wild diversity would have been even stronger.

Probably because of the unquestionable nature of this diversity in Troeltsch's mind, he does not spend much time trying to establish it. Rather, he seems most concerned to determine how the Christian cult has remained under control when divergent individual interpretations of Jesus are omnipresent and what prescriptive conclusions for Christology ought to flow from the recognition of this diversity. As we saw in the earlier discussion of faith's dependence on history, Troeltsch's argument for the proposition that faith needs from historical criticism only a "basic overall picture" of Jesus Christ is relevant here. The following passage speaks to this point and helps piece together Troeltsch's conception of the relation between Christology, cult, and the imagination of the Christian believer.

> When the historical existence of Jesus is looked at in its social-psychological significance and not as the only authority and source of power opposed to original sin, there is no objection to seeing it always in [a] broader historical context. Preparation and effects can be drawn into the interpretation. Preaching and congregational life do not depend upon philological exactitude in the details of the picture of Jesus. . . .
>
> But that must be accompanied by a consciousness of being able in all truth and honesty to see Jesus as the center of this living world. It must not feel or worry that it is composing a myth without object or basis in reality, for embodying an idea into which a thousand sources have flowed. Granted this presupposition it can interpret the picture of Christ in practical proclamation very freely and flexibly, using everything that flowed into him and everything which in the course of thousands of years has been accommodated and loved in him. Neither will it concentrate everything in Jesus. Other historical personalities too can receive their due and be seen in some sense as visible symbols and guarantees of faith that sustains our strength. . . . The Christian character and so the definiteness of the principle is preserved by everything being constantly related to the rallying-point, the personality of Jesus.[64]

Troeltsch evidently believed that orientation of the Christian cult to the historical Jesus is of the first importance in offering guidance to the development of the cult. In turn, the cult disciplines the individual Christian imagination to some extent. Just as important, however, is the fact that the cult is relatively independent of particular imaginative construals of Jesus by Christians. Not only does this independence produce greater stability in Christian worship and community life by freeing it from having to conform to divergent individual expectations, but it also enables greater freedom for individuals to adapt to their own needs and interests the symbol of Jesus Christ. This freedom is a liberty of the imagination under the creative, protective constraints of the structure and life of the cult, for it is the cult that presents the archetypes and authorities to which the imagination responds. Troeltsch describes this freedom in the following way: "As images of personal concrete life [archetypes, authorities, sources of power, and rallying points deriving from prophets and founder personalities] can be interpreted with a versatility and flexibility possessed by no mere doctrine or dogma. They also possess a vividness and plasticity never found in theory and understanding but only in imagination and feeling."[65]

As noted in the earlier discussion of the dependence of faith and dogmatics on history, the Christian cult functions as a "buffer" between the individual Christian's appropriation of Jesus and the stark and sometimes perplexing biblical and traditional pictures of him. This allows biblical research to proceed—and even to shift its center of opinion regularly or to produce indigestible results—without having too deleterious an effect on the life of individual believers. This is one of the keys both to the cult's importance and more generally to the immense diversity, versatility, and resilience of the Christian religion.

With this reconstruction, we can understand Troeltsch's affirmation of the role of Christian imagination in apprehending Jesus Christ. And this is the answer to that part of the question of practical theology that concerns the description of the relationships among Christology, believer, and cult. But what, we must ask, is the object of the Christian religious imagination? What exactly is being interpreted so differently? The earthly Jesus? The Gospels' presentations of him? The historians' reconstructions of his life? The tradition's abstracted allegiance to him? Is there not some strain of an eternally present, mystical Christ in Troeltsch's thinking appearing again here and evident especially in his speaking of the "personal-

ity of Jesus" in the above quotation? But then how is this personality to be
conceived? How is it continuous with the earthly Jesus? In what sense is it
living? Troeltsch's indebtedness to Herrmann may be relevant here, for
Herrmann had asserted that the Christ encountered in faith through the
biblical portrayals of him was in fact the personality of the earthly Jesus, in
dependence upon the superhistorical and supernatural establishment of
this coincidence. As we have seen, Troeltsch regards such an answer to
these pointed questions as unhistorical, and also unrealistic, for it does
not give due weight to the actual diversity of portraits of Christ that the
tradition has in fact produced.[66] Yet, against his better judgment, Troeltsch appears on occasion to slip into the Herrmannian mystical outlook
when he is at the limit of his ability to explain the power of the "personality of Jesus Christ." But what will Troeltsch offer in place of the solution he
halfheartedly rejects?

Here again the answer for Troeltsch lies somewhere in the region de-
marcated by the conception of Jesus' vivid, authoritative personality, the
idea of Jesus as a revelation of God and of the divine love, and the idea of
the spirit of Christ, as this is borne on his rich philosophy of history. It
does seem to include the denial of any kind of resurrection and any sense
in which Jesus has an objective, ongoing life. But, as we have seen repeatedly, pushing for precision beyond this general summary exceeds the
hermeneutical resolution of Troeltsch's writings.

It is obvious, then, that Troeltsch's thinking about human imagination
and the cult of Christ begs for elaboration that it cannot now receive from
the theologian himself. However laudable Troeltsch's devotion to the
plight of his country, from the point of view of plumbing the depths of the
promising theological suggestiveness of his Christology, we might wish
that he had not turned his attention so wholeheartedly to history and politics upon his move to Berlin in 1915. Nevertheless, even to hold a position that implied a *positive* construal of Schweitzer's negative description
of the quest for the historical Jesus—"while Jesus maintains the central
position each age interprets him really quite differently and puts its own
ideas under his protection"—is to move in a profoundly startling direction. It is lamentable that more of twentieth-century Christological reflection has not followed Troeltsch's lead, for he moved in the direction he
did under the impetus of his determination to take seriously history and
the human sciences, and not on a theological whim. While many other
areas of Christian theology have begun to pay appropriate attention to the

human sciences, contemporary theology has failed to emulate Troeltsch by doing the same for Christology.[67]

The entire world picture fostered by alertness to social psychological realities finds the very concept of 'absolute meaning' of any sort highly suspicious—and doubly so when this concept is applied to a historical figure whose archetypal function at the center of the Christ-cult is so powerful. The implausibility of absolutist Christology established in this way is greatly magnified by the capacity of an interpretative perspective conversant with social psychological dynamics to produce a compelling explanation of the process whereby a cultic life grew up around the memory of the figure of Jesus and absolute revelatory and salvific significance was ascribed to him. Thus it was that Troeltsch was rightly unable to conceive of an adequate response to the massive implausibility of absolutist Christology apart from abandoning the cause of that implausibility: the fascination with absoluteness. His Christological approach—generalized appropriately to allow for the possibility of incarnational as well as inspirational, nonincarnational antiabsolutist Christologies—remains to this day the most intellectually and religiously tenable response to the crisis induced in contemporary Christology by the inability of absolutist proposals to establish credibility in the face of social psychological realities.

The Problem of Norms for Judgment

The series of issues we have been considering leads irrevocably to the question of *theological justification*. This question is not as sharp in the presence of an absolutist Christology. But when the situation of Christological doctrine is adequately grasped—as afloat on a sea of historical contingencies; without the assurance of supernatural guarantees or definitive, unchanging norms; and to some extent always at the mercy of the projective impulses of human imaginations and social customs—then the matter of theological justification becomes especially pressing and most insistent of all in relation to the problem of norms for judgment. We encountered a similar issue in the discussion of the history of doctrine, and it needs to be discussed in closing this chapter.[68]

We considered above Troeltsch's proposal for solving the problem of criteria for the development of Christian doctrine, ethics, and institutions. In relation to Christology, and consistently with his metaphysics of history, the argument was that Troeltsch was committed to a minimalist solution that (1) denied any definitive norms; (2) affirmed traditional norms such as the personality of Jesus, the biblical pictures of Christ, and others deriving from the Bible and the tradition of the church, but in a weaker sense, as contingent, contextual, and mutating norms; (3) admitted a role for social psychological dynamics, human ingenuity, and contingency; and (4) proposed that the traditional norms themselves were subject to social psychological dynamics in their creation, application, and development. The pressing issue is whether such a minimalist solution can support theological justifications of the shape taken by Christian ethics, doctrines, and institutions in various contexts. Put sharply, the question is whether Christianity *should* continue at all or, in relation to Christology, whether Christianity should continue intimately tied to the person of Jesus.

The great problem with Troeltsch's approach to norms for Christian doctrinal, ethical, and institutional developments was that he could not give a definitive, detailed answer to this basic question. He could say— and did say repeatedly—that Christianity is the highest religious development that can have significance for Europeans. But Christianity so conceived was still merely an approximation to the transcendent absolute, and so there is a natural impetus to *improve* it, by radical means if necessary. He could say that Christianity was "true for us." But when we know that there are parallel religious truth claims and that wish fulfillment and projection are active parts of our religious experience, what blocks the tendency toward changing religions, except that it is more convenient to go to church than to mosque or synagogue? What blocks the move toward skeptical withdrawal from the church, except that religious participation might for some be socially advantageous, interesting, or enjoyable? Where is the clarion call of the gospel in this messy absence of definitive norms? Where is the decisive command of God in a world of partial truths, group enthusiasm, projection, father-obsession, and wishful thinking?

Troeltsch was perfectly well aware of this multidimensional problem, as his lifelong concentration on the challenge of norms for ethical and religious judgments shows. So it is crucial to keep in mind his two-part answer, aspects of which already have been mentioned in other contexts.

First, as we have seen, exposure to a massive amount of detailed historical material compelled Troeltsch to adopt this minimalist position. The variability and diversity, contingency and individuality of all historical events and developments had become the leading features of history in his interpretation of it. Troeltsch's intuition at this point is difficult to evade. The challenge of finding an absolute must be pursued in and through this relativity for Troeltsch and for us; it cannot be circumvented.

Troeltsch came to this decision even before *Social Teaching*. It is expressed in the following quotation from the 1902 edition of *Absoluteness*.

> The problem faced by the modern approach to history is not that of making an either/or choice between relativism and absolutism but that of how to combine the two. This is the problem of how to discern, in the relative, tendencies toward the absolute goal. Or, to state the problem more accurately: How does one work out a fresh, durable, and creative synthesis that will give the absolute the form possible to it at a particular moment and yet remain true to its inherent limitation as a mere approximation of the true, ultimate, and universally valid values?[69]

Thus, whatever was to be said about norms and the problem of providing theological justification for Christianity, the presupposition of it had to be *Relativismus*, with everything that entailed. This is not an obviously hopeless task. It involves a certain amount of confusion and calls for a good deal of creativity, determination, and organization. But arguments for why Christianity should continue and why Jesus should remain central to Christianity can and must be made in every new situation. Such arguments do not fall from heaven; they must be laboriously, ingeniously crafted in whatever way is relevant for the context for justification, which in our time will include simultaneously church and culture.

The second aspect of Troeltsch's answer to the question of the justification for the continuation of Christianity emphasizes the importance of the subjective realm of faith. We saw this earlier in the review of *Absoluteness*. Any historical enterprise, and a religious enterprise most of all, requires a commitment of faith, a risk-taking that is commensurate with the real contingencies and ambiguities of the historical process. Troeltsch intuitively understood that the adventure of life, and of religion, is rendered facile and cheap if it is embarked upon with pat assurance, as if the envisaged goal were already in hand. One of the glories of religious experience is that there can be such a naïve sense of assurance at times. Such comforts have their place, but they must never be given a naïve *explanation*, lest a sense of the risk of life be not only temporarily forgotten in a moment of assurance, but also systematically obscured by misguided intellectual construction. As the final chapter of *Absoluteness* resoundingly shows, Troeltsch regarded the absolutist interpretations of revelation and salvation—expressed preeminently in absolutist Christology—as just such a misguided construction: an "artificial, scholarly, and apologetic" abstraction designed to protect naïve religious experience from the truth about the ambiguity of life and the relativity of history.[70]

Conclusion

Troeltsch raised so many new issues and brought so many old ones to a head that designating him to mark the beginning of the contemporary period in Christology is entirely justified. A whole new agenda for Christian theology, and Christology in particular, was forged in his dense, unsystematic, evolving, often inconsistent, but exceedingly rich writings. In particular, the rejection of absolutist Christology was given tremendous impetus by Troeltsch, and some appreciation for the importance it was to have in the twentieth century can be glimpsed already in his writings.

Troeltsch's thought not only set an agenda for twentieth-century Christology; in retrospect it also highlights noticeable failures. Outstanding among these are the relative sloth with which the twentieth century has approached the problems clustered around Christology in the light of the human sciences and the ongoing failure in many circles to come to terms with contemporary physical cosmology and the crisis of plausibility into which it plunges absolutist Christology. Doubtless, had Troeltsch's work not been swamped by the arrival on the European scene of neoreformation theology, as vital as that shift seemed to be for the church at that time, twentieth-century Christology would have found itself working out his envisaged agenda for it consciously and explicitly, rather than accidentally backing into that agenda as it has repeatedly throughout the century.

In spite of frenzied Christological activity for many decades, and in spite of the relative flourishing of nonabsolutist Christologies toward the end of this century, this interpretation of Troeltsch suggests that the twentieth century has been in some ways a Christologically retrograde movement after the nineteenth. It is just this perspective that has led one of Troeltsch's interpreters to the curious characterization of him as the first theologian of the twenty-first century.[71] Surely it is enough to regard him as the first great contributor to the twentieth-century Christological discussion. But this is already a large claim by contrast with the assessment of Karl Barth who, on the basis of his own distinctive agenda, depreciated the dogmatics of Troeltsch as "formally the nadir of the Neo-Protestant development which commenced at the beginning of the 18th century"[72] and announced that, with Troeltsch, "the doctrine of the faith was on the point of dissolution into endless and useless talk, and . . . Neo-Protestantism in general had been betrayed onto the rocks, or the quicksands."[73] With such remarks as these, Barth made a dreadful error in judgment about both Troeltsch and the value of the tradition of mediating liberal theology within which he stands.[74] It is impossible to reconcile Barth's sweeping negative judgment of Troeltsch with the immense creativity and insight that Troeltsch displayed in so many areas.

However, to give Barth his due, we have seen that there is much to be dismayed about in Troeltsch's thought, both because of what it portends for theology and, even less happily, because of Troeltsch's immensely suggestive but frequently ineffective constructive theological efforts. Troeltsch's outstanding contribution to Christian theology lies, therefore, not in what he achieved in the way of constructive theological synthesis, but in his honest declaration of some aspects of the intellectual environment for future theology: dependence of faith on history; *Relativismus;* history of religions; the recognition of social psychology, cosmology, and evolutionary biology; and, as an inevitable concomitant of this environment, a Christology that reclaims intellectual viability and religious authenticity by leaving behind absolutist habits of mind. Those absolutist Christologies may have greater superficial continuity with the classical Christological tradition, but they betray the very tradition to which they profess allegiance by squandering the power of the Christian proclamation on the illusory comfort of absolute assurances. The true inheritors of the classical Christology are those Christologies capable of preserving the realism, plausibility, and efficacy of that great tradition: the modest Christologies.

Modest Christology and the Resolution of the Crisis of Plausibility in Contemporary Christology

Introduction to Part II

Part I argued that the critique of hermeneutical absolutism in Ernst Troeltsch's Christological thought (*not* his anti-incarnationalism, and *not* his cynicism about the classical Christological tradition) points the way to the only satisfactory resolution of this crisis induced by the collapse of traditional lines of justification for Christological assertions. Since Troeltsch's time, this crisis of plausibility has both deepened and eased.

On the one hand, a crisis that remains unresolved in too many circles intensifies, provoking the scattered variety of reactions that is evident in contemporary Christology: a vast number of more or less independent, unsystematic Christological forays that tend to be narrow in scope but extremely creative in applying Christological insights to a multitude of individually pressing problems. Moreover, other challenges to the plausibility of Christology that were peripheral at the beginning of the century have since come to the center of attention, especially ethical concerns and a more sophisticated understanding of the psychology of religious experience and the sociology of religious groups.

On the other hand, the solution to the crisis advocated here is being creatively exploited in many kinds of Christological work, enlarging the circle of theologians who see overthrowing absolutist Christology (often

143

under other descriptions) as the optimal way to maintain continuity with the classical Christological tradition. Indeed, in some spheres of reflection, such as interreligious dialogue and most feminist Christology, the consensus appears to be firmly on the side of anti-absolutist Christology. These changes represent a significant easing of the crisis, though the efforts tend to be scattered and connections between sympathetic points of view unexplored.

Both the persistence of the crisis and the lacunae evident in its easing constitute a clear call for a more systematic approach, the satisfying of which is the goal of Part II. Such tension as arises between the systematic and historical interests in Part II is resolved, as in Part I, by giving priority to clarifying the conceptual structure of the positions and arguments treated rather than discussing in great detail historical patterns and influences.

Chapter 4 delineates the problem of Christological absolutism with greater precision. The result is a distinction between two ideal classes of Christology—absolutist and modest—together with a discussion of some characteristics of the modest class, a version of which Troeltsch espoused. An especially important point is the distinction between the two major kinds of modest Christology: the inspirational, nonincarnational type and the more traditional, incarnational type. In a preliminary way, this chapter also indicates the sense in which the absolutist tendencies of the classical Christological tradition ought not be judged essential to it and begins to show how the classical tradition fairly can be regarded as better represented overall by modest than by absolutist Christologies.

Chapter 5 is an in-depth investigation of two of the most well developed and influential modest Christologies of recent years. John Hick is far and away the best known representative of the inspirational (and nonincarnational) type of modest Christology, which has been defended in theological literature only rarely since the time of Troeltsch, its other famous advocate. Far more commonly espoused, because of its greater evident continuity with the classical Christological tradition, is the incarnational form of modest Christology. John Cobb has been selected for review from among many possible representatives because his Christological project is carried out in vivid awareness of the problematic character of Christological absolutism, particularly as this bears on a Christian response to religious pluralism, and because of the metaphysical thoroughness of his proposal.

Chapters 6 and 7 explore the various dimensions of the crisis of plausibility as it appears in the contemporary situation, showing how modesty improves Christological prospects in each case. Treating all of these aspects of the crisis in a short span gives a good indication of just how daunting that crisis is when it has to be faced by theologians equipped only with absolutist Christologies, and it also demonstrates the constructive potency of modest Christologies. The argument to be made in these two chapters has a large scope and calls for a method that is comparably ambitious; the approach to theological and historical material is different from the rest of the book, accordingly. Whereas all of Part I focused for the most part on a single theologian, and investigated others only insofar as they illumined the issues raised by Troeltsch; whereas chapter 4 is analytical in character; and whereas chapter 5 is an intensive investigation of two modest Christologies; chapters 6 and 7 deal with a great many figures and themes in rapid succession. These two chapters present, therefore, not a close reading of the figures and themes mentioned, but an overarching interpretation of them in relation to the specific purposes of the argument. The detailed work leading to the overarching interpretation cannot be presented in a book of this size. Such a fast-moving and broad-ranging method of argument has a distinctive value when the logic of the case to be made and space constraints demand it.

4
The Absolutist Principle and Modest Christologies

Modest Christology is Christology without absolutism, but in a particular way. After all, to make Christological affirmations at all is to affirm in some sense that the absolute, however that is to be understood, is disclosed. Moreover, the mode of personally appropriating Christological assertions often has the character of an absolutely passionate, absolutely serious commitment. The critique modest Christologies level at absolutism is aimed not at the possibility of the conditioned appearance of the absolute in history, nor at the absolute risk and passion that sometimes attend reception of such appearances, but rather at the way Christological assertions are made and meant. It is simultaneously a hermeneutical critique of Christological totalization, and a religious critique of Christological idolatry.

The Origin and Structure of the Absolutist Principle

The Scandal of the Christian Gospel

The Apostle Paul's correspondence with the church at Corinth contains the following passage:

> For Christ did not send me to baptize, but to preach the gospel—not with words of human wisdom, lest the cross of Christ be emptied of its power. For the message of the cross is foolishness to those who are perishing, but to us who are being saved it is the power of God. For it is written, "I will destroy the wisdom of the wise; the intelligence of the intelligent I will frustrate." Where is the wise man? Where is the scholar? Where is the philosopher of this age? Has not God made foolish the wisdom of the world? For since in the wisdom of God the world through its wisdom did not know him, God was pleased through the foolishness of what was preached to save those who believe. Jews demand miraculous signs and Greeks look for wisdom, but we preach Christ crucified: a stumbling-block (σκάνδαλον) to Jews and foolishness (μωρίαν) to Gentiles, but to those whom God has called, both Jews and Greeks, Christ the power of God and the wisdom of God. For the foolishness of God is wiser than man's wisdom, and the weakness of God is stronger than God's strength. (I Cor. 1:17–25, NIV)

In speaking of Christ crucified as a σκάνδαλον to Jews, Paul was referring in part to the difficulty they had in imagining God sanctioning the crucifixion of the purported Messiah. By citing Isaiah 29:14, part of a song of woe for Jerusalem, Paul was making a connection to the legendary obstinate pride of Israel so forcefully attacked in that lament. It is difficult to determine the extent of the suggestiveness of the connection with Isaiah. Paul may also have succeeded in calling to mind Isaiah's images of the suffering servant from Deutero-Isaiah, which were touchstones for alternative interpretations of the messianic hope in Judaism after the Babylonian exile.

In speaking of Christ crucified as μωρίαυ to Gentiles, Paul was referring to the pagan intuition that it was absurd to ascribe ultimate saving significance to a single instance of divine revelation, especially when the locus for that revelation was a human being and, what was worse, an executed human. A similar theme appears in Paul's address to a group of

Athenian Stoic and Epicurean philosophers at a meeting of the Areopagus, as recorded in Acts 17:16–34. In a city accustomed to celebrating numerous revelations of divinity, and pondering the nature of all things in discussion, Paul is said to have spoken of the one and only God, who will "judge the world with justice by the man he has appointed" and whose intention was made known by raising Jesus from the dead. The author of Luke-Acts goes on to comment, "When they heard about the resurrection of the dead, some of them sneered, but others said, 'We want to hear you again on this subject.'" Here the cause of both derision and curiosity is the extraordinary claim about the resurrection, though it may also be Paul's attempt to authorize his message by appealing to it.

In these two passages about and by Paul, we have the primary biblical material relevant to the description of the gospel as a "scandal" or as "foolishness." This designation must be understood in the first instance as an affirmation of the loving provision of God for human salvation, made available to those who believe, but not especially amenable to the power and wisdom of the self-assured. It also refers to several substantive issues within the proclaimed gospel itself: the availability of salvation through but only through faith in Jesus Christ, the significance of the crucifixion of Jesus for effecting that salvation, the impact this had on the interpretation of the messianic hope, and the authorizing import of the resurrection. All of these ideas could be thought scandalous or foolish in various ways.

Expressed in these ways at the deepest level is the scandal of the very conception of the transcendent-immanent God—a creator God whose interest in our finite world, in human pain and longing, in human salvation, finds expression within history and nature. The distinction between Creator and creature, between time and eternity, is from one point of view an infinite qualitative one. Yet the creaturely experience of communion with God bespeaks great intimacy. One of the most familiar characteristics of religious experience and reflection is the awareness of the scandalous character of this contrast. This scandal of divine concern is sometimes called the "scandal of particularity" but could equally well be called the "scandal of universality." It was rightly detected in the encounter between Jesus and his disciples, and this scandal was thereafter rightly celebrated in the worshipping community of Christians as somehow definitively expressed for them in Jesus Christ. Indeed, to speak of the scandal of divine concern in the Christian way is to be committed to both the possibility and importance of Christology.

Absolutizing the Scandal of Divine Concern

Even before the apostolic era had drawn to a close, the resolutely scandalous character of the Christian gospel began to take on new shades of
meaning. In this process the fundamental scandal of divine concern was
profoundly absolutized in its connection with Jesus Christ. That is, to
make the etymological connection, the scandal of divine concern was applied "away (from all other instances), by itself" to Jesus Christ, making
the revelatory and salvific significance of this symbol uniquely, exhaustively, unsurpassably rich. This did not happen instantly, however, but in
several lines of development with complex interconnections; I will describe a number of these developments in what follows. The idea of incarnation, which by itself need not be given an absolutist interpretation,
played a crucial role in all of them.

First, the Pauline corpus includes a number of Christological formulations. It is important to note that the most basic Christological reflections
found there—the remark from I Corinthians quoted above, for example—
are affirmations of the scandal of divine concern and do not entail Christological absolutism. They could be affirmed by any Christology whatsoever,
for Christ crucified is a centerpiece in almost any Christology, and only
the simplest claims are made about it in the passages mentioned. Elsewhere in the corpus, however, more adventurous claims are made about
the significance of Jesus. This is the case in Romans 8, for instance, and in
the kenosis hymn of Philippians 2, the meaning of which remains controversial.[1] The boldest formulations are found in Colossians (written about
60 CE). Here is the passage thought by some to have been an early Christian hymn:[2]

> He [Christ] is the image of the invisible God, the first-born over all cre-
> ation. For by him all things were created: things in heaven and on earth,
> visible or invisible, whether thrones or powers or rulers or authorities; all
> things were created by him and for him. He is before all things, and in
> him all things hold together. And he is the head of the body, the church;
> he is the beginning and the firstborn from among the dead, so that in
> everything he might have the supremacy. *For God was pleased to have
> all his fullness dwell in him*, and through him to reconcile to himself all
> things, whether things on earth or things in heaven, by making peace
> through his blood, shed on the cross.[3]

Again, even more dramatically, "For in Christ all the fullness of the Deity lives in bodily form" (Col. 2:9, NIV).[4]

There are hints of subordinationism in these ideas, hints that Christ was a created being ("the first-born over all creation"), and many more questions raised than settled by such phrases as the last one quoted. Complete analysis of these Christological formulations requires a detailed study of the cosmology within the terms of which Paul was theologizing, but that is not needed here. It is enough to note that the developing Christology of the second and third centuries followed the lead of the Colossians formulation, regarding Jesus as a man in whom dwelt the fullness of deity. Though this Christological focus marginalized Christological images with stronger roots in the Synoptic Gospels, its advantages were clear. On the one hand, the more general Pauline Christological insights bearing on the scandal of divine concern could be expressed powerfully in terms of the incarnation. On the other hand, the incarnational scheme enabled theologians to explain, with Paul, how Jesus Christ could have been a being with sufficient power to break through the oppressive principalities and powers dominating the cosmic spheres of the world (according to the common world view of the day), thereby to be the firstborn among many of those who would follow his saving path back to God: he could do this because he was the fullness of deity in bodily form.

Second, in the Johannine circle, even bolder attempts were afoot. The Gospel of John (probably written about 90–100 CE) speaks of the Word being with God in the beginning, saying that God was the Word, and that all things were made through the Word (John 1:1–3). Then it asserts that the Word became flesh and dwelt among us, full of grace and truth (John 1:14). Here we have an astonishingly clear-headed attempt to articulate the significance of the early Christians' experience of salvation through Christ in cosmological terms. The incarnation is important here, as in the parts of the Pauline corpus just discussed, but the cosmological contextualization is quite different because the Word that became flesh in Jesus Christ is itself the ordering, generative principle of creation. Admittedly, these ideas are merely introduced in the Gospel of John without being systematically filled out, and they draw on extant cosmological visions; but it is a mistake to underestimate the degree of innovation involved with regard to the interpretation of Jesus Christ. Moreover, this incarnational-cosmological view of Jesus Christ became determinative of future Christological developments to such a degree that the simpler Christological trial balloons of the Synoptic Gospels were left hovering close to the ground. It far surpasses in cosmological audacity even the adventurous incarnational imagery of the Pauline corpus.

Third, the widening of the incarnational interpretation from the Pauline corpus to the Gospel of John's cosmological grandeur opened up many possibilities for systematic philosophical development of Christological ideas that were not possible in Paul's more obviously mythological understanding of the incarnation. These were exploited by the early Christian apologists and theologians who were anxious to forge connections between the Christian view of the world and the impressive intellectual resources of hellenistic philosophy. Particularly notable is the concept of λόγος σπερματικός (germinative Logos or, in the plural, Logos seeds) that appeared in a number of writings, including Justin Martyr's *First Apology* (about 155 CE). Justin's aim was to characterize Christianity as the true philosophy, as the decisive culmination of prior philosophical insight in which the wisdom of the Logos is apparent. The apologetic point is sharp, of course, but Justin perceived continuity as well as discontinuity between Christianity and pagan philosophy. Thus, he found a way to affirm the scandal of divine concern by means of the incarnation, yet without absolutizing the significance of Jesus Christ in an extreme way.

Fourth, only a few decades after Justin, in the writings of Tertullian (about 160–225 CE), we see Christological absolutism affirmed using almost the same resources. There is no dramatic change in the intervening years. Rather, this is evidence that more and less absolutist interpretations of the incarnation coexisted in the late second and third centuries. Isaac A. Dorner, in his vast treatment of the history of Christological reflection, dwells at length on Tertullian's fascination with the incarnation. In discussing the early father's arguments against the view that Jesus cannot have suffered in being crucified, Dorner cites the following passage:

> Did a mere phantom suffer, "*quod vacabat a sensu passionum Dei?*" Then is our faith a lie, and our hope a phantom. Oh, spare the only hope of the entire world! Why dost thou destroy the necessary reproach of the faith? Whatever is unworthy of God, is for my benefit: willing am I to be shameless and blessed as a fool, and I require the material thereto. God's Son was crucified; I am not ashamed (to avow it), for it is worthy of shame: and the Son of God dies; it deserves all faith, because it is foolish.

He was laid in the grave, and rose again: it is quite certain, because it was impossible.[5]

Tertullian's view expresses indirectly what elsewhere is more explicit, namely, that the significance of revelation and salvation in Jesus Christ is unique, universal, absolute, and definitive, to the point that it cannot be subjected even to ordinary canons of rationality. Christological absolutism and such suspicion of human reason are not necessary partners, for neither view implies the other, but this is one of the principle ways by which Tertullian chose to express his absolutist Christology. This furnishes some insight into the reason for Tertullian's absolutism: he assumed that nothing else had any possibility of giving adequate expression to the hope of salvation that is the gospel of Christianity.

Interpreting the Process

What can we learn from this brief tour of some of the highlights in the emergence of absolutism in Christology? First, there were many Christological formulations in the literature of early Christianity, some exploiting foreign elements such as incarnation and others staying closer to traditional Jewish conceptualities of Messiah and prophet. But the incarnational trajectory of Christological interpretation was evidently felt—especially by those whose influence most shaped the Christian tradition as it came to exist—to do best justice to the experience of salvation and transformation through Christ as these were celebrated in early Christianity. This, therefore, was the conceptual sphere within which absolutism was to develop. Second, absolutist Christologies were only propounded in conjunction with, and probably could not have arisen without, the concept of incarnation. But the incarnation does not demand an absolutist interpretation, nor were all incarnational Christologies absolutist in fact. Third, there is a trajectory of development in Christology toward incarnation—beginning a generation or two after Jesus, running for about a century, and associated with the waning of the influence of other biblical Christological images. The trajectory that yields widespread acceptance of absolutism in Christology, however, is quite different: it begins much later, perhaps in the middle of the second century; it does not culminate probably until the fifth century; and it is so much less uniform that it is difficult to describe it as a trajectory at all. Fourth and finally, as we have just seen, absolutist incarnational interpretations of Jesus Christ coexisted in the late second century with more moderate incarnational Christologies, and there does not appear to be any debate specifically on the issue. Nor does debate arise later; even battles surrounding subordinationism in Christology were due more to differing responses to Neoplatonic emanation metaphysics than to any worries about absolutist interpretation of the significance of Jesus Christ. That is, in the context of the early centuries of the Christian church, Christological absolutism appears to have been a nonissue, an unthematized matter of taste. Its liabilities were not recognized at that time, but neither did it receive the explicit theological attention needed to assign it the same elevated status that the incarnation has within Christological doctrine.

All this said, it does appear that there was a convergence of Christological taste in the direction of absolutist judgments of the revelatory and salvific significance of Jesus Christ. This might be called a trajectory, though perhaps a "gradual drift" might avoid the causal connotations of "trajectory." I see no signs that anything obvious was thought to depend on this gradual development at the time. However, the absolutist style of incarnational interpretation steadily attained dominance, and—inevitably, because of its in-built conceptual liabilities—it began to disfigure as well as elucidate the scandal of divine concern. The scandalous elements of the gospel persisted, but they were contextualized and actually superseded by the thought that "in Christ all the fullness of the Deity lives in bodily form." Jesus' supremacy passed from being a poetic and contingent affirmation based on an overpowering experience of salvation to being an assertion whose metaphysical pedigree carried with it the implication of absolute, unconditional supremacy, characteristics customarily reserved for descriptions of divinity. Likewise, Jesus' human characteristics—his biological specificity, personal attributes, activities, likes, and dislikes—passed from being the contingent features of the one through whom God's salvation is encountered to marking out the forum for the literal presence of divinity. In many cases, this understandably produced the denial that Jesus could have been truly human, or the denial that he could have suffered in dying. Even when the docetic tendency was checked, however, the churches found it genuinely difficult to affirm the true humanity of Jesus Christ in an intelligible way and equally hard to maintain the distinction that seemed necessary between Jesus Christ and God.

There were other problems, also unrecognized at the time. The immense absolutizing of divine interest, activity, and presence in the single person of Jesus fostered the affirmation of Jesus' uniqueness and of his universal significance, and this in turn induced anti-Jewish reactions. Early Christian interpretation of the Jewish Scriptures expresses this development, for the historical expressions of divine concern sacred to Jews were subordinated to the events of Jesus Christ: they were regarded both as anticipations of him and as fulfilled in him. This hermeneutical strategy was useful for the Christians in forging their self-understanding as "not necessarily Jewish," but it also clearly indicates their conviction that any expression of the divine concern was intimately related through being subordinate to Jesus Christ. Correlatively, Jesus Christ's significance is ever more fervently interpreted as unique, universal, final, and unsurpassable. All of this, naturally, is accompanied and fostered by the development and intensification of the Christ cult. The anti-Judaism associated with these developments seems linked particularly to the absolutist tendencies in Christology, and not to Christology, or even incarnational Christology, as such.

By the time of Augustine in many parts of the church, and certainly by the middle of the fifth century, the scandal of divine concern itself simply was understood in absolutist terms. Alternative biblical and conceptual ways to express it in incarnational Christology (let alone nonincarnational Christology) were unexplored. The universal and particular had become welded together in the interpretation of Jesus Christ with unjustified definitiveness, the problematic character of which always has exceeded, but especially in the modern period exceeds, the warrant for it when considered out of the scandal of divine concern alone. Yet the problems were neither appreciated nor discussed.

One way of expressing the transformation in the scandal of the Christian gospel that is entailed by these developments is to speak, therefore, of a shift from the *scandal of the concreteness of divine concern* to the *scandal of the absoluteness of divine presence and activity*. In other words, it is one thing to admit that Christ crucified is, from some points of view, a preeminently scandalous or foolish way to conceive of God expressing saving love for humanity, and it may have been ambitious to explore ways of speaking about Jesus Christ as, in some sense, participating in divinity, even perhaps God incarnate. All this is a natural theological outworking of the scandal of divine concern, and precisely to that extent it was an appropriate avenue of Christological exploration. But it is not possible to justify from these resources the supposition that Jesus Christ is the unique, absolute, definitive, unsurpassable locus of divine revelation and, still odder, of the presence of God. Yet, this daring trajectory toward illegitimately absolutizing the scandal of particularity in the Christological reflection of early Christianity was the one that most effectively captured the Christian and more particularly the theological imagination.

How could so many Christians, and eventually almost all Christian theologians, venture such an interpretation of Jesus? There are two reasons for this, both of which have been mentioned in passing. First, we have seen one of the crucial reasons for the ascendance of the absolutist principle: it was mistakenly and *tacitly* assumed to be required to account for the experience of salvation, a reason that presupposes the role of the Christ cult in defining and intensifying that experience. A better analysis of the Christ cult and the experience of salvation through Christ would readily have deconstructed this assumption, and early Christian theologians may even have had the resources to do this, though that is debatable. What is clear is that absolutism trails along quietly behind arguments about what is necessary for salvation.

This point emerges in general terms in the debates between Arius and Athanasius, who were arguing over a conception of salvation and trying to preserve the Christological means for explaining that salvation as they variously understood it. Arius appears to have viewed salvation as mystical ascent to God through union with Christ, so Christ was best understood as part of a hierarchy of being, and the firstborn before time of all creation. The inevitable subordination of Christ to God in this vision of salvation is repeated frequently when salvation is viewed as mystical union and the ruling metaphysics presumes a hierarchy of being. These two conditions are fulfilled preeminently in Origen's Neoplatonic vision of salvation, for instance, so it is unsurprising that there are subordinationist tendencies in his Christology. By contrast, salvation was for Athanasius the overcoming of a chasm between humanity and God created by human sin. Only God could bridge the chasm, and God was believed to have done so in Jesus Christ, so the closest relationship between Christ and God was called for, free of any hint of subordination. So the debate is *explicitly* about subordinationism in Christology and its effects on the explanation of salvation. *Implicitly*, however, Christological absolutism also is being supported by this argument, at least for Athanasius: his view of salvation, together with his unawareness of any reason to proceed more circumspectly, made absolutist interpretation of Jesus Christ the natural Christological hypothesis. The same pattern appears much later in Anselm's *Cur Deus Homo?* in which the unique God-man was argued to be a hypothesis necessary for giving an adequate account of the incontestable actuality of salvation, understood in a way somewhat similar to that of Athanasius. Absolutism comes along for the ride in such arguments and attaches itself to a Christological understanding of salvation.

It is important to stress, however, that there is no *necessary* connection between a particular conception of salvation and Christological affirmations, for much turns on the metaphysics within which a Christological explanation of salvation is sought, as well as the way the metaphysics actually is invoked in the explanation. We cannot now know Arius' thought well enough to determine whether he affirmed the absolute uniqueness and comprehensive, absolute finality of Jesus Christ, but this is not *ruled out* by what is suspected to be his view of Jesus Christ; in fact he may well have affirmed it, such was the extent of the drift toward this assumption in his time. How is this possible? In the Neoplatonic hierarchy of emanations within which Arius did his theology, the Logos readily could be conceived as both uniquely related to God and uniquely, unsurpassably incarnate in Jesus Christ. In this case the absolutist Christology would have a good metaphysical basis. But the Neoplatonic metaphysics is readily adaptable to the idea of multiple incarnations or some other more moderate Christological scenario. The general rule seems to be that, whereas metaphysics can suggest a Christological approach, the conception of salvation demands one. Almost all metaphysical systems, when tweaked appropriately, are flexible enough to produce a desired Christological conclusion, avoiding unwanted ones; it is the conception of salvation—a conception most directly defined and maintained within the life of the Christ cult—that determines what conclusion is desirable. As a result, it is by means of the conception of salvation that absolutism crept into Christology.

The other reason for the willingness of Christian theologians to maintain the absolutist principle cannot be separated from the role of conceptions of salvation as determined by the Christ cult: the absolutist principle simply was not recognized as sharply problematic in the apostolic, patristic and medieval periods as it is felt to be now. Three considerations support this. First, the liabilities of absolutist Christology discussed above were evidently not apparent at the time (as with anti-Judaism in theology)

or were thought to derive from other sources (as with the difficulty of trying to articulate the incarnation in a Christologically absolutist framework—the absolutist interpretation impossibly exacerbated the problem,
but this factor was never thematized and debated explicitly). Second, the
cosmological grounding of absolutist Christological affirmations was more
plausible on an ancient or a medieval view of the universe, before the
movie screen of the night sky gave way to a three dimensional vision of
awesome, galaxial depth; before Immanuel Kant realized that some of
those lights were themselves galaxies of uncountable stars, immeasurably
deepening the vision.[6] Third, the absolutized idea of incarnation—as a definitive, unsurpassable, once-for-all event of cosmic dimensions—gradually became, under the impact of the Christian affirmation of it,
metaphysically more acceptable than it had been for many when it was
first applied to Jesus Christ. Metaphysics is as contextual an aspect of
human reflection as any other.

Absolutist Christology

The Absolutist Principle

The absolutist principle is a formalized statement of the conceptual core
of absolutist Christology. It has a distinctive internal conceptual structure,
involving two distinguishable claims:

1. the *Significance Thesis*: that the symbol of Jesus Christ, referring as it
    does to the divine presence in the life of Jesus, is uniquely, exhaus-
    tively, absolutely, unsurpassably rich in its signification. That is, the
    significance of the symbol is such that it is uniquely capable of having
    all meanings with religious import ranged around it, structuring those
    other meanings according to the internal relations of meanings in the
    symbol of Jesus Christ itself; and
2. the *Fact Thesis*: that God was, in fact, uniquely, exhaustively, ab-
    solutely, unsurpassably present in the historical figure of Jesus.

This principle is an absolutization of the scandal of divine concern, which
already offered profound ways of speaking about revelation and salvation.
Each of the four key adverbs in the definition plays a role in defining the

significance of Jesus Christ: uniqueness indicates its importance relative to other meaning structures, exhaustiveness expresses the universal scope of its applicability, absoluteness connotes its internally self-sufficient and independent quality, and unsurpassability bespeaks its definitive, once-for-all character.

The metaphysical implications of both the fact and the significance theses are debatable (for instance, do they entail the two-natures version of the doctrine of incarnation?). *Some* metaphysical claim is being made whenever one of these two theses is asserted, though how such claims are expounded may vary dramatically. It should be noted immediately that the second thesis implies the *metaphysical possibility* of the absolutist principle, for the obvious reason that the possibility of something is entailed by its actuality. Thus the fact thesis is partly historical and partly metaphysical in character.

The significance thesis requires a number of remarks. The first one is prompted by the fact that it is less obvious what is intended by it than by the fact thesis. Consider the theologian trying to express the absolute significance of the symbol of Jesus Christ. She or he will seek to show that any aspect of human meaning with religious significance can be comprehended by the symbolic meaning of Jesus Christ. So the religious significance of the human experience of sin and estrangement, the creation of the cosmos, the shape of the historical process, and the theologian's own personal fate must be brought into significant, structured contact with the symbol of Jesus Christ. The significance thesis asserts that the symbol of Jesus Christ is sufficiently rich and comprehensive that all such meanings will find a home under its umbrella of meaning, that they will in fact derive their ultimate meaning from being so comprehended, and that these meanings will be integrated with one another as a result. So, for instance, Jesus Christ may be thought of as the redeemer by whom deliverance from the power of sin is accomplished; as the Word by and through whom the creation was brought into being; as the decisive, orienting central point as well as the origin and eschaton of the historical process; and as the guarantor of eternal life and the resurrection of the dead by being himself the firstborn from among the dead. In such affirmations, the meanings of revelation, sin, evil and salvation, creation, the historical process, and eternity are all brought into decisive focus, as well as into relation with each other, through their being defined and oriented by the powerful symbol of Jesus Christ.

The second note to make about the significance thesis is that its assertion of the universal significance of God's unique, definitive presence in the historical figure of Jesus is made with reference to the *symbol of Jesus Christ*. But the universal significance of this revelatory life conceivably could be expressed in other ways. For instance, it could be put in terms of the stipulation found in various parts of the New Testament that salvation apart from Jesus Christ is impossible or—one of a number of possible specifications of this point—in terms of the necessity of a God-man for an adequate atonement. It also could be expressed as a metaphysically necessary event with the aid of an appropriate philosophy of history. The thesis about the universal significance of Jesus' life is expressed in terms of the power of the *symbol* of Jesus Christ in order to avoid committing this analysis of the absolutist principle to an unnecessarily narrow perspective. For instance, the absolutist principle does not imply the necessity of an atonement or of a particular metaphysical conception of the person of Jesus Christ such as the two natures or of a particular kind of philosophy of history, though it may well be impossible to avoid all of these in an adequate systematic Christology affirming the absolutist principle. Avoiding preempting such issues in the statement of the significance thesis is helpful, and speaking of the symbol of Jesus Christ achieves this goal.

Finally, the problem ought to be addressed of how speaking about the symbol of Jesus Christ translates into talk about the historical figure of Jesus himself. Should not the universal significance of the divine presence in the life of Jesus be expressed in terms of Jesus' person, rather than with reference to the universal comprehending power of the symbol of Jesus Christ? Indeed, this often, even usually, has been done: phrases such as *Jesus Christ is uniquely, truly divine* invest in the historical person Jesus a maximal degree of significance. But there is something odd about this admittedly common procedure. It is seems to be a *derivative* way of expressing the significance of Jesus. If we ask about the cash value for us of the assertion that Jesus is absolutely significant, we actually mean something closer to the significance thesis. To say that the historical person of Jesus is significant universally cannot mean what it says unless we are enabled by our talk about Jesus to comprehend all other relevant meanings, including especially our own experience of salvation, in an intelligible, religiously effective way. Thus, to speak about absolute significance in terms of the symbol of Jesus Christ is a more accurate way to proceed.

Now, it is plain that a great many affirmations about the historical person of Jesus might be entailed by the significance thesis in actual Christological presentations. The symbol of Jesus Christ, after all, must refer back to the historical person Jesus. This reference is essential for Christology in general, as well as for the absolutist principle. But the generality of the absolutist principle is expressed best by not limiting the range of possible assertions about the person of Jesus in advance. A particular Christology therefore can be understood as expressing the absolutist principle without requiring of it that it meet a predetermined battery of stipulations about the person of Jesus. This allows us to apply the absolutist principle to an important class of contemporary Christologies that prescind from making many claims about the person, Jesus—including those of Karl Barth and Schubert Ogden, which will be discussed later. Likewise, the absolutist principle as formulated here requires nothing by way of stipulations of ideas of salvation, either in interpretations of the work of Jesus Christ or in the philosophy of history.

To be more concrete about this point in relation to the person of Jesus Christ, consider the ancient teaching of the two natures. Though technically the two-natures are predicated of the divine Logos, the two natures teaching is also an assertion about the historical person of Jesus to the effect that he was truly human and truly divine, together with some specifications of the relation of these two natures, including conceivably that the appearance of someone with these two natures was a unique and salvifically decisive event within the history of creation. The two-natures doctrine understood in terms of this last clause expresses the absolutist principle (though it could avoid this implication if presented differently). However, to require of any contemporary Christology that it entail the two-natures doctrine if it is to be held to affirm the absolutist principle would be an interpretative mistake. There are many theologians in the modern period who seek to distance their Christologies from the traditional two natures doctrine, usually by reformulating what they take to be its underlying point, but sometimes also by repudiating it altogether. Yet many of these same theologians also claim to find universal and final revelatory and salvific significance in the symbol of Jesus and try with more or less success to exhibit that significance in the exposition of their Christologies. That is, they make the claim of the significance thesis stated above. When, then, they also assert the fact thesis, they affirm the absolutist principle.

Theological Sanction

After its fragmentary beginnings, its unthematized attachment to Christological interpretations of salvation, its invisibility in early theological debates in which it was actually a crucial factor, and its gradual acceptance as the preferred mode of Christological thought, the absolutist principle became established as the dominant interpretation of official church teachings about Jesus Christ. It was a silent coup. Resources for nonabsolutist Christological interpretations, including incarnational alternatives, then remained languishing in the Synoptic Gospels and in the letters of Paul, never having received the attention they required to become robust and ecclesially useful for that stream of the Christian church that became dominant. Moreover, once the New Testament sources for alternate Christological views became subject to being systematically read through the lens of the dominant Christologies, most of which eventually affirmed the absolutist principle in various ways, it was to be many centuries before alternate views could even be expressed in theology, though art and liturgy found their own ways to preserve the rich biblical heritage. The Socinian movement of the Reformation period constitutes the first widespread theological reclamation of those alternate Christologies after the Christologically decisive ecumenical councils of the fourth and fifth centuries—in part because of a renewed sense of the importance of paying careful attention to the variety of theological perspectives in Scripture.

Having said this, it is crucial to point out that the central credal statements of the fourth and fifth centuries cannot be read as affirming the absolutist principle in any straightforward way. It is the dominant theological interpretations of the creeds, and not the creeds themselves, that sanctioned the absolutist principle. There is little question, of course, that the framers of the creeds affirmed the absolutist principle. But the very fact that it does not find decisive expression in the creeds is an indication that they were most interested in other matters: the ones they did choose to speak about. This is the basis for my claim that we preserve what is *most important* in the credal tradition when we affirm the classical Christology even while rejecting the absolutist interpretation it typically received from the theologians of that era.

It is vital to be clear about this point. There is no suggestion here that a Christology rejecting the absolutist principle can claim complete continuity with *all* of the intentions of the church fathers and the framers of the creeds. That would be anachronism of the worst kind. Rather, the point is that such a Christology reasonably can claim dialectical continuity with what the framers of the creeds and many of the church fathers thought was *most important* about Jesus Christ. The disagreement between now and then over the absolutist principle is genuine but relatively minor compared to the agreements that exist.

To see that this continuity is genuine, consider the Definition of Chalcedon (451 CE):

> Therefore, following the holy Fathers, we all with one accord teach men to acknowledge one and the same Son, our Lord Jesus Christ, at once complete in Godhead and complete in manhood, truly God and truly man, consisting also of a reasonable soul and body: of one substance [ὁμοούσιον] with the Father as regards his Godhead, and at the same time of one substance with us as regards his manhood; like us in all respects, apart from sin; as regards his Godhead, begotten of the Father before the ages, but yet as regards his manhood begotten, for us men and for our salvation, of Mary the Virgin, the God-bearer; one and the same Christ, Son, Lord, Only-begotten, recognized in two natures, without confusion, without change, without division, without separation [ἐν δύο φύσεσιν, ἀσυγχύτως ἀτρέπτως, ἀδιαιρέτως ἀχωρίστως]; the distinction of natures being in no way annulled by the union, but rather the characteristics of each nature being preserved and coming together to form one person and subsistence, not as parted or separated into two persons, but one and the same Son and Only-begotten God the Word, Lord Jesus Christ; even as the prophets from earliest times spoke of him, and our Lord Jesus Christ himself taught us, and the creed of the Fathers has been handed down to us.[7]

This is essentially about incarnation, not the absolutist principle. Eutyches, a monk of Constantinople, (and others) had argued that "Our Lord was of two natures before the union [with human flesh], but after the union one nature" and that this one nature was that of the Son of God. [8] The Chalcedonian Definition addressed the monophysite challenge of Eutychianism by asserting that Jesus Christ had two natures. In so doing, the Council of Chalcedon affirmed in a distinctive way a Christological position suggested in the writings of many early Christian theologians, and firmly in place at the Council of Nicea (325), the Council of Constantinople (381), and the Council of Ephesus (431).

Moreover, the affirmation of the two-natures doctrine does not by it-self imply the absolutist principle, for the obvious reason that the ques-tion about the two natures is inevitable whenever incarnation is affirmed and so must be asked even, say, in a metaphysical scenario admitting mul-tiple incarnations. The problem is rather that the Definition was naturally interpreted in terms of the absolutist principle, and to that extent con-ferred upon the absolutist principle sanction almost equivalent to that of the Christological dogma it interprets. More specifically, speaking of "our Lord Jesus Christ, at once complete in Godhead and complete in man-hood, truly God and truly man" carried with it the implicit understanding of a definitive, absolute disclosure of God within history for more or less everyone writing or reading the creed, and yet the same form of words would be needed even in an incarnational Christology rejecting the abso-lutist principle.

The same line of argument, though with greater difficulty, can be ap-plied to the Nicaeno-Constantinopolitan Creed, officially recognized at Chalcedon in 451:

> We believe . . . in one Lord Jesus Christ, the only-begotten Son of God, Begotten of the Father before all the ages, Light of Light, true God of true God, begotten not made, of one substance with the Father, through whom all things were made; who for us men and for our salvation came down from the heavens, and was made flesh of the Holy Spirit and the Virgin Mary, and became man, and was crucified for us under Pontius Pi-late, and suffered and was buried, and rose again on the third day ac-cording to the Scriptures, and ascended into the heavens, and sitteth on the right hand of the Father, and cometh again with glory to judge living and dead, of whose kingdom there shall be no end.[9]

In this case, the attempt to check subordinationist tendencies led to the formation of a credal statement that rules out virtually any attempt to in-troduce metaphysical distance either between the God the Father and the only-begotten Son of God, or between the Son of God and the historical figure of Jesus.

Again, the absolutist principle is not explicitly stated here, though its hermeneutical definitiveness is doubtless the natural interpretative lens through which the creed was both formulated and used. The driving in-tention is to uphold the "truly divine, truly human" formula by implicitly ruling out various threats to it, and proponents of incarnational Christologies rejecting the absolutist principle rightly claim a significant degree of continuity with this intention. The claim of significant continuity is slightly less clear-cut in this case compared to that of the Apostles' Creed, because so many Christologies rejecting the absolutist principle have in practice elected to posit metaphysical distance in some sense either between God the Father and the only-begotten Son of God or between the Son of God and the historical figure of Jesus. Nevertheless, the classical Christological tradition, in this respect at least, can fairly be thought of as extended in a meaningful way by Christologies affirming the creed while rejecting the absolutist interpretation it was given by so many theologians at the time of its formulation and for many centuries afterwards.

Even though the Chalcedonian Definition was prompted by a particular controversy, and the Nicaeno-Constantinopolitan Creed may well have been, too, their applicability beyond the confines of the crises which gave rise to them was rapidly acknowledged. The anti-Arian anathemas of the Creed of Nicea (325) were dropped (along with other modifications) in the Nicaeno-Constantinopolitan Creed, for instance, not only because the Arian controversy had ameliorated somewhat, but because the creed itself remained a valuable statement of the Christian faith. In fact, the creeds were already normative for most Christian confession and theological reflection (especially in the West) when they were promulgated, and they continued to be so throughout the Middle Ages and beyond. Accompanying the explicit acceptance of the creeds was implicit but decisive embrace of the absolutist principle's hermeneutical perspective on them. In this way, the absolutist principle rode on the coattails of the creeds, receiving theological sanction and normative, albeit unwarranted, status. It is with an enormous amount of momentum, therefore, that the absolutist principle was propelled by official church teaching—though not *as* official church teaching—into subsequent Christological reflection.

The results of this propulsion were spectacular. The meaning of every individual human life, of the history of humanity, and indeed of everything sentient and not, past and future, in all of creation was thought to be expressed in the concrete life of Jesus, the son of Mary, and this meaning was believed to be particularly focused in his redeeming achievement. Moreover, this expression and recreation of meaning was linked to Jesus' life in such a way that the concrete person of Jesus was indispensable. This had the understandable result that dramatic metaphysical assessments of this person became ineradicable touchstones of Christian tradition, evident in much of the art, music, liturgy, and theology of virtually every Christian communion. Thus many matters, from the explicit Christian teachings of the incarnation, the doctrine of the two natures, and the Trinitarian conception of God, to unspoken assumptions concerning the significance of Jesus' maleness, were interpreted in exclusive and absolutist fashion.

The absolutist principle arguably inspired some of the most astonishing intellectual and creative achievements in Western culture, including numerous heart-rending works of art and music; the sweeping philosophies of history that we find in Schelling and Tillich, Hegel and Pannenberg, Rahner and Teilhard; and perhaps even the distinctive modern Western view of history as a whole. Unfortunately, the personal and cultural confidence naturally inspired by seeing the world through the lens of the absolutist principle also arguably has been distorted into exclusivistic intolerance and the most abhorrent moral obscenities on both small and large scales. But the idea itself, insofar as there ever is such a thing, has been powerful enough to drive multiple cultures for more than one-and-a-half millennia, to captivate generation after generation of religious imaginations and, in short and without exaggeration, to be a major force in the transformation of the planet.

The Problem of the Absolutist Principle

In the period of the absolutist principle's dominance—beginning fragmentarily in the second and third centuries, as noted above—the burden of meaning making imposed upon Jesus Christ by yoking the concreteness of his life with the whole of creation was carried with style. It is understandable, then, that the absolutist principle has been celebrated as much as it has. Within Christian theology as such, there are thousands of examples of authors who articulate it within their Christologies, hymns, and sermons. This plethoric enthusiasm for the absolutist principle testifies to its formerly unquestioned capacity to bring comprehensibility to large swathes of human experience by fusing harder-to-assimilate fields of meaning with the more readily understandable concrete life of Jesus.

How does this meaning-making process operate? It is arguable that meaning in history can only flow from a paradigmatic joining of the universal and the particular in a historical event.[10] This is so for smaller fields of interpretation than that encompassed by the events of Jesus' life. For instance, citizenship of a nation can take on existential importance when ideas like democratic rights and responsibilities are interpreted as embodied in the lives and activities of founding fathers, as is the case for many citizens of the United States of America with Presidents Washington and Lincoln. In much the same way, all Christology subsumes aspects of the significance of the ultimately universal in, through, and under the concrete conditions of a human life, and this is supposed to bring *comprehensibility* to the dimensions of the universe and the diversity of cultures. This marks the sense in which the scandal of divine concern in Jesus Christ is appropriately, joyously, and actually inevitably, paradoxical. It is when this hermeneutic process is absolutized to the point that every aspect of the universal, every religious-existential meaning in all times and places, is definitively and exhaustively subsumed under the significance of the symbol of Jesus Christ that the absolutist principle is being affirmed. The absolutist principle is hermeneutic totalization of Christology taken to the extreme; in religious terms, it now appears to be a species of idolatry. It has shown itself, nonetheless, to be an enormously powerful conception in human history, because this absolutist process of meaning making has been so effective for so long a period within cultures strongly influenced by Christianity.

However, given what we now know about the size and age of the universe, and the diversity and independent integrity of human cultures and religions, it is questionable whether this meaning-making process is still working. The universal dimensions of meaning that a Christology affirming the absolutist principle has to comprehend through the concrete life of Jesus have expanded in the modern consciousness to the point that they are rendered intelligible and existentially relevant only by violating or artificially minimizing their naturally universal sense. To us, the absolutist principle must involve the claim that the mysterious divine, the ultimately universal ground of being, is completely, uniquely, utterly concrete in a single, culturally, and religiously circumscribed mammalian biological form, dwelling in just one of a plethora of civilizations on one planet of a minor solar system in a vast galaxy, just one of literally too many to count.

We must ask, then, has the reach of the absolutist principle as far as meaning making is concerned begun to exceed its grasp? Correspondingly, has the traditional marriage of Christology with the absolutist principle been disclosed as intellectually inadequate by the discoveries of the contemporary world, to the point that the scandal of divine concern is disfigured by Christologies that extol the virtues of the absolutist principle? A diverse range of contemporary theologians rightly answer yes to these questions and so wish to modify or dispense with the absolutist principle while still propounding Christologies that in most cases rightly can claim to be contemporary representatives of the classical Christological tradition.

I am calling Christologies embracing the absolutist principle "absolutist Christologies." There are problems with any term that might be chosen to name the class of Christologies affirming the absolutist principle, and two in particular should be mentioned here. These two problems notwithstanding, "absolutist" is a natural term with no greater liability than any other candidate. And *some* name is needed, for the absolutist principle demarcates an important fault line of controversy in the contemporary Christological landscape, as we shall see in more detail as the argument continues.

The first problem of nomenclature is the risk that the narrowing of focus of the word *absolutist* primarily to its hermeneutical dimensions might be overlooked if talk of "absolutist Christology" becomes careless. It must not be forgotten that neither the reality of the absolute nor the legitimacy of describing the existential risk of faith in absolute terms is necessarily called into question by criticism of the hermeneutical excesses of absolutist Christologies.

The second problem is this: the degree of diversity among contemporary absolutist Christologies is so high that it may seem imprudent to try to characterize them as a class. After all, this class probably includes the majority of Christologies published this century; covers a variety of metaphysical perspectives; and encompasses a wide range of views about God, revelation, salvation, anthropology, the world and the nature of Christian doctrine. Moreover, though the absolutist principle may be defined clearly, the class of absolutist Christologies has some characteristics of an ideal type, with borderline cases, and sufficient internal complexity to prevent useful univocal characterizations of the entire class. Yet their common characteristic, whether or not it is the result of an explicit intention, is that they affirm a single, putatively normative Christological insight: the absolutist principle. The absolutist principle can be affirmed in a variety of ways, so simply specifying that this affirmation is made implies little about other substantive features of an absolutist Christology, such as its view of

God, the cosmos, human nature, history, salvation, or the nature of doctrine. The concomitant loss of nuance would therefore make such a characterization of little use for examining individual absolutist Christologies. But the identification of such a class of Christologies is an ideal first step to considering the possible virtues of an alternative Christological approach.

Proponents of absolutist Christologies may be divided into two groups: the repristinators and the reformulators. The repristinators are the smaller group. They are contemporary theologians who use traditional—especially Chalcedonian—terminology to preserve patristic Christological insights, including their assumption of the absolutist principle. In so doing, they are not merely indulging an antiquarian impulse. They are exercising a considered judgment in light of the undisputed fact that the world of modern knowledge seems to rule out automatically some or all of patristic wisdom. According to this perspective, some temporary loss of acceptability incurred by adherence to Chalcedonian terminology would be a small price to pay for preserving the insight of the absolutist principle. Eventually, it might be hoped, changes in contemporary thought forms could allow for a doctrinal presentation in prevailing conceptual categories that does not intolerably compromise those insights. Or the traditional terminology may be thought of as invariantly normative for all subsequent theological discussion.

For many centuries, however, and especially in the modern period, most theologians have unhesitatingly and imaginatively robed and re-robed classical absolutist Christology—associated preeminently with the Chalcedonian Definition and dominant in the Christological tradition—in contemporary language. This is the path of the reformulators. The motivation for these reformulations is the same one that drives the impulse to enliven the Chalcedonian language without reformulating it, namely, that the classical Christological tradition is not immediately intelligible in the contemporary world. The model for reformulation rather than preserving the Chalcedonian language comes, of course, from the Chalcedonian Definition itself, which was at the time of its formulation the result of creative terminological compromise, double valency of terms, and concept stretching, all in relation to language then current.

The unprecedented strength of the reformulating impulse in nineteenth- and twentieth-century Christology indicates the presence of a lack of fit between contemporary forms of thought and absolutist Christology.

Almost everyone writing in Christology has been trying to do Christology in an imaginatively different way, in order to inspire believers and nonbelievers for whom traditionally absolutist Christology has become problematic. The reformulators of the Christological tradition in the contemporary period can be seen as assuming that this inaptness is superficial. They believe that the veil hiding the powerful relevance of Jesus Christ for the contemporary world can be lifted, providing that the Christian tradition and some of the tendencies of modern Western thought can be reconciled. Such reconciliation presupposes that both sides of the tension must be taken seriously. However, according to the perspective of absolutist Christology, a satisfactory resolution can be reached only if Christology takes its *fundamental* cue from the dominant tradition of Christological reflection. To be sure, this tradition must be received critically and reformed in places in the light of contemporary insight, but its essential core has proven itself flexible and resilient, and alteration or abandonment of it is not justified. Still less is alteration justified if the core insights of Christology—including the absolutist principle, on this view—are thought to be revealed in some final and unconditional sense.

The lack of fit between absolutist Christology and contemporary Western assumptions about the world also can be interpreted as a profound, perhaps unbridgeable, chasm, and very far indeed from being merely a superficial awkwardness. In this case, no reformulation, no matter how sweeping, can solve the "lack-of-fit" problem. Two theological approaches espouse this view. First, the repristinators mentioned above believe that the modern Western way of seeing the world is intellectually and spiritually derailed, so that negotiation with it is wrongheaded. Staying close to the Chalcedonian terminology is probably the only viable strategy for such theologians. The second approach holds that, in spite of the extremities and flaws in Western assumptions about the world, absolutist Christology's core principle is the main source of the lack of fit. The usual argument in this case is that the absolutist principle—a longstanding though not necessarily well-examined accompaniment of much of the classical Christological tradition—needs to be dropped rather than reformulated or simply restated. Why? Those who retain the absolutist principle overestimate both the quality of its links to the classical Christological tradition and the degree of distortion in the presuppositions of the admittedly mixed up modern West, with which the absolutist principle is in conflict. And the reformulators are not paying enough attention to the radical nature of the lack of fit between the absolutist hermeneutical habits of traditional Christology and the contemporary world.

Well, the reformulators might say, exactly how serious can this lack of fit be? Surely not disastrous enough to warrant jettisoning what is perhaps the core insight of a normative understanding of Jesus Christ's person and work that has flourished, except perhaps lately, for well over a millennia and a half. This is a powerful reply and a good reminder of the *a priori* unlikelihood that such rejection as these revisionist Christologies advocate could be warranted. However, as our exploration of the origins of the Christological crisis of plausibility has shown, and as will be argued systematically in the remaining chapters of this book, the case against absolutist Christologies is strong. Moreover, the Christian tradition itself offers ancient and biblically grounded Christological alternatives to absolutist Christology that are also more conceptually sound, historically responsible, faithful to the credal tradition, and ethically viable. Rejecting the absolutist principle is a choice for the present day—one that an increasing number theologians are electing to make—but it is one that can be made with the aid of supportive if usually overlooked resources from within the classical Christological tradition itself.

Modest Christology

Modest Christologies and the Classical Tradition

A modest Christology is one that rejects the absolutist principle. As such, a modest Christology is fundamentally revisionist. It does not merely receive the classical tradition of Christological reflection critically, with a view to reconceiving it in up-to-date terms, like the classical reformulators. Rather, it holds that the dilemmas of Christological lack of fit can be solved satisfactorily only if one of the standing insights of this tradition—the absolutist principle—is broken with in a significant way. Of course, since a modest Christology is not a *non*-Christology, proponents of the revisionist approach usually argue—with wide variations—that their proposals capture a *deeper* Christological core, one more faithful to the original Christological insights of the biblical authors, or freer of unhelpful philosophical accretions, and therefore more responsive to the mystery of Jesus Christ in every time and place, particularly here and now.

In dispensing with the absolutist principle, advocates of a modest Christology must relinquish some of the familiar assumptions about the person and work of Jesus Christ made in absolutist Christology. At the same time, however, they wish to retain Christological symbols as a central focus for interpreting the contemporary world and the history of the cultural streams that have been impacted by the historic Jesus through the Christian churches. Furthermore, they wish to do this by paying attention to the significance of Jesus' *person and work*, for they are convinced—as are the defenders of absolutist Christology—both that the experience of salvation common to Christians is significant and that it cannot be understood adequately unless it is related to the person and work of Jesus. This task is not merely reflection on the fact that Jesus was proclaimed lord and savior in the early churches, nor merely a matter of explaining the events that occurred under the impact of the faith of believers, events which secured the eventual historic significance of Jesus. Advocates of a modest Christology seek to connect the reality of the contemporary Christian experience of salvation to the person, teaching, ministry, and fate of the earthly Jesus of Nazareth. That is, they wish to do Christology.

Theologians advocating modest Christologies are aware of the wondrous dimensions of the absolutist principle and of its formerly outstanding hermeneutical capacity to make all creation as meaningful as a human life. One is never so keenly mindful of a concept as when it no longer successfully performs the function that made it important in the first place. However, they are content to find in Jesus Christ an expression of the scandalously paradoxical mystery of divine concern. Some attempts to moderate the absolutist principle while retaining some of its less indefensible absolutist elements in a generalized form have been made. However, whether or not there is a complementary preservative movement, theologians advancing a modest Christology are determined to root out the sharpest form of the absolutist principle.

From the absolutist perspective, of course, a modest Christology has its own scandal, namely, that it is not scandalous enough. A modest Christology exchanges the razor edge of the Christian gospel for an allegedly bland amalgam of historical and religious insight about Jesus of Nazareth, or about something less concrete. As a result, according to the criticism, everything most tangible, sacred, and ecclesially useful is foregone. Proponents of modest Christologies believe that it is impossible to make good on this criticism, and they are convinced of the sufficiency of the hermeneutical and religious power of the scandal of divine concern. Moreover, from the modest perspective, the abandonment of the absolutist principle in its sharpest form is an intellectual and moral imperative; the truth about Jesus of Nazareth and about the nature of creation is at stake, as are fidelity to the classical Christological tradition and the moral effectiveness and institutional longevity of the Christian churches. In fact, only by disengaging the paradoxical and mysterious scandal of divine concern from the distorting force of the absolutist principle can the deeper, older, truer scandal be reenvisioned by Christians in the contemporary world.

It is instructive to inquire in a more precise way as to the connection between modest Christologies and the classical Christological tradition. The word *classical* is used commonly to designate the Christology of the Nicaeno-Constantinopolitan Creed and its clarification in the Chalcedonian Definition, together with their conceptual categories and terminology. This is essentially how John Macquarrie formally defines the term in his survey of Christian thought about Jesus Christ.[11] There is no question that this is an appropriate use of the word *classical*. But the term so defined is lost as a useful category for describing contemporary Christologies, since few of them confine themselves to the Chalcedonian terminology. Moreover, even Macquarrie often uses the term in a more helpful and informal way to designate an entire tradition, to which contemporary Christologies abandoning Chalcedonian terminology could also belong, for example. The key to a Christology's membership in the classical Christological tradition appears to be the firm intention to so belong, together with a successful demonstration that the candidate Christology exhibits substantial continuity with that tradition. This invariably involves finding an interpretation of the enormously complex classical Christological development against which "substantial continuity" can be measured. As a result, many Christologies can and do make the claim to be "classical," including some that are decidedly not Chalcedonian.

On this basis, modest Christologies justifiably can claim membership in the classical tradition if they can fairly and successfully interpret the classical Christological tradition so as to make clear their significant continuity with it. I have tried to indicate my own way of doing this here. The absolutist principle runs deeper in the classical Christological tradition than does the Chalcedonian teaching of the two natures, however. As we have seen, it appears long before the Nicaeno-Constantinopolitan Creed and the Chalcedonian Definition, the fourth- and fifth-century center-pieces of the classical Christological tradition. It is therefore *prima facie* more difficult for a modest or nonabsolutist Christology to establish conti-nuity with the classical tradition than for an absolutist, non-Chalcedonian Christology. However, interpretations of the classical Christological tradi-tion that attempt to envision at least some sorts of modest Christologies as belonging to the family of rightful heirs have been offered, Macquarrie's own partially developed offering being one of the impressive recent examples.

Two Types of Modest Christologies

There are two schemes for elaborating a modest Christology—one inspi-rational and the other incarnational. The inspirational type attempts to go back beneath the entire patristic Christological tradition and to build a Christology on an interpretation of Jesus as a religious genius of some kind. Naturally, an inspired Jesus is a kind of minimal basis for almost all Christologies.[12] The inspirational modest Christology endeavors to con-strain itself to this modest minimum. In so doing, Jewish categories of prophet or messiah, or analogies with contemporary inspired religious ge-niuses such as Gandhi, usually prove to be of more use in articulating Jesus' significance than Hellenistic-Jewish categories of Logos and sophia, or Greek metaphysical categories of incarnation and two natures.

   This approach to Christology is compatible with a large array of views of salvation, ranging from mystical ascent to God to striving toward au-thentic humanity. However, it does rule out any view of salvation for which a different kind of savior would be needed, such as a morally im-peccable savior for a perfect sacrificial offering, or a God-man for an ade-quate satisfaction in Anselm's sense. It does not, notably, render superfluous divine grace in cooperating with humans for their salvation. The scandal of divine concern is preeminently grace; it is the mysterious ground of the world—the world's otherness—turned in love toward the world and its creatures. Moreover, historical events of salvific significance can and should be interpreted as outworkings of this gracious divine impulse of love, however this divine activity is to be understood in detail. Even as the Jews have always understood the Torah to be a gracious expression of the loving initiative of God for salvation, so Christians understand this same gracious initiative to be expressed in the life and work of Jesus of Nazareth.

Constructive modest Christologies can be developed with little regard for criticizing the absolutist principle.[13] When an inspirational modest Christology does engage the dominantly absolutist Christological tradition, the characteristic strategy is a direct attack on the conceptual coherence of the absolutist principle. Its conclusion is that God was *not specially present* in the actual historical figure of Jesus at all—let alone uniquely, exhaustively, absolutely, unsurpassably present—because God cannot be present in this way in any creature. At best, a human being can be exceptionally aware of and responsive to the divine, which is what is meant by inspiration. As we saw in Part I, Troeltsch offers a Christological explanation of the significance of the symbol of Jesus Christ of this kind, and John Hick is the leading exponent of this approach in the contemporary period.[14]

From another point of view, a modest inspiration Christology prescinds from invoking principles that transform the essentially historical judgment of Jesus' inspiration into the claim of the absolutist principle. This claim lies beyond the bounds of historical research and, if made at all, should be principled. An inspirational modest Christology is unaware of any principle sufficiently compelling to induce theological reflection so far beyond the boundary of what can be historically confirmed or disconfirmed that it might see fit to advance the claim of the absolutist principle. In fact, proponents of inspirational modest Christologies see numerous reasons for resisting such a temptation.

For example, Albert Schweitzer's argument in *The Quest of the Historical Jesus* is that there is no justification for applying the God-human idea to Jesus, because it is nonsensical for historically-minded people. In fact, he claimed that the impossibility of the God-human idea as traditionally understood had been more or less universally accepted by the German life of Jesus researchers of the nineteenth century.[15] For them, simply taking seriously the proposition that Christological statements had to be about the actual historical figure Jesus of Nazareth implied that the two-natures doctrine (Schweitzer's particular irritant) could be affirmed only violently, in disregard of Jesus' evident humanity. An inspirational modest Christology with a powerful mystical cast was the result in Schweitzer's case, for he could see no principled way to assert the incarnation.[16]

Unlike the inspirational variety of modest Christology, the incarnational type assumes a world for which incarnations are thinkable, but absolutist readings of incarnation unjustifiable. If a modest incarnational Christology sees fit to engage the absolutist principle, the most common strategic criticism is that the absolutist principle distorts the scandal of divine concern by making exclusive the historical particularity of the divine in Jesus of Nazareth. There are two main ways in which this conclusion is usually secured.

On the one hand, the special presence of the divine in Jesus Christ may be affirmed (*against* the characteristic strategy of inspirational modest Christologies) while attacking the adverbial qualifiers of the fact thesis that describe the *mode* of that presence (uniquely, exhaustively, absolutely, unsurpassably). For example, Raimon Panikkar affirms that the divine was incarnate in Jesus of Nazareth but that the divine mystery is not limited to this one manifestation. The same is true of the diverse Christologies of H. Richard Niebuhr, Stanley Samartha, John Macquarrie, John Cobb, Gordon Kaufman, and Robert Neville, among others. This amounts to applying Christological predicates in the first instance to Christ, thought of as the principle of incarnation, and only secondarily and derivatively to Jesus of Nazareth, with a clear distinction maintained between the two.

On the other hand, the *locus* of the divine presence can be moved away from the historical person of Jesus to something else. Friedrich Schelling has been the customary guide for thinkers exploring this path, such as Ferdinand Christian Baur, David Friedrich Strauss, and Ludwig Feuerbach: they applied Christological predicates to the whole human race thought of as the ideal or eventually actual culmination of its development through the historical process. For the theists among them, the divine presence is the force driving or luring the historical process, and the Christological aspect of its impact on humanity is the establishment of a vision of human potential in the living symbol of Jesus Christ. Such Christologies are rare at any time, and the twentieth century exhibits no examples of them by major theologians as clear cut as those just mentioned.[17] Strauss offers perhaps the most infamous example, his distinctive argument being that the traditional Christological affirmations apply to Jesus only in a derivative sense, and primarily to an idealized conception of humanity as a whole:

> This is the key to the whole of Christology, that, as subject of the predicate which the church assigns to Christ, we place, instead of an individual, an idea; but an idea which has an existence in reality, not in the mind only, like that of Kant. In an individual, a God-man, the properties and functions which the church ascribes to Christ contradict themselves; in the idea of the race, they perfectly agree. Humanity is the union of the two natures—God become man, the infinite manifesting itself in the finite, and the finite spirit remembering its infinitude; it is the child of the visible Mother and the invisible Father, Nature and Spirit. . . . This alone is the absolute sense of Christology: that it is annexed to the person and history of one individual, is a necessary result of the historical form which Christology has taken.[18]

Both the *mode* and the *locus* versions of the critique of the absolutist principle usually found with modest incarnational Christologies move the primary referent of Christological predicates away from its traditional object—the historical person of Jesus—toward something else: Christ as the principle of incarnation, an idealized conception of humanity, or an archetype (variously actualized in Jesus or purely ideal) of human potentiality. And yet the metaphysical possibility of special divine presence in history, either in a person or in an idea, is affirmed in this view. Thus leverage is gained against the problems incurred in any Christology affirming the absolutist principle, and much of the classical Christological language is preserved at the same time.

The temptation to which those exploring this strategy can succumb is to appeal for authorization to the classical Christological tradition, based on the fact that there is a good deal of verbal continuity. However, such an appeal can be disingenuous because of the large conceptual shift required to make the traditional language meaningful in an incarnational modest Christology. For example, rejecting the absolutist principle involves rethinking the traditional idea of a single metaphysical mechanism for cosmos-wide salvation, set in motion by Jesus Christ's saving work—and even this calls for the dubious supposition that "salvation" is a cross-culturally applicable category. Thus it is misleading for the incarnational

type of modest Christology to claim continuity with the classical Christological tradition in an untroubled way, though the argument certainly can
be made judiciously.[19]

Strategies for Critiquing the Absolutist Principle

So far we have seen criticisms of the absolutist principle that naturally lead
to expounding an inspirational or incarnational modest Christology. But it
has become increasingly common—especially in debates over Christology
and religious pluralism—to see direct attacks on the absolutist contention
of the universal, unsurpassable significance of Jesus Christ in isolation
from any explicit concern with constructive Christology. In the language
of the formal definition of the absolutist principle, this corresponds to attacking the significance thesis directly and allowing the chips to fall where
they may with regard to the fact thesis. A word about these arguments is
in order here, since they evenhandedly further the cause of both the incarnational and the inspirational types of modest Christology.

   Denying *any* significance to Jesus Christ would be tantamount to
abandoning Christology as such, so the argument in question appears in
different forms depending on the envisaged *scope* of the significance of
the symbol of Jesus Christ.[20] For example, as we have seen, Ernst
Troeltsch was deeply troubled by the tension he sensed between the
claim of a qualitatively unique revelation of the divine and the localization
of that revelation in a particular member of an obscure culture within a
tiny corner of a vast and ancient galaxy, one of so many in a universe of
magnificent proportions. As a result, he sought to affirm the absolute significance of Jesus Christ *for Christians* or *for European culture*, while resisting the Christocentric "temptation" to posit Jesus Christ as absolutely
significant for revelation and salvation even when non-Christians (or non-
humans) would reject this analysis. Other "scopes" for the significance of
Jesus Christ can be assigned, taking into account time as well as space.

   The general motivation for limiting the scope of the significance of
the symbol of Jesus Christ bears especially on trying to secure a more
plausible rendering of salvation, which is why this strategy appears most
commonly in religious pluralism debates involving Christians. The most
common and most powerful arguments turn on the implausibility of
"anonymous-Christianity" explanations for the reality and independence
of what Christians are content to call "revelation" and "salvation" in non-

Christian religions and, by extension, in other parts of the universe. Such a Christocentric solution to the problem of religious pluralism is a genuine solution, in the sense that it addresses the problem in terms appropriate to it. But the Christocentric solution heightens rather than alleviates the problematic character of the absolutist principle, so a modest Christology characteristically affirms a vision of revelation and salvation that is not absolutely tied to Jesus Christ. The phrase *theocentric salvation* is used sometimes to express this shift, though theocentrism is almost as problematic as Christocentrism when it is used as a description of salvation in any religious tradition. However, though the jury is still out on the possibility of finding a universally acceptable way of translating between descriptions of God, Nothingness, Ultimate Reality, Transcendent Ground of Being, or Abysmal Mystery, the strategy of enlarging the ontological center of salvation away from Jesus Christ in the direction of this Unnamable Mystery is present in all types of criticisms of the absolutist principle and all types of modest Christology. Only this, it is thought, simultaneously can do justice to what Christians call the "scandal of divine concern," to the fact that Christians encounter salvation in Jesus Christ, and to the reality of what Christians are willing to call "salvation" in other religious traditions.

In all, then, we have seen three strategies for criticizing the absolutist principle. There are, in fact, only three such strategies, and they can be described in terms of the formal language of the definition of the absolutist principle. Either the fact thesis needs to be the focus for criticism (the two critiques leading to inspirational and incarnational Christologies) or the significance thesis does (the approaches just mentioned). And if the fact thesis is the primary focus of criticism, the natural options are to reject any special presence of God in Jesus of Nazareth at all (the first strategy, discussed above, leading to an inspirational modest Christology), or to affirm that special presence but to qualify and constrain it in various ways to avoid entailing a strong form of the absolutist principle (the second strategy, also discussed above, leading to an incarnational modest Christology). Note that the significance thesis may be thought to bifurcate in the same way that the fact thesis does, with a fourth family of approaches to Jesus denying any great degree of significance to Jesus at all— but then these would not result in Christologies.

These three strategies have interestingly different structural characteristics in regard to their sponsoring of constructive modest Christolo-

gies. In the first strategy, the assumption of the metaphysical or logical impossibility of the absolutist principle leads to the specification of a starting
point for a modest Christology and introduces a permanent constraint
into its development. It will never be possible on this view to suppose that
reality is such that an incarnation could occur in it, nor even that divine
presence in people could be exceptional, as the classical Christology
claims was the case with Jesus of Nazareth. While this is a significant constraint on a Christology, the first strategy provides little in the way of further indications about how a modest Christology should be concretely
expounded. Jesus will be interpreted as inspired in some sense, of course,
but the concrete content of the idea of inspiration remains to be determined. That proves to be a complex historical problem, as we shall see
when we come to an analysis of John Hick's attempt to solve it.

The second strategy, by contrast, is more specific with regard to the
development of a modest Christology, since it admits incarnation as an intelligible category. It is less reliant, however, on one particular argument
against the absolutist principle.

The third strategy of directly attacking the significance thesis, as we
have seen, is compatible with either of the two types of modest Christology. It is important to note, however, that there are modest Christologies
that clearly adopt the third strategy as their primary stance toward the absolutist principle and prescind from advocating a clear position on the fact
thesis. This will be the case whenever the theologian in question is uninterested or unwilling to cash out statements about the significance of the
symbol of Jesus Christ in terms of metaphysical statements about the person and work of Jesus of Nazareth. This reluctance sometimes appears in
theologians deeply influenced by existentialism, or those fascinated with
functionalist accounts of Jesus Christ. Obviously, modest Christologies
can be developed in the presence of this kind of stance toward metaphysics—be it a matter of principle or taste or perhaps simply lack of ex-
plicitness.

Retrieving the Christological Tradition

It was noted earlier that rejecting the absolutist principle is not an all or
nothing affair. As we shall see in due course, Schubert Ogden and Paul
Knitter represent interesting middle cases—Ogden more absolutist than

modest and Knitter more modest than absolutist—and elements of the third strategy for critiquing the absolutist principle are present in Paul Tillich's otherwise absolutist Christology. Such mixed cases are not uncommon.

It follows that "modest" and "absolutist" are not categories to which Christologies *always* can be assigned in a hard and fast way. Nevertheless, they constitute a classification rather than a set of ideal types, for there is a single principle defining (positively and negatively) each category, whereas ideal types have independent, positive principles for each type. However, like ideal types, this classification is *ideal* because of the existence of mixed cases. Many Christologies are relatively easy to classify one way or the other based on the strength with which the absolutist principle is finally affirmed. But many Christologies still bear elements of the opposing class within their conceptual structure.

Now, this is not at all surprising. The contemporary context for theological reflection on the significance of the symbol of Jesus Christ necessarily involves trying to come to terms with a changed conception of the universe, a more positive judgment about the independence and authenticity of other cultural-religious streams of human history, and a series of more or less urgent social and ethical crises. Since the absolutist principle is a major stumbling block in the case of the first two challenges—and some argue in the third, also—it is to be expected that every Christology that seeks to engage its context inevitably would contain at least a discussion of the problematic character of the absolutist principle, even if affirmation is the final path chosen. What is surprising is that *so few* contemporary Christologies engage these problems as directly as they ought. The suggestion here is not that these problems are dealt with in only a tiny minority of Christologies. On the contrary, it is safe to say that at least one of the three is a concern in most contemporary Christologies. The point is rather that the treatment of these problems is frustratingly *indirect* and even at times *evasive*.

Consider the fact that it is not hard to state the problem for the plausibility of Christology posed by modern cosmology's discovery of the size and age of the universe (even after allowing for the cosmic anthropic principle). So why does not every Christology with an interest in plausibly justifying Christology (as against, say, a more immediate concern with its efficacy, as in various kinds of liberation theology) state the problem clearly and deal with it as straightforwardly as possible? In fact, such an approach is still not common. The situation is better with regard to the problem of religious pluralism, where a number of theologians are developing Christologies appropriate to this challenge. A solid proportion of these Christologies are modest, but it is not the desirability of modest Christologies that is the point here. It is rather the shocking fact there are Christologies *whose priorities include plausibility in relation to the contemporary world* that do not engage the problem of religious pluralism at all.

How are the reluctance, indirectness, and evasiveness on the part of many Christologies concerned to be plausible and coherent with contemporary knowledge to be explained? It can hardly be maintained that cosmology and religious pluralism are irrelevant to the plausibility of justification for Christology. It seems therefore that this state of affairs can be explained *only* by the hypothesis that absolutist Christology does not present itself, *even to some of its advocates*, as a potentially fruitful context for the articulation of a solution to these problems. To solve these problems in the terms of absolutist Christology necessarily involves making immeasurably stronger the dependence of Christology upon the absolutist principle, an option even those who wish to affirm this principle are loathe to choose.

These Christological challenges have been before Christian theologians in their maximally sharp form since Ernst Troeltsch's articulation of them at the beginning of the twentieth century. Partial forms of the problem are present a century earlier, most famously in the Christological reflection of Kant, Schelling, Hegel, and Schleiermacher, but they have been *undeniably* pressing for at least eighty years. Potential solutions to these problems exist in the shape of modest Christologies, so they need to take their place alongside of their absolutist counterparts as legitimate Christological options. In fact, this has been happening for some time now, especially with regard to the problem of religious pluralism. But then we are doing scarcely more than picking up the reins where Troeltsch left them at the beginning of the century, with more experience than he could have possessed, to be sure, and perhaps even with more driving skill, but having made only a little progress in the interim. From this point of view, twentieth-century Christology ought to be understood as a quest for a believable Jesus. Furthermore, this book aims to show that it is a quest for which the only satisfactory prize is a modest Christology.

Clarifying Remarks about Modest Christologies

It will be worthwhile here to forestall potential misunderstanding with a series of remarks addressing fundamental questions raised in the definition and discussion of modest Christologies to this point.

First, it seems wise to anticipate an objection to the definition of modest Christology, namely, whether a *modest* Christology, defined as it is here, rightly can be called a "Christology" at all. Obviously enough, if the *definition* of a Christology includes the affirmation of what has been identified here as the core of the frequently absolutist classical Christological tradition—the absolutist principle—then modest Christologies are *non-Christologies* right from the start. But this would be a grossly prejudiced definition. We can recognize talk about Jesus Christ that shows no concern with the tradition of Christological reflection beginning in the Christian Scriptures, that fails to acknowledge the partial validity and evocativeness of traditional credal affirmations about Jesus Christ, that does not intend to refer to the experienced reality of salvation through Jesus Christ spoken of by the Christian churches, that excises God from the picture as if there were not something religious at stake in discussing Jesus Christ, or that does not relate this salvation and religious significance to the actual *person* of Jesus. Such talk is common enough, and it *ought* to be thought of as non-Christological in character. But modest Christologies do not proceed in this way.

On the contrary, proponents of *Christologies*, whether modest or absolutist, attempt to appropriate critically the theological tradition, to cultivate openness in the form of willingness to engage alternative interpretations of Jesus Christ, to account for the actual experience of salvation through Jesus Christ familiar in various ways to so many human beings, to keep the religious significance of Jesus Christ in view by seeking to uncover the activity of God in and through his earthly person and his historic influence, and to relate the salvation proclaimed by and experienced within the Christian religion to the person of Jesus. For any Christology, the symbol of Jesus Christ has crucial significance. While the significance thesis of the absolutist principle must be rejected, therefore, delimited assertions of Jesus' significance are always required by Christology, properly understood. Doing justice to the scandal of divine concern in Jesus Christ demands this. A modest Christology conforms to this condition.

Second, I have spoken generally about a "lack of fit" between the absolutist interpretation of the classical Christological tradition and contemporary understandings of the world. It has been argued that this lack of fit is severe enough to warrant abandonment of the absolutist principle in order to liberate the classical Christological tradition for renewed relevance. How does this relate, a troubled inquirer might ask, to the question of the truth of absolutist and modest Christologies? If the widely acknowledged lack of fit is as extreme as you say, they might continue, would it not be simpler to say that absolutist Christology is false?

Indeed, it would be simpler, but not necessarily clearer. To speak of "lack of fit relative to a particular era's thought" is to beg a horde of difficult epistemological questions, including the infamous set of issues surrounding cognitive relativism. While offering an opinion on those controverted questions here is not practical, it is possible to indicate how reticence about judgments regarding the final truth or falsity of absolutist and modest Christology can be consistent with decisive advocacy of a modest Christology. This result follows from a particular understanding of theological statements that can be briefly outlined here without necessitating a thorough treatment of the character of religious knowledge.

(1) Christological statements about Jesus Christ, though complex and possessing many noncognitive aspects, do nonetheless make truth claims, and therefore may be true or false. This conclusion presupposes an epistemology that affirms such fundamental points as the following: that there are historical events, that events can be known, even though never in a presuppositionless way, and that true and false statements can be made about historical events and their significance. It also presupposes that theological statements have a cognitive component among their other ethical, aesthetic, exhortative, and expressive functions, so that they, too, can be true or false. These points are not immediately granted in some contemporary theological circles, but they are very likely to be granted by anyone raising the challenge that it would be clearer to say simply that absolutist Christology is false—and this is the problem being addressed here.

(2) The sources for our knowledge of that which we express through Christological statements include external sources such as Bible and tradition and the equally obvious internal given of individual religious experience. There is the worship and practice of the Christian community and our understanding of the world garnered from these sources and many more. All of these factors play into the process whereby we come to know

that, for example, "Jesus Christ is Lord." But these factors do not present themselves independently of our grasping and interpreting them. Therefore, we must be committed to a view of human knowledge that accepts the *conditioning* roles of a number of factors: the knowing subject, historical context, social embedding, and reality external to the human mind that is capable of offering correction to human beliefs. This is a less controversial point for contemporary theology. In fact, it is probable that this understanding of the conditioned character of human knowledge—even and perhaps especially of theological propositions—has become a commonsense view of human knowledge in the modern period.

(3) What must we conclude about the nature of the warrants for any *particular* truth claims in theology, and Christology in particular, given the first two points? One way to approach this question is to ask how pervasive is the conditioning influence of the factors just mentioned. Can these factors be described as unavoidably partly *constitutive* of theological statements, or can they be allowed for when theological statements are formulated, so as to minimize or nullify their unintended or unwanted consequences? It has become clear—especially through hermeneutics, ongoing study of the history of ideas, and the philosophy of science—that the historicized and social character of human knowing is such that complex truth claims can be extraordinarily difficult to settle. This result is supported by considering the same phenomenon in the sciences, and in any other area of human knowledge with an empirical aspect, as well as in theology. That scientific theories are discovered and tested in social and historical contexts which irrevocably condition the material content and handling of those theories has been established beyond question by historians and philosophers of science, even though there remain many controversies about details. Even in disciplines such as physics, which are methodologically committed to excising every conditioning influence of the knower's context from the theorizing and testing process, contextual factors prove to be vital influences. It is impossible, it seems, to be free of our historical and social contexts, and even to allow completely for all of our unconscious assumptions in a sensible way. Truth is hard enough to discover in physics. In a field such as theology whose existential dimensions are as important as its empirical or otherwise objective nature, the pervasiveness of contextual factors makes truth seeking even more difficult.

Therefore, it is within the bounds of possibility that a long-standing, widely held, even beloved conviction of a religious community, a conviction that involves truth claims about the nature of reality, could be false. It is likewise possible that this falsity may be discoverable—in a provisional way, like all knowledge about such matters—if only enough were known about reality to cast the community's conviction into a more adequate light. We think this way about what has come to be called the "plenary verbal inspiration" of the Scriptures, for example: it was a widespread belief, discovered to be mistaken when our understanding of history became sufficiently rich. However, unconditional, absolute knowledge of the truth or falsity of such a conviction is also out of the question. Yet, in the context of and for the sake of a religious community, arguments can be considered about such convictions, and provisional conclusions can and must be reached.

The issue of the absolutist interpretation of the classical Christological tradition—the absolutist principle—is another such conviction. The context for our reflection on this idea has changed, even as the turning earth moves objects from shadows into light. We are obliged for the sake of the Christian churches and in the name of intellectual honesty to consider the possibility that some of the hermeneutical habits guiding our interpretation of the classical Christological tradition may have been mistaken in this important respect. John Hick often has urged that we must learn to leave behind our theological fundamentalism, as painful as that process will undoubtedly be, even as we have struggled to leave behind our biblical fundamentalism. Though such remarks are, for Hick, somewhat narrowly (and questionably) focused on the mythological nature of the classical doctrine of the incarnation, he nevertheless offers a pointed reminder that even large-scale traditions can be mistaken in ways that only become significant and evident when the context of its interpretation shifts.

Third, the definition of modest and absolutist Christologies does not duplicate any of the famous extant Christological distinctions. Without entering into a detailed discussion of numerous definitions, the easiest way to see this is by noticing that the modest-absolutist classification bears on the *results* of Christology. By contrast, the "from above-from below" distinction bears on Christological *starting points*; the terms cosmological, anthropological, eschatological, and dialectical refer to *schemas* that are capable of guiding the expatiation of entire Christologies; historical-ideal and ontological-functional are distinctions referring to the *style* of a Christology—and neither starting points, schemas, nor styles bear directly on the *results* of a Christology. In fact, there have been or can be both modest and absolutist Christologies to which each one of the above terms can be applied.

In fact, the only popular distinction bearing on the *results* of Christology is the notorious "low-high" pair, whose most important function appears to be a rhetorical one: it is the premise for the essentially derogatory term *low Christology*. Because vagueness is essential to the effectiveness of a slur, it is remarkably difficult to define the terms *low* and *high*. That is a sufficient explanation for their disappearance from most serious Christological literature in recent years. Suppose, however, that a guess at a definition could be arrived at by averaging the various uses of these terms. We might then hazard that the pair of terms is a classification having to do with whether or not a Christology affirms the divinity of Jesus Christ. But this classification, besides being very difficult to apply in practice, is obviously a very different distinction from the modest-absolutist classification. While a "low Christology" (if our somewhat arbitrary definition of the term can be trusted) might likely be a modest Christology, modest Christologies can be both "high" and "low." Incarnational modest Christologies, for instance, would characteristically make a clear affirmation of Jesus' divinity, though this is done in so many different ways that not much is conveyed by pointing that out.

In any event, the central point is clear: the modest-absolutist classification does not duplicate the work of extant Christological distinctions and is, in fact, significantly different from all of them. Its great virtue is that it succeeds in grounding an interpretation of contemporary Christology in which many superficially dissimilar Christological projects may be seen as related to one another through their dissatisfaction with the absolutist principle.

Fourth, there are other kinds of revisionism in contemporary Christology besides that of modest Christologies. David Tracy uses the term *revisionist* to describe a kind of Christology. Many who do not use the exact term make a similar point. Schubert Ogden carefully declares his own Christology to be "revisionist,"[21] and he is willing to give many less adventurous Christological efforts the same designation. But his Christology is substantially absolutist, in the way that term is used here, as we shall see in a later chapter—and this is so even though it imparts considerable impetus to the project of modest Christologies. Much of what is described as revisionist Christology is, in fact, still largely absolutist, being the result of a strong reformulating impulse, especially in regard to the problem of faith's dependence on history. No rejection of the absolutist principle is envisaged in many of these discussions. In fact, in some cases—here again Ogden is an example—the aim of the reformulation is to *warrant* a strong statement of the absolutist principle. It follows that modest Christologies are revisionist in a different sense than this word usually carries in contemporary Christology.

Some of the most profound kinds of Christological revisionism appear among the liberation Christologies, construed broadly as those interpretations of Jesus the Christ pursued in connection with liberation themes, be they Latin American, African, Asian, feminist, black, gay, or others. Liberation Christologies adopt a complex posture toward traditional interpretations of Jesus Christ, and the connections to modest Christologies are intriguing.

The most obvious remark to make about liberation theology relates to its distinctive methodological emphasis, which is particularly evident in the priority accorded to orthopraxis over orthodoxy, and the insistence upon reflection emphatically grounded in concrete social and personal activity. This perspective corrects a bias in traditional theological methods, which have sometimes tended toward reflection isolated from everyday, practical concerns, or ignored the sociopolitical context of the church when framing Christologies. The image of a lens is used often to put the point of the shift in the method of liberation theology effectively. As we have learned—not from liberation theologies so much as from the emergence of hermeneutic sensitivity through two centuries—everything we do and think presupposes and enacts the fact that we inevitably view the world through a lens, the embodiment of our cultural, social, and personal specificity. In a number of ways, we in the contemporary era have come to believe that awareness of this lens of specificity is essential for intellectual and moral responsibility. So, according to liberation theologians, the methodological decisions of theologians ought to reflect as starkly as possible ethical and practical commitments. Not only do the liberation theologians urge this open self-awareness upon theological activity, however; they also invite the exchanging of one lens for another, namely, one that takes the view of the poor, the disenfranchised, the exploited, women, and minority groups, and develops Christology from that perspective.

This call for Christology to bubble up "from below" (in a different sense from the one these words usually carry in the context of Christology), and the attendant reevaluations of traditional interpretations of Jesus Christ, is one of the distinctive contributions of liberation theologies to the contemporary Christological complex. A consequence of this shift in viewpoint is the inevitable posing of a series of challenging questions: for whom are Christological controversies important, whom do they serve, and whom do they marginalize, ignore, or silence? These considerations raise a general critique of projects like this one, whose appreciation of the liberation perspective is limited to craning the neck to try empathetically to look at Jesus Christ through the lens of the poor or otherwise ill-treated, rather than actually giving up the traditional interpretative lens being used for the sake of complete solidarity with them, which would involve taking on instead one or another of the lenses of liberation. There is no reply to this general critique except to hope to make ethical commitments sufficiently clear and to insist that thinking of all kinds ought to be free to specify its own methodological basis and to proceed unfettered by interests alien to its own.

More profoundly, liberation Christologies from and for the third world have customarily had little interest in reevaluating the tradition of Christological reflection beyond the scope of the urgent practical crises from which they are the reflective fruits. This is completely understandable, but problematic. It is conceivable that liberation Christologies attempting to move the process of theological reflection from eviscerating, dehumanizing crises in the direction of a reconstructed doctrine of the person and work of Christ might produce a Christology that undermines motivation for change instead of rallying Christians to seek justice. Perhaps some modest Christologies could have such an undermining effect, because of their disruption of the customary alliance between absolutist modes of thought and ecclesial rallying power. Thus, many kinds of liberation Christology have an inherently conservative bias concerning the question of Christological reconstruction that balances their ethical revisionism. If the traditional Christology can be made to serve the practical ends that every just-minded person agrees are vital, why revise the Christology, or even contemplate such action? The fact that there has been so little specifically *doctrinal* revision in third world liberation Christology is partly explained by this analysis.

Nevertheless, there is a potentially highly fruitful relationship possible

between the modest Christology and liberation projects, precisely because of the impulse toward *ethical* decentering fostered by modest
Christology's *theological* decentering of Jesus Christ. This decentering effect may well undermine the rallying power of a Christology, at least according to conventional assumptions about what makes for ecclesial
cohesion, but a modest Christology is well suited for undermining all
kinds of ethical absolutism, too. And it is forms of ethical absolutism that
preserve and ideologically warrant both oppressive regimes and the conscious and unconscious economic exploitation of the third world by the
first world. Modest Christologies are potentially highly useful, if actually
under-tested, partners for theologies of liberation.

The same remarks can be extended to most other spheres whose liberation has become a matter of theological interest. The connection to
feminist theology is especially interesting. Obviously, modest Christologies
are helpful partners in inducing a shift away from absolutized interpretations of the maleness of the historical person Jesus. Modest Christologies
commonly are found in feminist theology, as a result, though the repudiation in many such theologies of the classical Christological terms makes
the identification difficult to establish formally. What is more important,
as I shall argue later, the shift in consciousness being wrought by feminist
reflection of all kinds promises to be of the first importance for the ecclesial viability of modest Christologies. As we have seen, Troeltsch recognized the socially cohesive value of absolutist Christology in its ability to
provide a rallying point for Christian believers. He seemed doubtful that
another Christology—including his own—would fare as well in the essential task of uniting a diverse, multicultural Christian community. But this
ecclesial attachment to absolutist visions of salvation and the world is precisely what most feminist theologians critize and seek to change. If their
vision of the world is substantially realized, the anti-absolutism of modest
Christologies will be precisely what is needed for securing the unity and
ethical energy of the Christian Churches.

5

Incarnational and Inspirational Modest Christologies: Two Case Studies

This chapter analyzes two well-known contemporary Christologies that exemplify the two types of modesty. The aims are to reach a clearer characterization of the two types, in terms of both their conceptual structure and their relationship to absolutist Christologies, and to explore the senses in which these modest Christologies can be regarded as belonging to the classical Christological tradition.

The discussion turns first to John Hick's understanding of Jesus Christ, which he has described as an "inspiration Christology."[1] Until recently, Hick's view has received only limited treatment in several of his published essays and addresses. His monograph on Christology does not change the basic point of view, though adjustments here and there, all toward the goal of a more systematic approach, are evident.[2] We shall see that Hick's is a modest Christology of the first type, which is to say, a Christology whose positive affirmations turn mainly on the inspiring ethical and spiritual power of Jesus of Nazareth, one that confines the significance of Jesus Christ entirely to the creative, contingent flux of history, denying that it can be grounded in any literal assertion of Jesus Christ incarnating, instantiating, or expressing a universal metaphysical principle. According to Hick, Christological statements asserting or implying such a grounding are to be understood strictly as metaphorical expressions, the continued use of which is justified primarily by reason of their expressiveness and cultic usefulness. Ernst Troeltsch's Christology was also of this type, and what we learned in the examination of it in Part I is useful background for appreciating Hick's attempt.

Hick is far and away the most influential of the few well-known, contemporary advocates of this type of Christology, though experience suggests that it is more common among academic nontheologians such as biblical critics, historians, and scholars of religion—academics, that is, who do not publish specifically in Christology.

John Cobb's interpretation of Jesus Christ in *Christ in a Pluralistic Age* is the second Christology to be examined in this chapter. Espousing a modest Christology of the second type, Cobb admits the possibility of incarnation, instantiation, or expression of the Logos; argues that this possibility is actualized in the case of Jesus; and makes this historical actualization the primary basis for warranting Christian assertions of the significance of the symbol of Jesus Christ. However, Cobb denies that this particular (or any) incarnation, instantiation, or expression can be regarded in principle as uniquely, exhaustively, unsurpassably significant. Thus, in the case of both Hick and Cobb, the absolutist principle is rejected, and they are properly regarded as modest Christologies. However, it is their differences, rather than their similarities, that are of most interest for present purposes.

As we saw in the last chapter, among Protestants involved in interreligious dialogue, the incarnational type of modest Christology (in a variety of forms) is probably the most widely supported. It seems to be gaining ground within Catholic theological circles, also—especially because of Paul Knitter's advocacy of a form of it—though support for it in that sphere does not yet appear to surpass that of its main family of competitors: inclusivist, absolutist Christologies modeled after Karl Rahner's Christology. The main reason for the improving fortunes of modest, incarnational Christology is its valuable contribution to a solution to the problems of competing interpretations of the human condition and descriptions of reality among the religions that does justice to two profound experiences: the experience of commonality among the religions that seems to demand an inclusivist explanation, and the experience of strangeness and independence of cultural expressions that seems to demand a radically pluralist explanation. Cobb's work shows how both of these needs can be met simultaneously within the context of his modest, incarnational Christology.

Panikkar, Samartha, and Macquarrie (among others) are well-known advocates of the same type of modest, incarnational Christological position as Cobb—though obviously from varying perspectives and with different results. Any of these would have been appropriate objects for discussion in this chapter. Macquarrie, however, does not contextualize his acceptance of the possibility of a variety of instantiations of universal principles of ultimate reality in the systematic way that Cobb, Panikkar, and Samartha do; Samartha's approach is interesting but for my purposes does not illustrate as well as the others the flexible potential of modest incarnational Christologies; and Panikkar will be discussed later—so Cobb's Christology is a natural choice. Moreover, Cobb's *Christ in a Pluralistic Age* was a ground-breaking book that set—and in regard to metaphysical clarity still sets—the pace for systematic discussions of this type of Christology.

John Hick: The Logic of Modest Inspirational Christologies

Hick's Christological approach follows what was earlier called the first strategy for developing a modest Christology, which has a characteristic critique, but specifies no more than a starting point for a constructive Christology. Hick specifies the negative starting point for Christology by saying that the classical metaphysical understanding of incarnation must be regarded as a poetic, mythological conception that is of no use for systematic theological articulation of the nature and significance of Jesus Christ. To move any further, Hick, and any other explorer of the first strategy, must devise positive principles for the development of a modest Christology.

Hick proceeds from this starting point along two complementary ways in his various writings, which he supposes finally join at his inspiration Christology. One of these ways focuses on the character and activity of the historical Jesus as a means of pointing to the sense in which he was so specially inspired as to be a worthy referent of properly interpreted

Christological assertions. This is the primary positive principle used to develop Hick's Christological outlook. That this principle is defined in terms of the historical realm is an indication of the sense in which Jesus can be said to be significant: this significance must take shape within, and remains limited to, the historical process. For the same reason, the significance of the symbol of Jesus Christ can be lost if historical circumstances conspire so as to release the Christian religion to the graveyard of history in the way it has the vast majority of the earth's religious traditions.

Hick's other path involves attaching a theological interpretation to what he is able to reconstruct historically about Jesus, with the help of his modified and relativized Kantian anthropology, and under the carefully monitored guidance of the tradition of Christological reflection. He reconstrues traditional Christological assertions such as "Jesus Christ is God incarnate" in terms of the conception of "incarnate divine love." In this way, Hick tries to show that many of the traditional assertions are meaningful statements, despite what he takes to be the failure of all types of metaphysical construals of them to secure this conclusion. Having satisfied himself of their meaningfulness, Hick is in a position to parse their logical status: they are classified early on as mythological statements and later as metaphorical statements.

This process of argumentation has two purposes. On the one hand, it allows Hick to justify his commendation of the traditional Christological language to the worship of the Christian cult and to the piety of Christian believers. On the other hand, it allows him to mount the argument that his Christology can be seen as partially continuous with the classical Christological tradition, even as any unconventional interpretation of a complex historical chain of events is strengthened by providing a convincing reconstruction of a dominant interpretation. This strategy is identical in form, though ironically opposite in result, to the one adopted by early Christian writers such as Justin, Tertullian, and Origen, who argued that their interpretations of Jesus Christ—soon to be dubbed "classical" in honor of their triumph over, and eventually their complete suppression of, the "heretical" alternatives of such Christians as the Ebionites, Marcion, Valentinus, Sabellius, Arius, and Apollinarius—were continuous with divine revelation to the Jews by reinterpreting the Septuagint using the prophecy/fulfillment motif and allegorical methods.

The First Step: The Myth of God Incarnate

Hick's aim in "Jesus and the World Religions," his contribution to *The Myth of God Incarnate*, was to establish that there are many ways to conceptualize the significance of Jesus and that the conceptuality of incarnation was adopted simply because of contextual contingencies. On this basis, he urges that in our time "it is proper for Christians to become conscious of both the optional and the mythological character of this traditional language."[3] As he says in that article,

> We should never forget that if the Christian Gospel had moved east, into India, instead of west, into the Roman empire, Jesus' religious significance would probably have been expressed by hailing him within Hindu culture as a divine Avatar, and within the Mahayana Buddhism which was then developing in India as a Boddhisattva, one who has attained to oneness with Ultimate Reality but remains in the human world out of compassion for mankind and to show others the way of life. These would have been the appropriate expressions, within those cultures, of the same spiritual reality.[4]

Hick adduces a series of arguments against both absolutist and incarnational Christology, the cumulative effect of which is intended to be the making of conceptual and rhetorical space for his alternative Christological viewpoint. These same arguments are reproduced—in most cases without much modification—in several of Hick's subsequent writings. Hick's arguments are of mixed value, those against absolutist Christology being much stronger than those against incarnational Christology. In view of the importance of this step in Hick's overall Christological scheme, however, a brief summary of the arguments is in order, for which purpose their arrangement in "Jesus and the World Religions" is most helpful.

The History of Religions and Social Psychological Perspectives

Hick begins that article by adducing the parallel between the deification of Jesus in Christianity and the exaltation of Gautama in Mahayana Buddhism as evidence for a cross-cultural "tendency of the religious mind" toward "exaltation of the founder," leading "the developing tradition to speak of [the founder] in terms which he did not use, and to understand him by means of a complex of beliefs which was only gradually formed by later generations of his followers."[5] Here we see the theory of the development of doctrine being sensitized—as it was already for Troeltsch—to two considerations: the history of religions and social psychology.

Hick anticipates the objection that the resurrection of Jesus implies that Jesus was proven to be divine and that the development of thought about him as a result ought not be subject to the same social psychological patterns that appear to apply in the parallel Mahayana case. He argues that a physical resurrection is extremely unlikely when the stories on which it is based "refer to an event nearly twenty centuries ago and when the written evidence is in detail so conflicting and so hard to interpret."[6] Hick does not engage the "conflicting evidence" to which he alludes. With the help of a quote from John Caird, however, Hick does argue that a physical resurrection would not necessarily be "a proof of divinity" or even a "stamp of authenticity" for Jesus anyway. But this is a somewhat lame rider because everything turns on *who* was resurrected. If it were Hick's fairly ordinary and hypothetical next door neighbor, according a stamp of authenticity to everything he or she ever did or said on the basis of a resurrection would be less sensible than if it were a person, such as Jesus, who on any account said and did some fairly remarkable and controversial things. In any case, Hick's aim here is clear: he is attempting to short-circuit any attempt to make a social psychological exception of early Christian development by means of an appeal to the resurrection.

Reinterpreting Christological Development in Early Christianity

The way is cleared by these preliminary arguments for Hick to offer a positive interpretation of the development of the early church's Christological views. In short, how did the deification of Jesus take place? After a brief examination of some of the titles that were applied to Jesus in an ongoing attempt to think of him "in a way that was commensurate with the total discipleship which he evoked," Hick draws his conclusions about this process of development in the following passage:

> It seems likely that this deification of Jesus came about partly—perhaps mainly—as a result of the Christian experience of reconciliation with God. . . . The early Christian community lived and rejoiced in the knowl-

edge of God's accepting grace. And it was axiomatic to them, as Jews influenced by a long tradition of priestly sacrifice, that 'without the shedding of blood there is no forgiveness of sins' (Hebrews 9:22). There was thus a natural transition in their minds from the experience of reconciliation with God as Jesus' disciples, to the thought of his death as an atoning sacrifice, and from this to the conclusion that in order for Jesus' death to have been a sufficient atonement for human sin he must himself have been divine.

Thus it was natural and intelligible both that Jesus, through whom men had found a decisive encounter with God and a new and better life, should come to be hailed as son of God, and that later this poetry should have hardened into prose and escalated from a metaphorical son of God to a metaphysical God the Son, of the same substance as the Father within the triune Godhead. This was an effective way, within that cultural milieu, of expressing Jesus' significance. . . . And because of the inherent conservatism of religion, the way in which the significance of Jesus was expressed in the mythology and philosophy of Europe in the first three centuries has remained the normative Christian language which we inherit today.[7]

Hick's reconstructive interpretation in its specifics is shaky. His assumption that Jews would naturally apply their understanding of atoning sacrifice to Jesus in such a way as to require Jesus' divinity for the sacrifice to be sufficient is highly questionable. Hick's argument is not without force, however, especially when supported by other contributors to *The Myth of God Incarnate*, such as Frances Young and Michael Goulder, who offer fuller, more plausible reconstructions of the same process.[8] Its effect is to level the Christological playing field by overcoming the traditional exegetical advantage of absolutist Christologies, after which Hick's modest construal of the development of Christological reflection in early Christianity is certainly no less historically plausible than a similar construction based on an absolutist Christology. In addition, it has the inestimable advantage of being able to interact substantively with the history of religions, with sociology and psychology, and with general human religious dynamics such as founder elevation, which stands in marked contrast to the sharp problems that the absolutist Christological rendering of the same period of development encounters on the same issues.

The Logical Status of Classical Christological Language

At this stage in the argument of "Jesus and the World Religions," Hick turns his attention away from Christian origins and toward the patristic developments of Christological doctrine. However, rather than asking the question of the legitimacy of the pronouncements at Nicea, Constantinople, and Chalcedon, Hick presses a new line of argument: the issue of the status of the Christological language in those conciliar decisions. Focusing particularly on the "God-man" formula, Hick asks "whether it has any non-metaphorical meaning."[9] He argues that, while it is literally meaningful to speak of Jesus as a man, to speak of him in the terms of the conciliar pronouncements is to use "a form of words without assignable meaning."[10] It is an expressive utterance, thinks Hick, not a metaphysical assertion, regardless of how it was intended.

This leads directly to Hick's use of the word *myth* to describe what is valid in the language of the two-natures doctrine and divine incarnation. Thinking of a myth as "a story which is told but which is not literally true, or an idea or image which is applied to someone or something but which does not literally apply, but which invites a particular attitude in its hearers,"[11] Hick allows a certain kind of truth to a myth: it is "a kind of practical truth consisting in the appropriateness of the attitude to its object."[12] The application of incarnational language to Jesus is mythological because it has "no literal meaning," but it

> gives definitive expression to his efficacy as savior from sin and igno-
> rance and as giver of new life; it offers a way of declaring his significance
> to the world; and it expresses a disciple's commitment to Jesus as his
> personal Lord. He is the one in following whom we have found ourselves
> in God's presence and have found God's meaning for our lives. He is our
> sufficient model of true humanity in a perfect relationship to God. And
> he is so far above us in the 'direction' of God that he stands between
> ourselves and the Ultimate as the mediator of salvation. And all this is
> summed up and given vivid concrete expression in the mythological lan-
> guage about Jesus as the Son of God.[13]

There is much in this chain of argument that does not win agreement from many contemporary theologians. Notwithstanding acknowledged problems with the "truly God, truly man" formula, they think that the metaphysical terminology can be straightened out, or translated into other, more capable, terms. Consider Schleiermacher's surgical deconstruction of the traditional teaching that "in Jesus Christ, divine nature and human nature were combined into one person,"[14] or Harnack's argument that "the Nicene Creed was a victory of the priests over the faith of the Christian people."[15] These famous criticisms are respectfully echoed by a number of the doctrine's contemporary defenders—Wolfhart Pannenberg, John A. T. Robinson, and Douglas F. Ottati, to name a few[16]— who yet go on to offer reformulations that they think are intellectually viable. It is hardly surprising, then, that Hick's view has been attacked repeatedly in the controversy surrounding *The Myth of God Incarnate*, as well as by others not directly involved in the controversy, such as Schubert Ogden.[17] However, while Hick is swimming against the current with this line of argument, as it were, given certain presuppositions about the nature of reality, it possesses some plausibility. These assumptions are none other than those made by the theistic naturalism that often goes hand in hand with a modest Christology of the inspirational, nonincarnational type. Modest Christologies in general, however, are equally at home in metaphysical environments more hospitable to the concept of incarnation.

Breaking with the Incarnational Tradition

Another argument is broached at this point in Hick's presentation. Since the Christian churches uniformly took the mythological terms of incarnation language as literal metaphysical designations and have continued to do so almost uniformly right up to the present, Hick needs to give good reasons for breaking this pattern. After all, ecclesial tradition is most definitely not weak-minded, and to propose a change implying that a vast theological mistake has been made is decidedly to suggest otherwise. This is perhaps the thorniest difficulty with advocating modest Christologies of the nonincarnational type, and Hick handles it with straightforward directness. He argues that the mistake involved in incarnation Christology was possible because it did not have dramatically obvious negative consequences: it "did little positive harm so long as Christendom was a largely autonomous civilisation with only relatively marginal interaction with the rest of mankind."[18]

Drawing a parallel with biblical literalism, Hick notes that from a

twentieth-century point of view, "this use of the bible was always mistaken; but nevertheless it probably did comparatively little harm so long
as it was not in conflict with growing human knowledge."[19] Just as the
growth of human knowledge threw the traditional attitude toward biblical
interpretation into new relief, however, so does contemporary cultural
and religious pluralism bring a new perspective on the theological literalism of incarnational Christology. It is as if the light shaft of traditional
Christology were being refracted by a new-found lens, prompting the discovery of an alternative, richer, more complex way of looking at the symbol of Jesus Christ, a discovery that could not have been made without the
help of a developing culture to function as the lens. Of course, proponents of nonincarnational Christologies argue that the lens of ancient Judaism was always sufficient to avoid this Christological mistake. But once
the fateful decision had been made to commit theological and ecclesial resources to the Hellenistic world, the opportunity to make use of that lens
was lost, until historical criticism could recover it.

Hick's arguments against the possibility of a literal interpretation of
the incarnation are as relevant to undermining incarnational Christologies
of the modest type (e.g., Cobb's, below) as to the more traditional absolutist incarnational Christologies. But as arguments against the viability of
a literal interpretation of incarnation, they are not impressive. Such force
as they do possess is expressed more clearly by reformulating the arguments to make their target absolutist, rather than incarnational, Christologies. This is essentially the same pattern we noticed in Troeltsch's
Christology. The one argument that cannot be reformulated, and has relevance only for attacking incarnational Christologies, is the charge that the
idea of incarnation is incoherent. But such an argument is convincing only
in the right metaphysical milieu, so that the choice between incarnational
and nonincarnational modest Christologies appears to reduce to a metaphysical decision between visions of reality.

The Second Step: Jesus as Inspired

The Problem of Historical Judgments of Inspiration

Hick's view of Jesus as an inspired individual is presented briefly in "Jesus
and the World Religions," at slightly greater length in "An Inspiration

Christology," and in chapter 2 of *The Metaphor of God Incarnate*. Hick thinks that an assessment of this type is one that must be made according to the canons of historical research. It is the kind of judgment on which devout Christians and those neutral or antipathetic toward Christianity ought to be able in principle to reach substantial agreement. It involves a partial reconstruction of the general historical circumstances of Jesus' life, reaching back from the understandably enthusiastic and biased sources we now possess, through the communities and oral traditions that produced them, to the person whose words and actions, passion and spirit inspired them.

Hick is well aware that this is not an easy task. It was argued in the discussion of Troeltsch's view of the same problem that the nature of the sources themselves introduces an irreducible cloud of uncertainty into every stage of the analysis and a correspondingly high degree of imprecision in the results that can be obtained. In spite of the fact that biblical critical expertise has discerned the limits of the sources, however, Hick still produces a description of Jesus as inspired. It is crucial to understand the way in which Hick does this.

Many works, including those of recent authors who see themselves as having passed beyond the tendency toward excessive projection evident in earlier lives of Jesus, attempt to plot ingenious, compelling courses between the rocky snags thrown up by the sources and across the vast stretches of open water about which the sources have nothing to say. Such partially speculative works foster the impression that biblical criticism can achieve more precise results than its own best analyses of the limits of the sources allow. Some degree of distance from the mass of these works, however, leads to the conclusion that a large margin for error remains, since there are many comparably plausible but mutually incompatible speculative reconstructions, all of which weave a more or less feasible path through the same space marked out by the sources. Hick's attempt is *not* of this sort, for he unwaveringly maintains that such constructions are underdetermined by the available data. His reconstruction of the sense in which Jesus was inspired is explicitly, self-consciously speculative.

Hick's speculative construction relies heavily upon the rather general and very nearly incontestable historical hypothesis that standing behind the communal memories of Jesus inferable from the early Christian writings was a man of exceptional personal charisma and wisdom, who believed himself to be brokering a powerful message on behalf of God. That this powerful personality was the prime indirect cause of the development of the early church is also a reasonable supposition; Ralph Waldo Emerson's insight that "an institution is the lengthened shadow of one man"[20] is as apt here as anywhere, even though Jesus probably had no intention to create and saw no need for a religious institution.

With so strong a result in place, however, why does Hick insist that his reconstruction needs to be speculative? Hick thinks it quite dubious that the churches' inspiration—for their liturgies, their Christologies, their practices, the piety and martyrdom of their members—derived significantly from knowledge of the *specific details* of Jesus' character, as against the general fact of his life and death in conjunction with integrated interpretations of his supposed significance spread by compelling preachers and the compiled memories of particular ecclesial traditions, which included our Gospels.[21] More specific details appear to have become dislocated from their contexts or completely dropped out quite early, since we have few of them preserved in the extant texts and fewer that agree across the various memory pictures of Jesus that survive. It is widely agreed that this thinning of biographical specifics was fostered by the apocalyptic expectations of the early Christians. The sayings of Jesus have survived best, but even those that are thought attributable to him with some confidence by the scholars of the Jesus Seminar are radically decontextualized as we meet them, frequently pressed into service by the gospel compilers for their own redactionary purposes, and of little use for reconstructing a detailed personal profile. Hick is at some pains to point out to his readers this problem of reaching behind the plausible hypothesis of an inspired Jesus to reconstruct the kinds of details about his life that would give concrete intelligibility to this idea of inspiration.[22]

It is important to be clear about the extent of the problem that Hick rightly points out. We do not know specifically, nor can we suppose the Christians of the period of the Gospels knew specifically, the circumstances or location of Jesus' birth and early childhood; his family's occupation, social status, religious fervor or political views; the formative influences of his siblings and parents upon his self-understanding and view of the world; the kind of friends he made and kept; the circumstances of his father's (implied) disappearance from his life; the influence of his social and religious context upon his political and religious views as well as his personal style; his education and how he came by the knowledge especially of Deuteronomy, Psalms, and Isaiah attributed to him in the Gospels; the key formative events that shape any human's self-understanding; the decisive moral and intellectual decisions that shape any human's personal development; his contacts with intimate friends and lovers; the circumstances of his natural separation from his family; the nature of the corporate religious and social influences to which he was subsequently exposed; the process of development of his understanding of his message; the circumstances of the emergence of his public ministry; his manner of speaking; his bodily frame and appearance; the status of his health; the way in which he was experienced as compelling by those who became his full-time followers; the development of his self-understanding as his ministry unfolded; his view of the world and what was possible within it; his working theological interpretation of God, Israel, and the world as he knew it; the degree of public enthusiasm for his teaching in the various places to which he traveled through the duration of his ministry; the development of his apparent abilities to heal and exorcise; his self-understanding of these abilities; the intellectual and spiritual influences on the content of his message; his personal spiritual development and practice; how he looked and acted when he was angry, irritable, hungry, tired, elated, depressed, content, stressed, or deeply moved; the nature and effects of his apparent ecstatic or mystical experiences; his opinion of and social location within any or all of the many groups within Judaism; the relationship of his self-understanding to the key titles attributed to him in the Gospels; the nature of the decision to make the final trip to Jerusalem; whether he had envisaged and cultivated the opportunity for his own execution; the specific legal reason for his arrest, conviction, and execution; the year of his death; his attitude to his own death when it was imminent; his anticipation of the effect of his death; his expectations concerning his survival of and exaltation after death.

This is exactly the kind of information we would want to have if we were to gain a basic understanding of the sense in which Jesus could be said to be inspired. The facts we have, sketchy though they are, are sufficient to mark out a space within which we can imagine definite answers to all of these questions. However, notwithstanding the fact that there is no shortage of argument and attempted reconstruction around many of these questions, the figure of Jesus remains biographically enigmatic. In the case of Jesus, therefore, there is no chance of constructing very much at all of the modern biographer's prized possession: a personality profile and timetable of activities correlated with heritage, life influences, crucial events, and self-interpretation. Correspondingly, there is currently no hope of giving a nuanced and historically assured answer to the difficult question of the sense in which Jesus was inspired, including the way he affected people, the kind of character that accounted for those effects, and the biographical and circumstantial reasons for the emergence of such a character.

While Hick stresses the difficulty of reaching a *specific* understanding of Jesus' inspiration with reasonable confidence, it is precisely such an understanding that would seem to be the necessary first step in his Christological program, for it would bring concreteness to the rather abstract assertion that Jesus was an inspired religious genius. Without this tangibility, it remains obscure why anyone ought to consider Jesus a person worthy of allegiance in the twentieth century, and similarly opaque why anyone ought to bother with Christology at all. It follows that a speculative reconstruction is needed if the assertion of inspiration—held with justifiable confidence in general terms—is to gain definite content.

Hick's Speculative Reconstruction of Jesus As Inspired

How, we may ask, does Hick assure himself that his own spiritual needs and cultural perspective do not thoroughly distort his speculative reconstruction? Hick's method is to examine the inspiration of religious founders, prophets, and saints both ancient and modern, adopting them as models to guide speculation about the spiritual inspiration of Jesus. Hick anticipates the objection that answers to the above litany of questions in regard to other figures would be irrelevant to understanding Jesus as inspired because Jesus was not like other humans. Hick replies that whatever else Jesus was, the Christian tradition always has declared (albeit with mixed success) that he was truly human, so there must be continuity between his spiritual experience and that of other humans. Spiritual inspiration in other cases can therefore be informative about the nature of Jesus' inspiration.[23]

Hopefully safeguarded from the excesses of projection to some extent by this method, Hick proceeds by drawing analogies with Jesus from the lives of Gautama and Gandhi and by inferring what an encounter with Jesus must have been like from the early history of the churches and the Gospels' communal memories of Jesus, as these had been handed down from his followers. The results are meager, compared with what might be wished for, but they are sufficiently full and reliable, Hick thinks, to ground his Christological reflections.

At the most general and least speculative level, which is most characteristically the tone of *The Metaphor of God Incarnate*, Hick summarizes as follows:

> So what I myself see when I try to peer back through the New Testament documents to the person who lies at a distance of some two generations behind them is a man, Jesus, whose immensely powerful God-consciousness made God, and God's demanding but liberating claim upon men and women, intensely and startlingly real. He did not intend to found a continuing church or a new religion, and he was mistaken in his expectation of an early end to ordinary human history. Nevertheless he was so transparently open to the divine presence that his life and teaching have a universal significance which can still help to guide our lives today.[24]

More specifically, and more speculatively—which is typically the tone of "An Inspiration Christology" and "Jesus and the World Religions"—Hick imagines Jesus as a person "intensely and overwhelmingly conscious of the reality of God," with such resonance to the divine life that "his hands could heal the sick, and the 'poor in spirit' were kindled to new life in his presence." He would have deeply challenged all who met him with the "absolute claim of God" on their lives and inspired "a dynamic joy, a breakthrough into a new and better quality of existence, in harmony with the divine life." Were we in Jesus' presence, Hick thinks, "we should have felt that we were in the presence of God—not in the sense that the man Jesus literally *is* God, but in the sense that he was so totally conscious of God that we could catch something of that consciousness by spiritual contagion." Or else we might find ourselves "turning away from this challenging presence, being unable or unwilling to recognize God's call as coming to us through a wholly unpretentious working-class young man."[25] In short, we would have been arrested by the claim of God upon our lives, unable to remain indifferent or impartial, and compelled to make some response that involved the whole of our being. "For the very existence and presence of an authentic saint focuses the liberating divine claim upon others."[26]

This Jesus was not only an impressive person conveying a divine challenge, he was also a preacher and teacher who expressed his powerful experience of God in an intellectually compelling, memorable way, through parables, aphorisms, authoritative pronouncements, and an expectation of the imminent end of the age as the divine kingdom was established on earth. He was a man of action, too, in whose psychic healing activity the divine love was expressed in such a way as to reinforce his preaching and intensify the experience of being in his presence. Thus Hick envisages that "a close encounter with Jesus in first-century Palestine would be a conversion experience. . . . And it would grow into a profound sense of the sovereign goodness and love of God, relieving us of anxiety for ourselves and empowering us to love and serve others, gladly bearing witness to the divine power that had thus changed us."[27]

Continuing his suggestive reconstruction, Hick ponders the question of Jesus' self-understanding, for the Nazarene cannot have failed to notice the intensity of his consciousness of God by comparison with the faintness of this awareness in all those he met; indeed, this is the source of the authority with which he spoke. "So powerful was Jesus' awareness of the heavenly Father in comparison with the awareness of those around him, including the official religious leaders of his time, that he was aware of a unique calling and responsibility to communicate the reality of God by proclaiming the imminent coming of the divine kingdom and the insistent divine claim upon each man, woman and child."[28] Hick speculates that Jesus may have expressed his awareness of his unique position among his contemporaries "by accepting the title of Messiah or, alternatively, by applying to himself the image of the heavenly Son of Man—two categories each connoting a human being called to be God's special servant and agent on earth."[29]

In all, this is a compelling specification of the well-warranted, generalized assertion that Jesus was a religious genius inspired by his vivid awareness of the reality of God. It is a plausible historical inference from what can be supposed were the memories of Jesus that inspired parts of the second- and third-generation Christian writings that we now possess in the New Testament. It would be a mistake to suppose that it is historically secure, however, even though we can be fairly certain that some such account of Jesus is required. At every point, as Hick is completely aware, the exegetical problems passed over are enormous. Likewise, it would be a mistake to suppose that Hick's account is free of projective distortions.

But it is an account that seems significantly synchronous with what we know of other religiously impressive figures, consonant with a large part of contemporary biblical scholarship, and thus more stable than if it were merely an interpretation of the gospels unsupported by such external considerations. What is most important, this speculative reconstruction brings at least some degree of concrete intelligibility to the assertion that Jesus was inspired. It is capable of captivating the imaginations of contemporary Christians and is susceptible of presentation from Christian pulpits, and so serves at least to some extent the purposes Hick intends for it: to motivate and partially justify his Christology.

The Logic of Basing Christology on an Inspired Jesus

From some points of view, this is not a favorable result. The theologian, for instance, may wonder if Christology can proceed on the basis of historical inferences that are irreducibly speculative to a significant degree. Is the cult not undermined by this kind of indefiniteness? And is not this too weak and shifting a foundation for supporting the part of theology that is most decisively Christian? The historian may likewise wonder if historical duty has been done. How can concrete intelligibility be brought to a conception of inspiration by a partially speculative historical reconstruction, especially when the material content of what Hick supposes to be the case about Jesus is suspiciously consonant with his own cultural perspective and personal interests and thus immediately subject to the criticism that he has succumbed to the anachronistic distortion of projective wishing? And, more subtly, is the historian not going to cry foul when a Christology claims to be firmly grounded in a general way on the results of historical criticism yet simultaneously allows the specific content of this historical foundation to be determined by a series of partly speculative inferences?

We do well to ask, then, whether Hick can do any better. Hick is trying to work constructively with the problematic fact that the sources call for *some* explanation of Jesus' character and impact, even though they resist being drawn into support of any concretely detailed version. The procedure is based on a fundamental conclusion about the nature of the sources, namely, that, in spite of the problem of reconstructing details on the basis of the sources, "we do nevertheless receive, mainly from the synoptic gospels, an impression of a real person with a real message, lying behind the often conflicting indications preserved in the traditions."[30] By his own admission, therefore, Hick cannot hope to draw any more probable historical conclusions about the precise sense in which Jesus was inspired. This would require historical critical results of higher resolution than the sources can supply. Yet the general fact of this inspiration is not in doubt in the same way as are the specific details. Furthermore, thinks Hick, Christology can—and must, because it has no better option—proceed on this basis.

Far from being a problem Hick alone must face, this is the logic of the guiding principle for *any* modest Christology of the first type, and indeed any Christology that crucially depends upon the inspirational character of Jesus. Such Christologies are intimately dependent on the actual historical Jesus and the sources that afford access to him. They are not dependent upon the potential of those sources to permit detailed reconstruction, however, but only on the refusal of the sources to allow any interpretation of Jesus that fails to explain his tremendous impact with close reference to the power and inspiration of his character. We have seen that this was Troeltsch's conviction about the theological value of the New Testament sources at the beginning of the twentieth century, following Ritschl's brilliant intuitive grasp of the same point, and it is as sound today as it was then.

No Christology has a stronger connection to history than a modest Christology of the first type. Absolutist Christologies and incarnational modest Christologies both derive some support from speculative metaphysics, the philosophy of history, or some other source, which perceptibly reduces reliance on the historical sources for Jesus' life. Modest Christologies such as Hick's and Troeltsch's have no recourse. They have the most to gain by the discovery of hitherto unknown texts and archeological sites, as well as the most to lose. They are Christologies that have no good reply to the thought experiment of the time-machine historian who transcends the problem of the sources only to discover that Jesus was a sociopath whose fame was due solely to historical fortune. Under such circumstances these Christologies would almost instantly collapse, such is the strength of their dependence on history—which is not to say that the worship of Christ would instantly collapse. Other types of Christology under the same circumstances, being more theoretically flexible, would still have a chance—albeit a slim one—to parse the new historical evidence differently but still consistently with their guiding metaphysical convictions. They might then survive. Hick's Christology could not.

This degree of dependence upon history can be regarded as a weakness or a strength. It is a weakness if theoretical resilience and unbroken support for the cult and its self-understanding are prized highest. It is a strength if the concrete intelligibility of theological assertions—an advantage for reasons of both the theoretical and the cultic variety—is deemed the leading concern.

In all of these considerations, then, we are brought to an important conclusion. Hick is effectively throwing down the gauntlet to two common Christological approaches. On the one hand, there are Christologies that seek to establish a more embellished historical critical foundation for Christological reflection, such as Schillebeeckx's, Küng's, Moltmann's and Pannenberg's.[31] Such Christologies are in violation of a basic historical result, namely, that the sources do not permit results of the fine resolution being sought. On the other hand, there are Christologies that ground the definiteness of Christological assertions in spheres other than history and yet still intend to take Jesus of Nazareth as somehow referred to by whatever Christological assertions are advanced. In both of these cases, Hick implicitly urges greater historical realism. If Christology has to do with Jesus of Nazareth, then it is committed to the adventures of history, no matter how uncertain they be.

The Viability of Hick's Christology

One final crucial question needs to be pressed on the logic of Hick's Christology and so on the logic of the first type of modest Christology. How can tying Christology to a historical interpretation of "Jesus as inspired," whose specific content can be established only by speculative historical inference within rather broad historical limits, guided only by analogy with other religiously exceptional figures, be *beneficial* for Christology? Does this not signal rather the doom of Christology, so long as it is construed as having to maintain dependence upon history in the way that Hick thinks is required? After all, is it not intellectually evasive to claim a historical basis for Christology that, given the nature of the available sources, is *necessarily speculative*? Would it not be clearer to abandon Hick's conception of the historical reference of Christology, hypothesizing instead that Christological assertions refer not to the historical Jesus but to a supra-historical Christ? After all, we have more direct historical access to early understandings of this Christ, since the foundational Christian documents testify directly to this Christ. Moreover, it is this supra-historical Christ (in some sense) that is arguably the referent of statements describing contemporary Christian experience of "Jesus Christ." Interpreting the Christological assertions of the early Christian sources, as well as those of every era, as referring to a supra-historical Christ is a positive asset when trying to warrant the claim of continuity between the early Christian reception of Jesus Christ and our own reception today. Rudolf Bultmann was fully aware of this, and it is also systematically exploited as an asset by John Macquarrie through his consistent orientation to "the Christ event" in *Jesus Christ in Modern Thought*.

Hick does not take up this question directly, but the question needs to be pressed anyway. We saw when we examined Troeltsch's reflections on the many Christs of Christian faith that Troeltsch rightly regarded the conception of a supra-historical Christ as intolerably vague. In trying to specify what is meant by this supra-historical Christ, it obviously is necessary to register connections of some kind both to Jesus of Nazareth and to the multiplicity of readings of this Christ evident throughout the richly diverse history of Christian worship and piety, as well as in historical critical reconstructions of the life of Jesus. Troeltsch was never satisfied with his flirtations with Christ mysticism as a way of securing continuity between Jesus of Nazareth and the many Christs. This is one indication of its highly problematic character. Another indication is that this is simply not a popular topic for Christological reflection in the contemporary period. In any event, it presents a telling objection to any attempt to take the supra-historical Christ—however this is understood—as the primary referent of Christological assertions. This approach would invite not only historical but also sociological and psychological unrealism. The reference of Christological statements must include Jesus of Nazareth to avoid this kind of unchecked fantasy. To say "Jesus Christ is Lord" or "Jesus Christ is risen" may not be to speak *only* of Jesus of Nazareth, but these statements cannot be made without some reference to that man, no matter how difficult the process of understanding him is.

Thus Christology is inevitably involved in historical research. Hick's strategy is to begin with the historical Jesus and to worry about theological interpretation later. The precedent for his procedure is the obvious one that the actual Jesus was *encountered* and not the product of speculation. To be sure, his followers and detractors alike brought to their encounters with Jesus certain preunderstandings. But the concreteness of a person is never exhaustively captured in general, preexistent categories, and the apparent category-breaking impressiveness of people's encounters with Jesus underlines this. So Hick places consideration of the actual earthly Jesus at the head of his Christological agenda, making it the primary principle for the positive development of his modest Christology. If the sources make such a venture problematic, then so be it. It is best to be methodologically clear about the inevitability of dependence of Christology on history and respectful of the limitations of the sources.

The Third Step: Jesus' Inspiration as Divine Love Incarnate

Incarnate Divine Love

On the basis of his partially speculative historical reconstruction of Jesus as inspired, Hick embarks on the third stage of his Christological project: the interpretation of this Jesus in a manner at least partly continuous with the Christological assertions of the Christian churches. This leads to the second positive principle for the development of Hick's modest Christology: the significance of the symbol of Jesus Christ derives in the first instance from the significance of Jesus as a person imbued with the divine spirit to an extraordinary degree, though not in principle uniquely. "The basic thought," writes Hick, "is that to speak of God's love becoming incarnate is to speak of men and women in whose lives God's inspiration, or grace, is effectively at work so that they have become instruments of the divine purpose on earth. . . . Incarnation in this sense has occurred and is occurring in many different ways and degrees in many different persons."[32]

This is probably the weakest possible sense in which the word *incarnation* can be used without being disingenuous. Hick does not speak of "God incarnate" but of "God's love becoming incarnate." He does not speak of "God's presence" but of "God's inspiration." He does not speak of "God's inspiration" in this sense as unique or even rare, but as incarnate "in many different ways and degrees in many different persons." It seems, then, that incarnation is a common, perhaps even a familiar, occurrence. Yet Hick maintains a distinction between incarnation in his special sense and merely being inspired or talented or good in the way we usually understand these human characteristics. He speaks of "God's inspiration" as an active principle, for it is "effectively at work" and is instrumental in conforming earthly events to "the divine purpose."

This leaves open many questions. Foremost among these is whether the idea of a person being specially imbued by the divine spirit is itself a mythological or metaphorical conception with no specific metaphysical content, as Hick takes the literal interpretation of incarnation in the usual sense to be. Is the attribution of intentionality to the divine inspiration that led Jesus meant by Hick to be literal? Or is it merely a figure of speech? Hick does not clarify this point. To see the importance of this question, consider the consequences of regarding this principle of divine love as figuratively "active" in and through many humans, through whose lesser love the divine love is at work in the world. This would be analogous to a generation of young basketball players buying sneakers endorsed by a basketball superstar because they are inspired by him, which purchases enhance the superstar's reputation (among other things). In this case, there is no metaphysically distinct transfer or connection of inspiration between superstar and fan; the superstar could, for example, be quite cynical about the whole marketing process.

If Hick were to resolve the ambiguity of his position along this line, then the language of "divine love incarnate" would appear to be arbitrary and optional, since it would be a common occurrence, familiar in a first-hand way to most humans, albeit to a lesser degree in most cases than was presumably the case with Jesus. And if Hick wishes to postulate a more metaphysically definite connection between divine and human love, then he would seem to be committed to the paradoxical position of denying (literal) metaphysical, physical, or psychological incarnation at the same time as asserting a spectacular kind of (literal) "incarnate love" that seems itself to beg for another principle of explanation. In this way, the just-dismissed "God incarnate" is readmitted subtly as the reason why "incarnate divine love" can be so unusual and disclosive of God in the case of Jesus. Disappointingly, even the more extended treatment in *The Metaphor of God Incarnate* does not resolve this ambiguity in decisive fashion. However, while this is a kind of theological failure, it is important to note that it is not the kind of problem that adds credence to the absolutist Christologies against which Hick rails so energetically. Hick's arguments against the absolutist principle are sound; it is only his argument against the intelligibility of metaphysical incarnation that is being challenged here. This problem in Hick's position is thus a consideration that bears on the decision between the inspirational and incarnational kinds of modest Christology.

Hick's Religious Anthropology

While the question about how to interpret the inspiration explanation of Jesus' efficacy is never resolved clearly in Hick's writings on Christology to date, a few remarks about his anthropology may help to place his discussion of inspiration and incarnate divine love into a fruitful perspective.

We have seen that, in Hick's view, all of the great founding figures of the world's religious traditions, not to mention prophets, shamans, and mystics, are indwelt by the divine spirit—the "absolutely Real," as he calls it—in a more or less distinctive way. Orientation to this ultimate Reality, which spiritually imbues many people to various degrees, results in an especially strong consciousness of the Real, a compelling spiritual character, and also in many cases an irrepressible drive to work for the realization in societies of the Real and the personal liberation and social harmony and justice associated with it. But this pattern of human existence is not different in kind from the way all humans are. For all human beings are potentially oriented to ultimate Reality, which they encounter in the midst especially of their own moral freedom and religious experience.

Hick's transcendental anthropology is rather muted, compared to Rahner's or Tillich's, but it exists in his thought nonetheless and is pressed into service in two ways. On the one hand, it lies at the heart of his interpretation of religion. It is the basis for Hick's contention that orientation to the Real is an aspect of almost every religious tradition. It is decidedly not the essential heart of religion, as he is at some pains to point out at the beginning of *An Interpretation of Religion*, and it is also conceived in fundamentally different, perhaps incompatible ways.[33] But it is an undeniably common feature in religious experiences and traditions and needs to be explained. On the other hand, it is the key, thinks Hick, to understanding Jesus' distinctive significance for Christianity and his commonality with other great religious figures. Thus it provides interpretive clues to the meaning of his inspiration Christology.

Hick follows Kant's theory of reality as not perceived, experienced, or thought about apart from being "filtered" by the human perceptive apparatus and the categories of the understanding. Hick, however, like most advocates of transcendental anthropology, modifies Kant's scheme to allow for the possibility that the Real (the absolute, or God) is also experienced in the same mediated way:

> The Real is experienced by human beings, but experienced in a manner analogous to that in which, according to Kant, we experience the world: namely by informational input from external reality being interpreted by the mind in terms of its own categorial scheme and thus coming to consciousness as meaningful phenomenal experience. All that we are entitled to say about the noumenal source of this information is that it is the reality whose influence produces, in collaboration with the human mind, the phenomenal world of our experience.[34]

This filtering process takes place through the medium of Kant's categories of the understanding in relation to perceiving the physical world. Hick argues that the categories relevant to "religious experience are not universal and invariable but are on the contrary culture-relative. It is possible to live without employing them; and when they are employed they tend to change and develop through time as different historical influences affect the development of human consciousness."[35]

Hick regards this as a consistent extension of Kant's theory of the categories of the understanding. He does not attempt to rebut Kant's argument in *Critique of Pure Reason* that the categories of the understanding are invariable and limited precisely to those treated there. Hick appears to believe that Kant did not admit or was not concerned to explain specifically religious experience and that this oversight is the only reason why Kant could have thought his categories limited to twelve and culturally invariable. From this analysis it follows for Hick that humans can respond to their experience of the absolutely Real and, when they do so, they will necessarily do so within the scope of the particular categories made available to them by their cultural and religious embeddedness.

This anthropology makes possible the conception of a person who is exceptionally aware of the absolutely Real, we might suppose, even as some people are exceptionally sensitive in other realms of human experience. Religious genius is not an unfamiliar kind of giftedness, parallel in many ways to intellectual or artistic genius. Moreover, a person religiously gifted in this way can intensify that sensitivity by taking it with profound seriousness, to the point that being in harmony with experience of God becomes the overriding goal of life. In that exceptionally responsive life, the absolutely Real, being the source of human love, would be expressed as loving action, and being the source of human wisdom, as profound insight. Such is the case with every religious genius, according to Hick, and he believes it makes sense to suppose that this was the case with Jesus.

Obviously this kind of approach to Christology is consonant with a pluralistic interpretation of the diversity of religious traditions, for it offers a way of thinking about Jesus as related to an absolute Reality that underlies all religious experiences and traditions, without involving exclusive elements in that conception. At the same time, it presents the possibility of speaking literally of a person with an exceptionally strong sensitivity to the absolutely Real, on which basis *metaphorical* language about "incarnate divine love" is applicable. It does not, however, provide any basis for interpreting "incarnate divine love"—much less "God incarnate"—in a structured, metaphysical sense.

The Contrast with Absolutist Inspiration Christologies

Inspiration Christology—sometimes occurring under the name of *pneumatological* or *spirit* Christology—has not been an uncommon approach in modern Christian theology, owing to its explicit and varied exploration in a series of Christologies, beginning in the modern period most famously with Schleiermacher, and extending into the last half of the twentieth century with the Christologies of D. M. Baillie and Geoffrey Lampe.[36] Hick plausibly suggests that others have pursued the same theme in a less explicit way, listing Küng, Schillebeeckx, and Rahner.[37] An inspiration or spirit Christology is a natural option for Christologies conforming to an anthropological schema, be they absolutist or modest, since the idea of being specially imbued with the divine spirit, if it makes sense at all, does not require making an anthropological exception of those who are so imbued, such as Jesus.

The fact that Baillie's and Lampe's inspiration Christologies—two of the clearest examples—are absolutist calls for some explanation, however. Hick somehow generates a modest Christology from roughly the same conceptual approach to Christology according to which Baillie and Lampe discovered a Jesus who was uniquely inspired, and decisively, finally significant for human salvation and the revelation of God. Hick's explanation of this anomaly is the correct one: Baillie and Lampe were simply methodologically inconsistent.[38] On an inspiration Christology, the finality and

uniqueness of Jesus Christ cannot be deduced from a preexistent conception of incarnation; it must emerge from the historical study of Jesus as inspired. But the field of history does not admit of the conclusions about
uniqueness and supremacy that they drew; rather it allows only comparative investigations to settle such questions, assuming even then that such
comparisons are meaningful.

> Whether [incarnation in this sense] happened more fully in the case of
> Jesus than in that of any other human being, or even perhaps absolutely
> in Jesus, cannot properly be settled a priori (though that seems to be
> how Baillie and Lampe settled it) but only on the basis of historical infor-
> mation. This means in practice that it cannot be definitively settled, for
> we lack the kind of evidence, touching every moment and aspect of
> Jesus' inner and outer life, that could entitle one to make such a judg-
> ment.[39]

In short, Baillie and Lampe allowed their bias toward an absolutist Christology to determine the results of the historical study, to the point of fla-
grantly transgressing the limits of what is possible within historical
inquiry.

In the case of Rahner, with whom Hick does not deal in detail, we
have the same absolutist conclusion as Baillie and Lampe but in a methodologically consistent fashion. For although Rahner's Christology is an inspiration Christology, the result about Jesus' decisive uniqueness derives
not from historical inquiry but rather from his Christocentric philosophy
of history. Thus Rahner's method is a hybrid of the historical and metaphysical from the beginning, whereas Hick's method emphasizes historical investigation, and so is narrower in scope and less audacious. The
difference between absolutist and modest inspiration Christologies can be
put in this way: an inspiration Christology whose theological interpretation remains maximally tied to the results of empirical history rules out by
definition the possibility of an absolutist interpretation of Jesus' inspiration. This is because assertions of uniqueness and finality, to be explicable
at all, must be principled, by appeal to an understanding of the world, of
history, of revelation, of what is necessary for salvation, or to some other
guiding principle capable of introducing the absolute into the realm of
contingencies that is history.

John Cobb: The Logic of Modest Incarnational Christologies

By way of introduction to Cobb's incarnational modest Christology, some general remarks are in order. These remarks bear on the logic of incarnational modest Christologies and illuminate the relation between the inspirational and incarnational types of modest Christology.

Theological Affirmation of Incarnation Must Be Principled

The second type of modest Christology begins from a premise diametrically opposed to the one defining the first type, namely, that "this human being is God incarnate" is an intelligible proposition when it is construed literally in the context of some metaphysical scheme and true in the case of Jesus and possibly others. Hick argues the opposite, as we have seen, and is able to make sense of the idea of incarnation only when it is interpreted as a metaphor for describing the significance for us of a person inspired in the way that Jesus was, an encounter with whom is an experience of ultimate value and challenge for us.

However, affirming the intelligibility of the incarnation of the divine in a human life, in something like the way this was done in the doctrine of the hypostatic union, does not entail affirming the uniqueness of such an event. Other principles would have to be invoked to reach this conclusion. For example, if the argument of Anselm's *Cur Deus Homo?* were sound, an atonement by a single God-human would be required for human salvation, and a second God-human would be superfluous for salvation and so incomprehensible. Or if Hegel's philosophy of history, as appropriated by Rahner, were correct, a God-human would be the center of the entire flow of history of the cosmos. Or if Brian Hebblethwaite were right, then the Christian idea of God as personal can be maintained only in the presence of a *unique* incarnation; nonuniqueness of incarnation compromises the intimate, singular personalness of God.

However, if no such uniqueness principles are invoked, then the metaphysical category of "God-humanhood" might conceivably be full of exemplars, or perhaps not exemplified at all, remaining a mere possibility. Experience of or testimony to a person of whom it might be said, "this is a God-human" would be a matter for public scrutiny and historical examination. The criteria and warrants for admission to such a category might be drawn differently by different people or within different traditions, and changing historical results might cast a hypothetical candidate in more or less favorable light for inclusion. In all, identifying a "God-human" would necessarily be a contingent, relativized, communal process of interpretation within the sphere of history. This can be expressed by saying that it is a matter of historical judgment.

Thus it is that Christologies affirming a literal metaphysical incarnation can be modest. What is more interesting, this is the reason that Christologies affirming a literal metaphysical incarnation and prescinding from the invocation of uniqueness principles *must* be modest. Even if it be thought that, as a matter of contingent fact, there had been only one instantiation of God-humanhood in human history, the absolutist principle rationally cannot be secured unless some principle is invoked to cover our ignorance of vast stretches of space and past time, our lack of detailed knowledge about what we think we *do* know, and the contingencies of the future. The case for modest Christologies turns on a series of arguments to the effect that there are no good reasons for asserting such uniqueness principles and that there are a number of compelling reasons not to assert them.

Two Ways of Affirming Literal Metaphysical Incarnation Modestly

Modest incarnational Christologies proceed differently depending on how the problems such a Christology is to solve are conceived. The most common arena at present for exploring such Christologies is, naturally enough, interreligious dialogue. We may proceed by imagining how Christians are to do theological justice to their respect for and appreciation of the fact that vast numbers of people find ultimate reality intimately tied to and expressed in the image of the Buddha. How are Christians to understand the man, Gautama of the Sakyas, of whom it is said, "He is the Buddha"? There are at least two major options, whose implications favor quite different incarnational modest Christologies.

First, Gautama may be thought potentially to be a candidate for description under the Christian category of God-humanhood, perhaps on the basis that the earthly Buddhas sometimes have been described as incarnations of the *sambhogakaya*, or transcendent Buddhas, which themselves are all one in the *dharmakaya*, which is Absolute Reality.[40] Then the Greek philosophical model for incarnation can be thought of as directly relevant for understanding Gautama, even as it has been fruitful for understanding Jesus. The principle of incarnation, often described in Christianity as the divine Logos, is thought of as expressed in different ways in Jesus and Gautama. This separation of the classically welded principle and instantiation of incarnation helpfully resolves a major crisis for Christian theology. A similar move may be made in relation to other world religions, though it may not be in a human life so much as in a revelatory history or sacred writings that the divine Logos reveals itself. Obviously, this abrogates the absolutist principle while retaining the idea of incarnation. This type of modest Christology appears in Raimon Pannikar, Stanley Samartha, and others engaged in interreligious dialogue.[41]

Second, the religious traditions of humanity might be thought of as too individual, and translation between them too difficult, to justify finding a general, cross-cultural category such as God-humanhood that applies in the cases of both Jesus and Gautama. This is the view of John Cobb, among others. "What is supremely important to the Buddhist is not what appears supremely important to the Christian. 'Christ' and 'Buddha' do not name the same reality. Christians must come to understand Christ in a world in which they deeply appreciate and respect those who do not find Christ to be what is supremely important to them."[42]

This frank admission of profound interreligious difference is invoked by Cobb to prevent the theologian from hastily subsuming the religious mystery of any religion into the conceptual comprehension of Christianity. It is not that translation and understanding are impossible, nor that adjustments and subsumptions can never be the result of understanding. It is rather a matter of giving due consideration to the rich complexity and internal variegation of religious traditions. The parallel between Buddhism and Christianity noted above is valid, but it is far from being an adequate basis for proclaiming a unifying theory of religious truth that comprehends Buddhism and Christianity in one sweeping glance. Such comprehension is worked out in the same way and on the same time scale as traditions themselves evolve, for which process the infinitely diverse and intricate engagements and abandonments of history are the steps along the way. The starting point, according to Cobb, must be to confess openly the differences as they appear.

But how does this effort to take religious pluralism more seriously lead to a Christology that actually answers to the problems raised by pluralism? Does it not lead simply to affirming whatever has been said about Jesus and reaffirming this as a kind of mantric guide for Christianity as it wends its way through the historical process of interaction with the religious traditions of the world? Something like this appears to be Wolfhart Pannenberg's approach, for his tentativity in principle with regard to doctrinal formulations does not find expression in the *content* of the doctrines themselves, remaining something like an external methodological conditioning factor, almost with the quality of an afterthought in appearance (though not, we are led to hope, in reality). By contrast, Cobb correctly believes that the methodological conviction about the experimental nature of Christian doctrine—which he shares with Pannenberg—ought to lead to reformulations in Christological doctrines themselves. In *Christ in a Pluralistic Age* Cobb argues that "when Christ becomes a principle of closedness, exclusiveness, and limitation, he ceases to be what is most important for the Christian and the appropriate expression of the efficacy of Jesus."[43] Thus Cobb attempts to present a Christology that could do justice both to the radical differences between religious traditions and the manner by which these traditions are slowly transformed by interacting with each other. Christ is identified as the principle of this creative transformation and of every kind of creative transformation, and thus Christology is presented as authorizing and even propelling Christianity into the process of creative transformation through interaction with other religious traditions.

The similarity between these two varieties of modest incarnational Christologies—represented by Pannikar and Samartha, on one side, and Cobb, on the other—should not be overlooked in drawing out their differences. They both adopt the strategy of understanding incarnation as the fusion of the concrete life of Jesus with a principle of incarnation that is applicable and equally active beyond the limits of Christianity. In Pannikar's case, this wider applicability is understood primarily in terms of its historical manifestation in human religious traditions of all kinds. In Cobb's case, it is interpreted in a highly general way as a metaphysical principle of creative transformation, which obviously extends to every aspect of human life and of the cosmos and not just to the development and interaction of religious traditions.

The First Step: Christ as Principle of Creative Transformation

The Obscuring of Christ in the Modern World

Cobb begins his argument with the familiar observation that the profane, pluralistic consciousness of the modern West has obscured Christ, rendering incoherent the Christ images familiar from the Christian tradition.[44] On the one hand, the profane consciousness drove Christ out of the world and into the shrinking circle of the Christian churches. To this, following many Protestant theologians of the twentieth century, Cobb responds that Christ is also found in much that is important to the secular world, after all. On the other hand, the pluralistic consciousness undermines the plausibility of traditionally absolute claims about Christ's significance. Cobb's response here is to embrace a radical pluralism at the same time as saying that Christ stands for the principle of openness and honest love of understanding within which the fact of plural centers of meaning does not become destructive.

This Christian response to pluralism, as we have already noted, involves rejecting the temptation to affirm that "Christ" names that which is of supreme importance to Christians, to Buddhists, and to the adherents of every religious tradition, on the grounds that it is unrealistic. Cobb's view of Christ also requires rejecting that tendency of Christians to close themselves off from the full richness of meaning in, for example, Buddhism, as if the fact that Christ and Buddha name different realities implied that they were not also individually open, inclusive, and universal in intent. Furthermore, since the name *Christ* has dubious status in the secularized modern context, Cobb argues for the use of whatever terminology successfully communicates with those to whom Christians address themselves. This may involve using philosophical concepts or generalized talk of ultimate reality. It may even require surrendering language with transcendent elements. But Cobb believes his primary task is to reconstruct the image of Christ so that the word *Christ* can again be used, at least for theological purposes, in a way that does justice to the power that has always been possessed by the reality to which the word refers.

Cobb's strategy is first to define a conceptually robust understanding of Christ as the principle of creative transformation and to defend the hypothesis that there is a distinctive way of being consisting in the literal, full, metaphysical incarnation of this principle as the Logos in a human life, which is rightly called "Christ." The second step is to argue that the historical Jesus instantiates that structure of existence, though it is probably not the kind of possibility that could have been imagined until it had actually been realized. Cobb goes on to identify Jesus the Christ as expressing the hope for transformation in the future. This interesting dimension of his argument need not concern us here.

Christ as Creative Transformation

Cobb finds an enlightening parallel between the history of art, as analyzed by André Malraux, and the history of Christian reflection on Jesus Christ. In both cases, the image of Christ passed from being well defined, though repeatedly transformed under the influence of changing historical circumstances, to being actually absent. In modern art the Christ image does not usually appear in concrete form. And in modern theology, Christ has been obscured in the senses just summarized. But the principle of continuity and transformation of styles woven through the long history of Christ images in art continues, according to Malraux, and is best understood as being that for which the long succession of Christ images stands. Cobb argues for the same conclusion in Christology: "The thesis is that Christ names the creative transformation of theology by objective study which has broken the correlation of faith and the sacred and made pluralism possible."[45]

Cobb is aware of how ironic it is to name as Christ that very drive toward pluralism and open-endedness that so often has been resisted in the name of faithfulness to Christ understood as divine reality, when this is assumed to be sacred, transcendent, and unchanging. Thus Cobb is fully engaged in revising traditional Christology even as he seeks to interpret Jesus as the incarnate Logos. The interpretation of Christ as the power of creative transformation in theology is traced through a number of changes in the twentieth century, beginning with Harnack's use of Christ as an honorific title for the historian's Jesus, through Barth's unrelenting identification of Christ with God, and Bonhoeffer's view of Christ incarnate in the being of Jesus as the ground of hope for humanity, to liberation theologies of many kinds. Though it is tempting to identify Christ exhaustively with the power of transformation in societies and human lives, Cobb points to what he takes to be a more profound truth, namely, that all of these theological transformations attest to Christ as the power of creative transformation of human imagination, in which "Christ breaks the relation to himself as objectified figure and becomes the principle of liberation at work in theology itself."[46] This process of creative transformation is especially evident in the impact on Christian theology of the study of other religions. This makes inescapable the conclusion—if it were not already obvious through the fact of multiplication of centers of meaning in a secular culture—that theology serves Christ "by allowing itself to be creatively transformed by those disciplines which relativize and desacralize every form in which Christ has previously been known."[47]

Christ as Logos Incarnate

It is arguable that anything as abstract as a principle of creative transformation in theology and art cannot be identified either with the man Jesus or with the traditional interpretation of this man as the Logos incarnate. Thus Cobb is faced with the challenge of relating the three realities named "Christ," Logos," and "Jesus." Cobb begins by speaking of Christ as an image that refers beyond its conceptual content to reality. Images "have as their referents vast and changing clusters of meanings that unite entities and concepts."[48] "Christ" names an image even as the richest words of all religious, cultural, and political traditions are images. Christ as an image in this sense refers to Jesus, to the ever-widening historical sphere of influence rippling out from him, to a movement of the transcendent into history, to a rich series of interpretations of Jesus Christ in the cultic and theological life of Christianity, and to a yearning for consummation of the ambiguities and frustrations of historical life. Without denying any of this rich field of reference, Cobb proposes to make the case that the "unity of entity and concept that 'Christ' names is creative transformation."[49]

Creative transformation so far in the argument has been identified only in the history of art and theology. Cobb invokes process metaphysics to argue that creative transformation is ubiquitous. Whitehead's understanding of the initial aim in every actual occasion is pointed to as the source of potential novelty in every moment and situation, and the ground of the drive toward discovering and creating the new in human affairs. Creative transformation therefore lies at the heart of reality and is most profoundly expressed in the striving of reality to produce order and beauty. The connection with the understanding of Logos as "the cosmic principle of order, the ground of meaning, and the source of purpose"[50] is unmistakable.

The ontological transcendence of the Logos is evident in the transcendent dimension of every experience of creative transformation in life. In Whiteheadian language, the Logos is the harmonized envisagement of possibilities that defines the Primordial Nature of God. Cobb concludes that creative transformation, as the urge toward the new that is active in all of reality, is both *transcendent* as an expression of the Logos, and *immanent* as the initial aim of each moment in the ongoing process of actualization. This, says Cobb, is the meaning of incarnation. "Christ is thus the immanence or incarnation of the Logos in the world of living things and especially of human beings."[51] The implication is that "God as Logos is effectively, if unconsciously, present and felt in all events. The Logos is truly incarnate in the world. Christ is a reality in the world."[52] This unthematized experience of God as Logos exists everywhere and is active independently of our recognition of its reality. " 'Christ' is not the name simply of Jesus or of God. Yet 'Christ' is not a figment of imagination."[53]

The Second Step: Identification of Jesus as Christ

Moving beyond an Inspiration Explanation of Jesus' Efficacy

This seems to be an ideal basis for an inspiration Christology, in which incarnation is construed not as a special possibility realized in the case of Jesus Christ, but (with Cobb) in a highly general way as the immanence of the transcendent Logos in all of creation. The historical evidence about Jesus could be accounted for by supposing that Jesus was a person with an exceptionally clear and powerful awareness of the divine Logos. He would be thought of as gifted in the same way that other great religious geniuses are, and he would be thought of as continuously related to all of humanity who, to various degrees, are responsive to the urge of the divine Logos in their lives and in the world. Being amenable in this way to an inspiration Christology, Cobb's argument to this point does not support an incarnational Christology in the strong sense needed to speak literally of Jesus Christ as "God incarnate." In fact, this is exactly the kind of construction that we saw was missing from Hick's account, and without which his talk of (literal) incarnate divine love seemed to undermine his rejection of (literal) divine incarnation.

Cobb, however, wishes to go further than this. So, as the second step in constructing his modest Christology, he examines the relationship between what we know of the man, Jesus, and what we know of Christ, the principle of creative transformation in life. Cobb readily admits that the interpretation of Jesus as Christ is a matter of historical judgment. Like Hick, he recognizes that most of what we know about Jesus is about his influence. And, again like Hick, he argues that this influence is so significant as to demand an explanation. Unlike Hick, however, Cobb thinks that the inspiration explanation does justice neither to Jesus' efficaciousness— though he gives no adequately worked out reasons for this opinion—nor to the authoritativeness and certainty of Jesus' teaching. Thus Cobb is led to seek a better account of Jesus' person than can be provided by an inspiration Christology.

Against Reductionist Explanations of Jesus' Efficacy

There is no need here to rehearse Cobb's marshaling of such knowledge as we have of Jesus' influence on his followers and of his life and activity. Cobb respects the limits of the sources for the most part, and Hick would be in substantial agreement with Cobb's historical summary. We may judge Cobb to overestimate the confidence with which we are justified in attributing forceful authority and unwavering certainty of purpose to Jesus, however. Cobb deals with the evidence in favor of his position at length but without his characteristically finely tuned historical suspicion,[54] handles the counterevidence rather clumsily,[55] and never succeeds in warranting his position with the strength needed to justify his subsequent use of it. At this point, Cobb would have done well to have admitted frankly, as we saw that Hick did, that there was an irreducible element of speculative reconstruction in these inferences about Jesus' authority and certainty of vision. In fact, these unduly sanguine historical conclusions seem to be guided by what needs to be historically the case about Jesus if Cobb's interpretation of Jesus is to be correct.

Setting aside this difference in historical judgment, it is nevertheless the case that Cobb provides a different explanation for Jesus' efficaciousness than Hick. There are two reasons for this difference. First, Cobb thinks that the obvious inspiration interpretation is inadequate, from two dubious points of view. On the one hand, Cobb asserts that the inspiration explanation of Jesus necessarily leads to the collapse of the institutional church, for if Jesus was basically like other people, we would have no reason to pay attention to him.[56] But Cobb's treatment of this complex question is far too cavalier in view of the importance of this point to his argument, even though an inspiration Christology's ability to support institutional cohesion may in fact be problematic. Moreover, the relevance of this point to his case is unclear, because supporting ecclesial institutions as they currently exist cannot be assumed without further ado to be a criterion for the assessment of Christological adequacy. On the other hand, Cobb cashes out his illegitimately strong historical inference about Jesus' authority and certainty of purpose by arguing that this can be explained only along incarnational rather than inspirational lines. We will return to this point presently. In any event, the very fact that there can be such different reactions to the ability of an inspiration account of Jesus' efficacy to account for roughly the same understanding of the historical material is startling. That must be set aside as yet another example of how personal location and religious sensibilities are ineradicable elements in interpreting Jesus.

The second reason for the difference in interpretation of Jesus' efficacy is that Cobb is able to imagine a way of being human that grounds the possibility of speaking of a person being different in *kind* from other people. An account of religious genius that relies on the hypothesis of degrees of inspiration needs no such audacious metaphysical hypothesis. In fact, thinking of humanity as essentially of one kind might be thought to be favorably economical with regard to the multiplication of metaphysical entities. Cobb considers an argument appealing to this virtue specious. He takes it to be unduly swayed by the reductive impulse of modernity that tries to regard something unexplained as of the same kind as something already understood—though it is as well to note that philosophers from Aristotle to Ockham with noted sympathy for this practice of metaphysical economy were decidedly not modern. The reductionist form of explanation is extremely useful, in the natural sciences and history alike, but it has its limitations. To cite a well-known example, this reductive impulse, expressed in the historiographical principle of analogy, makes a supposed resurrection "event" transparent to, and thus uninvestigatable by, conventional historical research. Likewise, Cobb observes that a unique or even a rare instantiation of a special category of human being would be rendered invisible to reductionist ontological explanations. Reductionist forms of explanation must, therefore, be checked by awareness of their significant limitations. The possibility of an ontological category without directly or indirectly experienced instantiations cannot be ruled out in advance. The correct way to proceed in the case of humans is on a case by case basis, always ready to see an exception to extant patterns of expectation.

The very abundance of living things, together with the fact that they evolved from inanimate matter, stands as stern confirmation of the wisdom of allowing one's standard methods of explanation to be surprised by the unanticipated, the unprecedented, the unique. Life has emerged from the lifeless realm, and self-consciousness from the biological. We know that reality is astonishingly fecund under the drive of the principle of creative transformation. Can we not imagine—under the impact of a person of extraordinary religious power—a structure of existence in which the incarnation of the Logos becomes the principle of personhood as well as the initial contributing factor in every actual occasion, a form of life that is the very essence of creative transformation itself, by which transforming and healing power is set loose in the historical process in a tangible, enduring way? Cobb can, using process metaphysics.

Incarnation as a New Structure of Existence

In a vital joint of Cobb's argument, he speculates about the nature of the fullest incarnation of the Logos, saying of incarnation in general that

> the mode and function of that incarnation vary. The Logos is now more, now less determinative in the constitution of occasions. Although the Logos is never entirely absent, resistance to creative transformation can be successful. What people believe, to what they attend, and what they decide affect how the Logos is incarnate within them. Structures of existence are correlated with different roles of the Logos.
>
> To assert that the Logos was incarnate in Jesus in itself, therefore, is true but insufficient. The Logos is incarnate in all human beings and indeed in all creation, but it does not provide all with certainty of God's will or the authority of direct insight. If Jesus is a paradigm case of incarnation, and if the structure of his existence as it incarnates the Logos is

explanatory of his assurance and authority, the possibility of a distinctive mode of incarnation should be considered. In the fullest incarnation of the Logos, its presence must constitute not only a necessary aspect of existence but the self as such. Embodiment of this structure of existence explains Jesus' certainty and authority.

. . . A person may conform to a considerable degree to the possibility offered by the Logos. But the Logos is felt as a force other than the self and as acting in relation to the self within the total synthesis that is the actual experience.

Although this is the most familiar structure of existence, it is not the only possible one. . . .

In another possible structure of existence the presence of the Logos would share in constituting selfhood; that is, it would be identical with the center or principle in terms of which other elements of experience are ordered. In that structure, the appropriation of one's personal past would be just that ideal appropriation of one's personal past made possible by the lure of creative novelty that is the immanent Logos. If this occurred, the usual tension between the human aim and the ideal possibility of self-actualization that is the Logos would not occur. . . . the "I" in each moment [would be] constituted as much in the subjective reception of the lure to self-actualization that is the call and presence of the Logos as it is in continuity with the personal past. This structure of existence would be the incarnation of the Logos in the fullest meaningful sense.[57]

In the second paragraph of this quotation we may note the appearance of Cobb's second dubious reason—alluded to earlier—for rejecting inspiration explanations of Jesus. Cobb uses the one overly confident inference from his historical analysis of Jesus—Jesus' supposedly overwhelming authority and unbroken, certain awareness of the divine purpose—as a criterion for assessing the explanatory power of the inspiration theory. This particular use of a historical inference demonstrates clearly that Cobb believes it can be drawn with maximal security. But such confidence is utterly unattainable with regard to so intimate a feature of Jesus' person. To think it is attainable is as psychologically naive as it is historically unduly optimistic. Therefore Cobb's reliance on it for rejecting the inspiration explanation of Jesus' impact and efficacy is more than questionable.

Logical and historical lacunae aside, has the concept of a full and literal metaphysical incarnation of the Logos in a human life been rescued by this speculation from the obscurity that Cobb says has overcome it? While it is certainly the case that all of the problems that have plagued the classical view of incarnation under the auspices of substance metaphysics arise again in a different voice in this case, it may be that the idea has been resuscitated to a considerable extent. Certainly Marjorie Hewitt Suchocki in *God, Christ, Church* concurs with Cobb that process metaphysics makes this rescue mission possible.[58] Let us grant this for the sake of argument, however, because we must now ask about the applicability of this structure of existence to Jesus and, further, about Cobb's view of its uniqueness. As he says, interest in the theoretical possibility of the incarnational structure of existence "has been that it fits with what we know of Jesus."[59]

Jesus as Christ, the Incarnate Logos

Does this structure of existence explain what we know of Jesus? Cobb goes to great lengths to show that the hypothesis that Jesus instantiated this structure of existence has the explanatory power asked of it.[60] The answer, in view of these arguments, is surely yes. But this hypothesis may well explain far more than we are entitled to ask of it on the basis of the small amount that we actually do know about Jesus' life, teaching, and passion. The most pressing question must therefore be whether we are *justified* in invoking such an explanation for Jesus' efficacy. For Cobb the method of approach to this question must be historical. And even though we must be open to the possibility of pattern-breaking structures of existence, the inspiration explanation of Jesus' efficacy, if it cannot be shown to be inadequate, is still surely the preferred explanation. Thus we are entitled to expect that Cobb will explain clearly what are the inadequacies of the more obvious and less audacious inspiration explanation of Jesus' efficacy.

Alas, Cobb obscures his own methodology by failing to produce such an explanation. We have seen that Cobb offers two reasons, but both are highly questionable. Together they do not gain even an inch of ground against the inspiration explanation of Jesus' influence and efficacy. We are left to draw the conclusion that Cobb simply believes that the inspiration version of his position, described earlier, does not do the job and that he is willing to maintain this mere assertion against advocates of inspiration

Christologies who think it does. This is an unfortunate lapse in an otherwise impressive argument.

In fact, Cobb appears to be goaded into his argument that the full incarnation structure of existence applies to Jesus as much by his concern to conform his presentation to the traditional understanding of Jesus Christ as by historical considerations or by the failure of alternative hypothetical explanations. There are a number of signs throughout the book of this agenda, including the normative function of remarks such as "Christianity cannot be satisfied with . . . ," and unparsed appeal to the need to sustain the churches' institutional longevity by remaining consistent with the Christological formula that has worked in the past. This artifice on Cobb's part is completely unnecessary, however, for there may be excellent reasons to appeal to a long-standing tradition of interpretation, especially one that has effectively fostered institutional cohesion. The criterial function of such appeals could have been made explicit, therefore, though it is likely this would have strained Cobb's attempt to maintain an empirical approach to history, undistorted by the philosophies of history that usually are needed to make appeals to extant institutional patterns workable.

Moving on, however, and now assuming that Cobb's account of Jesus as Christ is correct, we must ask whether this kind of incarnation is unique within the historical process. Returning to methodological consistency, Cobb says: "There is no *a priori* basis for determining whether others have participated in this structure of existence. That remains an open question. Perhaps there are fleeting approximations in the lives of some Christian saints, but of this we have no adequate evidence. There might be some of whom history has left no record who was constituted much as Jesus was, but that is an idle speculation. So far as we know, Jesus is unique."[61] That the possibility of other instantiations of this structure of existence must remain an open question is a sound conclusion. It is what we would expect given the immanence of the transcendent Logos in all of reality when there is no principled reason for asserting uniqueness of incarnation (as there is, for example, in the otherwise logically parallel incarnational Christologies of Rahner or Pannenberg). That is all that is needed to see that the absolutist principle is ameliorated to the point that Cobb's is a modest Christology. However, Cobb's passing remark about having inadequate evidence for fleeting approximations in the lives of some saints is a disastrous mistake. It implies that we both need and have adequate historical evidence for attributing this structure of existence to Jesus and raises the specter of historical evidence for anything about Jesus all over again. Since Cobb does not think that we can argue from knowledge of Jesus to the assertion of full incarnation of God as Logos,[62] and since he would want to maintain the same logic and standards of evidence in every particular instance, it is safe to assume that Cobb errs here. After all, we have far more and better evidence for the Christlikeness of many of the Christian and non-Christian saints—living and even some nonliving—than we do for Jesus. Here, again, we see Cobb's partiality for supporting traditional Christian doctrine at all costs leading him into methodological inconsistency.

In spite of these problems with Cobb's argument, it is clear that he offers a robust modest Christology that is at the same time incarnational in a sense consonant with that of the classical Christological tradition. We possess in Cobb's Christology, therefore, a counterexample to the common assumption that the affirmation of Jesus as God incarnate necessarily entails affirming the absolutist principle. As a matter of fact, the two assertions customarily have been affirmed together. But when there is a fully operational commitment to the contingency of the historical process, and no principle by which the incarnation can be legitimately thought of as unique, there is no basis for maintaining the absolutist principle. Incarnation, freed in this way from the absolutist principle, once again can be affirmed without immediately bringing down upon the Christology as a whole the problems of intelligibility and plausibility that plague absolutist Christologies.

The Third Step: Affirming Christian Uniqueness

How does Cobb's modest incarnational Christology advance Christian reflection on religious pluralism? Hick's modest inspiration Christology and modified Kantian transcendental anthropology allow him to espouse a universal theory of religion in which all religions are conceived of as apprehensions of, and approaches to, the transcendent. This theory has been called a "pluralistic theology of religions," owing partly to the fact that *The Myth of Christian Uniqueness*, which Hick edited with Paul Knitter, was subtitled *Toward a Pluralistic Theology of Religions*. The contributors to that volume, in various ways—including Panikkar with his modest incarnational Christology—shared the general orientation that a "pluralistic theology of religions" is possible, either in the way that Hick thinks it is, or in a related way. In the most general terms, this view asserts that the absolutely Real, being the transcendent toward which religions are oriented, grounds the understanding and acceptance of the pluralism of religions; dialogue can thus proceed toward mutual recognition of these facts, provisionally confident that conflicts do not correspond to irrational chasms in the Real, but to culturally conditioned apprehensions of it. As such, differences can be affirmed in, through, and under the overriding celebration of a common purpose that can ground both common work toward liberation and justice, and a theology of religions. The traditional Logos Christology, elaborated along modest lines, is an effective incarnational Christological complement to this view, and Hick's inspirational Christology is similarly complementary.

Cobb's version of a modest incarnational Christology, however, is ill-suited to such an application. By itself, this diversity shows both that modest Christologies do not imply a so-called "pluralistic theology of religions" and, what is more, that there is no correlation between types of modest Christology and views on the possibility of a pluralistic theology of religions. Being clear about this point is advisable because it is in the sphere of the study of religious pluralism that much of the interest in modest Christologies is being generated at the present time. But if not a pluralistic theology of religions, what approach to religious pluralism is Cobb justified in taking from his Christological viewpoint, and why? We may approach an answer to this question by way of Cobb's argument for rejecting a pluralistic theology of religions.

Objectivist and Pragmatic Criteria for Interreligious Comparisons

The possibility of a pluralistic theology of religions is roundly attacked by Cobb and others in a collection of essays styling itself as a response to *The Myth of Christian Uniqueness*.[63] Cobb argues there that a pluralistic theology of religions requires imposing on religious traditions an objective, alien norm: the effectiveness with which they express and afford access to the ultimately Real.[64] He objects to this norm because he thinks it presupposes an inappropriately essentialist view of religion, namely, that "the several major religions are, for practical purposes, equally valid ways of embodying what religion is all about."[65] Religions are far more than just orientations to the ultimately Real, he thinks; they serve social and practical ends for which they are uniquely adapted in their various cultural contexts. And these capacities are not merely simple specifications of some essence of religion that is common to all traditions; they are irreducible differences that affect every aspect of the sense in which a tradition may be said to be religious. Surely Cobb is right about the character of religion here. But most on both "sides" of this issue explicitly deny the essentialist view of religion Cobb attacks, including—in particular and not without irony—Hick, Knitter, and Cobb.[66]

It follows that the debate for and against a pluralistic theology of religions cannot turn on the essentialist issue. Nor can it be over the inclusivist versus pluralist question for Christian theology, for here, too, there are pluralists on both sides, Hick, Knitter, and Cobb again being examples. Rather, the debate appears to hinge on the question of whether or not there are objective, theoretical criteria by which the superiority or equivalence of religious traditions can be assessed.

On this question, Cobb wishes to defend a deeper relativism than the pluralistic theology of religions can support, a relativism in which there are no objective norms external to every tradition, but each tradition is judged only by its own internal norms.

> I oppose the "pluralism" of the editors of (and some of the contributors to) *The Myth of Christian Uniqueness*, not for the sake of claiming that only in Christianity is the end of all religion realized, but for the sake of affirming a much more fundamental pluralism. Confucianism, Buddhism, Hinduism, Islam, Judaism, and Christianity, among others, are religious traditions, but they are also many other things.
> . . . The issue, in my view, is not whether they all accomplish the same goal equally well—however the goal may be defined. It is first of all whether their diverse goals are equally well-realized.[67]

We saw that Troeltsch in the *Absoluteness of Christianity* held that there are objective criteria for assessing the value of religions and contended that historical and philosophical analyses of religious traditions could by themselves establish the superiority of Christianity. Troeltsch eventually rejected this extreme form of objectivism in favor of one that closely resembles Hick's form of objectivism, which asserts that some measure of the value of a religion can be attained with reference to the clarity of its orientation to the Real, or the effectiveness with which it directs its adherents to the Real, as judged by internal norms of that religious tradition. This does not presuppose that the essence of religion is orientation to the ultimately Real—not for Hick, at least, though Troeltsch may have assumed this for a while—but only that all religions have this characteristic in one way or another. In other words, it is one of the cross-culturally applicable categories that, when specified by each religious tradition, register something of importance in that tradition.

Does the existence of such generalized, cross-culturally applicable categories constitute a metalanguage rich enough to construct a pluralistic theology of religions, in the sense of a generalized religious point of view that expresses what every religion (and religion as such) is *really* about? Some, including advocates of perennial philosophy such as Huston Smith, answer this question affirmatively, even though neither they nor anyone else in recent decades is under any illusions about the teeming diversity of intermediate purposes, activities, beliefs, and self-understandings in religious traditions.[68]

Most religion scholars answer this question negatively, however, and then it is possible to raise the question apparently at the heart of the debate over a pluralistic theology of religions: Does the existence of such generalized, cross-culturally applicable categories yield a norm for judging the value of religious traditions? Hick answers this question affirmatively, even though *An Interpretation of Religion* would seem to answer the first question negatively. In fact, Hick appears to believe that all of the major religions are roughly equally valuable relative to the cultures in which they are embedded when judged by his norm of apprehension of, and fostering of orientation toward, the ultimately Real. Knitter, too, answers the first question in the negative and the second question in the affirmative, though the norm he derives is oriented more to praxis and justice than in the case of Hick. By contrast, Cobb denies even the kind of objectivism involved in answering the second question affirmatively. It is this disagreement that seems to constitute the debate over the possibility of a theology of religions.

Even when objectivism of Hick's mild kind is denied, however, as it is in Cobb's position, there is always the possibility of defining a criterion in terms of adaptability of a tradition in the face of other traditions. This is in effect a pragmatic rule of natural selection for religious traditions that corresponds to their survival value in a competitive, religiously plural situation. This is a more or less objective but minimal norm, applicable to large parts of each religious tradition. It is a "survival-of-the-fittest" criterion[69] that measures the extent to which traditions can adapt and appropriate the insights gleaned from mutual interaction. Here are parts of Cobb's argument concerning the possibility of an objective norm for the assessment of the validity of religious traditions.

> Are we forced to choose between an essentialist view of religion, on the one hand, and conceptual relativism, on the other? I think not. The actual course of dialogue does not support either theory. . . .
>
> The problem with conceptual relativism is not that it sees a circularity between beliefs and the norms by which they are judged. This is the human condition. The weakness is that it pictures this as a static, self-enclosed system, whereas the great religious traditions can be open and dynamic. This does not justify someone claiming to stand outside all the relative positions and to be able to establish a neutral, objective norm over all. But it does mean that normative thinking within each tradition can be expanded and extended through openness to the normative thinking of others. . . .
>
> Of course, the enlarged norms . . . that result from this dialogue are not universal and objective. . . .
>
> There is one relatively objective norm that can be abstracted from this process. It is relatively objective in that it follows from features that characterize all the traditions to the extent that they acknowledge the pluralistic situation in which all are plunged today.
>
> . . . [As the great religious traditions] are in fact transformed by interaction, the norms by which they both judge themselves and others are enlarged. The universal relevance of their own insights is vindicated as other traditions acknowledge their value. The comprehensiveness and human adequacy of their traditions [are] enlarged as they assimilate the insights of others.
>
> . . . [This norm] has to do with their ability, in faithfulness to their heritage, to expand their understanding of reality and its normative implications. A tradition that cannot do this is torn between . . . unsatisfactory options in this pluralistic world. . . .
>
> It may be that judged by this norm, all the great religious traditions

are roughly equal. On the other hand, it may be that some are more favorably situated than others to benefit from the radically pluralistic situation in which we are now immersed.[70]

Setting aside Troeltsch's early and extreme view, the two other
positions mentioned may be called the "objectivist" (Hick) and the "pragmatic" (Cobb) approaches to theoretical criteria for interreligious comparisons.[71] Cobb classifies both Hick and Knitter as objectivists, which seems
to be a clean mistake with regard to Knitter, though fair with regard to
Hick.[72] Furthermore, by contrast with Hick, Cobb thinks that there is a
place for claims of uniqueness and superiority, and that questions of interreligious superiority are finally only sorted out in the historical process of
interaction.[73] It is against this background that Cobb advances his tentative claim to Christian superiority. He thinks that "Christianity is well-
equipped to move forward to the fuller universality" he believes to be
desirable and hopes "that other traditions will compete vigorously with
Christianity." However, while refraining from disparaging other traditions,
he does curiously announce his hope "that the Christian advantage in the
competition is less than I have supposed."[74]

Christology and Criteria for Religious Superiority

Unsurprisingly, Cobb makes explicit use of his modest incarnational Christology in supporting his tentative claim to Christian uniqueness and
the superiority of its historical survival value as a religious tradition. This
may seem paradoxical at first, since Cobb's Christology is developed by
arguing more or less historically for identifying Jesus of Nazareth as the instantiation or incarnation of the metaphysical principle of creative transformation. Since other such arguments for identification cannot fairly be
ruled out, it seems that other traditions could conceivably be cultural per-
mutations of the Christian religion, with the principle of creative transformation embodied within them in the same or related ways. That would
render obscure any claim to superior historical survival value. It was argued earlier that Cobb's Christology does indeed rush too cavalierly to affirming the uniqueness of Jesus Christ, in violation of the historical
method Cobb uses. The systematic structure of Cobb's Christology is
flawed accordingly, and he does not adequately ground his rejection of
objectivist criteria for interreligious comparisons.

Setting this problem aside, however, the genius of the connection drawn by Cobb from Christology to his interpretation of religious pluralism has not yet been drawn out sufficiently clearly. Cobb's argument that Jesus instantiates the principle of creative transformation implies that Christianity is specially placed to adapt effectively to a competitive religious environment, absorbing the insights of other religions while remaining true to its own tradition. That is what creative transformation *means*. The tradition of Christianity itself is here reframed around the principle of creative transformation, with the result that remaining true to Christian tradition and adapting to religious competitors are *identified*. Thus Cobb's assertion on behalf of Christianity that it is superior according to his pragmatic criterion for interreligious comparisons is firmly grounded in his Christology.

Superficially, this may seem to be rather too neat a solution of the problem. Cobb's strategy might be interpreted as mere slight of hand, moving the category of creative transformation to the heart of the Christian tradition so as to make the assertion of Christianity's superior competitive versatility true by definition. On the contrary, Cobb's identification of Jesus Christ with the principle of creative transformation is grounded in a considered judgment that Christianity really has displayed an extraordinary ability to adapt and survive and that the tradition does in fact embody this principle to an unprecedented degree in the history of religions. Whether this judgment is sound is a matter for detailed interreligious comparison; it may be that it finally proves impossible to withhold from other traditions the judgment that they are similarly adaptable, perhaps with excellence in different areas than Christianity displays. I would be inclined to this more generous judgment in regard to the large-scale religious traditions of the axial age. Moreover, the immensely complex variegation of the Christian tradition itself demands that the judgment of superiority relative to Cobb's pragmatic "survival of the fittest" norm be parsed carefully according to denominations, locations, eras, cultural settings, and so on. But these problems do not undermine the powerful connection Cobb establishes between his modest Christology and his pluralistic, pragmatic assertion of Christian superiority, so much as set the agenda for its continued investigation.

6
Modest Christological Solutions
to Internal Challenges

One of the central arguments of this book is that the contemporary crisis in Christology is multidimensional and that modest Christologies offer effective resources—indeed, are indispensable—for resolving this crisis in all of its dimensions. This chapter and the next seek to bring this developing argument to a conclusion by exhibiting a number of areas in which Christological reflection has proven to be problematic and yet has been helpfully advanced by modest Christologies.

The applicability of modest Christologies to easing Christology's crisis of plausible justification is better understood in relation to some dimensions of that crisis than others. The problem of Christology in the face of religious pluralism, for example, has been a major cause of interest in and support for modest Christologies in the last few decades. To many at work in this area of theological reflection, the idea of a modest Christology will seem familiar, even perhaps *passé*. But this is only one of a large number of problems for which modest Christologies have already proven, and promise still more to demonstrate, their worth. By seeing the effectiveness of modest Christology in relation to *all* of these problems—*all at once*, ideally—the value and power of Christological modesty, and the usefulness of using the absolutist principle to distinguish two idealized classes of Christologies, can be more fully appreciated.

The various aspects of the Christological crisis can be divided roughly into two groups. On the one hand, some aspects are *internal* to the Christian tradition of theological reflection, in the sense of being raised by the ongoing process of self-interpretation within that tradition. These are the problems of Christology's dependence on historical knowledge of the historical Jesus, the development of Christology from Christian origins to the fourth- and fifth-century ecumenical councils, and changing judgments concerning the long-standing metaphysical discussion of the possibility of the universal lavishing itself upon the particular. In each case, an aspect of the evolving tradition has made the justification of Christology problematic, and the problem must be solved by reconceiving Christology.

On the other hand, some aspects of the Christological crisis are induced in Christology by considerations *external* to the Christian theological tradition itself. These include a cluster of problems having to do with ethical responsibility (especially in relation to feminist and ecological concerns), the natural sciences (especially in relation to biology and cosmology), and religious pluralism. External challenges to the plausibility of Christological justification are addressed in the same way as internal problems: Christology has to be reformulated or reenvisaged to solve them.

The distinction is less helpful than it may appear at first glance, because the indirect cause of "internal" Christological problems is very often some "external" development, such as changing understandings of history or shifting cultural-ethical norms. In fact, in the final analysis, the distinction breaks down from both directions for the simple reason that the Christian tradition is continually taking shape within, and influencing, its contexts. Blurring the internal-external distinction is helpful for clarity of understanding, therefore, but it does not rob it of usefulness, for the most direct cause of a challenge to plausibility and intellectual viability still usually can be identified as internal or external to the tradition of theological reflection. Internal dimensions of the contemporary Christological crisis will be discussed in this chapter, followed by external aspects in the next chapter.

History: Christological Dependence on Knowledge of Jesus

Reception of Troeltsch's Solution to the Problem of Faith's Dependence on History

It was argued earlier that Troeltsch pointed the way to a more effective solution to the problem of faith's dependence on historical knowledge of Jesus. Troeltsch's realistic appraisal of the cultic life of the Christian churches allowed him both to produce a convincing explanation of the fact that the problem of faith and history *is in fact* managed effectively (so long as cult-destroying forces such as individualism can be kept at bay) and to argue for the sociological feasibility of a specific level of dependence of faith and cult on history, namely, dependence on a "reasonable outline" of Jesus' life and teaching. Greater or less than this level of dependence is unsustainable by the cult in the long term, the level of sustainability being set by a combination of what historical research actually allows in terms of reliable knowledge of Jesus, and the need of individual faith and cult alike for a "mood of factuality" in perceptions of historical research. Modest Christology is essential to the *theological viability* of this proposed solution to the problem of faith and history, because it reduces historical requirements to a manageable yet religiously significant minimum, while simultaneously tying theological assertions maximally closely yet feasibly to historical information.

Has the value of modest Christology as a solution to this aspect of the contemporary Christological crisis been recognized and developed? The answer to this question in broad strokes is bluntly negative; in fact, Troeltsch has rarely been looked upon as an interesting resource for the problem of faith's dependence on history. This odd fact is cast in an ironic light, however, by a trajectory of twentieth-century theological reflection that, more or less unwittingly, has confirmed the decisiveness of the connection between Christological modesty and the problem of faith and history. This indirect form of support for modest Christology begins with Karl Barth's *Epistle to the Romans* (1918)—intensifying the irony, since neo-orthodoxy was more or less uniformly antagonistic to Christologies such as Troeltsch's. This support appears in neo-orthodox theology in a variety of forms, as well as in the responses this theological tradition evoked in later decades. It culminates, perhaps, in Schubert Ogden's *The Point of Christology* (1982). The aim here is briefly to indicate the nature of this most unexpected and still anonymous line of support for modest Christology. If this analysis is correct, then more thorough and open attention to the potential of modest Christologies as offering a solution to the problem of faith's dependence on history is long past due.

The Ambiguous Influence of Neo-Orthodoxy

The second and greatly revised 1921 edition of Barth's commentary on Paul's letter to the Romans and Troeltsch's 1923 lecture on "The Place of Christianity among the World Religions" are poles apart theologically. In spite of their historical proximity, and their common theological ancestry in the Protestant liberalism of Ritschl, Harnack, and Herrmann, they have little in common in terms of theological theme and method, conditions for plausibility, or criteria for being *Christian* theology. Nor does either work much resemble anything that the older liberal Protestants produced. Troeltsch faulted this common heritage for its confessional habit of refusing to engage contemporary problems vital to theological plausibility and Barth for its dangerously self-satisfied, and actually insipid, character, the result of the gradual loss of Christian identity while mingling with cultural luminaries. Both criticisms appear to possess some validity, though they are never as convincing when aimed away from the caricatures of Protestant liberals and toward their actual writings.

Barth was firmly opposed to ameliorating assertions of the significance and centrality of the symbol of Jesus Christ throughout his career. Adjusting the conditions for Christological plausibility in the way that modest Christology requires was, to Barth, tantamount to surrendering the central theological pillar supporting Christian identity, and would have represented a victory for the very culture Protestantism against which he inveighed. This is the origin of Barth's considerable influence *against* the acceptance and development of modest Christologies. However, while this pattern of negative influence is historically understandable, the theological objection to modest Christologies on which it rests is superficial. This superficiality must be unmasked, for the attempt to preserve Christian truth and ecclesial identity, though noble in itself, is intellectually incoherent and ecclesially self-defeating if it refuses to allow

cultural canons of plausibility to be contributing factors to judgments of
theological adequacy, as Paul Tillich was at some pains to argue throughout his career.

Barth was aware that the most powerful and interesting theological
approaches are not classifiable under the simplistic terms of trends and
theological fads. After all, in the preface to the English edition of *Romans*,
he begged his new readers to evaluate his work as it stands and not in
terms of their preconceptions about "Barthianism."[1] But the one-sidedness
of his unstinting rejection of certain traditional tasks of theology, particularly those concerned with the *plausibility* of theological assertions, was
itself a theological fad. Barth's so-called dialectical theology was simply
never—not even at the end—dialectical enough about the polarities
within the *task* of Christian theology: it must express truly the Christian
gospel and maintain Christian identity, but it also must be believable and
warranted in a broad intersubjective context. Forsaking wide-ranging engagement with cultural norms for intelligibility is actually impossible, even
if it generates enthusiasm in the short term, because our self-interpretation
as religious creatures does not come from an insulated ecclesial ghetto,
and the sneaking suspicion that our theological discourse is massively implausible cannot be held off by rhetoric alone.

Precisely because of the brilliance and exhaustiveness of Barth's theological work, there was no reason to think that confessional theology
could be done better than Barth had done it—especially with regard to
meeting the challenge of Christological plausibility without a critical re-
trieval of broadly intersubjective standards for intellectual adequacy. It
was a kind of theological *reductio ad absurdum* of the neo-orthodox
method: in view of the unsatisfactory result, what choice was there but to
return to the difficult and dangerous challenge of explicitly incorporating
cultural insight and knowledge into norms for doctrinal soundness? Again,
this procedure is inevitable for theology. Barth had carried it on surreptitiously, invisibly adjusting the accent he brought to his treatment of Christian confessional resources in the light of the very same cultural concerns
and insights that his successors found themselves once again making explicit in their work.

Thus it was that the theological programs conceived by neo-
orthodoxy soon outgrew their womb of origin and returned to previously
marginalized theological sources and tasks to make up the lack they
sensed in the insufficiently dialectical vision of theology they had inher-

ited. In fact, the great challenge of twentieth-century Protestant theology—even after neo-orthodoxy no longer seemed a promising context within which to pursue it—has been the attempt to meet both Troeltsch's and Barth's criticisms of Protestant liberalism simultaneously. Figures such as H. Richard Niebuhr and Paul Tillich are sometimes classified as neo-orthodox because of their embrace of this challenge, but already in their thought neo-orthodoxy had been utterly transformed into a theological program of mediation that closely resembled—with unspeakable irony—that of Albrecht Ritschl and his followers. The methodological one-sidedness of neo-orthodoxy, and with it the pattern of antagonism toward modest Christologies, has messily, but thoroughly, deconstructed itself.

Its theological questionableness notwithstanding, the negative influence of neo-orthodox thought on modest Christologies was very real. There is more to Barth's influence on modest Christologies than this, however, and this "more"—which first and most lucidly appeared in *Romans*—is not negative. To understand this, we need to make use of the two distinguishable component theses of the absolutist principle. Barth never for a moment allows the significance thesis to be weakened. But his approach to the epistemology of revelation, historical criticism, and biblical interpretation set in motion one of the most interesting and important trajectories in twentieth-century Protestant theology, one that was to sponsor the amelioration of the absoluteness principle through its fact thesis. Indeed, Barth himself in *Romans* begins this weakening. How is this so?

The understanding of the knowledge of God through Jesus Christ in Barth's *Romans* implies that the particular details of Jesus' life are formally irrelevant to his role as revealer, lord, and savior. He has this role because God decreed him to have it, and nothing about his own nature might have in principle or did in fact constrain God in his designation of the man Jesus as Christ. Bluntly, Jesus could have been a maniac or deluded or a sociopath or a saint or a sage or a genius, and this would be nothing more than a specification of the context for the divine decree of Jesus as Christ. In this epistemology, the divine decree carries over every instance of human frailty and human greatness, unhindered by the foolishness of human expectations about its mighty power to establish the word of God in history. True to the lack of any sign of Pauline fascination with the life and teaching of Jesus (apart from the major salvific events), Barth affirms

Paul's vision of the unconditioned power of God: it is not Jesus' being or life-achievement that makes salvation real for those who are called; it is God, and only God. When the divine decree so dominates the specific facts of history—Barth does not misrepresent the apostle here—it is appropriate to prescind from making claims about the person of Jesus such as the fact thesis does, and to speak about Jesus at every turn only in terms of his role as the one designated by God to be Christ.

Barth's astonishingly clear-headed and consistent epistemology of revelation provoked a storm of protest upon the appearance of the first edition of *Romans* in 1918. Barth rightly defended himself in the preface to the second German edition from charges that he was imposing his theological vision on Paul's letter to the Romans.[2] In fact he had discerned with seer-like profundity Paul's meaning, even as he had claimed to have done, and he had carried this off in such a way as to make sense of the famous conundrum of Paul's near silence about Jesus' life. Barth's early theological vision was as consistent as Kierkegaard's. Both saw clearly that the person of Jesus could in no way determine or condition the act of God: this is the meaning of Kierkegaard's infinite qualitative distinction between time and eternity. "Though we once regarded Christ [from a worldly point of view (κάτα σάρκα)], we do so no longer" (II Cor. 5:16).

Barth's patience for and fascination with traditional questions of Christology increased, as indicated by the space devoted in *Church Dogmatics* to the parsing of the consequences of the divine decree for the person of Jesus Christ. However, the fundamental insight of *Romans*—the essentially reformed one that God's decree unconditionally dominates human affairs, because the divine freedom is ever the precondition and context for the possibility of human freedom—remained constant throughout his career. It sponsored interesting shifts, and sometimes remarkable innovations, at every point in Barth's treatment of the doctrinal loci of the Christian theological tradition. And it paradoxically gave impetus to modest Christologies by sponsoring a way—Paul's way—of theoretically distancing the historical person of Jesus from the claims made about his salvific and revelatory significance. At no point does Barth's writing suggest a properly modest Christology, for the significance thesis is always unconditionally affirmed, and the fact thesis also gains strength in his thought with the unfolding of *Church Dogmatics*. Nevertheless, the music of his epistemology of revelation was to reverberate throughout neo-orthodox theology, producing a number of not necessarily harmonious overtones, even as it recalled many thematic elements from the painstaking playing out of melodic options in the problem of faith and history by Barth's liberal Protestant teachers.

If Barth rightly discerned in the Apostle Paul's theology a distancing of the Christian kerygma from the details of the life of Jesus, leaving the bare fact of the divine act in history as determinative of Jesus' significance, the theology of Bultmann extends this insight in a number of ways. He insisted that the Christian kerygma begins with the proclamation of Jesus as Christ by Paul and the Apostles, not with Jesus and his message of the Kingdom of God. Bultmann prescinds from requiring the saving action of God in history to include enabling the resurrection. And he advocates an existentialist reinterpretation of the power and content of the gospel. All of these features of his thought impart additional momentum to modest Christologies, for the fact thesis is further ameliorated through their sponsorship of a "don't ask, don't tell" policy with regard to mode and character of the presence of God in the life of Jesus.

Moreover, with Bultmann's theology, we even see hints of the significance thesis beginning to be moderated as a response to the moderation of the fact thesis. To speak of Jesus as risen in the spiritual vitality of the Christian church, and existentially to remythologize traditional Christian symbols and narratives, is indirectly to imply that the significance of Jesus Christ must be understood within, and solely within, the confines of the contingent flux of the historical process—even though history was understood by Bultmann to be the locus of inexplicable encounters with transformative divine power. This limitation of interpretative possibilities of the significance of Jesus Christ unmistakably prefigures amelioration of the significance thesis, and so ultimately of the absolutist principle.

It is unsurprising that neo-orthodoxy's tolerance for weakening the fact thesis induced an eventual weakening of the significance thesis. It is precarious in the long term to insist on the absolute revelatory and salvific significance of the symbol of Jesus Christ while maintaining a diffident attitude to the question of the metaphysical basis in the life of Jesus for such bold assertions about the significance of the symbol taking him as its partial historical referent. In Barth's developing thought, the significance thesis was protected by an eventual restrengthening of the fact thesis, whereas in Bultmann's thought the significance thesis was ameliorated in response to his refusal to shore up the fact thesis. The neoorthodox Christological position as represented by Barth's *Romans* was therefore an inherently unstable compromise between Christological absolutism and Christological modesty.

Other theologians profoundly influenced by neo-orthodoxy illustrate the same dynamic connection between the fact and significance theses. Herbert Braun, H. Richard Niebuhr, and Paul Tillich are especially interesting examples for present purposes. The Christological thought of Braun and Niebuhr never appears in sufficient systematic detail in their writings to permit an unequivocal interpretation. More precisely, and much like Troeltsch, there nowhere appears what can comfortably be called a "fully formed" doctrine of the person and work of Jesus Christ. Niebuhr appears to advocate in two essays a modest incarnational Christology, consistently with his generally historicist viewpoint.[3] Braun's laboring over the problems of New Testament Christology—especially the apparently gradual increase in the loftiness of the honorific titles applied to Jesus as the tradition developed[4]—is in part an attempt to secure a more coherent picture of the significance of Jesus Christ. Braun's presentation of the changing perception of Jesus in the early development of the Christ cult checks the tendency to make hermeneutically extreme Christological assertions in our own time.

Neither Braun nor Niebuhr was able to rest content with neo-orthodoxy's affirmation of the absolute significance of the symbol of Jesus Christ (the significance thesis) because of the defective strategy used to protect this affirmation, namely, distancing assertions of absolute significance of the symbol from the historical actuality of Jesus of Nazareth. Their response was to explore theological and historical means of bringing assertions of significance into line with what can be known of Jesus of Nazareth, so that those assertions would be properly grounded and able to withstand the natural charge of irrationalism forthcoming whenever the hermeneutical basis for an assertion of absolute significance is not evident. The solutions of both Braun and Niebuhr involved implicitly weakening the strength of those absolute assertions of significance, and so here again the neo-orthodox inheritance eventually issued in unexpected (and unintended, as far as Barth was concerned) support for modest Christology.

In the case of Tillich, the fact thesis was weakened in the same way as for Barth and Bultmann, but it was simultaneously strengthened from a metaphysical direction, for Jesus is New Being appearing in history. The bare fact of this appearance is more important than ever, and more is re-

quired of it, in the sense that the presence of New Being positively requires something in the way of appropriate behavior on Jesus' part. Even
so, it is infamously difficult to specify a hypothetical historical result that
would induce Tillich to admit the falsification of the assertion that New
Being appears in the history and person of Jesus of Nazareth. Thus, the
characteristically neo-orthodox strategy of separating absolute assertions
of significance from their referent still is being exploited by Tillich.

This is not the only pertinent aspect of Tillich's system, however. His
attempt to deal seriously with the reality of salvation in other communions led to a very different conclusion about the absolute significance of
Jesus the Christ. The significance thesis is stressed in the ontological
analyses but, in the social analysis of salvation in community, the significance thesis is ameliorated, the actual significance of Jesus being interpreted as relative to the community within which he is proclaimed and
followed, and his potential significance a matter of how that spiritual community enlarges and develops within the historical process. These two aspects of Tillich's thought, with the very different attitudes they entail
toward modest Christologies, are probably irreconcilable. Here again we
see the inherent instability of the characteristically neo-orthodox weakening of the fact thesis, for it evokes a weakening of the significance thesis—
in Tillich's case, at the cost of large-scale inconsistency, though this is to
be admired rather than chided in view of the significance of the constructive contribution involved.

Schubert Ogden

With the work of Schubert Ogden, we come to one of the finest attempts
in contemporary Christology to distance the constructive account from
traditional interpretations of the historical person of Jesus, expressed in
the two-natures doctrine, as well as to free Christological assertions from
having to claim the historically unverifiable about that person. This is the
most delicate and thoughtful development of the trajectory growing out
of neo-orthodoxy that we have been tracing. But Schubert Ogden's goals
in *The Point of Christology* are to be accomplished without threatening
the claim of the decisive significance of Jesus Christ, which is the tendency we have seen in different ways in the theology of Bultmann, Braun,
Niebuhr, and Tillich.

At this point we have seen how the neo-orthodox wrangling with the fact thesis at least potentially induces changes in the significance thesis, and thus we have discerned the positive element of neo-orthodoxy's influence on modest Christology. The question remains as to the strength of this inducement: if the fact thesis is sufficiently constrained, does resisting the induced tendency to weaken or relativize the significance thesis cause systematic strains—such as unprincipled, arbitrary affirmation of the significance thesis—within the resulting Christology? Ogden offers the clearest example of sustained delimiting of the fact thesis while resisting amelioration of the significance thesis. It is interesting to inquire, therefore, whether Ogden's Christological position shows signs of such systematic stress. The presence of such signs would be confirmation that the fact thesis and the significance thesis are interdependent, in the sense that sufficient weakening of the fact thesis demands at least some weakening of the significance thesis. It would thus justify our estimate of the positive influence on modest Christology of any theological position that characteristically weakens the fact thesis.

There is no question that Ogden intends to advance the claim of the significance thesis. Consider the following passage, summarizing three chapters of analysis of the question Christology answers, the subject of Christological assertions, and the conditions of asserting a Christological predicate.

> I have argued that, because the question Christology answers is an existential-historical question [rather than an empirical-historical one], the assertion that constitutes Christology explicitly as such must be an existential-historical assertion. Specifically, it is an assertion of the meaning of Jesus for us, or, to be more precise, of the decisive significance of Jesus for human existence. Thus any appropriate Christological predication is by way of asserting, in some conceptuality and symbolism or other, that Jesus is the decisive re-presentation of God, in the sense of the one through whom the meaning of God for us, and hence the meaning of ultimate reality for us, becomes fully explicit.[5]

Since the significance of Jesus for us (humans) is *decisive*, and is a *fully explicit* re-presentation of the meaning of ultimate reality for us (humans), Ogden's Christology declares the significance thesis every bit as much as more traditional absolutist Christologies.

What then is the position of Ogden's Christology on the fact thesis?

There seems to be a question about this, since Ogden carefully distinguishes between empirical-historical and existential-historical assertions and argues that Christological assertions are of the second sort. We may ask, then, does Ogden think that Christological assertions must answer to empirical history at all? Or are they merely a matter of expressing Jesus' significance for humans, regardless of what the historical person of Jesus did and said, or whether he even existed?

Ogden asks and answers precisely this question. His first step is to arrive at a statement of the conditions that must be met in order for a Christological assertion to be made truly. We have seen already that Ogden thinks of Christological assertions as expressing that "Jesus is the decisive re-presentation of God [in which] the meaning of ultimate reality for us becomes fully explicit."

> But if this is the constant function of even the most variable Christological predicates, it is not difficult to specify the conditions that must be satisfied if any of them is to be truthfully asserted. The only necessary, and therefore, the sufficient condition of any such assertion is that the meaning of ultimate reality for us that is always already presented implicitly in our very existence be just that meaning of God for us that is re-presented explicitly through Jesus.[6]

Ogden's second step is to draw out the implication that there must be an "a priori" or "transcendental" Christology, that the salvation "represented explicitly through Jesus" is implicitly present as an existential option to every person.[7] The third step is to show that the same criterion has an empirical-historical aspect. This is necessary, thinks Ogden, because some concrete historical encounter with Jesus is necessary for affirmations of his significance to arise. To that extent, therefore, justifying the central Christological assertion—that "Jesus is the decisive re-presentation of God [in which] the meaning of ultimate reality for us becomes fully explicit"—involves appropriate, empirical-historical inquiry.[8]

What aspects of the central Christological assertion would need to answer to such empirical-historical inquiry? The references to "particular experience of Jesus" and to the fact that God "is re-presented explicitly through Jesus" appear to assume Jesus' existence, significant contacts with him, and something about him that passes beyond merely what a casual observer may have thought about him. Furthermore, if his followers are thought to be the origin of the conviction that God "is re-presented explicitly through Jesus," then this too implies something about Jesus' life and work and is not merely a side-effect of the disciples' meaning-hungry imaginations.

We must be excused, for these reasons, for expecting Ogden to conclude that his criterion for the truthfulness of Christological assertions necessarily involves some assertions—minimal ones, at least—about the historical person Jesus. It is superficially inexplicable, therefore, when Ogden concludes as follows by emphasizing how important it is "that the empirical-historical inquiry that is required to justify the credibility of Christological formulations is exactly the same as that which is required to justify their appropriateness. In the one respect, just as in the other, what is necessary is not a quest of the historical Jesus, but rather a quest of the earliest Christian witness."[9] Ogden shows how seriously he means this, when he continues in the following way:

> To assert any Christological predicate of Jesus naturally requires that the condition of truthfully asserting it of any subject must be satisfied by the particular subject Jesus. But the conclusion reached in the preceding chapter was that the Jesus who is the real subject of the Christological assertion is the Jesus attested by the early Christian witness. This means that the condition of truthfully making the assertion in any of its formulations lies not in the being of Jesus himself that we still have to infer from this witness, but rather in the meaning of Jesus for us that this witness itself already normatively represents. Consequently it is by way of empirical-historical inquiry into what is meant by Jesus in this normative witness that the condition of asserting any Christological predicate truthfully can be known to be satisfied, insofar as this can be historically known at all.[10]

But this leaves many questions unanswered. How does the plausible supposition that "the Jesus who is the real subject of the Christological assertion is the Jesus attested by the early Christian witness" neutralize the impact of such claims about the person of Jesus noted earlier? To follow Ogden's point to its logical terminus, does he really intend to allow that Christological assertions make no actual historical claims about *Jesus' existence*? And if he admits such a basic historical claim as this, is he not also presuming at the very least some other kinds of minimal facts about Jesus? Was not Jesus male, for instance? a Jew? loved and hated? followed? a teacher? *executed?*

Ogden's reticence to acknowledge the implicit presence of historical claims about the person of Jesus (as against the normative early Christian testimony about his significance) in Christological assertions is unfortunate, but not inexplicable. Ogden begins *The Point of Christology* by drawing attention to a consensus among what he calls "revisionist" Christologies, by which he means especially Christologies that require and assume achievable a quest of the historical Jesus. These revisionist Christologies were supposed to escape the problem of faith and history as this had plagued traditional Christology by using empirical-historical research as the key to a more secure basis for Christological assertions. Ogden effectively shows that the revisionist Christologies are finally subject to the same problem that the traditional Christologies are and seeks to "talk about the point of Christology without becoming involved in the problems of typical revisionist Christology."[11] The attempt to make use of the neo-orthodox trajectory we have been tracing in order to find a new solution is what makes Ogden's book so important, even though his solution remains problematic in its specifics.

However, Ogden does not need to commit himself to so extreme a view. We get a sense for a more moderate position when he says, in a different summary, that "we have established that the conditions of asserting a Christological predicate in no way require that Jesus must have perfectly actualized the possibility of authentic self-understanding."[12] The same point appeared above when Ogden asserts that the condition of truthfully making a Christological assertion "lies not in the being of Jesus in himself that we still have to infer from [the early Christian] witness." Thus we see what Ogden is trying to avoid: committing Christological assertions to making empirical-historical claims that are in principle unverifiable. But then Ogden appears to conflate two distinguishable goals: freeing Christological assertions from unverifiable dependence upon historical claims about the person of Jesus and freeing them from *all* dependence. Admittedly this distinction is a difficult one to maintain, since there is no hard and fast criterion to which we can appeal. Having no choice in the matter, however, it makes no sense to suppose that the point of Christology can be made without having to answer to any empirical-historical research about the life of Jesus. At the same time, it is pointless committing Christological assertions to answer to empirical history for claims that lie outside of the historian's competence.

In this Ogden is surely correct. The problem lies, therefore, with the extremity of the assertions of significance that are to be made about Jesus Christ. Ogden's view remains problematic because he refuses to make this accommodation. Here again, therefore, we see a manifestation of the instability of assertions about the absolute significance of Jesus Christ in the presence of attempts to distance the person of Jesus from the historical implications of those assertions. Correlatively, we see the way that this instability lends support to modest Christologies. If Troeltsch was right— and I have argued that he was—the only way to solve the problem Ogden faces is to ameliorate the absoluteness of the assertions of Jesus Christ's significance.

Winds of Change in Life-of-Jesus Research

If this argument is sound, the potential of modest Christologies for solving the long-standing problem of faith's dependence on history, while still more or less unnoticed, is considerable and deserves sustained attention. In fact, there is even some urgency about the need for such attention in view of the fact that the problem of the dependence of faith and Christology on history has been as awkward throughout the twentieth century as it had been in the nineteenth. It did not help that Troeltsch's insights into these matters were effectively swamped by the arrival of neo-orthodoxy. Evidently, the lessons of the nineteenth century have not been learned well enough.

For example, the twentieth century responded to the late nineteenth century's—and Troeltsch's—courageous grasping of the faith and history nettle by thrice repeating the psychological over-optimism of Herrmann, Kähler, and Schweitzer, first in neo-orthodox theology, then in some sorts of theological existentialism, and finally in much of so-called narrative and story theology. In each of these cases, but in different ways, the question of reliable historical information about the life and work of Jesus is partially side-stepped, and the psychological need for faith to be informed by concrete historical facts is questioned, all under the auspices of an over-optimistic appeal to the indubitability of faith through one or another form of an immediacy of encounter with Christ.

Again, the twentieth century has seen the repetition of Harnack's determined historical optimism in the constructive Christological edges of the so-called second and third quests of the historical Jesus. The second quest was characterized by a struggling confidence that the authentic sayings, parables, and actions—and so aspects of the self-understanding—of Jesus could be distinguished from nonhistorical, legendary, or mythopoetically elaborated material originating solely by virtue of the devotion and enthusiasm of early Jesus traditions. This research stimulated a number of important Christological studies. Hans Küng's extended treatment of Jesus in *On Being a Christian* and Edward Schillebeeckx's *Jesus* and *Christ* are the most important Roman Catholic examples, both products primarily of the German scholarly consensus from the second quest. Another set of examples can be found in the Latin American liberation Christologies, perhaps most prominently in Leonardo Boff's *Jesus Christ Liberator*. The confidence of Boff's historical handling of the life and teaching of Jesus is exceptionally strong, perhaps in part stimulated by the importance of such access for his powerful ethical critiques. On the Protestant side, Wolfhart Pannenberg's *Jesus—God and Man* is generally more measured in its handling of historical material, except that his positive treatment of the resurrection was as astonishing to theologically versed Protestant audiences as Schillebeeckx's cautious distancing of his account from the assumption of a bodily resurrection was to Catholics.

In different ways, then, each of these exceptional works continues Harnack's excessive optimism with regard to the sources for a life of Jesus. But even as the second quest's enthusiasm eventually gave way to a renewed recognition of historical difficulties in the sources, these theological attempts also have had to face their unjustifiable optimism with regard to the New Testament sources. Pannenberg's study is the most hardy of the group with regard to surviving this failure of warrant for optimism. This, however, is mostly because his historical audaciousness is concentrated on the resurrection; that does not make any less unduly optimistic his contention that the extant evidence warrants an explanation along the lines of a bodily resurrection.

These several parallels to Harnack's overly sanguine enthusiasm notwithstanding, most Christological construction around the edges of the research efforts of the second quest does seem to have learned something from the nineteenth century's trials. Rightly sensing the danger of extensive dependence on historical details, such construction has tended to avoid overly systematic presentations and has concentrated instead on suggestive hinting. Most contemporary theologians, therefore, remain in a once burned, twice shy mode. Noticing that the diversity of historical interpretations of Jesus is *widening* and not *narrowing*, they patiently await the passing of historical euphoria and try to keep their systematic Christological efforts as independent of controversial historical results as they possibly can, all the while sensing with Harnack and Troeltsch that some kind of substantial connection between historical research and systematic Christological assertions must be maintained if faith and cult are to remain lively. While the systematic theologians in this way look most often with jaded interest upon the work of their biblical critical colleagues, the biblical scholars rarely enter into systematic territory at all. Occasionally biblical scholars will get serious about their Christological hinting, almost daring the nervous systematicians to jump on board and commit dogmatic assertions to their historical findings. At times like that, the wisdom of history is needed to avoid repeating tired mistakes.

This is especially the case in connection with recent life-of-Jesus research in the United States, represented by Jesus scholars such as Marcus Borg, John Dominic Crossan, Richard Horsley, Burton Mack, and Elisabeth Schüssler Fiorenza.[13] We are wise to think that the enthusiasm—reminiscent of Harnack's—among biblical scholars involved in the massive and relatively well-coordinated global research efforts of the third quest is inevitably temporary, in spite of the fact that many research advances from the second quest have endured and many more from the third will also survive the decline of elation. The third quest must finally yield to the problematically elusive character of the texts, notwithstanding its interdisciplinary grounding and its sophisticated socio-historical tools. Christologies that build too closely upon the results of the third quest naturally will be frustrated by this eventual fading of confidence.

It is arguable, however, that this danger ought to be risked from a theological point of view if the historical results are of sufficient promise for a Christology. Modest Christologies stand to gain a great deal by tying themselves to the new results of much work in the third quest, including the studies of each of the scholars listed above. A noneschatological Jesus understood as a Jewish-cynic teacher, a sage with alternative wisdom that undermines conventional assumptions, a social revolutionary, a peasant preacher, an egalitarian community builder, a shaman-like healer—all of these perspectives promise to bring a wealth of tangibility to Christological presentations of Jesus that have no use for the absolutist principle. So should modest Christologies jump on the third-quest band wagon, exorcising lingering demons of Harnack-induced suspicion about such enthusiasm, trusting that the new interdisciplinary methods really have procured a degree of reliable access to the texts formerly thought impossible?

On the other side of the coin, the twentieth century has repeatedly reminded itself of the theoretical advantages of not being able (so it was thought) to build a Christology too closely on historical results from life-of-Jesus research. One such reminder is found in the following judgment of Albert Schweitzer, made from his characteristically eschatological-apocalyptic point of view and with a positive tone that cannot have been representative of the views of many of his colleagues:

> Primitive Christianity was therefore right to live wholly in the future with the Christ who was to come, and to preserve of the historic Jesus only detached sayings, a few miracles, His death and resurrection. By abolishing both the world and the historical Jesus it escaped the inner division [between the life of Jesus and the idea of his spiritual significance], and remained consistent in its point of view. We on our part, have reason to be grateful to the early Christians that, in consequence of this attitude they have handed down to us, not biographies of Jesus but only Gospels, and that therefore we possess the Idea and the Person with the minimum of historical and contemporary limitations.[14]

Schweitzer correctly pointed out the value of the unfettered idea, which is useful for believer and cult alike. But surely the wholesale separation of the historical critical and Christological-theological spheres advocated in this quotation is extreme and far from being the best way to understand faith's supposed inviolability. Has not the assumption of faith's complete immunity from historical considerations always proven to be an unstable one, tenable only for short periods of time? Do not cult and piety alike have need of some assurance that the corporate and individual imaginations are not calling all the shots, running away on some flight of fancy while the difficult facts of history languish where they always were, awaiting imagination's return? Indeed, such assurance is essential. The feeling of historical tangibility is an essential part of the power and value of the Christological symbols. As Troeltsch argued, a Christ symbol unfettered by historical actuality leads in the long-term, especially in an era of heightened historical consciousness, to the dissolution of the Christian church, at least as it has functioned to date.[15]

Ought not Christology perhaps then ignore the warnings of excessive dependence on history and use the third quest to rekindle the amazing enthusiasm that surrounded Harnack's *What Is Christianity?* Is it not simply peevish of Christology to spurn purported research advances, in the way that Schweitzer seems to advocate? More than this, is it not strategically foolish of the underdog modest Christology camp to shun the historical results of Crossan, Borg, and the rest, with all they portend in the way of tangible, vividly historical support for modest Christology? No, on the contrary: Christology is right to *welcome* these winds of change in life-of-Jesus research. But they must be welcomed with caution, even suspicion; this much *must* be learned from Schweitzer.

Consider the complex research of John Dominic Crossan, for instance. In *The Historical Jesus*, Crossan advocates a more refined and purportedly objective method of stipulating criteria for determining which complexes of the Jesus tradition are the best attested and earliest. This involves classifying documents into one of four "strata" at varying temporal distances from Jesus himself and then counting independent attestations of various complexes. The material that hails from the earliest strata and that has multiple independent attestations is concluded to be the most reliable early information about Jesus. This material then can be used to construct a life of Jesus. The other major plank of Crossan's platform is his interdisciplinary embrace of a wider range of interpretative approaches than that furnished by historical criticism alone, including tools from a wide variety of sociological and anthropological disciplines. Jesus emerges through this process as Jewish peasant preacher after the fashion of the cynics, a wandering sage whose alternative and disruptive social vision is embodied in two remarkable activities: his magician-like healing, and his practice of communal meals in which conventional social distinctions were dissolved.

There is no questioning the remarkable achievement of Crossan's book. Its influence on the field to which it has contributed will force competing interpretations to match his methodological care with the sources and to follow the interdisciplinary example he sets. But the question here is how systematic Christology should respond. Crossan's eventual conclusions are possible, he thinks, because of discoveries about the relationships between and provenance of the sources; a more scientific method that moves research beyond the limitations its former subjectivity and haphazardness; and the application of a host of methods, models, and insights from the social sciences to the task of interpretation. But is

Crossan's method really so secure that the previously regnant apocalyptic interpretation of Jesus has been forever banished to the archives of oddities in life-of-Jesus research? Will there never again be significant adjustments in the dependence relations and priority of the sources? Are not the models and insights pouring forth from the social and anthropological sciences so rich and various that a wide range of interpretative possibilities will be supported in due time by scholars following Crossan's brilliant example of an interdisciplinary method of procedure?

The lesson of the last two hundred years is that, notwithstanding the ingenious research of current historians, the sources for a life of Jesus are deceptive. For theologians, Schweitzer's warning about the nature of the New Testament and related texts for reconstructing Jesus' life should have been received loud and clear. Christology must be carried on in an environment in which the reigning historical conclusions about the person of Jesus of Nazareth must ever be viewed with suspicion. No matter how enthusiastic historians may become at any given point, the historically minded theologian cannot fail to see the trend through the last two centuries of warranted decline of confidence in the usefulness of the sources for a life of Jesus. And yet Harnack's arguments—and Troeltsch's in a more limited way—for the necessity of historical tangibility in the symbol of Jesus Christ are also compelling.

Reflections on Skepticism

This pattern of scholarship, if interpreted correctly, confirms the late-nineteenth-century consensus around the need to grasp rather than avoid the problem of faith and history. But the element of historical contingency introduced thereby into systematic Christology still resists satisfactory handling. If an extended analogy can be introduced here, it appears that the two post-Ritschlian proposals, represented in their early forms by Harnack and Herrmann, still mark out the first- and third-base foul lines between which theologians hit their proposals. Each swing attempts to thread the Christological ball through the historical-critical fielders, while keeping it within the foul lines of the need of believer and cult for dependence of faith and history (Harnack) and the need to do justice to the irrefragability of Christian faith-experience and to a vision of true doctrine that changes less frequently than trends in historical research (Herrmann). Modest Christologies, by prescinding from making most of the problematic historical claims about Jesus demanded by the absolutist principle, may be likened in the baseball analogy to getting an easier pitcher than those against which most of the absolutist Christologies have to hit, where the quality of the pitcher is understood as corresponding to the difficulty with which historical research can make good on Christology's historical assumptions and assertions about Jesus. It does not change the game, but the chances of scoring are appreciably higher.

While most theologians try to hit the ball fair, accepting the terms of the problem of faith and history, some—the biblical positivists—refuse to play, while others recognize the importance of the game but believe the pitching and fielding is too good ever to get a hit. This is the skeptical view that disputes the contention of this part of the argument that the problem of faith and history does in fact possess a theologically feasible solution when a modest Christology is in the picture. In this skeptical group, concluding that Christian faith as traditionally conceived requires an attitude toward history that the rise of historical criticism has placed forever out of reach, stands Van Harvey's *The Historian and the Believer*.

In this work, Harvey tenaciously refuses to resolve the problem of faith and history in advance of locating satisfactory reasons for which to do so. Instead, he patiently exhibits the morality of historical inquiry—which "celebrates methodological skepticism and is distrustful of passion in matters of inquiry"[16]—in contrast with the *credo ut intelligam* morality of traditional Christian belief. It is this persistence that sets *The Historian and the Believer* apart as the premier twentieth-century example of taking the problem of faith and history *seriously* because, as Harvey shows, it is all too easy to yield to the natural claim of Christian faith that there must be a way to manage the provisional and tentative historical material to which it must ever be related. Harvey finds no such management technique, concluding that the faithful and the historical critical orientations of humanity have been since the beginning of the nineteenth century and are still in profound tension. Their *de facto* resolution in a person's life is a matter of existential commitment and practical decision; it is an irrational but understandable (and finally helpful) surd that comes into play both within and outside of religious contexts whenever theories are underdetermined by data or existential orientations underdetermined by reasons for choosing among them.

This is a powerful argument. However, the majority of the large number of twentieth-century works on the problem of faith and history assert, unlike Harvey, that it *is* possible to manage faith's dependence upon the shifting results of historical research, that this manageability is *theologically justifiable*, that the apparently conflicting stances of faith and of rational historical inquiry *can* be reconciled. But even the hosts ranged against Harvey's view seem to conform to his implicit prediction about them, namely, that they ought to show the marks of arbitrarily cutting short the wrestling with the problem of faith's dependence on history. Though it would be unfair as a characterization of any particular book, this hard working mass of literature can be likened, in a homey analogy, to the process by which parents develop strategies for managing conflicts between squabbling children with whom they are to be confined in a station wagon traveling a very great distance. There have been thousands of such discussions, aided by magazine articles and books on the topic, the most painstaking and creative preparations are made, and the same result always eventuates: the strategies never work completely, everyone gets frazzled and frustrated, and the station wagon and everyone in it almost always reach the destination anyway. The irony of the image—the merely limited usefulness of the frantic and maybe over-intense preparations for the long car trip and the irrelevance of that preparation for affecting the outcome—corresponds to the same irony in the literature on the problem of faith and history: these works seem to make a merely limited contribution to managing the problem of faith and history and, despite differences of approach, the same conclusion tends to emerge. It is as though the discussions of strategy are merely delusory rationalizations for the purposes of coping in comfort.

The conviction undergirding these works is that faith's dependence upon history is manageable: the historian and believer might be stuck together on a difficult journey, but the goal will be reached with both intact. But extant arguments for the theological justification of this conviction face severe problems, so why is the conviction so strong? Perhaps Harvey is right that there can in principle be no finally adequate theological justification for the conviction, and that it is purely an exigency for which theologians have happily been constructing their self-deluding rationalizations.

Thus it appears that Harvey's skepticism cannot be lightly dismissed and that he has put his finger rather gracefully on an element of the irreducible mystery in the faith-reason relation. Nevertheless, theological justification for expecting the relation of historian and believer to be manageable is not *always* contrived, though it very often may well be. In particular, the proposal advocated here in chapter 1 and explored further in this chapter produces a sociological explanation and a theological justification for manageability that solves problems competing approaches cannot solve. The theological rationale for this solution is not contrived, owing primarily to the fact that a modest Christology is an essential component. While anxious not to stomp disrespectfully over the mystery of faith and reason that Harvey has illumined, it can still be maintained that his skeptical arguments do not succeed in gathering into the fold of deluded but comfortable sheep a solution to the problem of faith's dependence on history based on modest Christology. This, as much any other phase of the discussion, is reason to take seriously modest Christologies as offering a solution to this dimension of the crisis of plausibility plaguing contemporary Christology.

Tradition: Reassessing Christological Development

In an earlier chapter we saw how theories of the development of Christian doctrine were impacted by the flourishing sense of history in the nineteenth century and its study of the history of religions. Troeltsch's argument was that a modest Christology is the only tenable option in the face of what must be supposed to have been the case about the way the ecclesial tradition and its Christological doctrines developed. In recent decades, those initial analyses of Troeltsch and others in the history-of-religions school have been greatly extended in scope and power, with the dual result that the Christological crisis of plausibility has been sharpened significantly and the potential of a modest Christology to solve this dimension of it has come more clearly into the open.

Contemporary reassessments of the Christological tradition have focused particularly on the New Testament and patristic developments in Christological doctrine. Two forms of argument have been explored. First, in their weaker, balancing form, these arguments have tried to nullify the significance of the fact that the tradition has predominantly assumed the absolutist principle. They show, for example, that the development of a patristic consensus around absolutist Christology is *understandable* even if the absolutist principle is thought of as *false*, thereby opening the way to other interpretations of those developments. Or they contend that the diverse tradition of Christological reflection was peremptorily narrowed by an extreme interpretation of Jesus Christ guided by the absolutist principle. Though the decisions leading to this narrowing of diversity may have been taken for what seemed at the time to be good reasons, they did not adequately reflect the diversity of Christological opinion in the churches according to the argument (recalling Harnack's opinion[17]). Or, in relation to the New Testament documents, the balancing argument notes that the biblical pictures of Jesus Christ are diverse, supporting many different constructive interpretations, including modest Christologies, absolutist Christologies, and no Christology at all. The absolutist principle, while not without some biblical warrant, attained a predominance and a strength of unbiblical proportions, leading to the unwarranted exclusion and even suppression of many alternative, biblically grounded views along the way.

In all instances, the balancing argument levels rhetorical ground, creating a conceptual and historical space for the consideration of alternative interpretations of Christological developments. The contention is, therefore, that the biblical pictures of Jesus, with their usually Jewish flavor, should be permitted more control over Christological reflection than they were allowed to exercise in the process that gave rise to the domination over the classical Christology of absolutist pretensions and the unwarranted concomitant of baptizing of the absolutist principle as "orthodox."

Second, the stronger, reconstructive form of reassessment attempts to exhibit evidence from the early centuries of Christological development that an absolutist Christology is an explanatorily inadequate doctrinal "hypothesis," in the course of presenting a superior interpretation of this crucial period from a modest Christological perspective. On the one hand, the basis for attacking interpretations of the developing tradition that construe it as supportive of an absolutist Christology tends to be that the absolutist interpretation was articulable only by departing from the Jewish conceptualities of Jesus and his early followers in favor of a Graeco-Roman framework within which the tensive "God in Christ" was too easily resolved into the unjustifiable "Christ is definitively, uniquely, unsurpassably God." Thus, analysis of the developing tradition does not support an absolutist Christology as an explanatory hypothesis, no matter how complete a consensus around that position eventually developed.

On the other hand, reconstructions tell the story of early Christological development on the hypothesis that a modest Christology is the correct account, with an eye to two requirements. First of all, the reconstructions must reinforce the balancing arguments by providing a detailed account of the forces that gave rise to the theological and political consensus around the absolutist principle. Second, they must show that the modest hypothesis is more explanatorily comprehensive, efficient, and fruitful than its absolutist competitor.

Reassessment of the Christological tradition has been the objective of many authors in recent years. It was the central focus of many of the essays in *The Myth of God Incarnate* (1977), a volume that triggered a controversy in the United Kingdom more substantial (if not more vigorous) than that surrounding Bishop Robinson's famous work,[18] and calls to mind the *Essays and Reviews* controversy of 1860.[19] The historical reconstructions of early Christianity developed in the works of Elisabeth Schüssler Fiorenza, Rosemary Radford Ruether, and Paula Fredriksen are especially impressive recent contributions to a scholarly task that looks to such figures as F. C. Baur and Harnack as its progenitors. The stream of modest reconstructions is deep and flowing rapidly.

Balancing Arguments: Biblical Christology and the
Diversity of Biblical Pictures of Jesus

The recognition of a wide diversity of Christological perspectives within the New Testament writings, and present in the early Christian communities from which those writings sprang, is an ancient one. For instance, Tatian's *Diatesseron* (c. 150 CE), a harmonization of the four Gospels, was composed in part to combat the pagan criticism that the gospel accounts were contradictory. In the twentieth century, there has been widespread agreement among scholars that there is a high degree of variation, and no clearly dominant Christological interpretation in the New Testament. Arguments about diversity have been advanced in numerous studies, representing almost the entire gamut of theological opinion.[20] There is also a significant consensus around the fundamental propositions that these interpretations developed in the different socio-religious contexts of the various early Christian communities; that the diverse interpretations developed primarily in the period beginning with the events surrounding Jesus' execution; and that the New Testament writings, especially the Gospels, give some insight into the patterns of development of these interpretations at a few particular times and places.

Beyond this, agreements are more fragile, both in the sense that they are not as widespread and in the sense that such concords as there are change with disconcerting frequency. For instance, debates continue over Jesus' self-understanding, the extent to which this understanding may have affected later interpretations of his person and work, how to classify the various socio-religious contexts of the earliest Christological reflection, how to classify the earliest results of that reflection, how to assess the respective impacts of Jewish and hellenistic conceptualities on Christological developments, the role of the Apostle Paul in those developments, and the degree to which the delay of an expected parousia and the need to redefine early Christianity over against Judaism affected Christological formulations.

It is understandably difficult to make a definitive presentation of the lines of development of interpretations of Jesus, with so little in the way of clear-cut positive historical results, and such an abundance of more or less controversial ones. Some negative results, however, are more assured. For instance, the collection of snapshots of this development afforded us in the New Testament itself does not approach uniformity, nor is it even reducible to a set of variations on a single, well-defined theme. It is arguable that there are family resemblance criteria among the various interpretations, so that Christological interpretations are combinations of ideas such as kingly messiah, suffering-servant messiah, eschatological son of man, prophet, healer, proclaimer of God's reign, revolutionary, rabbi, semi-divine wonder worker, logos, and so on. However, it is not easy to construe them as converging thematically or historically toward a single, specific interpretation. One of the most compelling recent presentations of this point of view is by Paula Fredriksen who argues that the diversity, contrary to the conventional habits of interpretation, is not explicable on the supposition that Christological reflection was developing on average in a particular direction.[21]

Of course, Christological uniformity was achieved in later centuries, and *some* process of development links that uniformity with the New Testament diversity, but this actual historical development cannot be deduced from the diverse New Testament data itself. In the words of Douglas F. Ottati, who wishes to affirm the intention of Chalcedon, though not its fractured metaphysical concepts, "there is sufficient diversity in the New Testament to render implausible the contention that Chalcedon represents a necessary development of what we find there. It can

and ought to be affirmed, however, that the Chalcedonian Definition represents a possible and appropriate development in meaningful continuity
with what we find in the New Testament."[22] This lack of necessity connecting the New Testament and the later conciliar decisions is confirmed
by the fact that the conceptual building blocks for the classical Christology
of the fourth and fifth centuries—the pre-existence of Jesus, the connection of Jesus to universal conceptions such as creation and redemption of
the world, and clear identification of Jesus as actually divine rather than as
merely a prophetic or messianic representative of the divine kingdom—
are elements only of a minority interpretation within the New Testament
as a whole, most famously represented by the Gospel of John. Other interpretations of Jesus, such as the anointed prophet of God, chosen to in-
augurate the divine kingdom, are more deeply and widely attested in the
New Testament, though each one of them, too, falls short of being the
center of gravity of the diverse understandings of Jesus found there.

These results do not by themselves offer the biblical theologian much
of a purchase on constructing a Christology. Indeed, this theological neu-
trality is doubtless a partial precondition for such wide agreement as
exists on the diversity question among contemporary historians in the
mainstream of biblical scholarship, whether conservative or not. For the
purpose of establishing the balancing form of the argument about
the Christology of the New Testament, however, *all that is needed are
these widely accepted results of research into early Christological development*, including especially the fact of diversity construed along such
lines as appear in Ottati's remark, above. This is sufficient to neutralize the
advantage that absolutist Christologies have traditionally had in regard to
interpretation of the New Testament, and to justify the exploration of alternative interpretations.

*Balancing Arguments: Disarming the Absolutist Consensus
of Patristic Christology*

The balancing argument designed to neutralize the over-ready appeal by
proponents of absolutist Christologies to a more or less uniform conciliar
and ecclesial tradition is not uncommon. For example, Paul van Buren offers this argument in the course of weighing the strengths and weakness
of the patristic legacy.[23] Noting that the patristic guideline of the God-man
formula "is really the legacy of the Johannine community only," he argues

that we must face the question of "whether we wish to abide by this primary patristic guideline. One argument for at least qualifying it is that it condenses the cloud of apostolic witness to what God has done in Christ into one drop: that of the Fourth Gospel."[24] And, in relation to the particular emphasis of Chalcedon,

> Certainly the relationship of Jesus to God and to humanity is a possible way in which to put the issues of Christology, and unquestionably they derive from the things concerning Jesus of Nazareth as these are presented in the Apostolic Writings. What is equally certain is that Chalcedon represents a remarkable narrowing of the rich diversity of those presentations. More importantly, the context was drawn far more narrowly than had seemed to have been necessary to the authors of those Writings.[25]

Van Buren's argument thus brings out the ambiguity of the patristic developments. On the one hand, as he argues, the conciliar curtailment of a meaningful, ongoing Christological discussion peremptorily narrowed the range of potentially viable Christological options down to an absolutist version of the classical Christology, which was itself highly problematical, as the debates about it show. The fact that the battle over this process of doctrinal solidification was so bitter, not to mention violent and ruthlessly political, is an indication of the strength of the alternate Christological viewpoints and also of the need from a theological perspective to keep the discussion going.

On the other hand, from both the ecclesial and secular political perspectives, arriving at some clear-cut decision was expeditious, for it was a distressing quarrel with unwanted side effects, and consumed much political energy that was needed in other areas. Nontheological factors come into play here, complicating judgments about warrants and errors. It is difficult, therefore, to argue that this cutting short of the theological debate was in the final analysis unwarranted or mistaken. Even from a theological point of view, *given* the undeniable drift toward affirmation of the God-man formula in general terms, it is possible that the conciliar decisions were in fact the most *theologically* appropriate moves to make. Of course, they doubtless would have been better delayed in an ideal world, allowing the theological discussion to percolate more. Those decisions in favor of what was to become, under the weight of an absolutist habit of interpretation, the paradigm instance of absolutist Christology, it must be admitted, approximated to the center of gravity of theological opinion at that time with tolerable accuracy, even though they did not accurately reflect the diversity of the New Testament.

This demarcates the lengths to which the balancing argument can be pushed. It cannot be used to argue that the conciliar solidification of a hermeneutically absolutist version of the two-natures doctrine was a theological or ecclesial mistake, in the context of those decisions. However, it can reasonably hope to establish that the general direction taken in the patristic developments narrowed the theological discussion of available options to an unwarranted degree, in the light of the original Christological diversity, partially preserved in the New Testament. Moreover, as we saw in an earlier discussion, careful historical analyses of the theological debates and the councils derail attempts to immunize the patristic process of development with the assumption of special divine shepherding, ensuring that taking those developments out of the field of history by invoking such shepherding will force the payment of a high price in plausibility. The same kind of analyses show that the influence of the person, teaching, and self-interpretation of Jesus himself were not, as they are sometimes supposed to be, a gyroscopic force leading the process of Christological reflection inevitably to its Chalcedonian terminus, absolutely read. There were too many powerful alien interests and conceptualities in place for that to be the case.

Recent patristic studies establishes all these aspects of the balancing argument's goal almost as a matter of course, though this was by no means always the case. Patristic truisms are fewer and fewer as new studies bring powerful reminders that the patristic era was extremely complex and highly fluid, with numerous practical contingencies and theological considerations informing every major decision. The groundbreaking works on Arius by Williams, Gregg, and Groh,[26] for instance, established that the dispute between Athanasius and Arius is best understood as an argument over different and very practically grounded conceptions of salvation rather than a bloodless metaphysical dispute, inducing a dramatic blurring of the suspiciously comfortable categories of "winners" and "losers," "orthodox" and "heretics." Such sensitizing achievements of patristic studies prevent the process of Christological development from being pressed into *automatically* favoring any given Christological interpretation—and this is the aim of the balancing argument.

It follows that modest Christologies need have no fear of the eventual near uniformity of patristic support for absolutist Christology. Nor should the classical Christological tradition's frequently absolutist presuppositions be taken to undermine support for modest Christologies. Modest Christologies cannot be kept out of the debate by the invocation of the rule of Vincent of Lerins, for absolutist Christology was not at first believed almost everywhere, always, and by everyone; and even if it had been, it still may be mistaken. More and more it appears that Christology espousing the absolutist principle is rightly described in such intriguing terms.

Reconstructive Arguments: Testing the
Modest Christological Hypothesis

Once the rhetorical, historical, and conceptual ground is hermeneutically leveled in this way by balancing arguments, the opportunity for advancing reconstructions of the early centuries of Christological development exists. This is not an easy task. For example, in relation to the New Testament, while the irreducible diversity of Christological reflection in early Christianity is for the biblical historian merely a widely established research result, it is a major problem for biblical theologians. Theirs is the complex task of deciding which interpretation of Jesus' person and work is best able to account for such development as exists in early Christological reflection, certain facets of which have been preserved in the New Testament. They must fit an overarching interpretation to the diversity.

It is troubling and fascinating that, with few exceptions, New Testament Christology in the last few decades has limited itself to articulating the process of Christological development, with biblical critical expertise—merely the first step for the biblical theologian—or to emphasizing generalized interpretations of the starting material with a more completely theological interest that shies away from the biblical critical details. This is one symptom of the much discussed malaise of biblical theology.[27] The complex reasons for this state of affairs include the fact that, without the interpretative bias induced by the predominance of the absolutist principle, formerly expressed in the lack of full recognition of the diversity of the New Testament witness, the plurality of related Christological interpretations in the New Testament does not resolve itself into a single, preferred Christology or even a definite line of Christological development. Moreover, ever-growing awareness of the complex diversity of patristic

theology, in conjunction with the breakdown of a "standard" interpretation preferring an absolutist Christology, has deepened the challenge of
making any hypothesis fit the historical data.

Modest Christological reconstructions of biblical and patristic Christological reflection have a crucial advantage, however: they do not *need* to
fit the historical evidence to any overarching trajectory of development as
part of an argument to construe as defensible narrow readings of later
conciliar decisions. After all, they hold the absolutist readings of those
later decisions to be distortions of the truth about Jesus Christ. This is not
much of an advantage if the connection between Jesus and an absolutist
rendering of Chalcedon actually possesses some sort of internal necessity.
The balancing arguments, however, demonstrate that it has become increasingly burdensome to argue along these lines. Thus, the plausibility of
historical reconstructions promises to be greater when they are freed
from having to defend an explanatory hypothesis that is expected to fit
the evidence point by point.

On the negative side, however, reconstruction from a modest Christological point of view lags behind. Justly hailed presentations of that data
such as offered by J. D. G. Dunn,[28] and recent masterful presentations of
biblical and patristic material such as John A. T. Robinson's *The Human
Face of God* (1973), Wolfhart Pannenberg's *Jesus—God and Man* (1977),
Hans Küng's *On Being a Christian* (1984), and Edward Schillebeeckx's
Jesus (1979) and *Christ* (1980), notwithstanding their innovative character
in other ways, all present the silent official embrace of Christological absolutism along with the conciliar decisions of the third and fourth centuries
as justifiable in the light of the prior process of development. Nevertheless, the modest hypothesis for guiding reconstructions of this period
have some superb representatives, such as Rosemary Radford Ruether,
and their number is increasing.

Ruether's modest Christological thought emerges almost incidentally
in *Sexism and God-Talk* and *Faith and Fratricide*. The primary purpose
of her reconstruction in these books is to attack patriarchy and anti-
Semitism, respectively, within Christianity and Christian theology. Here
the focus will be on the more detailed presentation in *Faith and Fratricide*.

In *Faith and Fratricide*, Ruether's aim is to show how the "negative
myth of the Jews" was absorbed from pagan sources into Christianity. She
shows how this myth is reflected in the New Testament, in the theology of

the church fathers, and in Christendom. The Christologically central part of her historical reconstruction is laid out especially in the second chapter, entitled "The Growing Estrangement: The Rejection of the Jews in the New Testament." There she argues that early Christianity, originally one Jewish sect among many, found itself rejected by Jews in both Jerusalem and the Diaspora when it tried to assert its primitive midrash, namely, that Christianity "was founded on the true cornerstone of God's people," the stone that had formerly "been rejected by the builders." This experience of rejection led to the opinion that Judaism "was hopelessly apostate and represented a heritage of apostasy which merited its rejection as the true guardian of Israel and the election of the Gentiles instead." Thus "the anti-Judaic tradition in Christianity grew as a negative and alienated expression of the need to legitimate its revelation in Jewish terms."[29]

Once alienation from Judaism and evangelization of the Gentiles became the pattern of Christianity—and this happened in the second decade after Jesus' death, according to Ruether—the Jewish sect found itself in an increasingly hellenistic context, less tied to synagogues. By itself, this sponsored the systematic muting of Jewish themes in Christological reflection and the amplification of Greek and pagan ideas. But this influence became especially important with the recognition of the failure of early Christianity's apocalyptic expectations. Ruether contends that Jesus' understanding of himself as Messiah had led to his disciple's eschatological expectation that the Messianic Age was imminent. But the expected apocalyptic cataclysm did not occur, and the Christian churches had, therefore, to find some new way to understand the significance of Jesus. They needed to distinguish the Christian interpretation of Jesus as the Christ from the apocalyptic Jewish concept of Messiah, which they achieved by what Ruether calls an "illegitimate historicizing of the eschatological."[30] By this, she means the shift in interpretation whereby the apocalyptic messianic hope is believed to be presently realized within history in the person of Jesus and then in the Christian churches, now clearly distinguished from supposedly apostate Judaism. Greek and pagan ideas were useful in providing materials for the reconception, as the Logos imagery of John's gospel demonstrates.[31]

It is at this point that the relevance for Christology of Ruether's discussion of the origins of Christian anti-Semitism becomes evident. According to her reconstruction, the developing Christological reflection both fostered and was shaped by anti-Semitic tendencies. In fact, she calls

Christology "the other side of anti-Judaism."[32] It is no accident, in Ruether's analysis, that the elevated conception of Jesus in John's gospel is accompanied by the severest anti-Semitic reflections.[33]

Ruether's reflections on the Christological implications of her historical analysis emphasize their relevance for Jewish-Christian dialogue.[34] She outlines a Christology that hinges on Jesus' resurrection as a paradigm for the hope of salvation and renewal, without ever transgressing her self-imposed line of illegitimacy by assuming that this hope had been realized. The work of salvation is not complete. Others must play their part. Final consummation is proleptically anticipated in Jesus' work, but never realized.[35] Ruether believes that a

> paradigmatic and proleptic view of the messianic work of Jesus is the only theologically and historically valid way of interpreting it consistent with biblical faith and historical realism. It is the only way we can reconnect Christianity with the context of this event in its original Jewish setting and so rediscover the real historical Jesus, who must ever elude an anti-Judaic Christianity. It represents the way we should have read the New Testament, if apocalyptic imminentism had not confused the early Christian sense of history. It is the way we needed to appropriate the apocalyptic expectation once its imminence had faded from sight, rather than transposing it into the messianic absolutism which generated Christian totalitarianism and imperialism.[36]

This, of course, corresponds to a modest Christology. The rich implications of Ruether's analysis for the negative ethical and anti-Judaic propensities of the absolutist principle are her primary focus, of course. But the main interest at this point is to note that Ruether offers a convincing reconstruction of Christian origins for which the hypothesis of an absolutist Christology cannot intelligibly account, but which is compellingly consonant with the supposition of a modest Christology.

A Rescue Attempt: Pannenberg on the Resurrection

Balancing arguments are in place, and the modest Christological hypothesis has been shown to be well supported by at least one reconstruction of the early centuries of developing Christological reflection. In order to conclude that the conventional, absolutist interpretation of this development cannot be rescued from the diagnosis of terminal implausibility, however, it is important to discuss the notable attempt to rescue the ailing reading by Wolfhart Pannenberg.

We may begin by noting that there seems to be a nearly complete correlation in the literature between the affirmation of modest Christologies and the denial that the development of Christian doctrine is well controlled—either by providential divine shepherding, or by the gyroscopic effect of the specifics of the personality, self-understanding, and teaching of Jesus. It is not hard to see why.

On the one hand, a confidence in controlled development is necessary to aid the interpretative resolution of the complex diversity of the early Christian traditions into a line of development whose climax can be legitimately construed as the conciliar pronouncements. Rahner, for instance, read the absolutist interpretation of the conciliar Christological pronouncements as having emerged from the welter of alternative interpretations as the most adequate expression of what was *implicitly believed about Jesus all along.* He held this in spite of his recognition that New Testament diversity allows the *deduction* of neither the classical nor the absolutist interpretation of Jesus from its pages.[37] And absolutist Christologies have almost always affirmed in the contemporary period something like Rahner's view of the development of doctrine.

On the other hand, it is safe to say that a modest Christology requires something like the view of the development of doctrine earlier attributed to Troeltsch and vividly illustrated in Ruether's thought. Ruether takes infinitely seriously the contingencies of history and the imaginative construction of doctrine by Christian communities to serve purposes partly defined by contingent contexts and partly to do justice to an increasingly normative interpretation of past events. The developments in those early centuries are interpreted by Ruether as not only contingent, with which construal Rahner could probably agree. But they are also interpreted as *not* truly guided by the nature of Jesus himself as human and Jewish, or by divine providential guidance, a view with which Rahner and most other proponents of absolutist Christology would be uncomfortable. It is this break, finally, that allows Ruether to conclude that the development as it actually occurred is defective in a variety of ways—notably with regard to the views of women, Jews, and Jesus to which it led—so that her modest Christological hypothesis is strongest when it *conflicts* with the absolutist result of the development, while still explaining the defective dimensions of the developing process. This pattern is quite general: a theory of the development of doctrine that tends to support absolutist readings of the conciliar decisions also interferes with the justification of a modest Christology.

The strength of the correlation between Christology and theory of development of doctrine is a serious problem for absolutist Christologies because "well-controlled" theories of the development of doctrine have to face the disabling difficulties discussed in Part I. A crucial question is therefore whether readings of patristic Christological developments that judge absolutist Christology to be justifiable *need* to rely so heavily upon a "well-controlled" view of the development of doctrine. Can they rescue themselves from gross implausibility by appealing to *other* evidence for the truth of the espoused Christological position, so as to avoid having to make inevitably weak appeal to partial and controversial ecclesial consensus?

No, they cannot; at least not by contemporary standards of evidence. The fundamental reason is, to put it baldly, that there is no longer any historical evidence, admissible by the reigning standards of historiography, that the absolutist principle is true. The consolidation of biblical criticism has forever placed out of reach the traditional strategy of appealing to the healing miracles, supernatural knowledge, and nature wonders attributed to Jesus in the gospels, which had formerly been thought, though dubiously, to be of help here. Neither is there any possibility of moving from the character of Jesus' teaching to assertions of his absolute, unique, and unsurpassable revelatory and salvific significance. With no historical evidence to support it, the assertion of the fact thesis of the absolutist principle has been forced to make appeal to the weakest form of evidence, namely, that testimony to the absolute revelatory and salvific significance of Jesus Christ was the eventual resting place of developing early reflection on Jesus' person and work. This only has force within a confessional community that stresses the importance of identification with absolutist interpretations of the fourth- and fifth-century conciliar decisions. In most cases, sensing the weakness of this appeal, anxious to forestall the objections to it mentioned here, and determined to remain as faithful as possible to the patristic teaching of the church, the absolutist reading makes vain attempts to secure greater robustness by drawing in analyses of religious experience, or undergirding it with a philosophy of history in which the development of early interpretations of Jesus is thinkable as well-controlled. Thus it is that absolutist Christologies usually and understandably bring to bear on the history of doctrine a theory of development similar to Rahner's.

It is precisely at this point that the importance of Wolfhart Pannenberg's emphasis on the resurrection emerges clearly. Perhaps, after all, there *is* some evidence for "Jesus' unity with God," or "Jesus' divinity,"[38] with the absolutist implications that such an assertion carries for Pannenberg. Admittedly, the connection between resurrection and unity with God, or divinity, connoting absolute significance, is far from obvious. But, if it were well enough attested, the resurrection would certainly be impressive evidence for *something*, and the divine nature of the one resurrected is not a wholly unreasonable candidate for that something. There is nothing new about this argument, obviously. Its roots can be traced as far back as the account in Acts of Peter's Pentecost sermon, in which he adduces the resurrection as evidence of Jesus' exaltation as Lord,[39] though there, of course, the resurrection is appealed to in support of a significantly different conclusion than Pannenberg wants to establish. But many theologians since the European Enlightenment, including Schleiermacher, his theological progeny, and a large part of the theological mainstream, have been skittish about the resurrection. Pannenberg traces this trend.[40]

Pannenberg, by contrast, is hardly skittish. Through a careful sifting of arguments and evidence, he concludes that

> the resurrection of Jesus would be designated as a historical event in this sense: If the emergence of primitive Christianity, which, apart from other traditions, is also traced back by Paul to appearances of the resurrected Jesus, can be understood in spite of all critical examination of the tradition only if one examines it in the light of the eschatological hope for a resurrection from the dead, then that which is so designated is a historical event, even if we do not know anything more particular about it. Then an event that is expressible only in the language of the eschatological expectation is to be asserted as a historical occurrence.[41]

Of course, this conclusion "has been opposed on the grounds that the resurrection of a dead person even in the sense of the resurrection to imperishable life would be an event that violates the laws of nature."[42] But Pannenberg warns that natural science expresses the general validity of the laws of nature but must at the same time declare its own inability to make definitive judgments about the possibility or impossibility of an individual event, regardless of how certainly it is able, at least in principle, to measure the probability of an event's occurrence. The judgment about whether an event, however unfamiliar, has happened or not is in the final analysis a matter for the historian and cannot be prejudged by the knowledge of natural science.[43]

In other words, the resurrection could be, for example, a suspension of natural law, or the first (or an unfamiliar) instantiation of a particular configuration of natural laws. The conclusion for the historian is clear: "If the historian approaches his work with the conviction that "the dead do not rise," then it has already been decided that Jesus also has not risen. . . . If, on the other hand, an element of truth is to be granted to the apocalyptic expectation with regard to the hope of resurrection, then the historian must also consider this possibility for the reconstruction of the course of events as long as no special circumstances in the tradition suggest another explanation."[44]

Pannenberg's direct treatment of the resurrection has great importance for Christology. Historical evidence for Jesus' divinity or the absolutist principle—formerly thought to be plentiful—has been reduced almost to nothing by historical criticism. Pannenberg's proposal offers the possibility of relieving the proponent of absolutist Christology from having to make inevitably weak appeal to the eventual and controversial patristic consensus about the absolute significance of Jesus Christ, supported primarily by a theory of the development of doctrine that carries no weight in secular historiography, with further dubious support from a tenuous interpretation of religious experience or from metaphysics or from the philosophy of history. In more rustic language, while it is risky to place all of the absolutist Christological eggs in one historical basket, the resurrection basket is far stronger than any alternative accommodation, and it is better than leaving them exposed to every kind of danger on the ahistorical picnic table, precariously supported by the single wobbly trestle of an unduly sanguine view of a well-ordered process of doctrinal development.

In assessing this bold reclaiming of history for the beleaguered absolutist Christology, two remarks are in order. First, an air of definiteness about the terms of Christology is created by bringing the resurrection within the field of history, in spite of its supposed unique and unprecedented character. The meaningfulness of the assertions of absolutist Christology is also improved by rendering them subject in principle to historical falsification. These are significant achievements. They underline the inadvisability of the half-heartedness with regard to the resurrection that has dominated critically minded Protestant theology for a long time. Rarely since the Apostle Paul and the early expansion of the Christian church has there been such clear-cut reason to think that anything would stand or fall by the historical reality of the resurrection. For Paul it was the truth of the Christian proclamation, but in Pannenberg's theology it is the plausibility of absolutist Christology.[45] In the final analysis, the stress on absolutist Christology induced by the massive incoherences under discussion in this chapter and the next far exceeds the tension-relieving impact of this new-found robustness. Ironically therefore, the resurrection's resuscitation, so to speak, by placing absolutist Christology into its most historically persuasive light, helps to make more clear-cut the final loss of plausibility of the absolutist principle.

The second remark bears on the effectiveness of Pannenberg's argument. It has severe problems, notwithstanding the benefits just mentioned. While it is true that he brings "falsifiability in principle" to his absolutist Christology, this is the weakest possible kind of falsifiability. It is completely impractical, since any conceivable historical information (with the speculative exception of historians with video cameras in time machines) cannot be brought to bear on the question of the resurrection. It would not be admitted as evidence in a Western court of law, for it is a matter of hearsay, multiply removed from the purported original events. The sole exception is Paul's account of his Damascus road conversion experience in Galatians, but that is too vague to be of evidential use in support of a bodily resurrection, and is not specifically supported by Acts' account of Saul's conversion. Moreover, while there is little consensus about an alternate explanation for the resurrection narratives in the New Testament—though the social psychological approach is becoming ever-more stable[46]—the evidence for the resurrection is hardly compelling, except to those for whom its factuality is already (and illegitimately) obvious on other grounds. Finally, the evidential import of the resurrection as establishing Pannenberg's claims for Jesus' divinity, and with this his absolute significance, is questionable. After all, what is to be made of the other reports of resurrections, even in the New Testament, let alone in the sacred texts of other religions? The history of religions ancient and modern has adduced such an impressive array of purported resurrections and similar events that Christian stories of Jesus' resurrection can no longer be regarded as unparalleled, as might formerly have been the case.

Pannenberg does not succeed in rescuing the absolutist Christology from precarious dependence on a thoroughly implausible theory of the development of doctrine, therefore, *even if he had succeeded in saving the resurrection*—and this he does not do either. Moreover, since this seems to be one of the last hopes for shoring up the plausibility of absolutist Christology, the impression of crisis in contemporary Christology is only deepened by its failure. Yet, here again in this dimension of that unwieldy, comprehensive crisis of plausibility, modest Christologies patiently point in the direction of an incontestably superior way forward.

Metaphysics: The Universal and the Particular

In an earlier chapter, we discussed the role of Strauss as one of the central figures in triggering the collapse of confidence in the uniform reliability of the Gospels and in raising the question of the extent to which faith's assumptions about actual historical events should and could be supported by historical research. The dramatic and controversial final chapter of his *Leben Jesu*, however, was only alluded to in that earlier discussion. Strauss was convinced that the absolutist principle, as present in absolutist Christologies, was impossible from the perspective of the metaphysic that guided his conception of history. *The significance of the human race, like all historical realities, could be grasped only in the totality of its historical unfolding; it could not be expressed in a single human being, as absolutist Christology urged that it was.*

This famous opinion of Strauss's is an answer to the question that most directly raises the issue of the metaphysical plausibility of the absolutist principle: can the universal lavish itself upon the particular in the way that the absolutist principle requires? The history of reflection on this question leads through many of the most creative theological moves made in the philosophy of history during the nineteenth and twentieth centuries, beginning with the classic era of German philosophy at the turn of the eighteenth and nineteenth centuries. The aim here is not to retrace this history but to examine the structure of the argument surrounding what will hereafter be called "Strauss's intuition"—it could be called Schelling's or Baur's intuition as well—with the aid of some conceptual tools furnished by Eugene TeSelle in *Christ and Context*.

Three Perspectives on the Archetypal Human Ideal

In TeSelle's analysis of what he calls the "archetype Christology"—the very phrase suggests what is at stake for Christology in the question at hand—he reviews each of Kant, Schleiermacher, and Hegel, drawing in Schelling, Baur, and Strauss, and compares their views on the question of whether the universal properly can be thought to lavish itself upon the particular, among other questions.[47] All of these thinkers grappled with the concept of an archetypal ideal of humanity, an ideal that expresses the profound capacity of humans for self-realization and cultural creation, while at the same time providing a sense of direction and hope in a world where this capacity is experienced in such familiar ways as blocked and frustrated. All of them are also concerned, in various ways, to connect their thought to their Christian religious context, which they rightly inter-pret as presenting such an archetypal ideal. TeSelle relates their various opinions and conflicts to three perspectives on the natural context for dis-cussion of an archetypal ideal for humanity, namely, the process of history in which that ideal is thought of as realized to greater or lesser degrees in response to the divine call or demand.[48]

The first perspective TeSelle identifies is that of the logical presuppo-sitions of humanity under God within the historical process. What does an analysis of humanity disclose concerning its potential? Kant's reflections on this question are indicative of this first perspective: the human ideal is implicit in the structure of human life. We are aware of our possibilities and experience the contrast between this vision of potentiality and the sad falling short of it as a moral imperative to realize the ideal of humanity in our lives. The archetypal ideal of humanity always has been present to human consciousness in this way and in every culture. Conceiving this ideal does not depend upon it being historically realized, for we do not need to have it suggested to us by its actual occurrence in history; it is al-ready perfectly clear. Nor does this human ideal need to be actualized pre-viously in order for us to realize it ourselves. We are incapable of realizing it and therefore must rely upon God to impute the satisfaction of the moral demand to us on the basis of our honest attempts to fulfill it, in a kind of semi-Pelagian justification by faith and works. But for this very reason, its realization in history is superfluous to our being empowered or inspired to conform our wills to the moral imperative.

This does not amount to an argument that the archetypal ideal of humanity cannot, in fact, lavish itself upon a particular historical human. Kant, for example, did not rule this out, though—with more candor than many theologians—he did note that, were this case with respect to Jesus, then it could not be known directly because of the inherent limitations of historical testimony. But even were the universal human ideal to have been realized in Jesus, this would be but a historical specification of universal principles that is not theoretically needed. The ideal itself, which is admittedly essential for an adequate human self-understanding, is present to our consciousness as definitely as are the intuitions of space and time. True, the thought of a concrete realization of the ideal may have practical relevance in forming a tradition in which the kingdom of God, the social locus of the effort to heed the moral imperative, would serve to promote moral interests. But the ideal itself is already fully present in our certain awareness of the moral imperative.

Schelling and Baur, less indifferent than Kant at this point, shared—or, more accurately, caused—Strauss's intuition. They believed that the archetypal ideal was intensely relevant to all of humanity but could not conceive of how an individual human could be the locus for it. From the position of the late twentieth century, we may express the point by pointing out that thinking of this ideal as realized two thousand years in the past seems to make of it a very limited thing, lacking in comprehensive vision for the true potential of humanity through technological advance and sociopolitical revolution. Have not the humanisms of the nineteenth and twentieth centuries been at great pains to articulate grand visions of the future based on their imaginative feeling for the content of this archetypal human ideal? And even if they were and are overly optimistic about the human capacity for realizing these grand visions, is it not still the case that their reflections demonstrate beyond a shadow of doubt that the archetypal ideal is far richer than ever could be contained or expressed in a single individual? Is it not so all-encompassing a vision that its realization is a matter of the accomplishment of the entire race in the course of its whole history? Correspondingly, is it not futile—risking both romantic projection and curtailing of the imagination—to return to an ancient man, hoping to find there the archetypal ideal fully realized?

From this first perspective—whether Strauss's intuition is affirmed or rejected, or Kant's agnosticism on the question holds sway—the salient features of humanity are its potential and freedom for self-actualization. The view is therefore first and foremost a prospective one, looking ahead to what might be attained on the basis of our current awareness of the tension between what is possible and what is actual. This tension between the archetypal vision and all too familiar failures to actualize it is the space within which life takes shape and possesses interest and challenge. In this sense, then, there is no room for final realization of the archetypal ideal. Such concrete historical realization, even if it were possible, is not only theoretically superfluous to our knowledge of the archetypal ideal and our struggle toward approximating it; it is also, so to speak, in metaphysical bad taste. The world is a fascinating place so long as the tension between ideal and actual is not collapsed. The realization of the universal human archetype in a human life is a flaunting of human potential that, being theoretically superfluous, is also unseemly. But if concrete historical realization were a superfluous and an unseemly idea for Kant, it was an unspeakably dull and finally an impossible one for Schelling, Baur, and Strauss.

The second perspective places emphasis on historical enactments, in which the ambiguous achievements of humanity are celebrated as evidence of the possibilities of self-actualization under the grace of God and failures are held up as reminders of the dependence of humanity upon redemptive events—events which have also been enacted within human history. The view in this case is that of the pilgrim, "confident that the resolution has already been offered, but also knowing that it remains outside oneself and can be appropriated only through struggle."[49]

In this case, the concept of the archetypal ideal of humanity can be formed well enough. But it is a concept that uncompromisingly presents itself as requiring concrete historical realization if humans are to actualize the ideal in their lives and societies. Our powerlessness to conform our will to the divine promise and command cannot be overcome by effort, but only by participation in the human ideal. The prior realization of the ideal is essential for our concrete participation in it, which occurs through social and mystical processes both in individual lives and in the sacramental life of the churches. Given this set of assumptions, it follows that the very possibility of the pilgrim struggle for realization of ideal humanity enables the deduction of the concrete historical actualization of this ideal humanity. Though history cannot confirm this, but can only indirectly suggest it, it is philosophically and experientially clear that such a perfect actualization must have occurred. This is the affirmation of Schleiermacher, Rahner, and Tillich, in their different ways.

Note that the possibility of perfect realization of the universal archetypal humanity is affirmed in this perspective, as is its necessity and thus its appropriateness. This is in obvious contrast to its impossibility or superfluousness in the first perspective.

The third perspective is from the position of the eschaton, the glorious culmination of the historical process. This imagined fruition provides inspiration for the confidence that something final and satisfying is always ready to break into the ambiguous, frustrating historical process. And this confidence is not often misplaced, as new life and new possibilities do indeed continually appear even in the darkest moments. Hope springs eternal finally because hope is rarely completely disappointed, even if it must be satisfied by fulfillment in other than expected forms. The human ideal is an active principle on this view. As history relentlessly propels humanity into the future, there is a real participation of humans and their societies in this powerful ideal. Humanity is thought of not so much as creating the ideal or being inspired by past exemplifications of it, so much as being drawn forward into the future *by* it and making it manifest in history even as it is already real in the eschatological fulfillment of history.

The view here is imaginatively retrospective, thinking of every moment as being drawn into reconciliation and fulfillment. In Hegel this reconciliation is accomplished within Spirit in and through its historical realization. But what, then, of the possibility of the lavishing of this universal archetypal ideal upon a particular person? For Hegel, this is an essential transition in the self-unfolding of Spirit in history. It corresponds to the divine recognition of itself in the other, in the creation and in humanity. As such, it both expresses the reconciliation in the divine life of the tension between potential and actual humanity, and prefigures the widespread realization in history of this same reconciliation, by functioning as the ideal to which Christians may approximate. The contemporary Lutheran critical renaissance of Hegel—in the work of Pannenberg, Braaten and Peters[50]—also regards this lavishing as an essential transition in the self-unfolding of the divine Spirit in history. But it is treated more realistically as a proleptic anticipation of the fullness of the eschaton, rather than an exhibition of that fullness as such within history.

Assessment of These Three Perspectives

By distinguishing these three perspectives, TeSelle enables key issues surrounding Strauss's intuition to be drawn into the open: Is the archetypal ideal of humanity artificially constrained by being envisaged as perfectly realized in Jesus? Is the concrete historical realization of the ideal necessary for humans to orient their wills toward the struggle to realize it individually and socially? Is such concrete realization superfluous to forming the concept of, and acting so as to realize, the human ideal? Moreover, by treating the various positions as perspectives on the historical process wherein the archetypal ideal of humanity is conceived and approximately realized, TeSelle at least makes a respectable attempt to bring out the validity of each, without requiring the submission of any of them to the excesses of the others.

Whether TeSelle succeeds in this attempt at coordination is debatable, however. The key issues just mentioned seem to split the approaches apart in a way that TeSelle's attempted reunion of them into a perspectival whole seems ill-suited to manage. For instance, consider the question of whether the archetypal ideal of humanity is artificially constrained by being envisaged as perfectly realized in Jesus. Is not this a sensible, well-formed question for which only one answer can be held to be correct? Schelling, Baur, and Strauss answer yes, in various ways; Hegel, Schleiermacher, and Rahner, no; and Pannenberg, Braaten, and Peters, yes, but proleptically. So does not treating these different answers as the result of different perspectives within the historical process of forming and realizing the concept of the human ideal only serve to mislead? Does it not cover a simple contradiction with affirmations of perspectival unity? It may well be that Schelling, Baur, and Strauss thought about the process of realizing the archetypal ideal from the point of view of looking forward to the dynamic process in which humans strive for its realization. Likewise, as TeSelle would have it, it may be that Schleiermacher thought about the same process from the point of view of its having been made possible by the historical act of the concrete, tangible realization of the archetype in a historical person. But then their different "perspectives" on this process are really different and *incompatible* interpretations: either the universal archetypal ideal of humanity lavished itself upon a concrete, particular person in the absolutist principle's sense, or it did not. If it did not, and it did not because it could not, then Strauss's intuition is right, and Schleiermacher's is wrong. If it did, then it could, and Strauss's intuition must bow to Schleiermacher's.

Nevertheless, TeSelle has laid his finger on something valid about the variety of perspectives on the process of humanity's grappling in history with the archetypal ideal of itself. Surely it is possible to regard this process prospectively, dramatically, and eschatologically-proleptically, with correspondingly different strands of meaning being teased out of the fact that there is such an archetypal ideal alive and well in human history.

How then can this valid insight about perspectives be reconciled with the fact that TeSelle's three perspectives involve contradictory views? It is surely not enough to say that "We need all of these perspectives, and there is no way to absorb one into another, because they have apprehended different points along the road from potentiality to actualization—or perhaps different aspects of the same point somewhere along that road."[51]

What is needed is to form some consistent coordination of these three views on the basis of which they may truly be called "perspectives." This is not a case of a mystery which resists analysis, thus necessitating a variety of mutually contradictory perspectives if it is to be spoken of at all. Rather, the contradictory elements of the three perspectives are the result of the coexistence among them of elements with metaphysical affinity for, and metaphysical allergy to, the absolutist principle.

The method being used here is unusual, and clarity about it is important. It is fruitless to argue *directly* against the metaphysical plausibility of the universal lavishing itself upon the particular in the extreme sense of the absolutist principle. Such an event is not unimaginable, and positing it even offers certain systematic advantages, adding force to the centralization of Jesus Christ in Christian theology and practice. And so, as pointed out above, such arguments can rapidly degenerate into a simple, unresolvable conflict of metaphysical tastes. But to show the metaphysical deficiency of the absolutist principle *indirectly* means to show that the supposition of such a lavishing conflicts with other, better founded, metaphysical intuitions. This kind of argument requires less in the way of common metaphysical ground with those views against which it is directed, and it does not need to make the dubious assumption that a metaphysical proposition can be rejected on the basis of the conceptual fragility of a given expression of it, a fragility that is supposedly objectively evident but actually is usually highly debatable.

If the set of mutually conflicting metaphysical intuitions TeSelle offers are not merely asserted as somehow complementary, as TeSelle himself does, but are turned on each other as competitive interpretations, then there are two results. First, the intuition that supports the possibility of the absolutist principle is overwhelmed by the stability and persuasiveness of more modest hermeneutical intuitions. Rejecting the possibility of "lavishing" in the sense of the absolutist principle enables the reconstruction of TeSelle's distinctions as a set of consistent perspectives on the human historical process as potentiated by the tension between possibility and actualization. Second, then, the new-found consistency of these three reconstructed perspectives is itself testimony to the advisability of rejecting the absolutist principle. Moreover, when all traces of the absolutist principle are removed, and the resulting adjustments in the three views made, they jointly constitute a powerful tool for describing and explaining different modes of theological reflection. The effectiveness of this tool likewise indicates the problematic character of the absolutist principle and confirms the advisability of its rejection.

A conception of the historical process as radically open, such as Troeltsch affirmed, has something vital to offer here. Given this openness, we might well ask TeSelle—or, more obviously, Kant—how it could ever have been thought that there was a single archetypal ideal for humanity. The empirical result even of Troeltsch's historical studies, now resoundingly confirmed and thoroughly superseded by cultural anthropology and religious studies, was that there is most definitely *not* a unique archetypal ideal for humanity. Archetypes are produced by the interaction of the human imagination with the depth of reality in a complex social context. They are created, they change and develop, they fall out of favor, they are extended, modified, critiqued, repudiated, clung to, and they may even die. They are, in short, symbols, in precisely Tillich's sense: they point to and participate in the reality of which they speak, namely, the potential of humanity.

The contrasts among the archetypal ideals of the cultural religious streams of the world are spectacular. There is the *chun tzu* of Confucianism, the *boddhisattva* and the *arhat* of Buddhism, the divinized human and God-man of Christianity, the Nietzschean *Übermensch* of secular atheism, the saint, the prophet; there is a world of diversity in ideal conceptions of the human. Hinduism even goes so far as to affirm this diversity explicitly, holding up the sage and the *sannyasin*, the mystic and the *brahmin*, and various other possible ideals for humans on the way to liberation. Within most traditions, the diversity is significant and not usually reducible to a single viewpoint. Most traditions tend to trivialize relevant differences between men and women—or emphasize irrelevant ones—in their formulation of ideals. The development and alteration of such human ideals is also a familiar fact. Indeed, the quest for the historical Jesus in its various forms during the last two centuries, and the varied images of Jesus from the beginning in Christian theology and art, testify unmistakably to variety and development in the Christian conception of the archetypal ideal of humanity.

The confident announcement of a fixed concept of an archetypal ideal for all human beings appears quite out of place, from this point of view. And the assumption that a fixed and absolute ideal has been realized in Jesus is similarly naïve. If Christianity has an archetypal ideal of humanity—and it seems to have at least one—then it was the imaginative result of many conflicting streams of interpretation of the hope of being human; it was powerfully impacted by numerous political, social, and accidental events and the activity and personal character of many people, including Jesus. To this extent, the dramatic view of TeSelle's second perspective is the correct one. But then this archetype could not remain fixed; it had to shift and develop under the influence of various norms, among which have always been the biblical pictures of Jesus as the Christ and, more recently, what can be discovered historically about him. This archetype still develops and changes even now, as secular visions of human life continue to aim jarring critiques, faithful to their own rational norms, at the Christian concept of ideal humanity. Thus the Christian archetype of ideal humanity is under constant transformation, as is every other symbol of the meaning and potential of human life and the cosmos that gave birth to it. Sometimes this transformation proceeds slowly, sometimes rapidly; usually norms from a familiar tradition guide its development and application, but sometimes alien norms create a tension that must be mediated or resolved.

From this perspective, the possibility of a historical, personal realization of the archetypal human ideal can be understood only in a narrowly circumscribed way. Such a realization could be rich enough to function inspirationally and normatively for a religious or cultural tradition, but must not be conceived so as to rule out the possibilities of developments and enlargements of the ideal, of intra- and inter-traditional diversity of the ideal, and of potential failure of the normative function of the ideal before subsequent challenges. This is a corrective to the view that Jesus Christ is the final and definitive expression of the archetype of ideal humanity. But it is also a corrective to the view expressed in Strauss's intuition, that this ideal can only be realized in the whole historical unfolding of the species. It affirms a middle way between these two extremes. It acknowledges that archetypes develop and are various, precisely to the extent that they are concretely relevant to people and cultures, and insists that the idea of a finally, absolutely definitive archetype is correspondingly a vacuous concept. But it also insists that archetypes of ideal humanity do exist, that they exercise normative functions within traditions, and that the best of them can be extremely long-lived and richly flexible.

There is little hope for an absolutist Christology in this atmosphere because the absolutist principle requires the elevation of a single archetype, however it might be defined, to a central position, there to be received as the final and definitive expression of the depth of human meaning and potential. Even if the possibility of its continual reconception is admitted, retraction of its claims to finality and definitiveness is not. A modest Christology, on the other hand, is at home in the historicized environment of contingent norms, mediated by traditions, articulating and adjusting human ideals so as to satisfy as far as possible both contextual demands and those traditional norms. The universal does not *lavish* itself upon any particulars, if the lavishing warrants assertions of the unlimited significance of the particular in question. Rather, it expresses itself in all particulars, and especially clearly in a few, in accordance with the principle that meaning in history is always and only a result of discerning wider meaning in particular instances of people and events.

A Modest Reconstruction of the Three Perspectives

In this light, TeSelle's three perspectives on the historical process wherein the ideal of humanity is conceived and approximately realized can be rendered more consistent with each other. Their various positions on the issue of whether the ideal had in fact received historical, personal realization made the three perspectives seem contradictory rather than complementary. But all three perspectives can acknowledge the *partial* concrete realization of the archetypal human in history, in accordance with the historicized viewpoint just described. All three can acknowledge the symbolic function of such realizations and the indispensability of this symbolic power for religious cult and community. All three must acknowledge, whether reluctantly or not, that there exists a diversity of human archetypal ideals and that there has been development, criticism, and adjustment of all important human ideals. All three perspectives can admit that hoping for historical confirmation of the claim that there has been a concrete, personal realization of a definitive archetypal ideal of humanity is an expectation based on a category mistake, for this is not an intelligible historical assertion. And all three can agree that it is impossible for historical research to offer substantial support for connected claims that, though historical in nature, exceed the inherent possibilities of historical sources, such as perfection of character, purity of intention, accuracy of self-understanding, and the like.

This amounts to a substantial general agreement. With this agreement in place, then, TeSelle's three perspectives can be articulated as truly complementary views of the historical process of conceiving and realizing archetypal human ideals, perspectives which emphasize some aspects of the relationship of that process to historically, concretely grounded norms and mute others.

The prospective view, for example, would speak about concrete, personal historical lives as vital influences on the formation of such ideals, rather than as theoretically superfluous to a purely innate awareness of them. At the same time it would stress that fact that our obviously culturally variable intuitions about human nature are partly formed by equally obvious cross-cultural structures of human existence. All humans have experiences of trying and failing, of wanting and being frustrated, of wishing with and without fulfillment. Such experiences set up the potential between possible and actual within which our conception of ideal humanity partially takes shape. But cultural values and understandings modify and specify these basic elements of the concept of 'ideal humanity.'[52] We bring those partly universal (as Kant saw) and partly culturally variable (as Lévy-Bruhl saw) intuitions to the interpretation of any concrete historical event, including Jesus' life. In this act of interpretation, we partly limit the possibilities of Jesus' significance for us by our intuitions about what an ideal human life might be like, and we are also partly astonished into the correction of our ideal for humanity by the factuality of this life, or by the boldness of the testimony to its significance. But we think of this significance as guide and inspiration for a path toward liberation that we anticipate prospectively and must walk without the source of our inspiration concretely present, trusting that God will complete our attempts to perfect ourselves out of the abundance of divine mercy and grace. Thus, this perspective suggests elements not only of an anthropology, but also of a view of salvation.

TeSelle's second perspective focuses on enactments. Here the first thought is about the facts that Jesus was received as bespeaking the depth of human possibility by his followers and that their attachment of such significance to him was a direct consequence of his personal impact upon them. We look at our pilgrimage toward realizing our full humanity as somehow assured by Jesus having enacted his own pilgrimage in such a way that we can think of ourselves as *following* him. We understand our own failures and successes as dramatically related to this following, and we attempt to model and to emulate the one we follow, as he is revealed to us in the stories about him that we tell and tell again. If we take Jesus to be our original inspiration in the first perspective, our primal memory for the pilgrimage, the second perspective presents Jesus as a companion on the road, leading the way, while we variously walk beside, or struggle to keep up, or perhaps even are carried when we become weary.

In the third, eschatological perspective, we conceive of Jesus Christ, the archetypal symbol of ideal humanity, as always in our future, calling us ahead. Here the primary assurance for our own pilgrimage derives not from the inspiration we draw from Jesus to trust the graciousness of God, not from the companionship of the Jesus whom we follow along the way, but from the proleptic character of the significance of Jesus Christ. What is realized historically is a promise for the future precisely to the extent that it is revelatory for the present. Because we find in Jesus Christ an archetype for our own potential humanity right now, we are led to the confidence that the universe can bear the historical realization of that archetype, and are borne on our pilgrimage by this confidence.

In all three perspectives, a different structural feature of the archetype of ideal humanity that Christians identify with the symbol of Jesus Christ holds sway. Each one corresponds to a different style of Christian theol-

ogy and a preference for a particular emphasis when speaking of salvation. What is more important for our purposes, in each case there is a
positing of an historical reality in correlation with the symbol of Jesus
Christ that justifies and makes efficacious talk about the person of Jesus.
But there is no historically unverifiable imputing of moral or personal
characteristics to the actual Jesus. Nor is there any need to elevate the actual Jesus to be the full, unique, and final historical actualization of ideal
humanity, accessible under the description of the biblical pictures of him,
as if this ideal were simply one thing.[53] Such an actualization is superfluous, because we can and must form partial conceptions of ideal humanity
apart from any realization of it, because we can and must live without certain historical knowledge of a perfect actualization of our ideal, and because the importance of our narratives about Jesus depends not on his
perfection but on his humanity. But a perfect actualization of the human
ideal is also impossible, because the variety of human ideals is not reducible to a set of alternative descriptions of a single life, no matter how
conceived, and because a perfectly realized archetype being ideal for us
means with an ironic certainty that it will not be ideal for others.

The idea of a perfect actualization of the archetypal human life is,
therefore, edifying insofar as it remains an imaginative expression of
hope, but a delusion if it is transmuted from a helpful projection into a
historical assertion. It is foolish, and in some sense immoral, to force history to bear the weight of human hopes. History tumbles along quite independently of our conceits, thinking that we have grasped its depth in
our lives and realized our depth in its process. It is an ambiguous process,
full of patterns and contingencies, amenable to control and shaping, but
finally breaking all constraints and defying all interpretations. What we
need in the way of an archetype of ideal humanity is what we have in the
symbol of Jesus Christ, as described in a modest Christology—no more
and no less—inspiration from the person, companionship with his God,
and the promise that the pilgrimage has a purpose.

7

Modest Christological Solutions
to External Challenges

The previous chapter showed that modest Christologies offer solutions to internal dimensions of this crisis of plausibility. However, internal challenges are arguably less telling in practice than the ethical, scientific, and interreligious issues discussed in this chapter—the external dimensions of the crisis. But the pattern is the same: whereas absolutist Christologies with wide variations are forced by their conceptual flaws to flounder in response to these challenges, Christologies dispensing with the absolutist principle can offer intelligible, poised solutions that demonstrate the continuing flexibility and power of the classical Christological tradition to relate the living symbol of Jesus Christ to the circumstances of our time.

Ethics: Christological Responsibility?

Exhibitions of purported ethical liabilities of traditional Christology have been plentiful in recent decades. Sometimes these charges, while well intentioned, have not been well argued, in the sense that the supposedly substantive connection to Christology remains obscure. The aim here is to trace out the connection between ethics and theology as far as Christology is concerned and to illumine the decisive role played by the absolutist principle. Now, any concept can be twisted to be destructive or oppressive, in the right circumstances. Therefore, the nature of the solution offered by modest Christologies to this aspect of the contemporary crisis in Christology is, by contrast with other dimensions of the crisis, practical. The argument is that Christology, when unburdened by the absolutist principle, is better placed to resist ethical distortions of many kinds than it is, and actually has been, otherwise.

The Ethical Impact of Christology

The range of charges that have been laid at the feet of traditional Christology is impressive. In several areas, Rosemary Radford Ruether has been one of the agenda setters. Her examination of the relationship between the traditional Christology of the church and both patriarchy and anti-Semitism, mentioned in the last chapter, led her to the conclusion that the hermeneutical absolutism of much traditional Christology has had an insidious effect in both cases and even that Christological origins are explained in part by the influence of such attitudes.

The feminist critique in Ruether's work has been explored and extended in many ways by theologians during the last couple of decades. Recently, for instance, several writers have pursued the connection between various understandings of the atonement and both child and spouse abuse.[1] A more long-standing and widespread area of investigation has been the practical, theological, and ethical implications of the fact that Jesus, who became God incarnate according to ecclesial doctrine, was a male member of the human species. Critics have argued that this initially expressed and then reinforced the bias that the male sex is solely worthy of being the vessel of divine self-disclosure, consolidating the subjugation of women. The widespread acceptance of this criticism among theologians has fostered interest in Christologies that deabsolutize Christology, perhaps by denying the incarnation altogether, or by allowing the possibility of *other* forms of divine self-revelation akin to the incarnation. This deabsolutizing entails a delegitimizing of ethical stances drawing support from Jesus' maleness.

The other aspect of Ruether's early work—the exploration of anti-Semitic tendencies in patristic Christology—also has been the focus of intensive research in the last two decades. An outstanding constructive

Christian theological response to this gnawing problem has been given by Paul van Buren.[2] He explores the benefits of a modest Christology for breaking the close correlation between traditional Christology and anti-Semitic action and theological rationalization.

Other ethical problems have come to light that are sometimes held to have Christological connections, though their Christological character may not be at the forefront of writers' interests. The abuse of animals and careless destruction of the earth's environment point to an anthropocentrism that could be partially Christologically grounded. Colonialism and the economic exploitation of poorer, so-called developing, countries by wealthier, so-called developed, nations bespeak a myopic, obsessive self-absorption that is conceivably supported and rationalized by absolutist Christological perspectives.

The question to be pressed here is why anyone would think that such a wide range of ethical issues—from child abuse to environmental degradation, from oppression of women to large-scale economic exploitation—could indict traditional Christology. How is this ethical impact of Christology conceived? *Are* there negative ethical consequences of affirming a traditional Christology? Are they such as to require its repudiation, or are they merely the result of deliberate or unintentional twisting of the true meaning of traditional Christology? In short, what does Christology have to do with ethics?

Some connections between practical behavior and an interpretation of Jesus Christ are obvious. Attempting to love one's neighbor and even one's enemies, for instance, is called for by moral maxims attributed to Jesus in the Gospels. And the compelling power of Jesus' person, as this is mediated by the gospel portraits of him, has inspired many to emulate what they have taken to be his attitudes and behavior. These connections, however, have little to do with the specifics of Christological interpretations of Jesus. Nor do they furnish insights into the interaction between theological concepts, individual behavior, and social policy.

Actions and thoughts are woven together in human life. Decisions about what to do are most often made against the background of a complex array of habitual practices and ideas about ourselves and our environment that defy exhaustive analysis. In practice, examination of the formative background material is rare; we almost always act without thinking, or without thinking very hard if the action calls for a preliminary decision, for this is essential for survival and efficient operation in the world.

Occasionally a large decision will require ethical analysis, whereupon we resort to rule following, trust our background-formed intuition, or more systematically try to expose the conceptual structure of this background to test its consistency and ethical soundness.

This hazy region of human existence is susceptible to all manner of ideas and actions that can have ethical significance in the appropriate settings. For instance, we learn one set of child-rearing practices implicitly from our families of origin and another from explicit training or reflection on our experience as parents. In an everyday crisis we may act in a negative or unhelpful way, and this act upon later reflection might seem to have been a result of habitual behavior grounded in our own childhood conditioning, habits that were insufficiently checked or adjusted by what we have learned as adults. A thought of this sort can fortify determination and increase alertness in such a way as to increase the chances of a better, more wholesome action or decision in future everyday crises. Again, our assumptions about our country and our conception of its heritage or destiny can greatly affect our actions, leading us to buy one product rather than another, to approve or disapprove of a decision to take military action, and to be understanding or intolerant of national differences. A final example is from the advertising industry, which in affluent nations channels enormous amounts of money to affect purchasing habits through conditioning the background of practices and ideas that consumers take with them to the market or to a car purchase. Theological concepts can affect actions, awareness of actions, and the ethical evaluation of actions in exactly this way.

Some of the most influential aspects of this background of assumptions and automatic practices are the pervasive ones that make us alert to some kinds of actions and oddly unaware of others or the deeply held ones that express and embody what is ultimately significant to us. National sentiment often participates in these influential aspects, as do religious ideas. A view of Jesus Christ that is imparted and reinforced by a worshipping cult can influence subtly or obviously many kinds of actions as well as interpretations of ourselves and our world. A culture, too, can consist largely of people in whom this formative influence has operated in more or less similar ways, to the point that Christological ideas are borne in cultural artifacts even without explicit recognition of any connection to their original source.

Given the complexities of the connections between the conceptual and the practical in human beings, those charging ethical liabilities against Christology are faced with the daunting challenge of connecting ethical complaints to Christology in a *detailed, compelling* way. Superficial analyses are as unconvincing as they are easy to produce. Effective critiques demand unusual skill in negotiating the dark alleys and getting behind the brightly lit street facades of the regions of our background held widely in common with others. They call for drawing attention to little-noticed actions, to connections among ideas and between concepts and actions, and to true origins of assumptions and behaviors whose pedigree has become uncertain. They are, therefore, very difficult to do well.

The Root of the Ethical Liabilities of Traditional Christology

In view of this, it is impossible here to engage each of the allegations mentioned earlier in the sustained, detailed way required to produce independent confirmation of their contention that traditional Christology is ethically problematic. What is in reach, however, is showing that the various individual charges have a common root: they all draw attention to unjustified absolutist elements in self-understandings formed by the Christian understanding of the world. These elements include assumptions of the native superiority or blessed destiny of the male sex, the "developed" world, the human species, the planet home of humanity, or non-Jewish Christians.

It is clear enough that the idea of God's personal self-revelation in a man—interpreted as a unique event of unlimited revelatory and salvific significance for the human species and the cosmos as a whole—is a dangerous one. It can be maintained that such a revelation might in principle have occurred in the life of a woman. Likewise, it can be maintained that the occurrence of this unique cosmic event within the human species does not denigrate the value to God of nonhuman species, that its occurrence on this planet does not make the one historical stream of which we are aware more important than the potential multitude of others in the cosmos of which we are not aware, and that its celebration as the decisive fulcrum of the history of creation is held in one and only one of that planet's religions does not invalidate other religions. These are solid replies. Watertight entailment, therefore, can never be established from these historical and conceptual contingencies to the ethical disasters in question.

Yet, as a matter of fact this all-significant event is permanently, irrevocably linked with the male sex; the human species and its planet home constitute the locus for it; the Western world has developed under its influence; and Christianity alone receives it for what it is held to be. The meanings of maleness, humanness, the West, Christianity, earth, and the cosmos are powerfully influenced by these linkages, and the coordination of these meanings in the intensely valued symbol of Jesus Christ adds to their conceptual and practical efficacy. These contingencies automatically impart an immense amount of momentum to any attempt to interpret as absolutely important that sex, species, culture, religion, and planet, and, in turn, to any attempt to legitimate personal behavior or social policy grounded on the premise of the absolute importance of these things. Moreover, this danger is not merely a matter of theory; such ethical legitimation often and infamously has availed itself of the rhetorical, conceptual, and practical energy associated with such hermeneutically absolutized symbols.

The logic of these connections is crucial. There is no implication here, for instance, that the maleness of Jesus automatically leads to sexism and patriarchy; after all, these devastating human practices are not caused by the fact of anyone in particular being male. Nor can it be inferred that a Christological appropriation of Jesus, with all of the power this brings to the symbol of Jesus Christ, is by itself enough to elevate the fact of his maleness into the dubious role of patriarchal sponsorship, though this is certainly far more likely on a Christological than a nonChristological interpretation of Jesus. It is only when the fact of Jesus' maleness is regarded as absolutely, definitively significant that the legitimation of patriarchy has ready access to the sponsoring power of the symbol of Jesus Christ. Now, when can Jesus' maleness be regarded as absolutely, definitively significant? This is *most likely* to occur when the symbol of Jesus Christ is regarded as possessing absolute, unique, final revelatory, and salvific significance—in the presence, that is, of the absolutist principle. The same logic holds for other specific facts that can be associated with Jesus: in every case, the absolutist principle is a most convenient and effective legitimator of ethical travesties. Those travesties may occur without Christological sponsorship, and they are avoidable even in the presence of absolutist Christology. When Christology *is* used in the rationalizations for them, however, it is too easily mediated and empowered by the absolutist principle.

Theologians have not usually held that the Christ event was contingent in any way; on the contrary, it was conceived in the mind of God before creation, and its historical definiteness is anticipatorily expressed in the trinitarian nature of God. This is one of the reasons that the discovery of undeniable contingency in the biological production of the human species has been problematic, a topic to be taken up in the next section. Theologians therefore usually have not said that the Christ event could have occurred in a woman's life, or within another planetary history, and until recently they have rarely assumed that other religions have revelatory and salvific significance comparable to that of Christianity. Theology has tended rather to give explicit theological support for the absolutizing of the particular details of the Christ event: he had to be a man because he belonged to the royal line of David and was a "second Adam"; he had to be a Jew because the history of revelation to the Jews reached its completion in Jesus; he had to be rejected by the Jews for the gospel to become efficacious for all humanity, and he had to be human for there was no other self-conscious species in the universe. These rationalizations for the necessity of the specifics of Jesus' life, the blighted children of the absolutist principle, are no longer compelling. But the absolutist principle has survived most of its spawn, and though vulnerable through being unshielded by offspring, it is still capable of vaulting into absolutely significant status the contingent facts surrounding the life of Jesus.

This suggests that the absolutist principle is the most prominent reason for the ethical liabilities of traditional Christology. Relinquishing Christological dependence on this unnecessary and distorting idea both removes many of the theological resources necessary for rationalizing such ethical travesties and helpfully improves the ability of Christology to resist being pressed into sponsoring them. But none of this constitutes an argument for the falsity of the absolutist principle, at least not without certain pre-understandings about the way we detect the truth. Anything, good or bad, can be distorted and used in the service of the ignoble, the sociopathic, and the violent. But a Christology ought not, if possible, be as conducive to such misuse as absolutist Christology is. When, therefore, there are other reasons to be suspicious of the absolutist principle (as there surely are), then there is strong motivation from the sphere of ethics to free Christology from its influence.

Driver: Ethical Reform through a Trinitarian,
Communitarian Decentering of Christ

A number of recent works at the intersection of theology and ethics have
been at some pains to develop what James M. Gustafson refers to in the
title of his two-volume work: an *Ethics from a Theocentric Perspective.* Insofar as Gustafson's ethical reflections engage Christology, the articulation of an ethics from a theocentric perspective resolutely embraces a
modest Christology.[3] His stance against what is here called the absolutist
principle is, however, only implicit. By contrast, the ethical case against
the absolutist principle is made in detail, though with different language
and a slightly narrower scope than proposed here, by Tom Driver in
Christ in a Changing World.[4]

This book appears to be a potentially unreliable guide, mixing aggressive polemics with an interesting depth of argument. However, by attempting to show how the absolutist elements in much traditional
Christology lead inevitably to negative ethical consequences, Driver offers
a perspective on the *general structure* of the problem of ethics and Christology instead of an extended argument against a specific negative ethical
consequence. This attempt is rare and deserves attention as an example of
the argument being evaluated here.

Driver's motivation in this book, as well as in other of his writings, is
well expressed in his dedication: "To all who have suffered at the hands of
people who claimed to act in the name of Christ." The traditional teaching
of the churches about Jesus Christ is, Driver believes, seriously ethically
flawed, so he offers analyses of the origin of this ethical derailing, its consequences in Christian history up to the present, and the options for reform. Using passionate and sometimes inflammatory language, Driver
argues that traditional Christology fosters what he calls "Christofascism."[5]
He means by this, first, the absolutizing of the past in order to legitimate
present injustices and inequities or to suppress evaluation and change of
the present situation. Second, Driver means the absolutizing of the idea of
"person" with the attendant consequences for the significance of implicit
"nonpersons." Since Jesus is the ideal, normative person, Jews (who "rejected" Jesus), women (who are not male, like Jesus) and nonwhites (who
are not white, as Jesus was supposedly long imagined by whites to be), are
second-rate or even nonpersons. Driver attacks Christofascist tendencies
as they appear in the concepts of Christ as center, model, and norm

(chapter 3); salvation as once-for-all (chapter 4); and the Bible as infallible (chapter 5).

Traditional Christology is not completely responsible for the horrors, subtle and violent, inflicted upon those without the power and voice to defend themselves, according to Driver. However, it *fosters* such injustice by the ease with which it can be bent to serve the interests of those with power. This bias toward ready coercion in support of injustice can be traced, he thinks, to the embodiment in much traditional Christology of a fatal ethical flaw: the regarding of Jesus Christ as center of creation, of human being, of history, of church, and of society.[6] This corresponds, of course, to what is conceived here more generally as the absolutist principle.

Driver's explanation of this flaw and of its origins owes a great deal to Rosemary Radford Ruether's *Faith and Fratricide*. In that book, as we saw in the last chapter, Ruether advances her argument against the "illegitimate historicizing of the eschatological" in the first century of the Common Era, by which she means the process of reconceiving Jesus and his redemptive work so that it was regarded as perfectly completed (and so already in history) rather than eschatologically immanent (and so drawing the Christian community toward its realization). Driver agrees with Ruether that this "paradigm shift" was primarily triggered by the failure of the early Christians' messianic expectations, but he points out that it also took place in the triple context of the extremely active life of the Christian communities, their ongoing struggles with non-Christian Jews, and their accelerating expansion into the Gentile world.

Each of these contextual elements played a role in fostering the absolutizing direction that the development of Christological thought took. Christian communities with Jesus as the focus of their intense hope were by and large amenable to absolutizing Jesus in their imaginations; Jewish Christians in conflict with non-Christian Jews were unlikely to admit that their messianic hopes had been mistaken; and Christians whose faith had a natural relevance to the Hellenistic world and beyond were ready and willing to conceive of Jesus in new categories, muting the messianic theme in favor of "a God-man who stood at the center of things."[7] This paradigm shift was given official legitimacy by the conciliar decisions of the fourth and fifth centuries CE, but was already an important factor as early as the last of Paul's letters and later in the formation of the Gospels.

According to Driver, the time has come for another shift. This time,

Christ must be decentered, and the Christian church needs to recover the "New Testament Christ" as "Christ future." Christ the center, model, and norm led and leads to ethical obscenities because of ineradicably absolutistic elements that are so easily used to the advantage of the powerful and shameless. Now, however,

> To be faithful to Jesus one must refuse him as model or central norm. He himself seems not to have needed a center of history. What he relied on was the power of a loving God. To be sure, that got him crucified; but if Easter means anything, it means the cross did not end or arrest the power of God. It need not mean that the love of God is focused forever on Jesus. To say so is to prescind from history and from the ethical decisions that are uniquely ours, having to do with matters that never occurred to Jesus.[8]

A simple recovery of a more primitive view of Jesus will not be adequate, however. Driver points out that the recovery of Jesus as our eschatological future could easily legitimate utopian symbols, rather than foster prophetic critique of degenerate institutions.[9] Therefore, he suggests a trinitarian and communitarian ethic as the context for an ethically adequate Christology.[10] Driver's constructive ideas are guided by three methodological principles:[11] (1) Christology must begin and end within ethics; (2) there must be freedom in the name of ethics from past formulations, be they biblical or traditional; and (3) the idea of relationality must be brought to the forefront of Christological thought—again in the name of ethics. This last principle corresponds to Driver's presuppositions that God changes through experiencing the world, and that Jesus Christ's relation with us is genuine and mutual. We must discern Jesus' action in our midst, therefore, and, in recognition of the mutuality of our relationship with him, take responsibility for what we say and believe about Jesus.

Driver's talk about Jesus "relating to us" and "acting" is not gratuitous. In a refreshingly realistic move, unusual in twentieth-century liberal theology, and quite consonant with Pannenberg's approach, Driver treats the resurrection of Jesus "not merely as a myth or a symbol but as a true historical event,"[12] and, in another inflammatory formulation, as "a quite real, 'objective' fact of history, as objective, let us say, as the slaughter of Jews in Hitler's Germany."[13]

While the ethical advantages of Driver's view of the resurrection are duly noted—a concretely live, decentered Jesus is probably as effective for stimulating ethical concern as the centered, just-barely-alive Jesus of some modern theology—there is a severe problem induced in his decentering strategy because of it. The resurrection, for instance, is one of the metaphysical-historical propositions most able potentially to confirm the absolutist principle, as noted in the earlier discussions of Hick's repudiation of the resurrection, and Pannenberg's affirmation of it. The same problem is raised by his talk of Trinity, which he explores without the aid of the kind of clearly stated distancing of Jesus from the second person in the inner divine life that is essential for the consistency of a modest Christology that affirms the Trinity. Granted the ethical travesties sponsored by traditional Christology's too easily distorted absolutist principle, and the effectiveness of his explanation for how this ethically dangerous interpretation entered mainstream Christology, could the absolutist principle nevertheless be true? Surely Driver's view of the resurrection and of the Trinity makes it very difficult to evade the irresistible conclusion that *Jesus is, in fact, the center of a very great deal of creation, if not all of it.* How is the resurrection to be theologically and metaphysically explicable from Driver's perspective otherwise?

The Problem of Loss of Moral Capital

This points up a severe problem with ethical critiques of the absolutist principle. How is moral force for personal transformation and social engagement to be generated from Christology if the main traditional metaphysical basis for it (the absolutist principle) is abandoned? Driver's proposed solution is to proceed with decentering Jesus Christ, while attempting to recoup lost moral resources by adopting a trinitarian, process doctrine of God and emphasizing the reality and presence of a resurrected Jesus Christ. The moral benefits of these aspects of Christian teaching are considerable, but Driver's constructions are conceptually fragile. Is there a consistent metaphysical perspective within which Driver can have his cake and eat it too? Perhaps William Ellery Channing, who held similar views about both Jesus and the resurrection, succeeded in this regard. For the purposes of understanding the problem of the loss of moral capital associated with rejection of the absolutist principle, it is instructive to draw some comparisons between Driver and Channing.

There are three telling differences between Channing and Driver, for present concerns. First, Channing rejected the trinitarian doctrine, making his position noticeably less strained than Driver's. It is hard to see how an appeal to the Trinity as the *vital* key for Christology and ethics could be effective in the context of a decentering Christological strategy. A modest Christology can be compatible with a trinitarian doctrine of God—this is relatively straightforward for an inspirational Christology, and an incarnational modest Christology merely requires a carefully maintained distinction between the principle of incarnation and the person, Jesus. But in this case, the Trinity is not quite the central, exclusively, intimately Christological doctrine that Driver thinks he requires.

Second, Channing did not have to reckon to the same degree as Driver with the naturalism of the contemporary world, which made an appeal to the resurrection less problematic for Channing—even though it was formally almost superfluous to his Christology, in the sense that it confirms but adds only a little new material to Christological affirmations about Jesus' person.

Finally, Channing could depend on the comparative strength and unity of Christian sentiment in the midnineteenth-century United States to generate moral capital. Driver, in the more secularized climate of the late twentieth century, cannot take this path. Christology, and indeed Christian theology as a whole, must attempt to be ethically self-contained, in the sense of generating and preserving on its own terms moral assets that can guide individual behavior and social policy and function as the basis for prophetic critique of the culture's moral assumptions. This is the only realistic option in a secularized, pluralistic culture that lacks enough commonly held moral convictions to guide itself sure-handedly and so has no surplus moral capital to share with ecclesial institutions whose own moral foundations are in a period of more or less radical transition.

Channing's attempt to team a supernatural construal of the resurrection with Christological modesty is being repeated by Driver. But while Channing's concerns were historical, metaphysical, and pietistic adequacy, Driver's focus is primarily ethical adequacy. This sensitizes Driver to the problem of generating moral capital within Christology—not an issue in the same way for Channing—which in turn leads Driver to risk conceptual inconsistency to secure a sound moral foundation. A decentered Jesus Christ who nonetheless is resurrected and properly described by the doctrine of the Trinity, in Driver's particular sense, is not utterly inconceivable, but it exacts a high price in theological consistency in exchange for the supposed ethical benefits. Thus, Driver's Christological doctrine seems to be an inherently inconsistent interpretation that could survive only as the teaching of the churches by constantly repelling more obvious construals of Jesus as somehow metaphysically unique, the very position that Driver wishes to attack for understandable ethical reasons. The probable ecclesial instability mimics the conceptual fragility.

The question remains, then, of how the absolutist principle can be abandoned, whether for compelling ethical or completely different reasons, without giving up all of the moral assets that absolutist Christologies have had at their disposal for centuries, along with the less welcome moral liabilities. Driver's need to throw down independent ethical roots, together with his deliberate forsaking of the absolutist principle as the source for moral energy and enthusiasm, is an attempt to protect moral capital that leads to conceptual unfeasibility. Yet Driver's problem is our own. It appears that this question will not be solved quickly. If, however, the absolutist principle is the liability that increasingly many theologians are arguing it to be, then it is a problem that will have to be answered rather than avoided. Advocates of modest Christologies do not suppose that Christian theology will find surrendering its "theological absolutism" to be an easy task, but they do assume that such a surrender, already underway, will have to continue. This involves pressing on into the future, giving up both known liabilities and known assets and actively waiting to see what develops.

The Impossibility of Ethical Renewal of Absolutist Christology

In concluding this section, a final possibility needs to be considered that promises a solution to the ethical liability of absolutist Christology, without changing the Christology itself. Perhaps absolutist Christology can reform itself, somehow protecting itself from the dangers of the absolutist principle, while retaining its well-established moral capital and its social rallying power. After all, does not the biblical exegesis of Latin American liberation theology discern in the Gospels a view of Jesus that is radically ethically effective, at the same time as conforming, in many cases, to an absolutist Christology? Is not the better proposal a recovery of the absolutist Christology—ignoring other objections to it for the moment—with its centered, normative Jesus Christ? This Jesus Christ advocated truly radical moral principles in what liberation theology reconstructs of his teach-

ing and activity. His eating with sinners, his treatment of women, his principle of turning the other cheek, his commandment to love one another
as God loves, to forgive as God forgives—these alone are a veritable mine
of moral gold. True, as Troeltsch has shown in his *Social Teaching*, these
principles were not sufficiently elaborated to solve many of the concrete
moral problems that quickly arose for the Christian churches, but they are
arguably sufficient to offset the potentially negative ethical consequences
of Jesus Christ as center, model, and norm. The fact that such disastrous
ethical consequences were actually realized—so goes the argument—is to
be attributed not to the centered, normative Christology itself, therefore,
but to the failure of the church to understand the *kind* of model and
norm that it possessed in Jesus Christ. So, is decentering really necessary?
Cannot the absolutist principle be retained?

The feasibility of this form of preserving while consuming one's cake
is a matter of practical judgment. Leaving aside the consideration that the
absolutist principle faces unwinnable battles on all of its many other
fronts, however, the hope that this strategy is feasible seems unduly optimistic. The historical pattern of the ethical corruption of absolutist Christology is consistent, so it does not seem viable for Christology to protect
itself from being co-opted by means of the absolutist principle into the
service of paltry rationalizations and disastrous sponsorship of ethical
travesties merely with the aid of occasional reminders. Ethical reminders
are always invaluable, regardless of the reigning theology, but intrinsic
conceptual disincentives to moral distortion are better.

Latin American liberation theologies do not offer a counterexample to
this judgment, for they have a vested interest in making use of the rallying
capacity for social transformation of a metaphysically and morally centered
Jesus Christ. This can foster the hesitancy of liberation theologies to draw
out the systematic Christological consequences of their general ethical and
theological stance. In other words, there may be a kind of failure to complete the hermeneutical circle from praxis back to reflection in liberation
theologies that blocks the perception of exactly how promising a decentered Jesus Christ would be for the problems of social justice in the long
term. Unless and until the hermeneutical circle is consistently closed in liberation theologies, their frequent recourse to the absolutist principle will
be too untroubled and their value as an illustration of the ethical renewal
of absolutist Christology limited. Furthermore, dangerous ethical situations are not effectively addressed by the absolutist Christology of many

liberation theologies, including especially the problems associated with anthropocentrism and earthcentrism. And the normative status of maleness alleged to flow from Jesus as the unique God-man is not blocked by observations about Jesus' supposedly unusual treatment of women, since even hypothetically second-class human beings presumably ought to be treated lovingly and fairly, in the manner of the best paternalism.

Naturally, it seems ill-advised to abandon the traditionally strong Christological core of Christian ethics, with all the disruption that would entail, if renewing that core is still possible. But the critique of the absolutist principle—in Driver's language, Christ as center, model, and norm—depends on nothing that could be affected by renewal strategies. This amounts to a strong *prima facie* case against Christological dependence on the absolutist principle. But that merely brings the matter to trial, as it were, and by itself does not warrant conviction. The prosecution has been tenacious in regard to anti-Semitism, patriarchy, ecology, and animal rights. Many scholars have been successful to varying degrees in showing that the absolutist Christology cannot be renewed in relation to these areas. However, in the case of contemporary ethics versus the absolutist Christology, the defense is strong and well developed, especially in Latin American liberation theology, in spite of the problems just mentioned. The prosecution's argument is therefore helpfully complemented by other arguments against the absolutist principle that establish that Christian ethics cannot proceed, at any rate, under the auspices of an absolutist Christology. Even without these other reasons to repudiate the absolutist principle, however, absolutist Christology faces a severe test in the face of these ethical critiques.

By contrast, a modest Christology offers fruitful resources for addressing the whole range of ethical dilemmas. These resources are especially and perhaps most obviously promising in the case of anti-Semitism, since a modest construal of the person and work of Jesus promises fructifying consonances with Jewish appropriations of Jesus. Such a Christology can be the basis for greater mutual understanding and may even help finally to uproot the anti-Semitic virus that repeatedly has misrepresented and maligned Jews and Judaism in Christian theologies and cultures. The immediate conceptual disabling of attachment to Jesus' maleness is another clear-cut advantage of a modest Christology. A new response to the exploitation of nonhuman species and wider ecological concerns is less decisively provided for in a modest Christology. To see this, consider the fact that the imagery of the Hebrew creation myths has been and will continue to be effective in sponsoring Jewish, Christian, and Moslem action on these fronts. Both customarily anthropocentric "stewardship" metaphors —most consonant with the absolutist principle—and theocentric "partnership" or "glory of creation" metaphors—most consonant with modest Christologies—are grounded there. It is arguable that the "glory of creation" and "partnership" images are better bases for ecological responsibility, but this is a difficult case, and, at this stage, any image that inspires appropriate action is to be applauded. Quite apart from whether the resources they offer are new and powerful, or simply variations of extant options, however, modest Christologies promise advances in regard to every aspect of the ethical dimension of the contemporary crisis of Christology.

Natural Sciences: Evolutionary Biology and Cosmology

Probably the bluntest challenges in the array of problems defining the contemporary crisis in Christology derive from discoveries in the natural sciences. While information theory and quantum mechanical discovery of wave-particle duality influence the *way* Christology is discussed at the present time,[14] neither has special relevance for the debate between absolutist and modest Christologies. The sharpest problems for Christological plausibility come from evolutionary biology and cosmology. The sharpness is due especially to the fact that it is not so much shifts in cultural values or hermeneutical customs that raise the problem in the case of the sciences, but discoveries about the way the world actually is. This distinction between interpretation and discovery in the sciences is no longer the completely clear-cut one that it used to be, but our modern belief about the size and age of the universe, for instance, is not a matter of interpretation that might later be changed. It is so powerfully warranted a belief that it must be regarded as a permanent addition to our stock of knowledge about the world, which is why we call it a discovery. This is not to say that it cannot be corrected in details or reinterpreted, but the discovery still remains, just as Newton's mechanics and his theory of gravity remained predictively accurate for ordinary experience even after they were interpreted as classical approximations to Einstein's theories of relativity, in which motion and gravity were very differently understood. It is the inherently irreversible character of the knowledge of the size and age of the universe that makes the fact of its conflict with the absolutist principle so forceful.

Modern cosmology challenges the plausibility of the anthropocentric and Christocentric tendencies of absolutist Christology mainly in the spatial dimensions, and the same challenge is pressed with respect to the temporal dimension by evolutionary biology. Because of this connection, the two scientific contexts for reflection upon Christology have much in common, but they are distinguished by one crucial feature. The temporal challenge to anthropocentrism has a one-dimensional character, in the sense that the human species stands in the temporal flow and can see the relevant parts both of the entire past history of the creation and of its future possibilities stretching out in opposite directions. Because of that, the temporal aspect of the problem of anthropocentrism is to understand the development and fate of the human species. This leaves open the possibility of regarding humanity as somehow the culmination to date of an immensely complex but meaningful process of development. That is, there remains the possibility of continuing to regard the human species as at the center of meaning of the developing process, though this must be done in such a way as to allow for the further developments that await us.

This possibility of retaining a central place for the human species appears to evaporate when the spatial challenge to anthropocentrism is brought into the picture. In that case, the human species is but one stream of historical development, alongside of possibly infinitely other such planetary streams, many of which may include civilizations of religious creatures such as ourselves, and interaction with which is decidedly not out of the question. It is the loss of one dimensionality that marks the difference in the tone of the two problems. The change may be put this way: instead of all roads leading through Rome, whereby the importance of Rome is secured, even though the ultimate destination may be elsewhere, it becomes a matter of all roads going wherever they go, which may or may not involve passing through Rome at all. The spatial problem is in the end no more difficult for Christology to deal with than the temporal challenge to anthropomorphism and Christocentrism, especially since a modest Christology is perfectly placed to deal constructively and creatively with both issues. The spatial challenge, however, has a more disconcerting initial impact, because it induces an immediate sense of loss of any natural way to preserve the centrality of the human species, which affirmation absolutist Christologies often require.

Evolutionary Biology: Finding a Whole-Hearted Response

There have been many attempts to reflect theologically on Jesus Christ and the nature of history from the perspective of evolutionary biology, whereas the same reflection from a cosmological perspective lags far behind. At root, this is for the reason stated in the analysis just offered: the temporal challenge to anthropocentrism offers possibilities for retaining continuity with anthropocentric and Christocentric tendencies in the absolutist principle. Evolutionary biology has therefore been fertile soil for creatively extending, rather than simply abandoning, those tendencies.

There are other reasons. Long before Darwin's *Origin of Species* and Lyell's *Principles of Geology*, there was an impulse encouraging a developmental view of history, namely, a growing awareness of the broad scope and diversity of human culture. This prompted philosophers to try to bring this diversity under a single descriptive analysis that would render it intelligibly patterned. Thus was the philosophy of history brought into the modern period, distinguished from similar, earlier tasks in part by the magnitude of informed appreciation for diversity that critical historical research had made possible. "Development" was the category pressed into service for explaining past and extant diversity and for giving that diversity a unified interpretation. German idealism—represented at its expansive peak especially by Schelling and Hegel—was one family of developmental approaches to the historical process. Romanticism's all-embracing interpretations of the world produced another, even more diverse, family not completely distinct from idealist philosophy of history, which it inspired and from which it drew many of its central insights.

When the science of geology gave reason to expand immensely the supposed age of the creation, therefore, philosophy of history and theology were not taken by surprise. There were pockets of resistance, but these centered on the infallibility of Scripture, and the rising tide of historical consciousness had already done most of the work necessary to reconcile the modern Western mind to the fact that human life came into existence on this planet only after an enormously long period of preparation.

The same point holds for Darwin's *Origin of Species*, insofar as evolutionary biology stressed the long time span needed for *Homo sapiens* to evolve. However, evolutionary biology had an additional impact on theological and Christological reflection by specifying the mechanism of that process of development. A myriad of random variations and the principle of natural selection together serve to place *Homo sapiens* squarely among all other species on our planet, inducing a decisively different understanding of human nature than had formerly held sway in many theologies. It was understandable that there would be more resistance to the idea that humans, primates, rodents, reptiles, insects, birds, fish, trees, flowers, and microbes had emerged from the same pool of genetic material. However, the outline of a philosophy of history that could profit from this new anthropology was already in place. Accordingly, in spite of the incomplete and problematic character of the results of evolutionary biology, resistance quickly became scattered into backwaters outside of the mainstream of theological reflection.

These were the reasons, then, that theological reflection readily took up the problem posed for the absolutist principle by evolutionary biology and developed constructive proposals with comparative ease. Thornton, James, Peirce, Whitehead, Blondel, Teilhard, Rahner, Tillich, and numerous other twentieth-century theologians and philosophers of religion sought to speak of God's presence in the creative, evolving process of history. Some of these attempts have preserved the absolutist principle. The contention here is that such constructions fail to come to grips with the problem in a whole-hearted way and that only rejection of the absolutist principle can.

The Nature of the Problem and a Modest Solution: TeSelle

Theologians pondering the impact of evolutionary biology have had to face special problems and doubly so when they have attended to Christology. Eugene TeSelle sets up his statement of these problems in such a way as to show the essential inadequacy of theological proposals that preserve the absolutist principle.

> Theologians have often talked glibly about the evolutionary perspective and its consequences for theology when they have actually done no more than make some observations about the chronological sequence of evolution and then suppose that it indicates a slow but steady movement of all things toward Christ and the eschaton. . . .
>
> It is not merely that we must now take seriously the dimension of time and acknowledge the slowness with which the present stock of

chemical compounds, flora and fauna, has been assembled; not merely
that the evolutionary process takes place step by step, that the outcome,
however exalted it may be, is the product of occurrences that have taken
place all along the way and continues to bear their stamp (as the morphology of the human body, for example, is conditioned by the many antecedent forms out of which it evolved). What is most shattering to our
theological presuppositions—but is so essential to the evolutionary theory, and so well verified, that it cannot be explained away—is that
chance, by which I mean the random coincidence of independent
chains of events, plays an irreducible role in the process.[15]

The role of chance is prominent in biological evolution, for large
changes in inherited genetic characteristics, and therefore in the gene
pool of a species, can be induced by the tiniest of chance incidents. For
instance, "the particular combination of chromosomes as two animals
mate, the damaging of a gene by a cosmic ray that set out from a distant
nova thousands or millions of years before, the capture of a particular animal by a predator, or its escape—these may have a permanent effect, either positive or negative, on the history of evolution."[16] To this list of
chance occurrences, we may add the most common cause of genetic
modification: chemical errors in replication of the genetic code.

Having thus prepared the way, TeSelle draws the challenge for theology in general by asking the following pointed question: "Now if religious
people are so eager to claim all of this for the wonders of God's creative
activity, where are they going to point to it?"[17] This is a sharp problem, for
which TeSelle believes the only workable solution is a view of divine action in which God is able to guarantee the successful progress of evolution not by detailed planning and manipulation but simply by being
present "to the matrix of potentialities that makes up our evolving
world."[18] The resemblance to Whitehead's doctrine of the divine provision of an initial aim to every actual occasion in accordance with its antecedent influences and its inherent capabilities is unmistakable. The
connection to Teilhard's conception of God drawing the creation toward
realizing ever more closely the glory of the divine order is also apparent.[19]

The theological problem that concerns us here, however, is specifically Christological. TeSelle expresses it well:

It has become impossible to hold to a Christocentric, even an anthropocentric view of the world in the strict sense. We cannot say that man,

as *this particular* species, the featherless biped with five-digited limbs, called *Homo sapiens*, is the goal of creation, or that Christ, as the presence of the Word in one human life, is the goal and center of all things. The process is more indeterminate than that, for there are many things that might have happened differently along the line of descent leading to man, and at every stage God can be thought to have only a limited range of specific goals in view, based on what *could* happen, given the potentialities then existing.[20]

This should not be understood as averring the *difficulty* of asserting a Christocentric or anthropocentric view. TeSelle means what he says: this is literally, logically impossible. This position obviously presupposes the kind of limits on divine activity that were just mentioned. The indeterminacy of the evolutionary process is genuine, according to him, and not merely an impression created by apparently chance events that are at some deeper level the direct expression of divine choices.

Recovering the traditional insight that the incarnation was planned before creation is difficult, on this view, but not completely out of the question. For example, the ancient interpretation of eternity holding that all of the contingencies of history are eternally present to, and pre-ordained by, God offers a way to articulate the possibility of divine ordination of the specific attributes of the God-man. This, however, is unappetizingly close to being either deistic or unintelligible. By contrast, TeSelle tries to retain a solider sense of God's participation in the historical process. Thus he notes, "Though the exact forms of life are affected by circumstance and coincidence, there is still the phenomenon of convergence: given a challenge to meet, life eventually meets it under the terms of the challenge, and the successful response, especially if it leads to a higher form and opens up further possibilities, can be said to be grounded in God and even led by his wisdom."[21]

Now, if God's general aim in the creative process is to realize the world's highest potentialities, and if it can be further assumed that such an aim would involve the development of finite intelligence and freedom, followed by social cooperation, cultural and intellectual activity, and religious dedication,[22] then "we would still not be able to say that Christ is the antecedent goal of the process, whether considered as a member of the human race or as the Word incarnate."[23] Rather, Jesus' religious significance must be affirmed as a part of a contingently emerging solution to a structural problem within the world (sin). If this is so, then there is no basis from the perspective of evolutionary biology for thinking that this solution should be unique in the way that the absolutist principle seems to require. The continued affirmation of the absolutist principle appears, therefore, to be arbitrary: it is an assertion outrunning the evolutionary biological facts that possibly could be invoked in its support.

TeSelle's modest Christology is developed briefly out of this background of argument. It centers around affirmation of interaction between an open universe and divine intentions that are only gradually formed as the contingent developments within the creation call them forth. Within this mutual flexibility and free development, the creation (in humanity, at least) becomes concerned with God, even as God is always concerned with the creation. The ideal for humanity arises in the space marked out by that concern, the initiative for which TeSelle carefully places on the side of the divine,[24] though we might have expected him to see it, too, as a mutually formed, and actually a changing, construction. In any event, this ideal—variously represented as the divine Word, or God's covenant—is gradually conceptualized and realized in various ways in the history of humanity. The central Christological question is, then, how Jesus relates to this ideal. TeSelle gives the following answer.

> The humanity of Jesus, though it is shaped by and attests to the Word, neither exhausts the Word nor is the sole means of access to it, for the Word is both knowable and efficacious elsewhere. The uniqueness of Jesus—a uniqueness which should not be seen apart from the uniqueness of Israel and the Church—will consist, then, in being the touchstone by which other responses are judged, the achievement by which their deficiencies are overcome, the center of gravity around which they cluster.[25]

The Normativity of Jesus Christ

This summary statement of TeSelle's modest Christology raises a question about the uniqueness or normativity of Jesus Christ. Granted (for the sake of argument, if necessary) that the unique and final significance of Jesus Christ for the entire cosmos is out of the question from an evolutionary point of view, can Jesus still be affirmed as uniquely and finally significant for his *species*? The level of species, after all, seems to be the natural forum for the disclosure of the divine Word, on TeSelle's evolutionary account of the matter. Tillich answers this question affirmatively, and we will return to his discussion below under the heading of cosmology, which is the context in which he raises it.

We may think of the uniqueness of Jesus Christ and so the scope of Christological normativity in a number of ways. Here the concern is with Jesus' significance for us and the degree to which we think it reasonable for us to suppose that this significance should extend in principle. We might experiment with the thought that Jesus is not uniquely significant for us in any way whatsoever, an impossible construal of the facts. Or we might suppose that Jesus is uniquely significant for us in our contemplation of reality at the largest scope imaginable: the entire universe and all possible realms of reality. This marks out two extremes of hermeneutical scope between which there are a number of possible middle positions: a denomination or religion, a historical trajectory of cultural proportions, a species, and a region of creation (a galaxy, say) including a number of hypothetical, eventually interacting religious civilizations (isolated from other such regions by the supposed impossibility of further communication).

In all of these cases the aim is to speak about the scope we ourselves can reasonably attach to our assertions of Jesus Christ as significant. It is not our concern to win agreement from others, when reflecting on uniqueness for us, but only to decide from our own perspective the scope of the historical trajectory for which we think Jesus Christ ought to be regarded as uniquely significant. Our reasons for drawing the scope at one point rather than another may vary. If we believe that Jesus initiates a new metaphysical possibility for creation as a whole, a possibility that is laid hold of by religious creatures only through explicit of implicit appropriation of the symbol of Jesus Christ, then we will choose the largest scope for Jesus' significance for us and think of the church as the principal mediator of this normative significance. If we believe that Jesus cannot be significant where his life and message cannot be learned about, then we will choose a scope that measures, at the largest, what scientists suggest can be the extent of our possible future communication with religious civilizations in our region of the universe. That may, conceivably, turn out to be no broader than our own planet. If we believe that the religious basis of a culture is additionally important for conceiving of the relevance of Jesus, then we may construe his significance for us at the scope of a culture, as Troeltsch did. In every case, the reasons are of quite different kinds.

A final dimension of variability in trying to answer the question of the scope we attach to the uniqueness or normativity of Jesus Christ's significance for us concerns the openness of the historical process. If a radically open view of history is held, as it is here, for instance, then there exists the ever-present possibility that the contingency of Jesus' normative influence—customarily partially hidden behind its normative function—may come even more into the open. This could happen if Jesus' normativity were to merge with other equally contingent norms, or perhaps even to be superseded by them. It could also happen if humanity was annihilated in one of the several ways its perverse ingenuity has constructed for itself in the twentieth century.

This is the basis for a rough morphology of positions that might be taken on the issue of the uniqueness or normativity of Jesus' significance for us. In the last quotation, TeSelle quite explicitly takes the significance for us of Jesus to be intelligible only for that cultural trajectory that has developed under the direct impact of Israel and the Christian church. This implies that TeSelle would allow that the divine Word might express itself in suitably different ways in other cultural streams. Thus TeSelle imposes a direct restriction on the scope of the absolutist principle's significance thesis, while simultaneously advocating a separation of the particular Jesus and the universal Word, as he calls it. TeSelle's position has much to commend it, though we need to keep in view the tentative character of all assignments of normativity or uniqueness, owing to the openness of the future.

There is a possible confusion about this conclusion, however. It might seem that TeSelle is committed to drawing the scope of Jesus' normativity at the level of species rather than cultural-historical trajectory. This is because of what he calls the "phenomenon of convergence": "given a challenge to meet, life eventually meets it under the terms of the challenge." Presumably, from the point of view of biological evolution, these challenges exist at the level of species. After all, it is at the level of a species that genetic information is negotiated and altered, rather than at the level of a culture, which is not primarily genetically, but almost exclusively socially and contextually, relevant to human life. Correspondingly, then, we would expect Jesus, who is held to be the meeting of such a challenge, to be relevant to the entire species. If this argument were sound, its conclusion would score against TeSelle's point of view on the scope of Jesus' normative relevance. Of course, the *potential* relevance of Jesus Christ is to the entire human species and possibly even beyond, but TeSelle's point is that it is currently theologically unjustifiable to speak of the normative significance of Jesus Christ in so broad a way, because the leading criterion for the feasibility of normative assertions needs to be the *actual* historic and present significance enjoyed by the symbol of Jesus Christ in the cultural settings it has influenced.

The argument against TeSelle's view is flawed in a number of ways. The most important mistake is that the phenomenon of convergence does not rule out the possibility of meeting challenges, including the structural challenge of sin (or existential estrangement, or suffering) in the experience of religious creatures, in more than one way. Even as the experience of the challenge is differentiated in a variety of social and cultural contexts, so the meetings of the challenge are tailored to those contexts. Interestingly, they would also have to be regarded as eventually mutually competitive, if the contexts of their development were to merge in significant ways. Such competition might well open up the possibility of specieswide relevance of the significance and normativity of Jesus Christ, but such an outcome cannot be thought to be any more likely than any of innumerable other possibilities of the same kind—the openness of the historical process forces a wait-and-see attitude at that point.

To return to the main point, and to put it in the strongest Christian terms, the problem of sin is decidedly not merely a challenge for the gene pool. This particular problem cannot emerge for a species apart from a comparatively rich social, cultural environment (compared with plant and animal species). Therefore, attempted solutions to the problem cannot be conceived at the genetic level either; they must take into account human tendencies toward sociability and cultural creation.

There are also technical problems with the argument we are entertaining against TeSelle's position. For instance, sociobiology has demonstrated at the very least that the physical and social environment of a species is an important factor in realizing some genetic potentialities rather than others. But these technical objections only reinforce the major objection by suggesting that genetics itself may be relevant to the social and cultural specifications of the challenge of sin, to which the person and work of Jesus Christ is thought to be an answer in kind.

The conclusion, therefore, is this: evolutionary biology throws two challenges up to the absolutist principle. The first is that it forces recognition of the facts that the historical, evolutionary process is contingent upon very small, chance factors and that literal anthropocentrism is absurd precisely to the extent that the emergence of the particular species *Homo sapiens* is a matter of chance occurrences. This in turn brings a large dose of contingency to Jesus' humanity. But then, as we saw, this merely plays havoc with the traditional belief that the incarnation was in the mind and being of God before all creation; this belief can be preserved by positing history as an open process with which God is intimately involved at every moment. In such a process, the absolutist principle still can be conceived. But then the second challenge must be met: the perspective of evolutionary biology demands that the scope of claims about the relevance of Jesus' normativity or uniqueness be limited at this time in history to the cultural level. Absolutist Christology is, in TeSelle's phrase, "nothing more than a speculative over-belief" that casually ignores far sounder explanations of the data.[26] By contrast, a modest Christology warmly resonates with evolutionary biology and offers a way to lay out with detail and plausibility a path for continuing the classical Christological tradition into the evolutionary future.

Cosmology: Breaking the Deafening Silence

Extant ground-based telescopes are capable of detecting more than one hundred thousand million galaxies, with each galaxy a panoply of at least as many stars. These are truly staggering numbers. It is *prima facie* inconceivable that life could not have developed in any other places in our own galaxy, let alone in the unimaginably large number of other galaxies. This inconceivability multiplies almost daily as understanding of biological life processes deepens and astronomical exploration—including especially the detection by the Hubble space telescope of solar discs, the early form of planetary systems, and radio astronomers' discovery of evidence for individual orbiting planets—accelerates.[27] Moreover, it is reasonable to assume for reasons broached in the discussion of TeSelle's Christology that intelligent life, even if very different in form from our own species, would be social in character, and therefore that culture and religion would develop in step with self-consciousness in other places than on our own planet. This is a wildly, richly different scenario for creation than that possessed by our Western medieval ancestors. It poses profound challenges to any tendencies in human thought that foster the view that the human species is somehow central to the meaning of creation.

We have seen that Troeltsch was profoundly influenced by the inescapable impression of the vastness of the universe and the patent absurdity of anthropocentrism and the Christological absolutist principle as conceptual pillars for interpreting the world known to possess such proportions. But the contemporary version of this problem is slightly different than it was in Troeltsch's time because of the cosmic anthropic principle. This observation of contemporary cosmology is complex: it has several versions, many aspects, and controversial implications for a number of philosophical issues. But its basic import for our concern here is simple to state. To get living beings of our kind, a number of conditions need to be met, including at minimum the possibility of stars, solar systems, planetary habitats, and stable macromolecules. These are not sufficient conditions for human beings by any means, but merely a few of the long list of necessary conditions. It turns out that a number of features of the cosmos as a whole can differ very little from what they are without interfering with these necessary conditions. For instance, increase the mass of the universe by much and there will not be enough time before cosmic re-collapse for the multiple generations of stars needed to create the heavier elements necessary for living creatures; reduce the gravitational constant by a small amount and the rate of cosmic expansion will be too rapid to permit stars and solar systems from forming; or alter any of a number of fundamental constants and chemistry is impossible, let alone stable, replicating macromolecules. It seems, then, that a universe of about the size and age of our own is necessary if we human beings are to exist at all thus the name: *cosmic* anthropic *principle*.

All this is quite straightforward and, at the level at which I have introduced it, not especially controversial. We may conclude from it that our very existence as a species implies that the size and age of the universe should be about what it is, and therefore that size and age *in themselves* ought not make Christological assertions any more implausible than our own existence. But none of this deflects the charge of implausibility leveled against the absolutist principle, or for that matter against the foolishness of any anthropocentric interpretation of the cosmos. Just because the universe has to be big for us to be here does not mean that the whole big cosmos is here for us. And just because the universe has to be old for

us to be here does not imply that we humans are somehow the culmination of the cosmic processes of complexification. The universe may be
teeming with life in innumerable forms, and we may find many kinds of
living beings at least as interesting as we find ourselves. The absolutist
principle falters not on the size and age of the universe in themselves—
not even for Troeltsch—but on the vanity of absolutizing the significance
of Jesus Christ in a cosmos with such dimensions.

The awareness of the vast age and size of the cosmos has become second nature to most educated people within Western cultures. Yet, as Paul
Tillich complains, Christian theology has been noticeably slow to reflect
creatively on this theme: it "has been carefully avoided by many traditional
theologians, even though it is consciously or unconsciously alive for most
contemporary people."[28] Such a glaring dissonance between Christology
and contemporary self-understanding deserves more attention than it has
received, and the relative muteness of Christian theology on this point
amounts to culpable negligence.

Not every one has completely ignored the problem, however, even
though few have given it sustained attention. TeSelle briefly draws a cosmological perspective into his argument.[29] And in very recent years the
deafening silence has started to break as theologians have realized that a
problem for Christology as easy to state as this one simply cannot be ignored permanently. Between the obviously compelling modest solution
and the stance of the many theologians who, whether or not they have
thought about the problem, remain content both with an absolutist Christology and with no attempt to wrestle systematically and explicitly with
the issue, there have been represented a number of important middle positions—positions that are either absolutist or not whole-heartedly modest, and finally unsatisfactory. Some have thought explicitly about the
problem and retained the absolutist principle (for example, Karl Rahner).
Others have arbitrarily reduced the scope of revelatory and salvific significance of the symbol Jesus Christ from its cosmic dimensions without due
attention to the systematic ramifications of such a move (Leonardo Boff,
for instance). The most impressive attempt of the not whole-heartedly
modest group is that of Paul Tillich, who was truly innovative in trying to
deal with this problem, even at the cost of introducing incoherence into
his system.

Since the main outlines of the argument from cosmology and the argument from evolutionary biology are identical, and the modest solution

is even more clearly compelling in the cosmological case than it was in the already presented evolutionary biological case, there is no need to restate the obvious modest solution. Here the aim will be simply to show that the extant alternative solutions are inadequate.

Immodest Straws and the Plausibility Camel: Rahner

Karl Rahner famously and influentially has argued that Jesus Christ can only be understood in evolutionary terms and that his significance, even so understood, must have cosmic dimensions.[30] The idea of multiple incarnations is out of the question in Rahner's case for the usual reason: perception of the fact that God is personal is distorted when we might even hypothetically point to more than one historical being with the confession that "this person is God for us."[31] That sharpens the problem of cosmic immensity by forsaking one (though the least attractive and certainly not the only) strategy for ameliorating the problems it induces in Christological plausibility. But Rahner's transcendental anthropology makes possible his assertion that the salvific significance of Jesus Christ is cosmic in scope and independent of the acknowledgment of Jesus Christ by those who are saved. This then places the absolutist principle in the most plausible possible light with regard to the challenge of cosmic immensity—though not of course with regard to the other problems it must face.

The picture Rahner paints is rightly renowned for its beauty, even as Teilhard's vision is: an entire universe striving toward the realization of its highest potential, a realization that does in fact occur in one place and time in the entire cosmos, with the liberating, transforming ramifications reverberating throughout. An audacious proposal, in continuity with the vast bulk of theological tradition, it is severely problematic yet not metaphysically impossible. After all, the evolutionary process of the universe had first to produce religious creatures somewhere on one of the likely billions of life-bearing planets, though this is far from being universally an inevitable culmination of the evolutionary process. That we live where this happened is a logical possibility, and the anthropocentrism attending Rahner's view would be justified better were our existence decisive evidence for the actualization of that logical possibility.

We must ask, therefore, how Rahner conceives of the eschatological future of the cosmos in relation to the species and the planet in the evolutionary development of which Jesus Christ, the God-man, appears. This will be the test of how serious Rahner is in his affirmation of the absolutist principle, for consistency in his scheme demands that a cosmic future is inconceivable without humans and their testimony to Jesus Christ. In *Foundations of Christian Faith*, Rahner's discussion of eschatology is mainly concerned to argue that individual eschatology that is, life after death is not enough and that collective eschatology also is needed. In the course of addressing this issue, he makes the following remarks:

> With regard to the question about the end of this history [of mankind], we have to repeat the reservation here that we may not allow the spiritual and collective history of the world to come to an end within a world-time which continues on. Purely a priori that would not be inconceivable in itself. The following is not very probable for anyone thinking in categories of development, given the unimaginable size of the cosmos, but if someone presupposes that spiritual, corporeal and free beings who work out their destiny before God exist only on our earth, and if he imagines that this total and collective history of the human race will come to an end through some cosmic or historical catastrophe for the human race, for example, by an atom bomb or by the biological extinction of the race, then of course he could readily conceive of the continuation of the world and its physical history. But this conception does not really take seriously the fact that, in spite of all the legitimate natural sciences, we know matter only as the seedbed of spirit and of subjectivity and of freedom. . . .
>
> Without a very clear view of the history of the material cosmos, the dogma itself says first of all that the history of the human race as a whole is moving in its history towards a fulfillment of the human race which will end history.[32]

Thus taking Rahner's world view "seriously" demands that cosmic history would have to end if human history did—on the assumption that "spiritual, corporeal and free beings" exist only on earth. But what if this assumption is rejected?

> If we presuppose that in the dynamism of God himself matter has transcended itself into subjectivity, unlimited transcendentality and freedom in other places in the cosmos besides on our earth, and if we assume that in fact this transcendentality in other places is also borne by God's

self-communication in grace, for grace is the reason for creation, then we could move towards the idea that the material cosmos as a whole, whose meaning and goal is the fulfillment of freedom, will one day be subsumed into the fullness of God's self-communication to this material and spiritual cosmos, and that this will happen through many histories of freedom which do not only take place on our earth.[33]

Rahner thus vacillates between inconsistency and implausibility. On the supposition of many religious creatures in many places throughout the cosmos, he imagines the consummation of the entire cosmos along a variety of different lines of historical development, which in turn obscures his interpretation of the cosmic significance of the evolutionary process that produced Jesus the Christ. But on the supposition that humans alone are the manifestations of subjectivity, unlimited transcendence, and freedom in the cosmos, *regardless of the potential for further evolutionary developments in other parts of the cosmos,* cosmic history can extend no further than human history. This is the straw of consistency that breaks the back of the plausibility of his absolutist Christology. It retains only its status as an inconceivably unlikely logical possibility, and that is simply not enough of a basis to defend the intelligibility of Christological affirmations.

Intriguing, Inconsistent Modesty: Tillich

A similar problem arises for Tillich in his *Systematic Theology* at the point of his discussion of the quest for and the expectation of the Christ. Tillich states the problem as one of "how to understand the meaning of the symbol 'Christ' in the light of the immensity of the universe, the heliocentric system of planets, the infinitely small part of the universe which man and his history constitute, and the possibility of other 'worlds' in which divine self-manifestations may appear and be received."[34] His answer to this statement of the problem is relatively self-contained and in need of no elaboration, so most of it is quoted here at length.

> The basic answer to these questions is given in the concept of essential man appearing in a personal life under the conditions of existential estrangement. This restricts the expectation of the Christ to historical mankind. The man in whom essential man has appeared in existence

represents human history; more precisely, as its central event, he creates the meaning of human history. At the same time, our basic answer leaves the universe open for possible divine manifestations in other areas or periods of being. Such possibilities cannot be denied. But they cannot be proved or disproved. Incarnation is unique for the special group in which it happens, but it is not unique in the sense that other singular incarnations for other unique worlds are excluded. Man cannot claim that the infinite has entered the finite to overcome its existential estrangement in mankind alone. Man cannot claim to occupy the only possible place for Incarnation. . . .

Perhaps we can go a step further. The interdependence of everything with everything else in the totality of being includes a participation of nature in history and demands a participation of the universe in salvation. Therefore, if there are non-human "worlds" in which existential estrangement is not only real—as it is in the whole universe—but in which there is also a type of awareness of this estrangement, such worlds cannot be without the operation of saving power within them. Otherwise self-destruction would be the inescapable consequence. The manifestation of saving power in one place implies that saving power is operating in all places. The expectation of the Messiah as the bearer of the New Being presupposes that "God loves the universe," even though in the appearance of the Christ he actualizes this love for historical man alone.[35]

Tillich is to be commended for allowing his appreciation of the problem, and his honest treatment of it, to lead him into even greater inconsistency than Rahner, even as both are to be commended for venturing a serious response to a theological problem for Christology that has been ignored too often. The view expressed by Tillich, however, while intriguing, remains unsatisfactory for two reasons.

First, Tillich's proposal grants religious autonomy without further ado to those religious creatures about whose existence we are unsure, but it fails to grant the same courtesy to those non-Christian religious creatures who share our own home. Moreover, his own principles demand that he ought to make this extra move, since the saving power of divine love, from Tillich's point of view, always is mediated by historical communities. His Christocentrism appears strained accordingly, even when limited to the scope of the human species.

It might be replied to this objection that this is a natural distinction to draw, for though we have contact with non-Christian religions, we have no contact with religious creatures of other planets. To this reply, however, it must be further objected that Tillich's solution assumes too much about the extent of interplanetary interaction. If we were able to contact religious species on other planets, if we were able to exchange goods and culture with them, then they would at once be brought into the same situation formerly applicable only to non-Christians on our own planet. This would force a reevaluation of the scope of Christocentrism, a reevaluation that would have to be repeated each time an alien religious culture came into substantial, ongoing contact with the earth. In short, the argument would have decidedly diminishing returns.

Moreover, it does no good to suggest that in encounters with alien religious beings we would discover a manifestation of New Being in their history that would trigger a mutual recognition and tolerance of different apprehensions of New Being for different historical streams. On the one hand, these streams would likely thereafter merge, invalidating Tillich's easy distribution of a unique manifestation of New Being to each stream of planetary history. On the other hand, we already have the opportunity of testing our capacity for mutual recognition and tolerance right here on our own planet, and the Christocentric view of salvation in that context suggests that the mutual recognition scenario is an unlikely one in the hypothetical interplanetary context.

A second, telling objection to Tillich's proposal is that it induces internal metaphysical inconsistencies in his system. In his ontology, New Being is understood to be universally, cosmically, and absolutely significant, and it must realize itself in history if it is to transcend its fragmentary and anticipatory preliminary signs. It is not a matter of simply realizing or becoming aware of something that always has been the case in the universe of being, namely, that it has a valid description under which it is New Being. The breaking into history of New Being is a definitive metaphysical occurrence with cosmic consequences, and not merely a socially mediated, epistemological happening, though it is that, too, through the community that testifies to the New Being, the Christian Church, and indeed through many other kinds of communities, in fragmentary and anticipatory ways. Tillich's philosophy of history includes the idea that something metaphysically final and decisive happens when the absolute ground of all being appears under the estranged conditions of existence. This is the definitive inbreaking and realization of the New Being that prompts Tillich to use the description "final revelation" for the process whereby it is disclosed and accepted. Moreover, his Christocentric concept of the "latent church" also involves a metaphysical basis for salvation, and not merely an episte-mological, socially and ecclesially mediated one. Within the bounds of Tillich's system, therefore, the absolute need only break definitively into history once in order to accomplish the means of salvation for all being—the universe as a whole—everywhere and at all times. And that one time becomes forever after a point of celebration, even as Jesus Christ has been celebrated for centuries for just this reason.

Now this points to a severe strain in Tillich's system. It is one of which he was increasingly and painfully aware, for he expressed misgivings about the consistency of the system as the marvelously suggestive third volume was taking shape.[36] Tillich structured the third volume so as to emphasize the socially mediated character of salvation—an attempt to do justice to the validity that he recognized in other religions—without ever losing sight of the more ontological interpretation of salvation developed especially in the first volume, but also in the second. In so doing, he be-came ensnared in a number of dissonances that we can only wish he had lived to explore further.

Given this conceptual fracture, we should note the significance of the fact that Tillich introduces the discussion just criticized in the context of a passage about the expectation of the Christ. The natural terminology to use in such a context is that of the "essential man" becoming the "central event" of all "human history." This terminology, with its orientation to the human species, is what gives to Tillich's proposal such plausibility as it possesses. But it also serves to disguise the ontologically fundamental and universal character of the appearance of the New Being in history, a per-spective that looms larger in other parts of the *Systematic Theology*, and better expresses the ontological foundations of his system. From the point of view of his ontology, therefore, it is proper to ask how Tillich be-lieves he can be justified in conceiving of this inbreaking as happening in multiple places and times. Yet from the point of view of his conception of human communities, multiple instances of divine self-realization in his-tory make sense. A resolution to this tension is not forthcoming, how-ever—at least not from Tillich.

Perhaps this tension is most neatly captured in Tillich's complex view of Jesus as the Christ. Thought of as the final revelation of essential God-humanhood, or essential humanity (which is the same thing), there ap-pears to be significant potential for dealing constructively with the reality of religious pluralism as well as the cosmological problem under discussion here. However, thought of as the final revelation of the unconditioned ground of being under the estranged conditions of finite existence, and as the basis of Tillich's concepts of New Being and latent spiritual community, the possibility of envisaging a limitation on the significance of the symbol of Jesus Christ is problematic. Yet such a limitation is precisely what is required for a satisfactory solution to the problems of cosmology and religious pluralism, as Tillich himself implicitly acknowledges by the form of his proposed solution.

Were another theologian to advance Tillich's position, one with a less metaphysically specific understanding of the implications of the appearance and reception of Jesus as the Christ, he or she might perhaps be able to avoid the particular problem that confronts Tillich's proposal. However, the fundamental advance of Tillich's Christocentrism is to relegate the understanding of salvation to the level of ontology, in order to furnish a comprehensive explanation of the fact of epistemic differences in interpretations of "salvation" among the world's religions. The very character of Christocentrism, then, implies that any Christocentric view that tries to limit the scope of salvation to a single species or a region or a time will also be subject to the same criticism of metaphysical inconsistency that applies to Tillich's proposal.

Unprincipled Modesty: Boff

In concluding this section, it is important to identify a form of pseudo-solution to the problem of Christology in cosmic dimensions. This occurs when, presumably out of a sense of the sharpness of the problem, a theological position apparently affirming absolutist Christology is qualified unexpectedly and arbitrarily to allow for the possibility of multiple incarnations scattered through the cosmos. Rahner's brief reflections at the end of *Foundations* are unfortunately of this type. Tillich also makes this move, though not in an unprincipled way, for the entire third volume of *Systematic Theology* (even though not the whole work) lays the conceptual groundwork for such a speculative proposal. The complaint here is rather against Christological offerings that simply "solve" the problem of cosmology and Christology out of a conceptual vacuum, without grappling with the absolutist principle that drives the problem.

Leonardo Boff offers a clear-cut instance of such a pseudo-solution.[37]

After considerable emphasis on the cosmic dimensions of the significance of Jesus Christ, and no sign in either terminological choices or conceptual linkages that this significance should be thought of as anything other than absolute, unique, and final for revelation and salvation, Boff asks the natural question, "Is Jesus important to the earth alone or to the whole cosmos?"[38] His answer is to make the typical move of an incarnational modest Christology, distinguishing between the principle of incarnation (the "eternal Logos of God, the Second Person of the Blessed Trinity") and the Logos incarnate in Jesus ("a human being like us . . . the Logos who assumed out human condition"), and then allowing that "Just as the eternal Logos, which fills all reality, appeared in our flesh and assumed evolutionary coordinates in our galaxy, nothing prohibits this same eternal Logos from having appeared and assumed the spiritual and evolutionary conditions of other beings in other systems."[39]

However, this laudable move of Boff is not accompanied by any treatment of the range of connected questions that it raises. For example, he adopts Rahner's anonymous Christian category in relation to other human cultures without asking why other creatures in the universe cannot also be so described. Nor does he pause to discuss whether granting that "the cosmos has other dimensions and consequently allows for relationships with God and his Word different from that realized in Jesus of Nazareth" should not also lead to similar recognition of independence being granted to other religious and cultural streams on earth. Furthermore, Boff offers no argument for his arbitrary limitation of the significance of the symbol of Jesus Christ to the human species on earth. Nor does he appear to envisage the possibility that the contingencies of history and possible technological developments in the future may well give Christianity the opportunity to prove that it is capable of subsuming the religious insights of religions elsewhere than on earth into its purview. Finally, Boff retains the absolutist principle with little or no discussion of the other dimensions of the crisis it has caused in contemporary Christology, temporarily and inconsistently relinquishing it only in face of this singularly pointed dimension of the problem.

This kind of half-hearted Christological modesty will not do, for it neither addresses soundly the problem of plausibility facing Christology nor continues the Christological tradition with the integrity it deserves. The Christological absolutism of Teilhard, Rahner (excepting his destabilizing excursus discussed earlier), and Pannenberg is infinitely preferable. A

Christologically modest response is demanded by the problem of cosmic immensity, but only a whole-heartedly modest Christology can resolve this aspect of the Christological crisis of plausibility in a dignified way.

Religious Pluralism: The Modest Consensus

The last external dimension of the contemporary Christological crisis to be considered is also the best known and most discussed: the Christological response to religious pluralism. In this case, the argument that needs to be made for modest Christologies begins from the recognition in Christian terms of the salvific integrity and independence of all religions, as well as the presence of recognizably Christian salvation or something somewhat like it in the lives of nonreligious people. On the basis of this recognition, the argument contends that either type of modest Christology—inspirational with Hick and Troeltsch, or incarnational with Cobb, Panikkar, Macquarrie, and so many others—is more adequate than any Christology wedded to the absolutist principle.

This entire argument is complex, with many phases. Aspects bearing on the logical position of modest Christologies in this debate will be kept in the forefront here, with some other parts of the case merely summarized and explained. The reason for this is that modest Christologies are already completely familiar in many circles where religious pluralism has sponsored revision of traditional Christological reflection, though under different names. Laying out the entire argument in detail seems superfluous, as a result. But one of the purposes of this book is to show that a modest Christology addresses *all* of the dimensions of the contemporary Christological crisis of plausibility, and the dimension of religious pluralism certainly cannot be left out of that picture.

To keep the presentation as concrete as possible, it will be launched in dialogue with what is probably the main competitor to modest Christologies in the sphere of religious pluralism: Karl Rahner's absolutist, inclusive Christology. The discussion will conclude with a review of two modest Christologies prominent in discussions of religious pluralism—those of Paul Knitter's *No Other Name?* and Raimon Panikkar's *The Unknown Christ of Hinduism*. This will serve as a further indication of how modest Christologies can be developed with a variety of accents in response to the theological challenge of religious pluralism.

Theological Impact of Recognizing the Integrity and
Independence of the World Religions

The existence of many religions besides Christianity on this planet was not
to be a problem for Christians until the following conditions were met:
(1) Christians had to know enough about those other religions for Christians to make a responsible judgment about what might be called their
"religious integrity" and "salvific efficacy"; (2) Christians had to come to an
actual positive judgment about the religious integrity and salvific efficacy
of those religions on *Christian terms*, even if the theoretical criteria for
this judgment remained elusive; and (3) Christians had to be under the
impression that Christian religious reflection and piety entail assertions
that are incompatible with such a positive judgment about the religious
integrity and salvific efficacy of other religions.

Condition (3) has been fulfilled almost from the beginning of Christian reflection on Jesus Christ and the salvation believed to be wrought
through him. Except for a few Christians on the margins of the Christian
churches, such as enlightened missionaries, fulfilling condition (1) has
been possible only since the rise during the nineteenth century of the systematic study of religious phenomena. Moreover, this study had to
progress a long way before some measure of freedom from preconceived
ideas was achieved, and thus the possibility of fair judgment has not really
existed in a widespread way until the middle of the twentieth century.
Condition (2) was met as a matter of course after the possibility of a serious judgment about the character of other religions was in place.

It is only in the last half-century, therefore, that the problem of other
religions has reached its maximally sharp form. Along the way, it had to
pass beyond the early-nineteenth-century attempts of theologians and
philosophers of religion such as Schleiermacher and Hegel both to define
an initial approach to Christianity in the context of other world religions
and to establish Christianity's definitiveness and supremacy in that context. It also had to pass beyond Troeltsch's admission—at first fumblingly
reluctant, then more definite—of the failure of all attempts to establish
the preeminence and absoluteness of Christianity among the world religions. It then had to pass beyond the attempts to manage the problem
that followed from the first genuine breakthroughs in constructive Christian theological reflection on the issue, represented most prominently by
Karl Rahner's "anonymous Christianity" and Paul Tillich's "latent church."

These concepts of Rahner and Tillich are so important that they mark out a whole class of responses to the Christian version of the problem of other religions, usually described as the Christocentric or inclusivist approach. They draw on older concepts such as the Logos Christology of John's gospel and the *logos spermatikos* of Justin Martyr and find echoes all through the history of Christian thought. They also are anticipated in less clear cut ways by a number of nineteenth-century figures from Schleiermacher and Hegel to Blondel and even, in a quite different way, Barth.

Rahner and Tillich make very much the same point, namely, that salvation of any kind, no matter how it is understood or where it occurs, requires the saving accomplishment that the Christian churches testify occurred in Jesus Christ, and in him only. All salvation participates in this central event of salvation, though the precise nature of this participation is understood differently. In this way, the Christian message is thought to testify most truly to the source of adequacy and efficacy of salvation in every religious tradition. Christianity merely testifies to this source, however; it does not embody it exclusively within the church. Therefore Christianity stands under the judgment implied in the finality of salvation in Jesus Christ every bit as much as any other religion does. Jesus Christ is broken for all, and Christianity enjoys no decisive advantage in regard to salvation; rather it is burdened with special responsibility to proclaim its message truly.

The Christocentric or inclusivist approach customarily is contrasted with the formerly dominant ecclesiocentric or exclusivist approach, the analogies of "center/periphery" and "inclusion/exclusion" being the two main ways this change has been characterized in the rapidly growing literature on the subject. The exclusivist approach affirms the uniqueness and finality of salvation in Jesus Christ, even as the inclusivist approach does. But it regards this salvation as mediated exclusively by the Christian church. Of course, God may make special arrangements for salvation in certain special cases, but we are not privy to knowledge of such contingencies. What is revealed in Jesus Christ is salvation for all, a salvation available through the sacramental life of the Christian church. This naturally requires the church to protect and nourish the salvation it mediates and to extend its influence throughout the world, if all are to hear the gospel and to have an opportunity to respond to the good news of the love of God.

The ecclesiocentric approach proves inadequate, and the Christocentric approach is required, in the presence of even a low level of recognition by Christians of the religious integrity and salvific efficacy of other religions. The inclusivist approach is found wanting, however, when Christian theology feels obligated to accord the fullest recognition of integrity and efficacy, that is, when Christian theology must explain the existence of salvation outside Christianity—assuming this even can be spoken of as "salvation"—that possesses the same degree of independence from Christian salvation as Christian salvation is thought by Christians to possess from all other kinds of salvation. The thesis that the *mechanism* of salvation is described truly only by Christianity, in spite of the belief of other religions that there is no such relation—the characteristic move of Christocentric approaches—is incompatible with this degree of recognition.

Once such a high degree of recognition has been achieved, the problem of other religions is fully formed and the question arises of how Christian theology should respond. The tension involved in continuing to affirm the inclusivist or Christocentric approach under these circumstances is thought by many to be an acceptable burden in exchange for maintaining the traditionally absolute and final character of the Christian understanding of revelation and salvation. But another class of responses is also possible at this juncture of the developing problem. These approaches are variously though not unproblematically described as "pluralist" or "theocentric," in continuity with the terminology used for the other two classes of responses mentioned already.

To appreciate the need for some approach other than the inclusivist one, it is as well to pause and review Karl Rahner's Christology, the greatest inclusivist Christology of the twentieth century. The exposition will show that Rahner's inclusivism is problematic *not in itself* but because it involves an embrace of the absolutist principle. This will be the basis for the subsequent argument that a more adequate response can be secured only by adopting a modest Christology, and *this* requires both a return to a form of ecclesiocentric view of salvation and a hermeneutical deabsolutizing of the transcendental anthropology necessary for an inclusivist approach. This amounts to a shift to a properly pluralist perspective. In fact, the argument will be that when the absolutist principle is rejected most of the approaches current in debates on religious pluralism conceptually merge to a significant degree.

The Traditional Inclusivist Position: Karl Rahner

The innovative Second Vatican Council had an ambiguous influence on the growth of modest Christologies within Roman Catholicism. The remarkable "Declaration of the Relation of the Church to Non-Christian Religions" (*Nostra aetate*) was construed in subsequent years along two significantly different lines, both staying true to the document's intention to do justice to the nobility of the religious quest and the presence of truth and goodness in other religions. Karl Rahner's Christocentric inclusivism was one kind of response, making a dramatic virtue of the absolutist principle. The other, and later, kind of response is represented by Paul Knitter, who moderates the absolutist principle and begins to explore the resources of modest Christology for responding to the challenge of *Nostra aetate*. We will come to Knitter's offering shortly.

While some consequences of Karl Rahner's Christology were raised in the last section, the purpose here is to expound the Christology itself, especially in relation to the challenge of religious pluralism. Rahner's theology is properly circular, so it is not possible to speak of it beginning with any particular theme. An exposition of his Christology must begin somewhere, however, so we take up his theological anthropology first.

For Rahner, humans are the creatures who experience themselves simultaneously as in the presence of absolute mystery and as radically threatened by guilt. As oriented toward mystery, humans experience transcendence and know the term of that transcendence unthematically, non-conceptually. Rahner says of this knowledge that it is

> that concrete, original, historically constituted and transcendental knowledge of God which either in the mode of acceptance or rejection is inevitably present in the depths of existence in the most ordinary human life. It is at once both natural knowledge and knowledge in grace, it is at once both knowledge and revelation-faith, so that distinguishing its elements is a subsequent task of philosophy and theology, but not really a reflexive act for this original knowledge itself.[40]

The possibility of this knowledge, then, is grounded in the graced character of the entire creation, but it is also not knowledge of an "individual object alongside other objects," which is why it is at once a matter of natural knowledge and knowledge in grace. This is also the reason, for Rahner, that the experience of the transcendent ground and the experience of creatureliness belong together and imply each other.[41]

The gracious character of what Rahner characteristically calls "the term" of the human experience of transcendence is the ground of the possibility of human freedom. This is as much a freedom to deny God as to affirm God, and Rahner sees an unthematic affirmation or denial in every human action.[42] The possibility of affirmation corresponds to the possibility of authentic self-realization. As Rahner neatly puts it, "In real freedom the subject always intends himself, understands and posits himself. Ultimately he does not do *something*, but does *himself*."[43] Humans as a matter of fact, then, are always becoming simply because they are free, but the orientation to mystery is the freedom and the responsibility to become authentically human, to be related to the transcendent ground of their creatureliness. This orientation also informs us that we frequently choose not to say "yes" to God, that such sin is an ineradicable aspect of our lives, and that, as a result, we cannot finally prevent ourselves from threatening and damaging ourselves.[44] Human freedom, therefore, "takes on for us in the concrete an inescapable importance and a radical seriousness."[45]

Consistent with Rahner's affirmation of this importance and seriousness, it is not enough for humans vainly to struggle to realize fellowship with their transcendent ground, out of obedience and a sense of responsibility to the ultimate mystery of the world. The fact of this struggle for authentic existence itself presupposes divine participation in the process. Thus it is that Rahner's theological anthropology eventually leads to Christology. But his analysis of the historical process, too, leads to the incarnation as the central event of that history, toward which it is impelled, and with reference to which humanity ever after understands itself.

Rahner's metaphysics of history has strong affinities with the classical German idealism of Hegel and with Whitehead's realist metaphysics. God, while infinite, does change and develop by interacting with the world. And that interaction is implied in the very fact of human self-transcendence: "We presuppose that the whole dynamism which God has instituted in the very heart of the world's becoming by self-transcendence . . . is really always meant already as the beginning and first step towards [God's] self-communication and its acceptance by the world."[46] Thus God is oriented toward self-communication to the world, even as humanity is oriented toward communion with God.

Under what conditions can God communicate with the creation, apart from establishing it in freedom and grounding it in mystery? Only in the history of free creatures, since free response is essential to real communion. How then can the divine self-communication reach its definitive, irrevocable expression? Through a human life. Thus Rahner is able at once to expound "what is really meant by the doctrine of the Hypostatic Union and of the Incarnation of the divine Logos," and to show that "it fits into an evolutionist view of the world."

> The Savior is himself an historical moment in God's saving action exercised on the world. He is a moment of the history of God's communication of himself to the world—in the sense that he is a part of this history of the cosmos itself. He must not be merely God acting on the world but must be a part of the cosmos itself in its very climax. This is in fact stated in the Christian dogma: Jesus is true man; he is truly a part of the earth, truly a moment in the biological evolution of the world, a moment of human natural history . . . It must be understood in this connection that the statement of God's *Incarnation*—of his becoming *material*—is the most basic statement of Christology. The divine Logos himself both really creates and accepts this corporeality—which is part of the world—*as his* own reality; he brings it into existence as something other than himself in such a way, therefore, that this very materiality expresses *him*, the Logos himself, and lets him be present in his world.[47]

Rahner thus regards the concrete appearance of the Logos in a human life as the climax of both the evolutionary process and of the movement toward definitiveness and irrevocability of the divine self-communication. The potential for free authenticity of humanity (the actualization of essential humanity), and for ultimate communion of God with the creation grounded in mystery by divine grace, is achieved in the incarnation.[48]

The Absolutist Principle Makes Inclusivism Problematic

Inclusivism with regard to salvation is founded on Rahner's transcendental anthropology; the activity of divine grace is at no point limited to the church's influence, but is rather interpreted as the ground of all human freedom. Profound differences among people raised in different cultural-religious traditions notwithstanding, some kind of transcendental anthropology seems required to do justice to the cross-cultural reality of responsiveness to the transcendent in human experience. The terminology in which such a transcendental anthropology is cast surely will be a contentious matter, since people experience being characterized in foreign terms distasteful, but the explanatory power of a transcendental anthropology is considerable nonetheless.

It is as well, then, that Rahner's transcendental anthropology and its attendant inclusivism do not entail the absolutist principle, for otherwise absolutist Christologies would have a plausible anthropology to appeal to in their support. In fact, Rahner's is possibly the most compelling and lucid articulation of the absolutist principle in the twentieth century. But its origin in his Christology is the striking merger of his theological anthropology with a historical vision of awesome breadth, under the auspices of fidelity to his assertion that "the goal of the world consists in God's communicating himself to it,"[49] which is applied in the strongest way to Jesus Christ. This is why the incarnation is, for Rahner, a metaphysically unique and definitive necessity, absolutely and unsurpassably significant for revelation and salvation. Furthermore, it is the presence of the absoluteness principle and not the transcendental anthropology that makes Rahner's inclusivism problematic as a Christian attempt to make theological sense of its own teaching in the face of religious pluralism.

To see this, consider that Rahner's absolutist, Christocentric approach possesses an irreducible element of exclusivity, because it withholds a certain level of recognition that adherents of other religions would prefer be yielded and thus creates a highly implausible lack of symmetry in the Christian analysis of religious pluralism. This sometimes is denied. A common strategy to secure this denial is expressed in a reported remark of Rahner himself, who, upon being asked how he would respond to being described as an anonymous Buddhist, said that he would be honored to be regarded as participating in the highest reality as understood by Buddhists. However, Rahner's metaphysics—in asserting a real redeeming transaction in Jesus Christ of definitive, unsurpassable significance, at least for the entire history of humanity—implies that anonymous Christians of non-Christian religions, once aware of the origin in Jesus Christ of the salvific efficacy of their religion, must accept the Christian gospel if the reality of their salvation is to be confirmed. That is, there is a time limit for confessing Christ that sets in after ignorance about the true nature of salvation has been removed. But then, we might ask, how can these two views be consistent? Is Rahner, as an anonymous Buddhist, also to be subject to a parallel Buddhist time limit? If so, then this contradicts his belief that the origin of all salvation is in Jesus Christ. If not, then his implicit claim of complete equivalence between anonymous Christianity and anonymous Buddhism is false.

The conclusion was obvious from the start: you can't have a fundamental metaphysical reality (namely, all salvation occurs only through Jesus Christ), to which one religion alone truthfully testifies, without also introducing a logical imbalance among the various competing accounts of "salvation." By itself, Rahner's transcendental anthropology is not problematic, for it would allow for a range of socially mediated forms of salvation. It is the hermeneutical absolutizing of the salvific and revelatory significance of Jesus Christ that robs Rahner's inclusivism of explanatory power and propels it headlong into the ditch of implausibility.

Supposing, then, that an attempt was made to preserve a transcendental anthropology—whether Rahner's or Tillich's, or another—while preserving it from being hermeneutically absolutized. The result would be an intriguing mixture of a number of stances in the religious pluralism debate under the sponsorship of a modest Christology. The anthropology itself would lead to a kind of inclusivism that finds commonalities among the various salvific processes (to use Christian terms, once again, for processes that may be more different than similar) based on biological and anthropological similarities alone, yet without positing a single metaphysical mechanism for salvation, as the absolutist principle requires. Moreover, these salvific processes must by definition be realized in social institutions and traditions in order to be salvific in the broadest sense, so the various forms of salvation would be irrevocably historically melded with traditions, recovering the best insight of the usually marginalized ecclesiocentric vision of salvation. And finally, the transcendental anthropology itself demands, from a Christian point of view, a theocentric explanation, and, from a sociological point of view, a pluralist explanation. Under the sponsorship of a modest Christology, therefore, the Christian response to the integrity and independence of salvation within and beyond the diversity of the religions of planet earth is able to coordinate what is best about traditional and more recent explanatory approaches.

The Consensus Position: Modest Incarnational Christology

The problems facing the absolutist, inclusivist proposals of Rahner and others have driven many theologians involved in interpreting interreligious dialogue in print to repudiate the absolutist principle, and with it planks of the absolutist, inclusivist platform such as a philosophy of history in which Jesus is not only the center of human history but also its beginning and end; the concomitant anthropocentrism and inexplicable emphasis on human history and the human planet; and the interpretation of the independence and salvific efficacy of other religious traditions in terms of the primacy of divine revelation as understood by Christians. For instance, contemporary theologians and religious philosophers such as John Bowden, Howard Burkle, John Cobb, Don Cupitt, Donald Dawe, Tom Driver, Christopher Duraisingh, Langdon Gilkey, Thor Hall, Monika Hellwig, John Hick, Gordon Kaufman, Paul Knitter, Hans Küng, John Macquarrie, Robert Neville, Raimundo Panikkar, Rosemary Reuther, John A. T. Robinson, Stanley Samartha, Dorothy Sölle, Leonard Swidler, Paul van Buren, and many others are exploring Christology without the absolutist principle as the key to interpreting religious pluralism.

One way to ameliorate the absolutist principle is to loosen the traditionally firm link between Christ, thought of in a lexically strained way as the second person of the Trinity, and Jesus, in whom Christ is incarnate, to allow for the possibility of Christians affirming other Christ events or analogues of Christ events.[50] In describing Thor Hall's way of doing this, Paul Knitter puts the point well: "Christians [need] to relativize the particularity of the incarnation (Jesus) and to universalize the principle of incarnation (Christ)."[51] Some of the authors just listed, such as John Hick and John Bowden, use modest Christologies of the inspirational, nonincarnational type as their entry point into interpreting religious pluralism. Most, however, pursue Hall's approach—the incarnational type of modest Christology in various ways—some emphasizing the nature of the universal, others the relativity of the particular, some motivated primarily by the need to stimulate interreligious dialogue, others by the need for Christian theology to be efficacious, and still others to establish an adequate metaphysics.

So wholehearted and widespread have been the acceptance and exploration of modest incarnational Christologies in this sphere that it is fair to say that they define the "broad consensus position" in the ongoing discussions surrounding religious pluralism. This is one of the few areas of contemporary theology in which the decisive edge modest Christologies have over the entrenched absolutist Christological opposition is already realized, the other being feminist theology. The absolutist, inclusivist position is far from being out of the picture, of course, but the number of its publishing adherents appears to be declining, especially in Protestant circles. In the third place, lagging behind as far as the number of its published exponents is concerned, are approaches based on modest inspirational Christologies, though many supporters of this view may not be publishing works specifically in Christian theology.

The logic of the argument to this point will be obscured unless it is noticed that this taxonomy of positions is not customary, the more familiar ones being the exclusive-inclusive-pluralist, and ecclesio-, Christo-, theocentric families. It has been argued that relinquishing the absolutist principle and allowing a modest Christology (of either type) to sponsor proposals for making theological sense of religious pluralism partially dissolves these sets of distinctions in healthful fashion. While exclusivism keeps its usual meaning and is rejected, inclusivism and theocentrism remain as concomitants of the anthropological continuities presupposed in a viable transcendental anthropology; and the necessity for historical, social mediation of salvific processes is expressed from various points of view in terms of pluralism, ecclesiocentrism and Christocentrism. Naturally, all of these terms have distinctive meanings in the presence of a modest Christology.

We are now in a position to consider two important variations on the modest incarnational consensus position. Paul Knitter's approach in *No Other Name?* is the complement of Rahner's as they are both able to trace their heritage to *Nostra aetate*. It is especially interesting because of Knitter's view of truth in that book as dialogical and relational, and the conception of the historical process thereby implied. A second and very different instance of the consensus position is by Raimon Panikkar.[52] The importance of Panikkar's book lies partly in its extraordinary mystical vision and partly in its author's desire to coordinate a trinitarian doctrine of God with his modest incarnational Christology.

The Consensus Position: Knitter's Relational View of Truth

In the process of providing an excellent survey of Christian attitudes to the world religions in *No Other Name?* Paul Knitter offers his own theocentric view. His view has not remained unchanged since this book, but it is the view of *No Other Name?* that most effectively expresses what I am calling the "consensus position," so I will limit consideration of Knitter's thought to that book.

The position of *No Other Name?* is more tentative and exploratory than most instances of repudiation of the absolutist principle. It is also not a constructive Christology, and it may not be completely unreasonable to suppose that a constructive theology with the kind of tentative assertion of Jesus' uniqueness that Knitter wishes to espouse may face significant internal tensions that demand resolution in terms of a more clear-cut stance toward the absolutist principle. In any event, Knitter's view as it stands emerges in the context of a pattern of criticism of other views. Some basic principles of what Knitter takes to be an adequate constructive Christology are disclosed in that process of criticism, which consists in analyzing characterizations of Jesus as unique and then asking about both the basis for the purported knowledge of Jesus' uniqueness and the adequacy of this claim to the facts of the world's religions.

Knitter points out that the uniqueness of Jesus is understood in two more or less equally unsatisfactory ways.

> The conservative Evangelical and mainline Protestant models hold to an *exclusive uniqueness*, affirming that only in Jesus can true revelation or salvation be found. In such an understanding, the Christ event is *constitutive* of any true encounter with God, anywhere in history. The Catholic model, dissatisfied with such exclusivity, proposes an *inclusive uniqueness* for Jesus; God's revealing-saving action in Jesus includes all other religions, either as an anonymous, cosmic presence within them or as their final fulfillment. In this view, Jesus remains, if not constitutive of, at least *normative* for, all religious experience, for all times. All these traditional Christian claims are insufficiently sensitive to the way they contradict contemporary awareness of historical relativity and to the way they impede authentic dialogue with believers of other faiths.[53]

Knitter's objection to the inclusive uniqueness thesis is of particular interest, since this view at least is aware of the need to explain apparent "salvation" in other religions. With relation both to Rahner's transcendental Christology[54] and to process Christology,[55] Knitter asks what reason there is to limit the incarnation to a unique occurrence. Does not the Christological structure of anthropology in both transcendental and process theology imply in principle the possibility that the realized, final essence of humanity, which is at the same time the climax of divine self-communication, might *not* be unique? Knitter's question is forceful indeed. He repeatedly states that the reasons for uniqueness in the context of human history offered by Rahner and the process theologians either are not clear, or are clear but not persuasive.

It is unfortunate that Knitter does not enter into more detail at this point, for it would be helpful to see him apply his criticism to the various reasons that are in fact offered. Rahner's philosophy of history, as we have seen, presents a substantial reason for Jesus Christ's uniqueness (within human history at least), and it does not derive solely from his transcendental anthropology. Even on the basis of such an anthropology, however, it is possible to think of Jesus as the firstborn of many, so that his uniqueness lies in being the first to realize authentically the essence of humanity and therefore the one under whose influence others would follow. But in this case, as in the case of the process Christologies that Knitter mentions (Cobb, Griffin, Ford, Mellert, and Pittenger[56]), the matter seems to come down finally to a dilemma: either Jesus' uniqueness is necessary, because of a philosophy of history or a divine decree or in some other way, or Jesus' uniqueness is contingent and a matter of historical judgment. But the contingency of Jesus' uniqueness offers no reason to limit the incarnation to Jesus and also invites the insurmountable problem of trying to say how this is to be known about Jesus. A divine decree or an over-riding philosophy of history, on the other hand, seems to run counter to the emphasis both of Rahner's transcendental anthropology and of process anthropology, in which the point of humanity is precisely to realize its essence authentically in the ambiguity of history.

Knitter rejects the possibility of any *categorical* assertion of Jesus' uniqueness. However, unlike some theologians who go on to reject the *possibility* of uniqueness, a move for which he likewise cannot find justification, Knitter tries to protect the possibility of a *tentative* assertion of the uniqueness of Jesus. This assertion would be tested in interreligious dialogue, under the ethical rubric of "doing before knowing."[57] Knitter calls this a confessional approach,[58] but this seems to be too broad a characterization in view of the fact that the inclusivist approach he attacks can be and is also held confessionally and can actually be a fruitful base for interreligious dialogue. The approach to Christian uniqueness Knitter holds to be most adequate is described in the following passage: "The theocentric model proposes what can be called a *relational uniqueness* for Jesus. . . . It affirms that Jesus *is* unique, but with a uniqueness defined by its ability to relate to—that is, to include and be included by—other unique religious figures. Such an understanding of Jesus views him not as exclusive or even as normative but as *theocentric*, as a universally relevant manifestation (sacrament, incarnation) of divine revelation and salvation."[59]

This approach to uniqueness is one of three foundational principles for Knitter's incipient Christology. The second is a methodological commitment to the idea, prominent in liberation theology, of *praxis*. Knitter applies this to the role of inter-religious dialogue, which he takes to be precisely the kind of context within which experience (doing) can inform Christian theology (knowing).

The third principle is a view of truth as relational. Knitter raises more questions than he answers in his brief remarks on this subject, encapsulated in the following quotation:

> In our world of historical consciousness, scientific relativity, and pluralism, human consciousness is being called to let go of its former securities and to affirm a new understanding of truth, including religious truth. . . . In the new model, truth will no longer be identified by its ability to exclude or absorb others. Rather, what is true will reveal itself mainly by its ability to *relate* to other expressions of truth and to *grow* through these relationships—truth defined not by exclusion but by relation.[60]

Knitter goes on to offer, in effect by redefining terms, a notion of absolute truth:

> The model of truth-through-relationship allows each religion to be unique; such uniqueness can even be called—if we are willing to redefine our terms—absolute. Each religion contains something that belongs to it alone, separately, distinctively, decisively: its particular grasp of divine truth. The truth it contains is uniquely important; it must not be lost. This uniqueness can be affirmed as absolute insofar as it calls for total personal commitment and claims universal relevance.[61]

This view is, in the opinion of some, hopelessly romantic. History is nothing if not littered with the remains of religious insights, "uniquely important" according to Knitter, but very definitely lost as existentially meaningful insights, embodied in living traditions. Knitter unnecessarily gives away part of a robust, historicized conception of truth with such sentimentalism. If history is to be the field upon which perspectives upon an absolute, divine truth are to vie with each other for supremacy, then let the games begin and give no more than a furtive glance to those who perish along the way. It is survival of the fittest, and the fittest are those that cannot only best make sense out of other perspectives, but also do the best justice to the one, divine truth. Freed from its faintly sentimental overlay, as we have seen in earlier chapters, this is Ernst Troeltsch's view of religious truth at the end of his life and John Cobb's as well.

With these three basic principles in place, Knitter has the foundation for a modest Christology in which, again like Cobb, the assertion of the unique salvific and revelatory significance of Jesus Christ is offered to the process of testing and truth seeking that is interreligious dialogue with existential determination but methodological provisionality. This position as sponsored by a modest Christology differs in two crucial ways from its visage when supported by the absolutist principle. First, it is never held with such definiteness that the prospect of future revision would necessarily be thought of as self-contradictory, as is the case with so many Christologies wedded to the absolutist principle—though not, notably, in the case of Pannenberg's absolutist Christology. Second, and more decisively, no denial is made at any point that *independent* revelatory and salvific significance is rightly attributed to the sacred symbols of other religions and nonreligions. Nor is the symbol of Jesus Christ thought to be superior *presently* to the meanings embodied in the symbols of other salvific traditions. The claim is only that the symbol of Jesus Christ can *adapt* in the process of interreligious dialogue to take account of the truths of other religious traditions. This claim is met with parallel claims from other traditions, naturally, and Knitter's relational view of truth—if it is coherent, a question not addressed here—mediates the dialogical process in the midst of such mutually competitive claims to superior adaptivity and symbolic richness.

It follows from this that Knitter rejects any assertion of the unique significance of Jesus Christ in the sense of hermeneutically absolute or exclusive significance, as if there were not other and independent religious meanings with irreducible significance and majestic truth of their own. But the second and third principles of Knitter's Christological foundation—the emphasis on the praxis of dialogue and on the idea of relational truth—demand that the claim about the unique (in the sense of *uniquely adaptive*) significance of Jesus Christ be advanced and tested, in search of that series of contingent and ever-provisional confirmations and, presumably, corrections that the historical process can bring. The contention that the symbol of Jesus Christ is adaptive enough to be potentially universal in its significance is held, in other words, in the context of an ethic of belief that apportions strength of belief in accordance with the degree of support that the belief in question can sustain from the dialogic process. Finally, therefore, it is Knitter's ethic of belief—an ethic grounded in the second and third foundational principles—that both demands rejection of the absolutist principle and fosters a provisional affirmation of the adaptive revelatory and salvific power within the symbol of Jesus Christ.

The Consensus Position: Panikkar's Mystical, Trinitarian Vision

Whereas Knitter uses an incarnational modest Christology to explain how Christian uniqueness can be spoken of in the context of the competing truths of the world's religions, Panikkar uses the same kind of Christology to elaborate a vision of reality in which what might be true about all of those religions emerges. There is no sense in which Panikkar reduces the distinctiveness of different religious traditions to the terms of Christianity, or to an overarching philosophy of religion, yet he does not shrink from making a bold attempt to paint a mystical vision of plurality in unity.

In the first edition of *Unknown Christ* (1964), Panikkar maintained that the incarnation of the divine mystery in Jesus was unsurpassable and universally normative. In the revised and enlarged edition of the same book (1981), after further reflection on his experience, articulation of that conviction dropped out. The necessity of divine revelation in Jesus for the socio-religious complex of Christianity is maintained, however. Though Panikkar may now have more radical views,[62] the major Christological step of relinquishing the normativity and finality of Jesus is fully taken in the 1981 edition of *Unknown Christ*. This step is prepared for by emphasizing Christ's theandric character:[63] as the depth of the infinite divine in the human, and the finite humanity of God, as "a living symbol for the totality of reality: human, divine and cosmic,"[64] as "the concrete connection between the Absolute and the relative."[65]

Panikkar is comfortable making appeal to the tradition of Christian thought for support at this point. He makes connections to the Christian teachings about Christ as sacrament and to the two natures of Jesus Christ. Perhaps the most important systematic connection, however, is to the trinitarian doctrine of God. "Within the Christian tradition this Christ is incomprehensible without the Trinity. A non-Trinitarian God cannot become incarnate. A non-Trinitarian Christ cannot be totally human and totally divine. . . . I am only reflecting the Christian tradition if I consider the symbol Christ as that symbol which 'recapitulates' in itself the Real in its totality, created and uncreated."[66] Thus, Christ is that through which everything is, the creative word of the infinite divine mystery, the Logos. As such, Christ necessarily transcends every description we might give of it and every concept that we might apply to it. Christ is the self-expression of absolute mystery and so is fundamentally mysterious. It is not thereby incomprehensible, however, as our concepts and words are themselves participants in the mystery of reality and so capable of at least pointing to the mystery of Christ. It follows that Christ is Unknown, as well as present in everything, and in every human.

> The thesis of the Unknown Christ is that, whether or not we believe in God or Gods, there is something in every human being that does not alienate Man but rather allows Man to reach fullness of being. Whether the way is transformation or some other process, whether the principle is a divine principle or a 'human' effort, or whether we call it by one name or another is not the question here. Our only point is that this cosmotheandric or Trinitarian, *purushic* or *isvaric* principle exists.[67]

The "Unknown Christ" functions in much the same way in Panikkar's thought as grace-grounded transcendental anthropology does in Rahner's. Both ideas make possible a conception of the universe as "graced," allowing humanity "to reach fullness of being." Christ is understood as the expression of the mysterious ground of all that is, and Christ's universal significance is given cosmic dimensions. However, whereas Rahner takes the immanent Trinity to be the economic Trinity, resulting in a maximally strong identification of Christ with Jesus of Nazareth, Panikkar resists this identification. Rahner could agree with Panikkar when he asserts that "the Christian, in recognizing, believing in and loving Christ as the central symbol of Life and Ultimate Truth, is being drawn towards that selfsame Mystery that attracts all other human beings who are seeking to overcome their own present condition."[68] But Panikkar goes further to insist that "the Mystery cannot be totally identified with Christ. Christ is but one aspect of the Mystery as a whole, even though he is *the* Way when we are on that way."[69]

This last comment needs further interpretation. Panikkar's view superficially suggests that the Divine Mystery can be given a number of names, corresponding to a variety of historical-cultural insights into the mode of approach to that Mystery. In this view of the matter, the Mystery is thought of as objectified through being sought and named in a multitude of Ways, and these Ways therefore as merely nominalistic conveniences. Panikkar objects to the relativizing effect of this perspective on the status of the various Ways: "I do not wish to defend the naïve and uncritical notion that 'there is' one 'thing' which Men call by many names—as if the naming of the Mystery were simply a matter of attaching such tags as culture or language puts at our disposal."[70] The point is that "our discourse is not 'about' something that merely 'is' or 'is there'. Rather it is a disclosure of a reality that I *am* and you *are*. The Mystery is not objectifiable because 'you' and 'I' are constitutively part of it. Nor is it merely subjective, because 'we', the subject(s), are not all there is to it."[71] Thus the Ways themselves are constitutive of the Mystery to and through which they lead. It is not a case of there being many paths leading up a mountain, an image that objectifies the Mystery as a mountain. Rather, there is no climbing in the abstract, for the Mystery is encountered only in concrete pilgrimage in a Way.[72]

This approach of Panikkar—he calls it "mystical"—sits somewhat awkwardly with his other, equally emphatic assertion, that "we are on the brink of a mutation in human civilization" in which "no religious tradition is any longer capable of sustaining the burden of the present-day human predicament and guiding Man in the 'sea of life.' "[73] If this is the case, how are Christians or Hindus to stay focused on their Way? Will not the "interpenetration, mutual fecundation—and . . . mutation in the self-interpretation of these . . . religious traditions"[74] make impossible the sort of single-minded devotion to a Way that seems to be presupposed by Panikkar's understanding of the inseparability of Mystery and Way? Unsurprisingly, this question is not adequately answered. It could not be, for the result of the sort of mutation to which Panikkar refers, and which he himself embodies in some ways, lies in the future, separated from the present by a mass of contingencies. Nevertheless, this does suggest a major challenge to be negotiated, for theology and pastoral work alike: how is a Way to be followed and continually reclaimed when it requires *both* single-minded commitment and openness to the validity of other ways? Perhaps Hinduism will offer Christianity a viable solution to this challenge, based on its traditional combination of commitment to a path and openness in principle (though not always in practice) to the paths adopted by other Hindus.

Panikkar uses this same potentially fruitful connection between Hinduism and Christianity to press a critique of Christian theology, which has "always been tempted to extrapolate in an over-zealous manner."[75]

> The predominantly Semitic mentality of Christian theology will reach the intelligibility of the ultimately ungraspable Mystery ascending to it from its concrete and visible manifestation: Jesus Christ. Thus, once the identification is made, it will with great difficulty proceed in the opposite direction; if Jesus Christ is the Mystery, any other real name or real manifestation of the Mystery will appear inadequate because it contradicts the Christian understanding. The predominantly Aryan mind of Hindu theology, on the other hand, will reach the affirmation of the ultimately ungraspable Mystery by *descending* to each of its concrete and visible manifestations: e.g. Rama, Krishna, etc. The identification will never be complete and closed, and thus there will be no difficulty in recognizing several identifications without destroying the identity of the Mystery.[76]

Here, then, is a model that Panikkar is prepared to commend to Christianity. It is a unified vision of plural religious centers and depends upon repudiating the absolutist principle. The ungraspable Mystery is the only finally determining reality, and every revelation of it is also relativized by it. It is in these terms that Panikkar addresses the issue of the relation between Christ and Jesus of Nazareth: "Christians have called the [cosmotheandric principle] Christ, and rightly so. My suggestion is that they should not give it up too lightly and be satisfied simply with Jesus—however divinized. It is in and through Jesus that Christians have come to believe in the reality that they call Christ, but this Christ is the decisive reality."[77]

In concluding, we may note that Panikkar's and Knitter's contributions show the value of a modest Christology for advancing the theological interpretation of religious pluralism to have two aspects. On the one hand, modest Christologies allow theological reflection to interact meaningfully with the challenge of religious pluralism, which interaction is unnecessarily curtailed when the absolutist principle is in the Christological picture. On the other hand, modest Christologies offer intriguing resources for specific constructive responses to religious pluralism. As in every other aspect of the contemporary Christological crisis of plausibility, therefore, modest Christologies promise, in a way that Christologies tied to the absolutist principle can no longer, to propel the rich tradition of Christological reflection into the future with a felicitous combination of conceptual poise and constructive power.

Conclusion

The first task of these concluding remarks is to bring the entire argument to an end by characterizing modest Christologies as the interim goal of a quest for a believable Jesus, as the search for a *Christological* way around (or through) the forbidding impasse presented by the contemporary crisis of plausibility facing reflection on Jesus Christ. From this point of view, the argument can be seen as laying out some unavoidable conditions both for the plausibility of lines of justification for, and for the practical efficacy of, contemporary Christology. This will involve summarizing and reinforcing a theme that has run throughout the argument: that modest Christologies do not represent a theological capitulation to the contemporary *Zeitgeist,* but are rather intellectually vigorous, poised, and religiously potent interpretations of Jesus Christ. As such, they have a legitimate claim to be the most adequate inheritors of the mantle of the classical Christological tradition in the contemporary situation.

The second task extends the argument in a more adventurous direction. At numerous points in this book, an effort has been made to show that modest Christologies are not what a superficial glance might suggest. For instance, they are not necessarily anti-incarnational (as some of the literature at the present time mistakenly assumes a plausible Christology must be); they are not necessarily low Christologies (if "low" means denial of Jesus' true divinity); they are very far from being ecclesially and spiritually impotent (as nonabsolutist Christologies might be supposed to be); they do not necessarily entail approval of a theology of religions or an overarching philosophy of religion; they do not necessarily rule out such "historical events" as the resurrection; they are not just "one issue" Christologies, solving one problem without regard to others; and so on. What they *do* rule out is the absolutist principle, which involves especially what has been called the "significance thesis": that the symbol of Jesus Christ is absolutely, uniquely, exhaustively, unsurpassably significant for revelation and salvation.

This negative characterization leads to the inclusion as "modest" of a wide range of otherwise very different Christologies. The same is true of "absolutist" Christologies. There are also borderline and mixed cases, because the classification is *ideal*. However, a positive characterization of the modest class would help to indicate in a general way the significance of Christological modesty. Moreover, if the absolutist principle is really the bone of contention in contemporary Christology that I have argued it is, then Christologies repudiating it ought to have deep conceptual connections with each other. The second task of this conclusion is, accordingly, to offer a positive conceptual characterization of modest Christologies in terms of the world views, the historical-metaphysical "styles," with which they resonate. Such world views are chiefly two, and both are allergic to the absolutist principle: ecstatic naturalism and impartial supernaturalism. This provides a way to warrant claims for the religious potency of modest Christologies, as I hope to show.

Modest Christologies and the Quest for a Believable Jesus

The Interim Goal of a Quest for a Believable Jesus

While the theologically interested historians of the last two hundred years have been engaged with more or less intensity in a quest for the historical Jesus, the historically minded theologians have been busy with their own, more comprehensive search: for a way to coordinate both the historian's Jesus and the Christ of Christian tradition with the living Christ of faith in the context of contemporary self-understanding—in short, a quest for a *believable* Jesus.[1] This is a quest simultaneously for convincing justifications for Christological assertions and for ways to speak of Jesus Christ that do justice to the transformative power the classical Christological tradition ascribes to him. This quest for a believable Jesus characterizes a great deal of the Christological activity of the twentieth century, be this activity practical and opportunistic or theoretical and systematic.

Naturally, the quest for adequately justified and efficacious ways of conceiving of the Christ of contemporary Christian faith experience is common to every era. During times of religious and intellectual ferment, however, this quest takes on a more urgent mood. In this sense, the modern era has affinities with the formative centuries of the church, the period of its emergence into the high Middle Ages, and the upheaval which was the Renaissance and Reformation. However, the Christological quest of the twentieth century has several features which distinguish it both from these earlier periods of cultural restlessness and from the rest of postenlightenment modernity. Some of these features are adumbrated by such nebulous words and phrases as inner-worldly interpretations of history (historicism) and nature (naturalism); the flowering of the social and natural sciences in the bed of critical thought; the partial collapse and transformation in the West of traditional structures of meaning and value under the impact of democracy, capitalism, and technology; and the rapid merging of cultural-religious traditions (cultural and religious pluralism). Modest Christologies have been propelled from obscurity into relevance by their aptness for comprehending and addressing this distinctive situation.

These characteristics underline the role of Troeltsch as one of the focusing lenses for twentieth-century Christology, because the questions associated with this new situation were fully present *simultaneously* for the first time in his theological reflection. In fact, to various degrees, Troeltsch was partly responsible for bringing many of these potent problems to a new stage of definiteness, thereby raising awareness in the church and among theologians of their importance for Christology. As we saw in Part I, those questions usually were not answered in a comprehensive, systematic way by Troeltsch and sometimes not even posed as clearly as they might have been. Nevertheless, they were trumpeted in his fragmentary theological offerings with great urgency. It is in this sense that he succeeded in setting part of the agenda for twentieth-century Christology, even for many of those theologians who do not trace their intellectual heritage through him.

Thus the dimensions of the Christological problem were well defined at the beginning of the twentieth century—and they were the dimensions of a looming crisis, which at that time was already well over a century in the making. This crisis is hard to characterize precisely, like all things that loom as large as it does, but I have spoken of a crisis of intelligibility or plausibility, a crisis of justification. When this crisis of plausibility has been recognized in the twentieth century, as it often has, it has only occasionally been in all of its dimensions. And when the whole problem is conceived at the same moment—as it has been perhaps preeminently in historically and sociologically minded theologians such as Troeltsch and H. Richard Niebuhr—both its daunting severity and its driving cause become evident. The core of the crisis is affirmation—sometimes deliberate, sometimes habitual and unthinking—of what here has been called the "absolutist principle."

I have argued that the solution to this crisis has been discovered again and again in relation to most of its various dimensions. Many theologians working on specific issues with Christological connections—from ecology to the liberation of economically exploited peoples, from child abuse to the ordination of women, from nuclear war to reclaiming eros for Christian spirituality—have been legitimately satisfied by such discoveries and have understandably seen no need to press beyond their various quests for Christologies adequate to the urgent needs with which they have been concerned, needs to which theology in general must pay more sustained and coordinated attention. However, until these many aspects of the Christological crisis and the many approaches to solving them are comprehended in a single unified glance, what is common among the conceptually problematic cores of each of the smaller problems remains hidden away, effectively protected by a "divide and survive" strategy.

By contrast, when the problem is seen as a whole and the common threads of the various extant solutions are tied together, the absolutist principle—as that against which so many Christological projects have been struggling independently—is disclosed and given a name. Then and only then do many of the problems of Christology resolve themselves into a much larger, more urgent, more persistent crisis of plausibility, and the common component of the individual solutions to all of these smaller problems is evident at once: the absolutist principle must be consistently resisted within Christological reflection. Part I of this book showed how the Christological crisis was formed under the impulse of what was called in chapter 4 the "absolutist principle." Chapters 6 and 7 demonstrated the role of the absolutist principle in causing or exacerbating a wide range of Christological challenges and the abundant benefits accruing to Christology when the penchant for absolutist formulations is overcome.

In this book, Christology without the absolutist principle is called "modest." This is not a great name, to be sure, for it threatens to obscure the ecclesial, ethical, and spiritual potency of a properly developed modest Christology; nevertheless, the name's natural meaning conveys the point, as a useful name should. At some point in a hypothetical future, when it is generally recognized that modest Christologies are the dominant representatives of the classical Christological tradition, the name *modest* will no longer be needed. There are, as I have shown, a number of ways to do Christology without the absolutist principle, from which it follows that "modest Christology" designates not a particular Christology, but a class of Christologies. Moreover, the distinction between incarnational and inspirational types (worked out especially in chapter 5) offers merely an indication of the diversity of approaches possible; this book has not been concerned to catalogue this diversity, but only to establish the most general characteristics of the modest class thought of as an ideal whole.

A modest Christology is the interim *goal* of the many and various paths in the quest for a believable Jesus because it meets the basic conditions for intellectual vigor and the poised combination of fidelity and plausibility that a contemporary Christology must in order to be adequate. It is the *interim* goal, however, because to announce a Christology meeting these fundamental conditions is merely to pass through the portal into the great hall of the classical Christological tradition, ready to join the ongoing task of Christology. The fact that no constructive Christology is presented in this book is a clear indication that the task has been a propaedeutic and preparatory one, one that invites and aids the working out of modest Christologies in detail.

As the interim goal of a quest for a believable Jesus, modest Christologies furnish the classical Christological tradition with a more viable form of Christological reflection than absolutist Christologies can offer: one that does not squander or distort the power of that about which Christol-

ogy seeks to speak in the way that I have argued a Christological embrace
of the absolutist principle requires; one that allows engagement with the
object and term of Christological reflection to transform the tradition
when it flags under the dead weight of misplaced loyalty to unworkable
formulations; one with the poise and charm to draw out the best of the
tradition while engaging the rich array of intersubjective contexts within
and by which Christology must understand and evaluate itself; one with
the historical rootedness required to remember its heritage and purpose.
The claim of modest Christologies to be the most adequate contemporary
representatives of the classical Christological tradition is grounded in their
superior potential for fostering Christological reflection with such desirable characteristics.

Avoiding Capitulation to the Spirit of the Times

However, it might be objected that this conclusion is purchased at too
high a price, because—all claims to the contrary notwithstanding—it requires capitulation to unquestioned assumptions of the contemporary
spirit of the times. By contrast, runs this objection, doing Christian theology means fidelity to a long-standing tradition, and such fidelity has the
great virtue of protecting theology from over-enthusiastic compromise
with the *Zeitgeist.* This objection has some superficial appeal but can only
be applied here with the help of a significant misunderstanding, for it is
precisely fidelity to the classical Christological tradition that is at stake in
the debate between modest and absolutist Christologies. The point of
chapter 6, "Modest Christological Solutions to Internal Challenges," was
to show that modest Christologies are at least as adequate to criteria of
continuity with tradition as are their absolutist counterparts, and the same
argument emerges in various ways elsewhere.

Furthermore, to move the counter-objection in a different direction,
the classical Christological tradition is never available in isolation from the
cultural contexts in which it arises; a self-standing Christological tradition
can be neither detected by historical analysis, nor created by a methodological commitment to carry out Christological discourse within the limits of a supposedly well-defined linguistic environment on the scale of an
entire tradition. On the contrary, Christian doctrine is always answerable
to criteria for plausibility that derive in part from the cultural environment
of ecclesial theology, for theology and culture cannot in principle nor in

practice be completely separated from each other. Securing the plausibility of lines of justification for doctrinal formulations—as judged by "external" criteria such as those discussed in chapter 7—is therefore a mandate *internal* to the tradition of Christological reflection.

Thus, managing the virtuous interests of plausibility and fidelity is a question of *balance.* In the case of modest Christologies, these interests are partially aligned, which is why modest Christologies can be thought to advance the classical Christological tradition. They are also partially opposed, in the sense that advocacy of a modest Christology entails a critique of the absolutist hermeneutical habit so closely associated with the classical Christological tradition. This balance can be achieved only in every new situation by creative determination to articulate a faithful, plausible vision of the significance of Jesus Christ. No completely secure path to such balance has emerged in the history of the relation between theology and culture, and absolutizing a contemporary cultural bias as a way of securing this balance is no more effective a strategy than absolutizing the revelatory and salvific significance of the symbol of Jesus Christ.

What is required, therefore, is methodological openness to the correction of theological proposals. Such openness is not the exclusive prerogative of modest Christologies; as noted elsewhere, it is formally present in some articulations of absolutist Christology—Wolfhart Pannenberg offers the premier example—and absent in some articulations of modest Christology—especially in those taking current cultural insights too much for granted, which is evident in some articulations of the charge that the idea of incarnation is incoherent. Openness is crucial, however, if a balance between plausibility and fidelity is to be achieved. When openness is present, a suitable methodological environment is established for making judgments about which aspects of cultural insight need to be the source of criteria for the plausibility of Christology, and which need to be critiqued out of the richness of the Christological tradition as one-sided and distorting. It is on this basis that modest Christologies and theology in general can avoid merely capitulating to cultural fads, and yet at the same time take cultural insights with appropriate seriousness.

But methodological openness by itself is not enough, for it merely sets the context for Christological debate by facilitating the achievement of balance between fidelity and plausibility. The debate itself must be carried on, and the arguments for modest Christology presented in this book are contributions to that debate. They have tried to establish that the interests of both fidelity and plausibility are obscured when Christology is wedded to the absolutist principle, and that modest Christology is the most faithful, plausible, and efficacious continuation of the classical Christological tradition in our time.

Measuring the Strength of the Cumulative Case

Precisely how strong is the cumulative case for modest Christologies? To answer this question, consider the following. If metaphysical arguments necessarily involve judgments about metaphysical plausibility, and if such judgments are made on the basis of coherence with other, purportedly indispensable perspectives, then a very great deal hinges on the idea of *indispensability*. A variety of perspectives have been shown to be dissonant with the absolutist principle and consonant with modest Christology's avoidance of it. But these purportedly indispensable perspectives are indispensable in different ways. The discovery of the age and size of the universe, and the attendant transformation in our cosmological assumptions, is one perspective that is indispensable in the strongest sense: it is not obviously a matter of interpretation that might later be reversed. It is a discovery in the sense of a permanent addition to our stock of knowledge about the world. On the other hand, a response to the ethical absolutism fostered by the absolutist principle is a less clear-cut issue. It is readily conceivable that ethical absolutism in some respect might some day in some place, as in the past, be thought of as a great virtue, in a way that some find hard to imagine here and now. This is indispensability in a weaker sense.

What is needed is some method to weigh the relative indispensability of the perspectives with which absolutist Christology is dissonant against the consonance that absolutist Christologies have displayed in relation to so many understandings of the world prior to the modern period. Alas, it is far from easy to assign measures either of degrees of consonance or of the relative importance of indispensable perspectives. Moreover, the required judgment is complicated by social and personal factors that are intangible and of which it is impossible fully to take account. This is the nature of theology and an illustration of how complex are judgments of fidelity to the classical Christological tradition.

However, consider what has been shown: the absolutist principle coheres with very little that the West has discovered about the world, about human nature, and about human societies since the medieval period yielded to the modern. When this principle is tested in the fires of the modern disciplines of history, anthropology, sociology, psychology, and natural science—as it has been continuously for the last quarter of a millennium, and especially in the last century—such theological justification as has emerged for retaining it is far less compelling than that adduced in favor of rejecting it. Moreover, the absolutist principle is not a harmless Christological distortion: I have argued that the contemporary vigor of the churches' proclamations is seriously damaged by it and that there have been and continue to be devastating, mostly unintentional ethical side effects. This lack of coherence has become more and more obvious and has been flagrant in the contemporary era.

In the language of some recent studies in theological method influenced by the philosophy of science,[2] therefore, Christologies wedded to the absolutist principle should be described as research programs whose explanatory power is spent and whose survival depends on *ad hoc* adjustments that are useful primarily for their face-saving value. The controversy in the philosophy of science about whether there can be clear-cut rational criteria for abandoning a degenerating research program (symbolized by the debate between Paul Feyerabend and Imre Lakatos[3]) is relevant here, either as metaphor or as theoretical parallel, depending on the working understanding of theological method. Conceivably, there may finally be no rationally coercive way to justify the abandonment of absolutist Christologies; the switch may be accomplished finally only by natural attrition of the boosters for absolutism. A kind of intuitive weighing of arguments is possible still, however, even though it is necessarily a vague and painstaking process. Similarly, even though the balancing of criteria for plausibility and fidelity cannot be achieved with ideal precision, the combined weight of the arguments presented makes it difficult to resist the conclusion that Christologies are untenable precisely to the extent that they affirm the absolutist principle.

We must ask frankly, therefore, whether theologians and ecclesial bodies are rationally justified in retaining Christologies that affirm the absolutist principle—notwithstanding the fact that its bare metaphysical possibility has been defended throughout this book. Under what weight of evidence would it make sense to take the step, say, of committing to a modest Christology—implicitly by avoiding, or explicitly by abjuring, absolutist formulations of the significance of Jesus Christ—in a pronouncement at the modern equivalent of an ancient ecumenical council? When would the World Council of Churches, a meeting of Roman Catholic bishops, or the World Alliance of Reformed Churches be rationally and ecclesially justified in following the (implicit) example of a very few smaller communions by making such a pronouncement?

I have argued that the evidential weight is *already* solidly on the side of modest Christology and against absolutist Christology, and has been for some time. Are we not, therefore, at that time when some decision about the viability of the absolutist principle needs to be made? The absolutist principle has run out of theoretical flexibility and is faced with long-standing, apparently insurmountable problems. The challenges to absolutist Christology are infinitely stronger and more coordinated than they have ever been. Waiting out the Christological crisis is exceedingly unlikely to be an effective strategy, as it has been on so many occasions through the church's history when an interpretation of doctrine has been under fire. Christian theology is indeed, therefore, at the very crossroads in which some decision must be made between absolutist and modest Christologies.

Continued affirmation of the absolutist principle in the form of absolutist Christologies requires a reversion to an earlier period of our culture, a period for which the rallying power of an exclusivist Christology was more important than it is now, historical sensibilities less pronounced, our knowledge of the world and of ourselves less detailed. Such a return is impossible, without some major disaster to trigger the loss of much of the contemporary world's knowledge, ambiguous and troubling as that knowledge is. The quieter, often suppressed, voices of the tradition of Christological reflection speak again in our contemporary setting, urging a return to older views of Jesus Christ and a decisive embrace of newer ones. It is past time to seek consistent interpretations of his person and work that leave the absolutist principle behind and allow Jesus Christ to recover the relevance and transformative power that the classical Christology claims for him.

A Final Objection: The Value of Absolutism

It is possible, even when the evidence is so strongly stacked against absolutist Christology, to cling to it as beloved, as aesthetically and religiously appealing, as the last bastion of resistance to the overwhelming stench of

Christian theological compromise with cultural insight. Even if it is fool-ishness, according to this objection, the absolutist principle must be af-firmed repeatedly against the wise of this world; indeed, precisely because it is foolishness, it stands as timeless testimony to the facts that God tran-scends human understanding and that faith in its deepest forms moves in realms of which a weak-kneed consistency with reason knows nothing.

Søren Kierkegaard will be cited in support of this, both for the cri-tique of Christianity that he issues and for his vision of religious faith.[4] The desire to achieve a poised coordination of the resources of Christian faith and more broadly based cultural insight into the world and human life is a perfect example of the aesthete's thirst—much maligned in Kierkegaard—for intellectual harmony. Likewise, the emphasis on balancing fidelity and plausibility in Christological construction expresses a not-so-subtle re-sistance to the possibility that there could ever be a teleological suspen-sion of the ethical, which is a deeply religious manifestation of the internal demand of faith to take priority over all human standards of the good, true, and beautiful. Fidelity in its deepest form, according to this critique, knows nothing of plausibility, even though it achieves an internal certainty of its own—possibly one that flies in the face of all canons of plausibility. The incarnation is the very heart of the Christian gospel because it be-speaks the breach of the walls between eternity and time; this breach is so contrary to reasonable expectation and rational assignments of plausibility that it must be described in the most extreme hermeneutical terms as ab-solutely, uniquely, comprehensively, unsurpassably significant for revela-tion and salvation. That is, incarnational Christology *must* affirm the absolutist principle; Jesus Christ must be the unique, unsurpassable, all-determining reality, or the very heart and soul of the incarnational vision of reality is squandered on placating the awkward feelings of timid theolo-gians who feel left out of the cultural fun.

It is difficult to assess such a critique without having recourse to the very standards of adequacy it repudiates as inapplicable. This is its genius, of course; it was the essential epistemological twist in the thought of both Kierkegaard and Barth, for it sets up the Christian gospel—and with it Christology—as an either/or proposition, even as Kierkegaard presented becoming a Christian in these terms in his masterful *Either/Or*. But the force of this vision of religious faith, properly construed, applies equally as a critique to *every* kind of theological thought, to every Christological in-terpretation, to every truth propounded about God. That is the point of a teleological suspension of the ethical; there are no rules when one transcends the universal insights of ethics and reason, even as there is no way to rationalize the offense of Abraham's willingness to sacrifice Isaac. Kierkegaard is devastatingly clear on this point in *Fear and Trembling:* whereas the aesthete is attracted by the possible and the ethical soul by the eternal, the truly religious person loves the impossible. There can be no doctrinal, psychological, social, or rational anticipations of the demand of faith. The experience of the infinite risk of faith, properly understood, does not—cannot—confer supremacy on particular theological doctrines or views of the world, which are subject to argumentation only within the earlier aesthetic and ethical stages of life. Indeed, one of the implications of Kierkegaard's doctrine of "truth as subjectivity" in *Concluding Unscientific Postscript* is that the deepest forms of subjective faith are independent of the content of that faith; the infinitely passionate faith that takes as its object a false teaching is infinitely preferable to the more restrained faith that limits itself to the objectively true. In other words, the greater the risk of faith in its love affair with the impossible, the less important doctrinal squabbles become.

The fundamental mistake of the objection under examination here is, therefore, that it does not take Kierkegaard seriously enough. It attempts to hijack Kierkegaard and press him into the support of a proposition that he rejects, namely, that a specific Christological doctrine (absolutist Christology) can receive rational support from the existence of a mode of faith in which infinite passion and infinite risk force the abandonment of canons of plausibility and the goal of poised balance between intellectual vigor and fidelity to the Christian gospel. I think that Kierkegaard's phenomenology of faith is profoundly insightful and even regard it as the most promising point of contact between Christian and South Asian forms of religious consciousness. But the attempt to use it in support of absolutist Christologies is tantamount to the nonsensical act of trying to achieve a rational deduction of Christological doctrine from the teleological suspension of all universal laws of ethics and reason. Kierkegaard's own fondness for absolutist interpretations of the incarnation must not be allowed to obscure the point that there can be no feedback from the realm of faith's infinite passion that is capable of confirming Christological doctrines of any kind, modest or absolutist. It is enough to be propelled toward the infinite risk of faith by the scandal of divine concern, the testimony of the gospel that the ultimate object of religious faith is concerned with us and our lives—and this lies at the heart of all Christology, and in modest Christology is least obscured by absolutist hermeneutical excess.

Approaching the Conceptual Heart of Modest Christologies

I turn in finally to the task of providing a positive characterization of the diverse class of modest Christologies. First, I shall describe two opposed but related visions of nature, history, and God that resonate with modest Christology but are antagonistic toward absolutist Christology. Many views of Ultimacy, world, and humanity are resonant with modest Christology, but these two—impartial supernaturalism (e.g., the perennial philosophy) and ecstatic naturalism (e.g., Troeltsch's naturalistic religious historicism)—are particularly instructive. Second, I will suggest how these two fundamental world views are resonant with each other, in spite of the apparent impossibility of synthesizing them. In this way, the conceptual core of modest Christology can be illumined. Third, I will make some remarks about the variations in historical style of modest Christologies as a way of deepening perceptions of their similarities and differences. Finally, on the basis of the previous steps, I will intimate my reasons for thinking that modest Christology is peculiarly well suited to capture religious imaginations and sustain ecclesial institutions in contemporary Western culture and beyond.

Two World Views Amenable to Modest Christology

It is admittedly odd to begin a process of elucidating the deep commonalities of Christologies in the modest class by showing that they are resonant with one or another (or perhaps both) of two fundamentally opposed views of Ultimacy, world, history, and humanity. Superficially, this would seem to guarantee the conclusion that the class of modest Christologies is a combination of several kinds of Christologies with no fundamental conceptual core. That, however, would be a hasty conclusion, as I hope to show.

First, then, consider impartial supernaturalism. This was discussed in Part I in general terms as supernaturalism without the biased supernatural apologetic for a particular tradition, so here it might be most useful to describe a particular impartially supernatural world view: perennial philosophy. This is a recent name for a class of closely related ancient views whose most famous representatives are Plotinus in the West and Sankara in India. Recent advocates are Aldous Huxley and Huston Smith, and there have been many diverse exemplars in between, including Western luminaries such as Meister Eckhart and Jakob Boehme. Perennial philosophy attempts what many think impossible, namely, to identify a fundamental metaphysical view present in every religious tradition that can be the basis for understanding all religious insight as ultimately and essentially about the same thing, no matter how dramatic the superficial differences might be.

The world view of perennial philosophy is a dramatically supernaturalist drama of spiritual beings and powers; of incarnations and revelations; of a personal, attentive deity; of salvation histories and divine acts. Its central affirmation is that our world and human beings are at the low end of a great scale of being and value whose infinitely wonderful peak is Ultimate Reality, beyond being and nonbeing, about which it is finally impossible to say anything directly. This Ultimate is variously called "The One" (by Plotinus); "Nirguna Brahman" (by the Vedanta tradition springing from Sankara, meaning "God-without-attributes"); "Godhead" (by some Western mystical traditions); and "Sunyata" (by Buddhists, meaning, roughly, "emptiness"). These names are boldly held to refer to the same Absolute Mystery. The first three names implicitly express the denial that the ultimate is God-as-highest-being, to whom may be attributed such qualities as goodness, justice, being-personal, love, power. and activity. Yet the reality of this God as highest being—the devotional object of most theistic people—is also affirmed at a lesser level; Vedanta calls it "Saguna Brahman" (God-with-attributes) and apophatic mysticism refers to it simply as "God," recognizing that it is the ultimate object of attention for kataphatic traditions.

Also overflowing from the One (a favorite image of Plotinus for such emanation is that of a fountain) are other realms of being, both nontemporal (Plato's forms, for example, or Plotinus' Mind) and temporal (angels, demons, the material world, and humans partly within it, and all manner of other possible heavenly beings and powers). Perennialists uniformly insist that the material world has a dim reality and power compared to the realm of the spiritual. Understandably, then, perennial philosophers have demonstrated little interest in spending a lot of energy incorporating detailed scientific insights into their point of view. Rather, they have been content to point out that the material world, presumably well described by science, is relatively unimportant in the larger scheme of things.

With regard to human salvation or liberation, the point of the perennial philosophy is that human beings must try to escape the preliminary material world of illusion and return to the source of all being, the One beyond being. The shape of world history in all versions of this view is relatively unimportant, therefore—a mere detail whose discovery (if possible at all) is nothing more than the satisfying of an irrelevant curiosity. Thus, the origins, directionality, and end point of the cosmic process, including cosmic and biological evolution, can be settled in any number of ways; perennial philosophy is neutral to the competing scenarios.

Second, ecstatic naturalism is a recent name for a class of naturalistic views, each of which affirms in one way or another that nature has a "depth dimension" (Tillich) that is the proper object of religious concern. This world view offers a religiously compelling vision of a natural world throwing up creatures with astonishing profusion who are naturally oriented to the religious mystery of nature and history and seek to engage it in one way or another; and it explains alternate convictions by means of natural social and psychological processes such as (often healthy) projection and (usually unhealthy) delusion. Because human beings are essentially oriented to this mysterious depth of nature, many such views involve a transcendental anthropology. There have been many forms of naturalistic religious historicism affirmed during the modern period, including pantheistic, panentheistic, world-as-God's-body, and mystical visions. They have in common a sparse metaphysic of Godhead (in the sense of perennial philosophy) and world, where Godhead is the infinite depth, the mysterious horizon of nature and history.

Naturalism (of which ecstatic naturalism is a specification) is an essentially post-Renaissance interpretation of Ultimacy, world, and humanity, though it has clear antecedents as far back as ancient times both in Greece (especially Aristotle and the pre-Socratic Milesian physicists) and in South Asia (especially Carvaka, the nonorthodox and eventually universally repudiated materialist school of Indian philosophy). Naturalism of all kinds came into their own in and after the Renaissance because of the rise of the natural sciences in their modern form. Formerly, too much about the natural world and history was unexplained for the belief in its independent, self-developing, and self-regulating character to be much more plausible than an intriguing thought experiment. The natural sciences change the balance of plausibility, however, and naturalism, though it flies in the face of virtually all of the great wisdom traditions of the world, has become (with the usual inconsistencies) the working world view of everyday life in much of the modern Western world, coexisting with various degrees of comfort with theism and other religious perspectives.

With regard to human life, naturalism typically adopts a "historicist" outlook under the impact of a number of realizations that deepened through the nineteenth century: that religious, ethical, economic, political, and cultural traditions were at least partly *constructed;* that human beings could to some extent *control* the natural world through technology and social organization; that history could be *molded* in the direction of human interests through fearless attacks on prejudice and the self-conscious embrace of responsibility; that *fate* was at least as much the result of ignorance and lack of self-conscious human will-to-power as it was the consequence of subjection of the cosmos to divine whims; and so on.

The developments sponsoring a historicist interpretation of human affairs did not rule out the religious perspective of ecstatic naturalism, but they did challenge familiar assumptions about the relative power of the divine and the human in the world. Thus, it is unsurprising that elevated anthropologies and dynamic philosophies of history were developed in Europe during the nineteenth century (from Schelling and Hegel to Feuerbach, Marx, and Nietzsche), some suggesting rapprochement with traditional religious insight and others violent repudiations of it. In the twentieth century, after Kierkegaard and Nietzsche in the nineteenth, existentialism has perpetuated the insight that human decision is fundamental, and it has done so in both religious and antireligious forms. The birth of the social sciences and the study of religion at the end of the nineteenth century likewise permit both religious and antireligious forms of naturalistic historicism. Naturalistic historicism, therefore, need not have the religious tone of ecstatic naturalism. When it does, it cannot be so through the affirmation of a supernatural governing divinity in some other realm than the natural world, merely reaching in from time to time to effect the divine will in accordance with the divine intention. Rather, naturalistic historicism gains an ecstatic cast through an affirmation of the religious mystery of nature and history against reductionistic attempts to deny it, while embracing this-worldly accounts of nature and history through the full recognition of the social-psychological, natural-scientific, and critical-historical dimensions of interpretations of reality.

Now, with regard to Christology, both impartial supernaturalism (represented here by perennial philosophy) and ecstatic naturalism (which might be represented by Troeltsch's naturalistic religious historicism) allow for its possibility. In fact, both incarnational and nonincarnational, inspirational Christologies are conceivable in the context of either worldview, and non-Christological interpretations of Jesus also are possible. However, both world views are allergic to the absolutist principle. Impartial supernaturalism, including the perennial philosophy, is not amenable to absolutist Christology because it excludes any rational basis for attaching unique, definitive, unsurpassable significance to the symbol of Jesus Christ. The story of revelation and salvation is broader than the Christ event, which neither defines nor triggers nor decisively culminates every aspect of that story, though the Christ event expresses and participates in it. On this view, the Absolute can never be expressed definitively within history and nature because they themselves derive from it.

Similarly, ecstatic naturalism takes a skeptical stance toward principles by which assertions of historical significance can be accorded absolutely unique or final status and gives preference to those assertions of significance that are rooted firmly in the contingent flux of historical meanings. It affirms norms with profound historic significance but is realistic about the socially interpreted and historical character of those norms; imagining that they were absolute or final would threaten to take them out of history and deny the role of human social imagination in creating them. The Absolute can and does disclose itself in history and nature, but *not absolutely*. By contrast, the absolutist principle presupposes that absolute finality and significance can appear decisively in history, be recognized there, and be embodied in traditions of discourse that continually testify to its appearance and reception. Ecstatic naturalism and the absolutist principle are profoundly dissonant, accordingly.

The Conceptual Heart of Modest Christology

Ecstatic naturalism and impartial supernaturalism, naturalistic religious historicism, and perennial philosophy cannot be synthesized. It is arguable that Paul Tillich made the most prominent attempt to forge a synthesis between them, a synthesis in which his concept of 'biblical religion' played a key role. Most of the (for Tillich, Neoplatonic) hierarchy of being was lost in the "synthesis," however, and his achievement ought to be described as the submission of perennial philosophy to ecstatic naturalism (a term Tillich himself used to describe his thought), and not a synthesis of the two. These two world views have never been synthesized without one or both being disfigured beyond recognition.

In spite of the apparent impossibility of an even-handed synthesis of ecstatic naturalism and impartial supernaturalism, the two views clearly have some affinity for each other. Both views envision Godhead and the world as mediated variously by metaphysically real or imaginatively projected realms of beings. To be sure, the world is conceived differently in the two cases as ontologically fundamental or as ontologically "less real." Godhead in both cases is Absolute Mystery, however, and the overall metaphysical geography of the two views is intriguingly similar. In fact, they are almost mirror images of each other, which suggests that the only possibility for a serious, even-handed synthesis of the two would lie in finding some way to regard imaginative projections as having greater reality than human beings through the participation of those projections in their ultimate referent, the Godhead. To say the least, an unusual theory of symbols would be needed were a synthesis to be achieved along these lines.

In any event, it is these general similarities of metaphysical structure that offer insights into the conceptual heart of modest Christology. These structural similarities can be described with the phrase *mediated Godhead-world relation*. Modest Christology is committed to such a mediated Godhead-world relation, though the form of mediation can be naturalist or impartially supernaturalist. The absolutist principle requires the sacrifice of mediation to the idol of absolute realization in history and nature. This sacrifice can be made in a number of ways, including by adopting exclusive supernaturalism, or by siding with Hegel against Schelling in affirming that the Godhead can lavish itself definitively and uniquely upon a particular. The mediated Godhead-world relation, no matter how it is conceived, is allergic to both kinds of sacrifice.

It is important to be clear that the mediated Godhead-world relation affirms that the Absolute can and does appear in history; it is only unique, exhaustive, definitive appearance that is ruled out; this is where the line of battle with the absolutist principle is drawn. I have insisted throughout this book that there are no knock-down arguments for the absolutist principle (thus: against the mediated Godhead-world relation), so modest Christology can afford to be—indeed, *must* be—open to the possibility of the truth of the absoluteness principle, even though it is a remote possibility. But while the absoluteness principle is neither inconceivable nor metaphysically impossible, the *working hypothesis* of the mediated Godhead-world relation is that absolute meanings do not appear definitively in history. The case for this hypothesis is by no means a weak one, as I have tried to show, but there is no knock-down proof available; implausibility and infidelity to the classical Christological tradition are the strongest charges that can be brought against the absolutist principle. The strongest representation of the absolutist principle in the contemporary era, therefore, will not be a Rahnerian strengthening of it against all evidence, but rather Pannenberg's methodologically open affirmation of it: an insistence based on the claim of deep fidelity to the Christian tradition and on the confidence that the historical process will bear out the extraordinarily audacious expression of hope for the entire cosmic historical process grounded on the interpretation of the life and, especially, the resurrection, of Jesus as a proleptic anticipation of final reconciliation. This view suffers from the implausibility that all absolutist Christologies do, and I have argued that its claim to deep fidelity to the Christian tradition is seriously one-sided, but it does at least continue to affirm the absolutist principle as convincingly as possible.

The Historical Style of Modest Christology

Just as the mediated Godhead-world relation is understood differently in ecstatic naturalism and impartial supernaturalism, so the mediated Godhead-world relation is consonant with a complex family of historical styles. The same is true of views of nature, as we have seen in the resonance of the mediated Godhead-world relation with both ecstatic naturalist and impartially supernaturalist interpretations. Here, however, I will concentrate on views of history.

Among many possible kinds of variation in historical style, consider that dimension of variation which bears on what can be called the "active or passive character" of the historical process. To explain this, recall the opposed positions of Hick and Cobb on the possibility of a pluralistic theology of religions, which were discussed in chapter 5. Hick and Cobb exemplify a passive and active view of ecstatic naturalism, respectively. Hick's view is that the capability of religious traditions for adaptation and survival has no final bearing on their inherent superiority or uniqueness. As a matter of fact, religious traditions perish all the time but are no less "valid" for that; their validity and value derive from the fact that they afford access to the transcendent.[5] Cobb's view, by contrast, is that the religious tradition that survives the best is the one that is the truest. Put differently, this view says that survival, though dependent to some extent on contingencies, is very much relevant to the question of assessing claims to uniqueness, truth, and interreligious superiority: we are engaged in a drawn-out fight to the death for the right to represent the religious aspirations of the entire race or sections of it, and the survivors survive because of inherent advantages, not merely by accident.

The difference may be pictured somewhat gruesomely as the contrast between the ancient Roman arena in which the gladiator who remains standing can interpret his survival as a sign of his competence as a warrior (the view of Cobb—and also Knitter and Pannenberg) and the process of random mutation and natural selection that characterizes biological evolution (the view of Hick). It is the difference between "might is right" and "might is might." It is the difference in principle between an active and a passive conception of the interaction between religious traditions in history and corresponds in the final analysis to active and passive versions of the philosophy of history connected with the mediated Godhead-world relation. In the former, truth, goodness, and beauty are unfolded through the chain of crisis and disaster, creativity and love that constitutes history. History is finally *maya,* or illusion, but it is also the glorious, increasingly intelligible *lila,* or play, of the Absolute. It retains a sense of active movement toward an unattainable goal, albeit a movement that suffers setbacks and could perhaps even be thwarted. In the latter, history is the passive context for the striving of creation. Here the emphasis is not on that toward which the creation strives within history, but on the relativization of historical activity and progress before Ultimate Mystery; the possibility that the divine *lila* will forever remain patternless and unintelligible is retained, and emphasis is laid upon the fact that *only* the Ultimately Real is *ultimately* real; every historical striving pales before that to which we are inescapably oriented.

Impartial supernaturalism (especially in the form of perennial philosophy) is most closely aligned with the passive view of history, and ecstatic naturalism, with the active view. This is not a hard and fast correspondence, however, but merely a conceptual affinity. Moreover, in spite of the different moods of these visions of history, both firmly embrace the mediated Godhead-world relation, as this has been defined. Therefore, both prefer a modest Christology or no Christology before an absolutist Christology. With regard to the types of modest Christology, the inspirational type seems more or less at home with either version of religious historicism, as the Christologies of Hick, with his passive religious historicism, and Troeltsch in his essay on "The Place of Christianity among the World Religions," with his active religious historicism, illustrate. The same is true of the incarnational type.

The Religious Potency of Modest Christology

A final issue bears on the aptness of modest Christologies for addressing the contemporary religious environment, particularly of Westerners and their religious institutions. How does the alleged ethical, ecclesial, and spiritual potency of modest Christologies manifest itself? I have already indicated in the Introduction that an adequate response to a question of this sort demands more in the way of detailed, systematic insight into the relations between religious people, religious groups, and religious ideas than presently exists. Nevertheless, it seems prudent in the conclusion of this work to give some brief, albeit necessarily vague, answer—which in this case has three parts.

First, as the need for social gravity in a religiously and morally pluralistic cultural environment sharpens, the choice facing us will become ever more clearly one between a futile return to ethical and conceptual absolutism and a poised embrace of anti-absolutist pluralism in such a way as to emphasize the orienting role of traditions and the ongoing methodological commitment to both intra- and intertraditional conversation.[6] This situation of decision was what Nietzsche had in mind when he spoke of nihilism, and he may well have been correct in his contention that this uncertain, interim phase of Western culture could be negotiated only in the presence of massive social disruptions—so far he certainly seems to have been partially right.[7] But Nietzsche's overly individualistic reading of this situation produced his own idealized self-image as an archetypal solution: the infinitely solitary hero, the *übermensch,* who could make moral decisions and take full responsibility for doing so in a morally ungrounded

environment. What is required—and what has emerged forcefully since
Nietzsche in a hundred ways—is a social reading of the same situation,
one that allows for human weakness and disagreement, one that takes account of political corruption and moral evil, yet one that envisages that
decisions can be made by communities and responsibility for those decisions can be taken without supposing an evident, absolute moral foundation or universal moral agreement, so long as conversation oriented to
inquiry within and among traditions of discourse is maintained.

This is the situation in which modest Christologies have immense
moral, spiritual, and social resources to offer. They facilitate the apprehension of ethical, spiritual, and social value by Christian individuals and
communities in an environment with contested ethical, spiritual, or social
norms. Moreover, they do so by means of the concrete symbols of a religious tradition of enormous power. Without some such symbolic resource, the human imagination and will falter for want of a language in
which to speak of the mysterious, wondrous, confounding environment
of human life.

This is not only the reason for the efficacy of modest Christologies in
our time, therefore; it is also the reason why religion itself never can be
eliminated: Feuerbach was partially right that religious symbols are the result of the projective impulse of the human imagination in a difficult
world, but religion is not *only* projection; Marx was partially right that religion is fueled by alienation and that overcoming alienation must be the
goal of human life, but religion is not *only* a result of human self-alien-
ation, and religion can help and not merely hinder its overcoming;
Durkheim was partially right that religion embodies powerful social mores
and values, but religion is not *only* the embodiment of the values of one's
society; Freud was partially right that religion inhibits growth into true
adulthood, but religion is not *only* a social realization of mass infantile
neurosis, and it fosters human maturity in a wide variety of circumstances.
The mystery of the world neither is explained nor is eliminated by pointing out our profoundly self-referential entanglement in it, and its irre-
ducibility calls for symbolic engagement and social embodiment. The
mediated Godhead-world relation is at home in this welter of partially accurate critiques of religion—indeed, it has been partial sponsor of some
of them—but it refuses to be distracted by the forcefulness of the critiques from noticing the religious depth of nature and history and testify-

ing to its ethical, social, and spiritual importance in human life. In such a context, modest Christologies are a boon for theology, for Christian churches, for piety, and for evangelism. They disarm the self-referentiality of human existence and allow for engagement of the mystery of the world in symbolic terms that are maximally adequate for that most serious of life tasks.

Second, the impression of the ecclesial, ethical, and spiritual potency of modest Christologies increases the more the contemporary situation of church and culture is diagnosed as one calling for an understanding of the world along the lines *either* of ecstatic naturalism *or* of impartial supernaturalism. As different as these two ways of seeing the world are, they independently supersede the anthropocentrism and absolutist hermeneutical tendencies of the absolutist principle and are natural environments for modest Christologies. The key to the religious efficacy of modest Christologies is the prevalence of impartial supernaturalism and ecstatic naturalism in Western culture. Very often these views even coexist; for instance, the movement between a naturalistic outlook on everyday, technology-filled life and a belief in personal angels is unproblematic for many people, doubtless because it is negotiated without much reflection. These two views are also present side by side within Christian churches. This plurality of religious viewpoints is not new in the least. In fact, the cultic life of mainstream Christian churches almost always has depended on a certain degree of vagueness in the way religious convictions are expressed in the cult for stimulation and guidance of the religious imagination (this is less the case in sectarian groups). Most Christologies within the classical tradition possess some degree of flexibility in this regard, and modest Christologies are no exception. They have sufficient flexibility to meet a variety of religious needs and inspire a large range of religious imaginations.

Third, while it is true that the flexibility of modest Christology is essential to its cultic usefulness, the ethical and religious potency of modest Christology emerges most clearly from consideration of what ecstatic naturalism and impartial supernaturalism have in common. This common content corresponds to the religious genius of the mediated Godhead-world relation. Both world views envisage human beings as engaged in a never-ending struggle to understand themselves spiritually, intellectually, and socially before a nameless mystery that eludes all actual names applied to it. Both insist that human life and theological reflection, indeed the whole cosmos, fall under the command and invitation, and finally the judgment, of this Ultimate Mystery. Both deny that it can be grasped definitively in any rational presentation, any religious vision, or any system of symbols. Both assert that this mystery is the all-determining reality, and both enjoin worship and humility upon those who reflect upon it. The fact that both ecstatic naturalism and impartial supernaturalism are well represented in Christian communities today shows that it is more vital for religiously potent liturgical and theological formulations to register these common thematic elements than it is decisively to present a consistent metaphysics.

This indicates the great ethical and religious strength of modest Christology, which takes its rise precisely from these themes and rejects the absolutist principle as their antithesis. In view of its intellectual, ethical, and religious advantages, therefore, large-scale ecclesial affirmation of modest Christology, particularly of the incarnational variety, is an intriguing thought experiment. To be *encouraged* by the church to resist the temptation to embrace hermeneutically absolutized renderings of reality, of personal development and salvation, of society and history, of ethics and sacraments—this would be a delight and a relief to many Christians, as well as to the hordes who avoid churches because of a praiseworthy, visceral allergy to absolutist blunderings through the mysterious delicacy and inexplicable brutality of life. On these points, both those inclined to an ecstatic naturalist view and those drawn by the vision of impartial supernaturalism can join in celebration.

Modest Christology does, however, require giving up the absolutist principle and the associated comfort of absolutist metaphysics and ethics, albeit an ultimately empty and idolatrous comfort. Though doubtless an unpleasant prospect for some, this is necessary, no matter which of the two above-mentioned metaphysical perspectives suits one's Christological tastes. The ecstatic naturalist world view defers in this matter to the insight that history supports rich structures of meaning guided by powerful, contingent norms, but that absolute, unchanging norms are an illusory hope borne upon denial of the ambiguity of life and sustained by inattention to historical details. The impartial supernaturalism point of view insists that only an immature spirituality can tolerate the gross hermeneutical excess of the absolutist principle, which for that reason has a limited, transitory place on the path toward spiritual wisdom that eventually leads to the relinquishment of such vain attempts to control Absolute Mystery. Abandonment of the grasping after absolutes is being forced steadily upon Christianity by an intransigent world that continues doggedly to refuse characterization in absolutist terms. Modest Christologies offer a way forward in this situation; indeed, the classical way.

Notes

Introduction

1. Sociological research both into congregational life and into the structure and transformation of beliefs of individual Christians, though not the kind of systematic work needed, has been venturing in these directions in the last two decades. Examples covering a variety of religious groups are Hammond and Johnson, eds., *American Mosaic*; Bromley and Hammond, *The Future of New Religious Movements*; and Hoge, *Converts, Dropouts, Returnees*. Of special relevance for understanding the spiritual efficacy and ecclesial viability of Christology in the United States at the present time is Hoge, Johnson, and Luidens, *Vanishing Boundaries*.

Introduction to Part I

1. Coakley, *Christ Without Absolutes*.
2. Troeltsch, "The Significance of the Historical Existence of Jesus for Faith," pp. 205–7 (italics added).

Chapter 1

1. Troeltsch, "The Significance of the Historical Existence of Jesus for Faith," pp. 182–207. In view of the context, "Geschichtlichkeit" in the title of this essay is rightly translated "historical existence," but its more general meaning of "historicality" expresses the content of the address rather well. Troeltsch's description of the problem posed by historical criticism for Christology indirectly indicates this context: "The crisis began when criticism and historical and psychological methods were introduced into research on the gospels. It has today found its sharpest expression in the silly question that is just now occupying many people, whether Jesus ever existed, and in the more justifiable concern whether we possess enough certain knowledge about him to understand historically the emergence of Christianity, let alone justify attaching religious faith and conviction to the historical fact" (p. 182). Troeltsch is referring to Drews, *Die Christusmythe*, which had stirred up controversy by trying to prove that Jesus never existed. Troeltsch had already responded to Drews' thesis in "Aus der religiösen Bewegung der Gegenwart," especially pp. 1179ff, reprinted in Troeltsch, *Gesammelte Schriften* 2, pp. 22–44, especially pp. 36ff. When it came to his Aarau address, therefore, though he thought the Drews controversy itself "silly," Troeltsch took the opportunity it presented to deal with the more profound issues at stake in the relationship between historical criticism and faith in Jesus Christ.

2. "The Significance of the Historical Existence of Jesus for Faith," p. 182. The translation's varied capitalization of "Christian" has not been preserved.

3. Apprehension was fueled early on in the process by skeptical or radical interpreters of the Gospels such as Baruch Spinoza (1634–1677), *Tractatus theologico-politicus* (1670); David Hume's (1711–1776) famous attack on miracles in *Philosophical Essays concerning Human Understanding* (1748); the early works in defense of deism by Voltaire (1694–1778); Anthony Collins (1676–1729), *A Discourse of Freethinking* (1713) and—an example of his Deistic attack on Christianity—*Discourse of the Grounds and Reasons of the Christian Religion* (1724). The philosophical outlooks of many of the rationalists and deists found a ready resonance with the possibility raised by the just–budding historical critical way of thinking that the New Testament did not *necessarily* provide an accurate report of the "things concerning Jesus." Understandably, conservative religious responses were at pains both to rebut the arguments of these interpreters and to criticize the methodological assumptions that allowed them to imagine that the New Testament could possibly be misleading or unreliable in the first place, or that it could even adequately be approached without prior faithfulness to the traditional assertions of the Christian faith. The conservative respondents included especially Joseph Butler (1692–1752) and William Whiston (1667–1752) in England, and Matthäus Pfaff (1686–1760), Lorenz von Mosheim (1694–1755), and Sig-

mund Jakob Baumgarten (1700–1757) in Germany. On this whole period, see especially Frei, *The Eclipse of Biblical Narrative*.

4. See Harnack, *What Is Christianity?* Lecture 3, especially pp. 51–52.

5. Harnack, *What Is Christianity?*, p. vi.

6. See pp. 79–101 on the question of asceticism and the social question.

7. Troeltsch makes this point: "Harnack correctly characterizes his book as a work of peace and unification. Even if it had no influence on the official church in this sense, nevertheless it has united thousands of Christians who were confused and distrustful of official theology and brought them closer again to the Christian community." See "What Does 'Essence of Christianity' Mean?" pp. 168–69.

8. See, for example, Bultmann's introduction to Harnack, *What Is Christianity?* pp. x–xi.

9. On the other hand, Claude Welch, in his survey of the problem in *Protestant Thought in the Nineteenth Century*, vol. 2, pp. 147–65, especially pp. 150–52, notes that others were even more optimistic about managing the problem, at times even to the point of suggesting that the problem itself was not especially serious. For instance, the Ritschlian theologian Theodore Haering, and English speaking theologians such as H. R. Mackintosh, P. T. Forsyth, James Martineau, G. B. Foster, W. N. Clarke, and William Adams Brown each thought that there was substantial consonance between the knowledge deriving from faith and the results of historical criticism, even though they differed on exactly how much of the traditional assumptions about Jesus were confirmed by historical research.

10. One of the most famous remarks on this subject was made by George Tyrrell about Adolf Harnack: "The Christ that Harnack sees, looking back through nineteen centuries of Catholic darkness, is only the reflection of a Liberal Protestant face, seen at the bottom of a deep well"; see Tyrrell, *Christianity at the Cross-Roads*, p. 49. The same point is made powerfully by Schweitzer: "Thus each successive epoch found its own thoughts in Jesus; that was, indeed, the only way it could make him live. But it was not only each epoch that found its reflection in Jesus; each individual created him in accordance with his own character. There is no historical task which so reveals a man's true self as the writing of a Life of Jesus" (*The Quest of the Historical Jesus*, p. 4). The same point is made in the conclusion of Schweitzer's study, ch. 20, pp. 398–403, and in Cadbury, *The Peril of Modernizing Jesus*.

11. This tendency appears in Christian mystical writings about Jesus Christ of all eras and is espoused by Schweitzer himself, whose so-called Christ-mysticism, together with his famous mystical-ethical stance of "reverence for life," places priority on the contemporary experience of Christ. This in turn deals with the problem of paucity of sources and adverse historical findings, both of which he thought applied in regard to the historical Jesus.

12. See, as one of many examples, the cook's tour of the place of images of Jesus in the history of culture provided by Jaroslav Pelikan in *Jesus Through the Centuries*. See also Harnack, *History of Dogma*, and the fiercer but more limited survey in Schweitzer, *The Quest of the Historical Jesus*.

13. Schweitzer, *The Quest of the Historical Jesus*, p. 401; the varied capitalization of spirit, obviously not present in the German, is unexplained in the translation. This kind of language appears throughout the conclusion of *The Quest of the Historical Jesus*, pp. 398–403. On this matter generally, see Fritz Buri's article on Schweitzer in Marty and Peerman, eds., *A Handbook of Christian Theologians*, pp. 112–124, especially p. 118.

14. There are only hints of Schweitzer's view in *The Quest of the Historical Jesus*, but it appears more clearly, though still not systematically, in his subsequent work, *The Mysticism of Paul the Apostle*.

15. Dahl, "The Problem of the Historical Jesus," p. 146.

16. Kähler, *The So-Called Historical Jesus and the Historic Biblical Christ*, was in the first instance an attack on the life-of-Jesus movement, from a different perspective than that of Schweitzer's attack fourteen years later. The second, enlarged edition includes an essay in reply to Herrmann. The ET by Carl Braaten includes parts of the 2nd edition, but not Kähler's reply to Herrmann. Herrmann's response to Kähler's book was published as "Der geschichtliche Christus der Grund unseres Glaubens" and reprinted in *Schriften zur Grundlegung der Theologie*, pp. 149–85.

17. It is Claude Welch's judgment that *Historie* and *Geschichte* were, prior to Kähler's distinction, "usually interchangeable." See *Protestant Thought in the Nineteenth Century*, vol. 2, p. 153. In practice even now they are sometimes used interchangeably, but Kähler's distinction made a permanent contribution to the understanding of the relevant issues.

18. Kähler, *The So-Called Historical Jesus*, pp. 56–57.

19. Herrmann, *The Communion of the Christian with God*.

20. Ibid., ch. 2, especially §§ 1–16.

21. Troeltsch, "Half a Century of Theology: A Review," p. 75.

22. Ibid.

23. See Blondel, *The Letter on Apologetics and History and Dogma*, pp. 145–67, 349–73, 433–58.

24. See Loisy, *The Gospel and the Church*.

25. Troeltsch, "The Significance of the Historical Existence of Jesus for Faith," p. 192.

26. Troeltsch, "Half a Century of Theology: A Review," p. 74.

27. Troeltsch, "The Significance of the Historical Existence of Jesus for Faith," p. 192.

28. Troeltsch, "Half a Century of Theology: A Review," p. 63 n. 4.

29. See Loisy, *The Gospel and the Church*, where, for example, he notes with disapproval that Harnack's "tendency is evident, to concentrate religion into a single point where the realization of the perfect is to be seen," (p. 124) and that this tendency appears in many different ways in *What Is Christianity?* with the effect that the history of Christianity is seriously distorted.

30. The establishment of this consensus centers especially around the work of Rudolf Bultmann (1884–1976), and was firmly in place by mid-century. See Bultmann, *Theology of the New Testament*, §§ 1–4, especially pp. 4–6. After mid-century, it is found in standard works ranging from biblical critic Günther Bornkamm's *Jesus of Nazareth* to theologian Hans Küng's *On Being a Christian*, which was based on his estimate of the consensus of German biblical scholarship at the time (see especially pp. 214–26). Other authors holding this view include Hans Conzelmann, R. H. Fuller, Joachim Jeremias, Werner Kümmel, and Norman Perrin, though they take various opinions on the issue of the apparent contradiction between Jesus' assertions that the kingdom of God was *immanent* and his other assertions that it was *imminent*. C. H. Dodd is an example of a British scholar who resisted the consensus, insisting that Jesus thought of the kingdom of God as already present, and in no way anticipated the end of the world in the way that the apocalypticists did. For estimations of this consensus, see Chilton, *The Kingdom of God in the Teaching of Jesus* and, more briefly, Marcus Borg, *Jesus, A New Vision*, especially pp. 10–14.

31. Marcus Borg describes this shifting consensus in "A Temperate Case for a Non-Eschatological Jesus," especially pp. 98–100, and in "An Orthodoxy Reconsidered: The 'End of the World Jesus',", pp. 207–17. His conclusion is based on a 1986 "mail poll of seventy-two active Jesus scholars, members of the Jesus Seminar inaugurated by Robert Funk and members of the Historical Jesus Section of the Society of Biblical Literature," all North American scholars, in which "59 percent of those responding think that Jesus did *not* expect the end of the world in his generation." Borg repeated the poll at the October 1986 national meeting of the Jesus Seminar "with even more decisive results. Of the thirty-nine scholars voting, nine said they thought Jesus did expect the end of the world in his own time, thirty said they did not." See Borg, *Jesus, A New Vision*, pp. 14–17, and p. 20 nn. 25–26.

32. An accessible and amusing presentation of examples in regard to everyday experience is Gilovich, *How We Know What Isn't So*.

33. See especially Troeltsch, "The Significance of the Historical Existence of Jesus for Faith," pp. 186–89, 191–93, 201–5; "Half a Century of Theology: A Review," pp. 58–70, 73–75; and *The Christian Faith*, pp. 16–17, 91–93.

34. Troeltsch, "The Significance of the Historical Existence of Jesus for Faith," p. 192.

35. See especially Troeltsch, "The Significance of the Historical Existence of Jesus for Faith," p. 198, quoted below.

36. Troeltsch, "Faith and History," pp. 134–35.

37. Troeltsch, "The Significance of the Historical Existence of Jesus for Faith," pp. 197–98.

38. Troeltsch, *The Christian Faith*, pp. 92–93.

39. Troeltsch, "The Significance of the Historical Existence of Jesus for Faith," p. 198.

40. Ibid.

41. Troeltsch, *The Christian Faith*, p. 92.

42. Troeltsch, "The Significance of the Historical Existence of Jesus for Faith," p. 198.

43. Troeltsch, *The Christian Faith*, § 8, p. 87.

44. Troeltsch, "The Significance of the Historical Existence of Jesus for Faith," p. 200.

45. Troeltsch, *The Christian Faith*, § 8, p. 88.

46. Ibid., p. 89.

47. Troeltsch, "The Significance of the Historical Existence of Jesus for Faith," pp. 198–99.

48. See especially Troeltsch, "The Significance of the Historical Existence of Jesus for Faith," pp. 201–4, in which Troeltsch contrasts his social psychological argument about the centrality of Jesus for the Christian community with the position—similar in final outcome, though very different in positive content, method, and "total religious attitude"—of what he calls "the Schleiermacher-Ritschl-Herrmann school type of mediation."

49. Troeltsch, *The Christian Faith*, § 6, p. 75.

50. Troeltsch, "The Significance of the Historical Existence of Jesus for Faith," p. 202.

51. For Troeltsch's presentation of these sociological types, see *The Social Teaching of the Christian Churches*, and "The Social Philosophy of Christianity," pp. 210–34. Here it is enough to note that a church defines itself by membership in the cult, whereas a sect defines itself by its adherents' personal confessions of faith.

52. This theme frequently appears in characterizations offered by Troeltsch of his contemporary German context, and corresponds to the somewhat despondent tone of his writing in those places, even before World War I. See, for instance, the final section of "On the Possibility of a Liberal Christianity," pp. 343–59; *The Christian Faith*, p. 294; and the conclusion of vol. 2 of *The Social Teaching of the Christian Churches*. For a more general discussion of individualism in the context of modernity as a whole, see "The Essence of the Modern Spirit," pp. 237–72, especially pp. 244–49.

53. Troeltsch, *The Christian Faith*, § 8, p. 89.

54. Ibid., p. 90.

55. Sarah Coakley's review of these attempts demonstrates that none of them worked to Troeltsch's satisfaction. See *Absolutes*, ch. 6. A brief discussion of some options appears in ch. 2, below.

Chapter 2

1. The article first appeared almost immediately after Troeltsch's lecture as "The Dogmatics of the Religionsgeschichtliche Schule." It appears in revised form as "The Dogmatics of the History-of-Religions School." The quote is from "The Dogmatics of the History-of-Religions School," p. 87.

2. Troeltsch, "The Dogmatics of the History-of-Religions School," p. 87.

3. Ibid., p. 88.

4. Ibid., p. 89.

5. Ibid., p. 90.

6. See especially Troeltsch, "Religion and the Science of Religion," pp. 82–123, and *The Absoluteness of Christianity and the History of Religions*, ch. 4, "Christianity: Focal Point and Culmination of All Religious Development."

7. See Troeltsch, "The Dogmatics of the History-of-Religions School," pp. 88–89.

8. See Troeltsch, *The Absoluteness of Christianity and the History of Religions*, ch. 2, "Reexamination of the Evolutionary Apologetic."

9. See Troeltsch, *The Absoluteness of Christianity and the History of Religions*, pp. 45–46.

10. Ibid., 158.

11. See Troeltsch, *The Absoluteness of Christianity and the History of Religions*, pp. 105–6.

12. Troeltsch, *The Absoluteness of Christianity and the History of Religions*, p. 158.

13. Ibid.

14. This ambiguity persists in the philosophy of religion today. Troeltsch rejects an essence of religion *within* history, but allows that every religion conditionally testifies in a historically fluid way to a revelation of an absolute reality beyond history. John Hick, as we shall see in a later chapter, while not espousing essentialism in his formal approach to religion as a family resemblance phenomenon, does seem to suggest it in a different sense by speaking of all religions as affording access to the ultimately Real. Hick's and Troeltsch's philosophies of religion are remarkably similar at this point.

15. Troeltsch, *The Absoluteness of Christianity and the History of Religions*, p. 107.

16. Ibid., pp. 42–44.

17. Ibid., p. 107.

18. Ibid., pp. 111–112.

19. Ibid., p. 112.

20. Ibid.

21. Ibid., p. 114.

22. Ibid., pp. 114–115.

23. Ibid., p. 115.

24. Ibid.

25. See, for example, Maurice Mandelbaum, "Subjective, Objective, and Conceptual Relativisms," and Chris Swoyer, "True For."

26. Troeltsch, *Der Historismus und seine Probleme*, vol. 1: *Das logische Problem der Geschichtsphilosophie*. The second volume was never written, though some of its envisaged content may be deduced from examining late lectures such as "The Place of Christianity Among the World Religions."

27. See Yasukata, *Ernst Troeltsch*, especially pp. 146–48. For a discussion of the origin of this term, which Yasukata thinks lies with F. von Hügel, see pp. 160–61 n. 139.

28. Troeltsch, "The Place of Christianity Among the World Religions," pp. 60–63.

29. See Troeltsch, "The Dogmatics of the History-of-Religions School," pp. 94–95.

30. Ibid., p. 91; Troeltsch's emphasis.

31. Ibid., p. 95.

32. Ibid., p. 97.

33. Ibid., pp. 97, 99.

34. Ibid., pp. 99–100.

35. Ibid., p. 100.

36. For a fuller assessment of Troeltsch's *The Christian Faith*, see Garrett E. Paul's introduction in Wyman, *The Concept of Glaubenslehre*, and Yasukata, *Ernst Troeltsch*.

37. This is one aspect of Troeltsch's "cumulative case against incarnational Christology"; other aspects of this case appear elsewhere in this chapter and in the last. For what has probably become the standard review of the case in detail, see Coakley, *Christ Without Absolutes*, ch. 4.

38. Troeltsch, *The Absoluteness of Christianity and the History of Religions*, pp. 157–58.

39. See Troeltsch, "The Dogmatics of the History-of-Religions School," p. 98.

40. This theme is developed at length in the argument about naïve ab-

soluteness in the final chapter of Troeltsch, *The Absoluteness of Christianity and the History of Religions*.

41. Troeltsch, *The Absoluteness of Christianity and the History of Religions*, p. 161.

42. Troeltsch, *The Christian Faith*, p. 91.

43. Ibid., p. 98.

44. Ibid., p. 276.

45. See, for example, Troeltsch, "On the Question of the Religious A Priori" in *Religion in History*, pp. 37, 43.

46. See, for example, Troeltsch, *The Christian Faith*, pp. 119–23.

47. Troeltsch, *The Absoluteness of Christianity and the History of Religions*, p. 161 (italics added).

48. Troeltsch, *The Christian Faith*, p. 100.

49. Ibid.

50. Ibid., p. 98.

51. Ibid., p. 100.

52. Ibid., p. 274.

53. See Barth, *Church Dogmatics* 3.3, p. 409, and see the discussion of Barth's assessment of Troeltsch in the conclusion of Part I, below.

54. It is clear from "The Place of Christianity Among the World Religions," written just before he died, that Troeltsch remained a religious thinker all his life, and enthusiastically so. But the absence of references to Jesus Christ in his spelling out there of his latest conception of Christianity's significance, even in contexts where formerly such references would have been central, is an indication that he was at least diffident about the possibility of Christology. On the assessment of Troeltsch's move to a philosophy chair in Berlin in 1915, see Yasukata, *Ernst Troeltsch*, especially pp. 171–73.

55. Wyman, "Theology After Ritschl: The Case of Troeltsch," p. 61.

56. Kattenbusch, "In Sachen der Ritschlschen Theologie," p. 77. Cited in Wyman, "Theology After Ritschl," p. 61; Wyman's translation.

57. Wyman, "Theology After Ritschl," p. 62.

58. Ibid.

59. Chapter 17, below, takes up the discussion of this work.

60. These works are roughly of two kinds. On the one hand, there is the very large number of theological forays, limited in scope, occasional in nature, or part of a larger project that is not itself a systematic theology. Such works are very often comparative in orientation and many can be categorized under the heading of comparative theology. The books and articles in the Orbis series *Faith Meets Faith*, Knitter, gen. ed., frequently are of this kind, but there are many others. Thought of as instances of systematic Christian theology, these offerings are un-

derstandably either partial or generalized, and lack continuity with the large-scale questions and arguments of the discipline. But they are frequently illuminating and suggestive of how the larger task of systematic theology in Troeltsch's sense might be carried out in detail. A mere sampling of such theological contributions is as follows: Clooney, *Theology After Vedanta*; Cobb, *Beyond Dialogue* and "Beyond Pluralism"; Dupuis, *Jesus Christ at the Encounter of World Religions*; Heim, *Salvations*; Kaufman, *God, Mystery, Diversity*; Knitter, *No Other Name?*, *One Earth, Many Religions*, and "Theocentric Christology"; Küng, *Christianity and the World Religions* and "Towards an Ecumenical Theology of Religions"; Neville, *Behind the Masks of God* and *The Truth of Broken Symbols*; Panikkar, *The Cosmotheandric Experience*; Swidler, *After the Absolute*. Also see the more theological essays in collections such as Cobb and Ives, eds., *The Emptying God*; D'Costa, ed., *Christian Uniqueness Reconsidered*; Hick and Knitter, eds., *The Myth of Christian Uniqueness*; and Thangaraj, ed., *The Crucified Guru*. On the other hand, there is the *very* small number of more comprehensive works in which the pattern of development is closer to Troeltsch's prescription. Following it most closely is Smart and Konstantine, *Christian Systematic Theology in a World Context*; more in the vein of comparative theology are Ward, *Religion and Creation* and *Religion and Revelation*. Works of this kind that are less thoroughly implanted in the world religions are more numerous, and include Kaufman, *In Face of Mystery*; and Neville, *A Theology Primer*.

61. Troeltsch, *The Christian Faith*, p. 89.

62. See Newman, *An Essay on the Development of Christian Doctrine*.

63. So Ian Ker in his foreword to the Notre Dame edition of *An Essay on the Development of Christian Doctrine*, pp. xx–xxii. There Ker notes Jaroslav Pelikan's general agreement with this judgment by quoting the following passage from Pelikan, *Development of Christian Doctrine: Some Historical Prolegomena*, p. 3: "[Newman's *An Essay on the Development of Christian Doctrine* is] the almost inevitable starting point for an investigation of development of doctrine."

64. For a review of thought about doctrinal development up to Newman's *An Essay on the Development of Christian Doctrine*, see Owen Chadwick, *From Bossuet to Newman*.

65. This is the rule for ascertaining the primitive tradition advanced by Keble in his sermon entitled "Primitive Tradition," quoted in James C. Livingston, *Modern Christian Thought from the Enlightenment to Vatican II*, p. 141 n. 23. The rule itself, the so-called Vincentian Canon, is from Vincent of Lerins (d. before 450).

66. Newman, *An Essay on the Development of Christian Doctrine*, p. 29.

67. The first, incomplete edition of Newman, *An Essay on the Development of Christian Doctrine* appeared in 1845. It was extensively revised, expanded, and rearranged—though the argument was not substantially changed—and appeared

in a second edition in 1878. The Notre Dame edition reproduces that second edition.

68. Newman, *An Essay on the Development of Christian Doctrine*, p. 29.

69. Ibid., pp. 29–30.

70. Ibid., pp. 52–53, quoting from the third edition of his *University Sermons*, pp. 329–32.

71. Ibid., p. 33.

72. These criteria are Newman's famous "seven notes" of a genuine development of an Idea: preservation of its type, continuity of its principles, its power of assimilation, its logical sequence, anticipation of its future, conservative action upon its past, and its chronic vigor. See *An Essay on the Development of Christian Doctrine*, ch. 5, pp. 169–206.

73. This is traced out in detail in Harnack, *History of Dogma*, especially vol. 2, Part 2. It is also exhibited more briefly in Harnack, *What Is Christianity?*, especially pp. 190–217.

74. Newman, *An Essay on the Development of Christian Doctrine*, pp. 35–36.

75. Harnack, *What Is Christianity?*, p. 51 (Harnack's italics).

76. See Bultmann's introduction to Harnack, *What Is Christianity?*, pp. x–xi.

77. This point is compactly expressed by Loisy, with his typical sense for the dramatic, as follows: "Past centuries regarded dogma as the expression and the rampart of the faith. It was believed to be immutable, although men were never weary of perfecting its formulas. Herr Harnack also teaches the immutability of dogma, but he finds but one dogma in the gospel, and the work of Christian thought since St. Paul is thus condemned totally, since its object, in the main, is other than the paternal goodness of God. The time-honored effort to define the truth of the gospel is therefore held to be entirely in vain, foreign even to the gospel it wishes to interpret. It is a fact, that the development of dogma is not in the gospel, and could not be there. But it does not follow that the dogma does not proceed from the gospel, and that the gospel has not lived and lives still in the dogma as well as in the Church. Even the teaching and the appearance of Jesus have had perforce to be interpreted; the whole question is to know if the commentary is homogeneous with the text or heterogeneous." *Gospel and Church*, p. 155.

78. This school developed from the so-called "little Göttingen faculty," where early in his career Troeltsch worked with the historians and New Testament scholars Bousset and Weiss. Troeltsch notes that it came to include "such diverse figures as Robertson Smith, Wellhausen, Lagarde, Gunkel, Weizsäcker, Wrede, Usener, Harnack, Holzmann, and Bousset," in the process of denying the existence of anything more organized than a history-of-religions method. See Troeltsch, "The Dogmatics of the History-of-Religions School," p. 90.

79. On this point, see Troeltsch, "The Dogmatics of the History-of-Religions School," pp. 89–90.

80. See Weiss, *Jesus' Proclamation of the Kingdom of God*.

81. Troeltsch's shifting thought on the matter of the essence of Christianity is recounted in Steven W. Sykes, "Ernst Troeltsch and Christianity's Essence," in Clayton, ed., *Ernst Troeltsch and the Future of Theology*, pp. 139–71.

Chapter 3

1. Troeltsch discusses Comte's positivism as a theory of religion alternative to those of Kant's critical idealism and Hegel's absolute idealism in "Religion and the Science of Religion," pp. 106–8.

2. Revised for publication in *Gesammelte Schriften* 2; ET by James Luther Adams as "Modern Philosophy of History." This article is really an extended review of Heinrich Rickert, *Die Grenzen der naturwissenschaftlichen Begriffsbildung: Eine logische Einleitung in die historischen Wissenschaften* [The limits of the concept formation of the natural sciences: A logical introduction to the historical disciplines] (1903), which was itself a follow-up of a 1902 article with the same name.

3. Troeltsch, "Modern Philosophy of History," p. 273.

4. Ibid., p. 274.

5. Ibid., p. 276. In the same place, and with similar anxiety, it seems, Troeltsch says, "Unless religious positions can be regained and strengthened, it will be impossible to establish norms in [every other sphere of life]."

6. Hegel, *The Philosophy of World History*, quoted in Hodgson, *God in History*, p. 117.

7. Hegel, *The Phenomenology of Mind*, p. 795.

8. Hegel, *Lectures on the Philosophy of Religion*, Hodgson, ed., p. 406.

9. Ibid.

10. Ibid., p. 109.

11. Troeltsch summarizes Hegel at this point as follows: "The goal [of history] was seen as lying in the complete self-comprehension of reason, in a uniting of the divine and human reason which would emerge out of the developmentally engendered division between them. For this reason the goal of the development of religion and reason was seen in the Christian doctrine of the incarnation, this doctrine of course being conceived of as a mystico-religious unification brought about by the recognition of world reason, while the only connection with ecclesiastical Christology is that it is an idea contained in but separated out from the imaginative dogmas of the church." See "Religion and the Science of Religion," p. 106.

12. Troeltsch, "The Dogmatics of the History-of-Religions School," p. 92.

13. Troeltsch, "Religion and the Science of Religion," p. 106.

14. Troeltsch, "Modern Philosophy of History," p. 293.

15. Troeltsch, "The Dogmatics of the History-of-Religions School," p. 94.

16. Troeltsch, "Christianity and the History of Religion," p. 84.

17. Troeltsch not only easily dismissed tribal religions as unimportant, but also offered the kind of wooden characterizations of other world religions that do not survive a moment's scrutiny from the perspective of late-twentieth-century religious studies. However, he had for the most part moved beyond the desire to protect the universality of Christianity's absoluteness—the reason for the violations of his own principles—by the time the *Social Teaching* was completed in 1912. His "The Place of Christianity Among the World Religions" (1923), as noted in the last chapter, is free of the sort of failures of nerve that plague *The Absoluteness of Christianity and the History of Religions*.

18. For the argument in relation to the history of religions, see Troeltsch, *The Absoluteness of Christianity and the History of Religions* (1902, 1912) and "The Place of Christianity Among the World Religions" (1923); in relation to the history of Christianity, see "What Does 'Essence of Christianity' Mean?" (1903, 1913) and *The Social Teaching of the Christian Churches* (1912); and in relation to the history of Western culture ("Europeanism"), see "The Essence of the Modern Spirit" (1907).

19. Troeltsch, *The Absoluteness of Christianity and the History of Religions*, p. 89.

20. See, for example, Troeltsch, "Historical and Dogmatic Method in Theology" (1898) in *Religion in History*, pp. 11–32, in which the "relativism" that is attacked is *Relativismus*.

21. It is rejected, for example, in Troeltsch, "Historical and Dogmatic Method in Theology." It is conditionally affirmed in Troeltsch's treatment of parallel, competing religious truth claims in "The Place of Christianity Among the World Religions" and in *Der Historismus und seine Probleme*.

22. Hodgson, *God in History*, pp. 118–20.

23. Ibid., pp. 127.

24. Hodgson is careful to point out that "it would be misleading to suggest that Hegel regarded microhistory itself as 'simply tragic.'" Rather, his criticism turns on the fact that Hegel "believed it could be *emplotted* only in the tragic mode," thus failing to ground, if not effectively undermining, the hope for liberating praxis that realizes freedom in the present. *God in History*, p. 128.

25. Ibid., pp. 129.

26. Ibid., pp. 131–32.

27. Hegel is mentioned in loose connection to Christology twice in Troeltsch's *The Christian Faith*; see pp. 67–68, 282–83. On the first occasion,

Troeltsch is discovered perpetuating (by criticizing) the mistaken interpretation of Hegel as saying that "it is of no consequence whether the symbol of the God-man ever lived or not; it is simply enough that the human race could express its ideal in this way." This is Kant's position, and Strauss's—derived in the first instance from Schelling rather than Hegel. On the second occasion, Troeltsch merely states Hegel's position on redemption in connection with Christ without offering a specific evaluation of it.

28. See especially Pannenberg, *Systematic Theology*, vol. 1.

29. Garrett Paul, the translator, provides the translation "three million," noting that "the text reads 'three hundred thousand,' but that probably reflects an error in notetaking, since Troeltsch was relatively scientifically literate, and he does speak in terms of millions of years elsewhere." On many occasions Troeltsch speaks of hundreds of thousands of years as defining the age of the *human species* on earth thus far. See, for example, "On the Possibility of a Liberal Christianity," pp. 343–59, 347–48; and "The Significance of the Historical Existence of Jesus for Faith," p. 189. He must therefore have regarded the *earth itself* as considerably older than that. A factor of ten hardly makes a difference to Troeltsch's point, of course, but Paul's deviation from the notes at this point seems justified. I have retained the original, however, as three million is still too small by a factor of a thousand or so, according to current estimates.

30. Troeltsch, *The Christian Faith*, p. 79.

31. Troeltsch, "On the Possibility of a Liberal Christianity," p. 347.

32. Ibid., p. 348.

33. One of these appears in the previous quotation from Troeltsch, "On the Possibility of a Liberal Christianity."

34. Max Weber, quoted in Troeltsch, *The Social Teaching of the Christian Churches*, vol. 2, p. 915 n. 388. Troeltsch cites *Schlusswort*, 31, p. 580. On this topic generally, see Weber, *Protestant Ethic*.

35. Troeltsch, *The Social Teaching of the Christian Churches*, vol. 2, p. 647.

36. On this topic, see Troeltsch, *The Social Teaching of the Christian Churches*, "Economic Ethic of Calvinism" and "Calvinism and Capitalism" in vol. 2, pp. 641–50, and the associated notes in pp. 911–19, many of which demonstrate Weber's importance to Troeltsch on this topic. For other examples of this type of thought, see the sections on "Calvinism and International Policy" (pp. 650–52) and the important section on Calvinism and democracy (pp. 628–41).

37. Troeltsch, "Meine Bücher" in *Gesammelte Schriften* 4, p. 11.

38. Troeltsch, "Meine Bücher," p. 11. Also see "Introduction and Questions of Method" in *The Social Teaching of the Christian Churches*, vol. 1, in which Troeltsch confesses that, "Since no history of this kind is in existence, I am forced to open up the subject myself' (p. 25).

39. In relation to Troeltsch, "What Does 'Essence of Christianity' Mean?" see

the note by S. W. Sykes appended to the article in Troeltsch, *Writings on Theology and Religion*, pp. 180–81.

40. See, for example, the strident opening of chapter 1 (vol. 1, p. 39) in which Troeltsch declares that "the preaching of Jesus and the creation of the Christian Church were not due in any sense to the impulse of a social movement." The categorical tone of this remark appears repeatedly in the early part of the book, as Troeltsch appears to be somewhat anxious to establish the independence of the Christian idea at the point of its origin. It is this tone that gives way as the work unfolds to a degree of tentativity about Christian origins in which the assertion of the independence of the teaching of Jesus and the early churches very properly remains but is accompanied by the recognition that even they could have been conditioned by social context in interesting ways. Remarks in "The Significance of the Historical Existence of Jesus for Faith" (1911), written when *The Social Teaching of the Christian Churches* either was finished or was nearing completion, illustrate this shift. For instance, "With every advance in history of religions research into the origins of Christianity we see so many related yet originally independent religious and ethical forces flowing together, that it is quite impossible to treat Christian faith as something absolutely separate" (p. 189). Twentieth-century research on Christian origins has repeatedly confirmed the wisdom of Troeltsch's amelioration on this point.

41. Troeltsch, *The Social Teaching of the Christian Churches*, p. 1013.

42. Troeltsch, "The Significance of the Historical Existence of Jesus for Faith," p. 190.

43. Ibid., p. 191.

44. Ibid., pp. 196, 197.

45. This argument appears in the second edition of Troeltsch, *The Absoluteness of Christianity and the History of Religions*, p. 161, and at numerous points in *The Christian Faith*, especially pp. 93–98. The same sociological principle is also a hallmark of Schleiermacher's *Speeches on Religion* and his *Glaubenslehre*. In fact, Schleiermacher's arguments about the "clumping" tendency of religious believers are as impressive as Troeltsch's.

46. Troeltsch, "The Significance of the Historical Existence of Jesus for Faith," p. 195.

47. Ibid., pp. 194–96. Troeltsch mentions nature religions, Platonism, Stoicism and Christian monastic orders as examples.

48. Troeltsch, "The Significance of the Historical Existence of Jesus for Faith," p. 196. It is important to note here that Troeltsch had a changing opinion about the stability of social and psychological laws. In 1911 as he writes the essay under discussion, Troeltsch apparently still holds that there must be invariant, universal psychological and sociological laws because history would not be understandable otherwise. This was certainly his opinion earlier, as a remark in an 1898

essay, reprinted in *Gesammelte Schrifte* 2, pp. 729–53, shows. In speaking about his belief that consensus about "ethical and religious matters" can be obtained amongst serious representatives of the "great cultural types," he says, "This conviction is based on a belief that is both religious and ethical, namely, that ultimately the essential uniformity of human nature provides a foundation for consensus in recognizing supreme standards of value and that, because of this foundation, consensus will prevail." This uniformity corresponds to social and psychological laws that are consistent across time and place. See "Historical and Dogmatic Method in Theology" in *Religion in History*, p. 25. Later in his career, and certainly by 1923 in "The Place of Christianity Among the World Religions," Troeltsch clearly believes that such uniformities of human nature as (obviously) exist may not be relevant to gaining consensus on ethical and religious matters. Thus he envisages a world without consensus: "It would seem probable that the great revelations to the various civilizations will remain distinct, in spite of a little shifting of their several territories at the fringes, and that the question of their several relative values will never be capable of objective determination, since every proof thereof will presuppose the special characteristics of the civilization in which it arises" (p. 62).

49. Troeltsch, "The Significance of the Historical Existence of Jesus for Faith," p. 194. Troeltsch's use of the helpful phrase "rallying point" appears, among other places, on pp. 195, 201.

50. This constitutes a correction to the faintly trigger happy but otherwise helpful criticisms of this mistake by Troeltsch. See *Christ Without Absolutes*, pp. 150–52, in which Coakley criticizes Troeltsch for claiming that all great religions of the spirit "center on the adoration of their founder" (p. 151). But Coakley declines to treat the generalization she is criticizing as an *application* of the more plausible generalization that Troeltsch speaks about the most. In fact, she barely mentions the latter, giving the suggestion that Troeltsch's mistake was egregious, not withstanding the qualification in fn. 39, p. 151, to the effect that "Troeltsch would presumably have conceded this point" by the time he published *Gesammelte Schriften* 3 in 1922.

51. The richness of Troeltsch's thought is so pronounced—especially in "The Significance of the Historical Existence of Jesus for Faith"—that, at virtually every point, it badly needs unpacking with distinctions that Troeltsch himself never provided. Signs of the applicability of the distinction between psychological need for an archetype and social psychological need for cultic cohesion are omnipresent in "The Significance of the Historical Existence of Jesus for Faith," but Troeltsch only formalizes his thought in terms of generalizable laws on the social psychological front.

52. Coakley, *Christ Without Absolutes*, p. 144. These remarks are scattered

through Troeltsch, "The Significance of the Historical Existence of Jesus for Faith" and *The Christian Faith*.

53. Troeltsch, *The Christian Faith*, p. 96.

54. Ibid. (italics added); see Troeltsch's larger discussion of Jesus relationship to the emergence of the Christian cult in pp. 93–98. The claim that religiously potent social and psychological dynamics can account for the transformation of the earliest followers of Jesus that followed the so-called "resurrection appearances" has remained vague until recently. Noting that overcoming this vagueness is not the same as proving the case, the most exhaustive work on the topic is Starkey, *The Easter Experiences*.

55. See, for example, Troeltsch, "Faith and History" (1910) in *Religion in History*, pp. 135–45, especially pp. 134–35.

56. Troeltsch, "The Dogmatics of the History-of-Religions School," p. 98.

57. Troeltsch, "The Significance of the Historical Existence of Jesus for Faith," p. 202.

58. Ibid., p. 195.

59. Troeltsch, "The Dogmatics of the History-of-Religions School," p. 98 (italics added).

60. Troeltsch, *The Christian Faith*, p. 275.

61. See, for example, the end of the third section of Troeltsch, "The Significance of the Historical Existence of Jesus for Faith," p. 201, quoted below.

62. See Troeltsch, "The Significance of the Historical Existence of Jesus for Faith," p. 194, for one of many complaints against the deleterious effects of individualism: "This lack of community and cult is the real sickness of modern Christianity and contemporary religious practice generally. It is what makes it so impermanent and chaotic, so dependent on who happens to be there, so much an amateur thing for enthusiasts, so much a matter of world-view and the intellect. It has no dominant centre from which it can be nourished, but just as many centres as there are sensitive individual seekers. But it is not just that modern religion has become chaotic and indefinite. It is also feeble and insipid because it lacks the effect which a total spirit and fellowship has upon the individual, with its power to encourage and sustain, intensify and diversify, and above all to set practical goals for the like-minded group." Also see the introduction and conclusion to *The Social Teaching of the Christian Churches*, in which his frustration and concern about the condition of the churches are evident.

63. Sarah Coakley's consideration of these and related issues is helpful; see *Christ Without Absolutes*, ch. 6, "Troeltsch and the Many Christs," pp. 164–87.

64. Troeltsch, "The Significance of the Historical Existence of Jesus for Faith," pp. 200–1.

65. Ibid., p. 195.

66. Troeltsch had many objections to Herrmann. One of the clearest, though early, statements that has some relevance for the issue of his supernaturalism is "On the Question of the Religious A Priori," in *Religion in History*, pp. 42–43.

67. Coakley's judgment is germane here: "It could be argued, then, that our greatest modern Christological aporia is . . . a vast and unspoken unclarity about the reference of 'Christ' language *in toto*, a confusion greatly compounded by the divorce between technical theological discourse and ordinary people's cultic behaviour: how, in so many and various ways, they actually apply the language of 'Christ', and what it means to them experientially, morally, sacramentally. Yet surely neither clarity of reflection on this, nor a theological tapping of the imaginative and emotional power inherent in it, can be achieved without the application of the appropriate analytical resources from the newer social sciences. Such at any rate was Troeltsch's intuition." *Christ Without Absolutes*, p. 195.

68. Troeltsch's philosophical work on the issue of norms is *Der Historismus und seine Probleme*; the specifically theological material relevant to the current context has already been presented.

69. Troeltsch, *The Absoluteness of Christianity and the History of Religions*, p. 90.

70. See especially the section on rational absoluteness in Troeltsch, *The Absoluteness of Christianity and the History of Religions*, pp. 152–57; the quote is from p. 153.

71. See Garrett E. Paul's introduction to Troeltsch, *The Christian Faith*, p. xvi.

72. Barth, *Church Dogmatics* 3.3, p. 409.

73. Barth, *Church Dogmatics* 4.1, p. 387.

74. In some places Barth is more generous to Troeltsch, as when he includes him in a list of nineteenth century theologians in the work of whom "theology met the test as a science, and brilliantly so" ("Evangelical Theology in the Nineteenth Century" [a 1957 address] in Barth, *The Humanity of God*, p. 29), and again when he remarks that "Troeltsch was a gifted and, in his own way, a pious man" (*Church Dogmatics* 4.1, p. 386). But he regards Troeltsch's theology as demonstrating beyond doubt the failure of nineteenth-century mediating theology's assumptions that "relatedness to the world is its primary task and . . . there is a possibility for general acceptance of the Christian faith." Not that Barth had an objection in principle to the *attempt* to present the gospel beginning "from below" with the human situation in the world, struggling "its way upward to an authentic explication of the Christian faith." The problem was that this trajectory in nineteenth-century theology had made its method of thinking "exclusive and absolute" and so had failed "to validate the Christian message as God's act and word, the ground, object, and content of faith" (see "Evangelical Theology in the Nine-

teenth Century," pp. 23–25). At the beginning of that trajectory stood Schleierma-cher, in whose work Barth saw focused engagement with the proper task of theology, which Barth designated "a basic consideration on what the Church may, can and should teach in its prevailing present, in connexion with the biblical norm upon the one side and with the Church's past on the other." At the end of the same trajectory, Barth saw only a degeneration into the "thorough distraction" of Troeltsch's work (Barth, *Protestant Thought*, p. 312), whose life-work, according to Barth, in true Romantic fashion, "consisted chiefly in the proclamation and ever-renewed proclamation of programmes" (p. 231).

Chapter 4

1. The interpretation of Phil. 2:6–11 continues to be a matter of debate. Against the traditional view that the kenosis refers to the shedding of divine attributes in Christ's becoming human, J. D. G. Dunn, John Macquarrie, and others argue that understanding Paul as referring to Jesus' embracing of his servant role is more consistent with his "second Adam" Christology; whereas the first Adam strove to be like God, the second Adam forsook this misbegotten quest and so was authentically human.

2. Bultmann espouses this opinion in his *Theology of the New Testament*, vol. 2, p. 134, pointing out that it was first suggested by Ernst Käsemann.

3. Colossians 1:15–20, NIV, italics added. The striking reference in v. 19 reads: ὅτι ἐν αὐτῷ εὐδόκησεν πᾶν τὸ πλήρωμα κατοικῆσαι (Nestle-Aland, 26th ed., 1979).

4. In this case, the passage spells out the connotation of πλήρωμα, which appears in the previous passage from Colossians, with an explicit reference to deity: ὅτι ἐν αὐτῷ κατοικεῖ πᾶν τὸ πλήρωμα τῆς θεότητος σώματικος (Nestle-Aland, 26th ed., 1979).

5. Tertullian, "de carne Christi," 5, cited in Dorner, *Doctrine of the Person of Christ*, Division 1, vol. 2, p. 57. Dorner, anticipating a certain level of discomfort among his readers at such an affirmation of irrationalism, adds, "Those whose nerves are too weak to bear the utterances of such a πληροφία of faith, will find a tonic in the preceding chapter, where he speaks of the divine folly, which confounds and puts to shame the wisdom of the world, and where the ethical nature of God, love, is made the standard of the truly reasonable" (p. 57 n. 1).

6. Steven Weinberg suggests that it was Immanuel Kant in *Universal Natural History and Theory of the Heavens* (1775) who first suggested that some of the nebulae (at that time famously problematic) "are really circular disks about the same size and shape as our own galaxy. They appear elliptical because most of

them are viewed at a slant, and of course they are faint because they are so far away." See *The First Three Minutes*, p. 26.

7. Bettenson, ed., *Documents of the Christian Church*, pp. 51–52.

8. Ibid., pp. 48–49.

9. Ibid., p. 26.

10. See Harvey, *The Historian and the Believer*, ch. 8, especially pp. 257–58, in which the notion of paradigmatic events as the fusion of concreteness and wider meaning, or of particularity and universality, is helpfully developed.

11. See Macquarrie, *Jesus Christ in Modern Thought*, especially ch. 7, "The Rise of the Classical Christology," pp. 147–72.

12. Karl Barth's early Christology and those like it are the obvious exceptions; *The Epistle to the Romans* presents a view of Jesus Christ in which such matters as the moral perfection and self-understanding of the historical person Jesus are subordinated to his revelatory significance as the locus of the disclosure of the divine incognito.

13. A criticism of the absolutist principle need not be present in a modest Christology. However, since modest Christologies *usually* have the explicit aim of finding some way to ameliorate the absolutist principle, they *usually* engage absolutist Christologies, and the absolutist principle, directly. This aim may be present only implicitly when a modest Christology is constructive from the beginning, in the mode of traditional systematic theology. At one level, this is the difference between a positive, often biblically engaged, modest Christology that attempts to expound the religious significance of Jesus Christ directly (as Paul Van Buren's *A Theology of the Jewish Christian Reality* does in the main) and a modest Christological analysis that seeks to define itself *over against* the dominant tradition of absolutist Christologies (as, *par excellence*, in William Ellery Channing's and John Hick's writings). It is difficult at the present time to advance a systematic modest Christology without engaging the absolutist principle; systematic theology's respect for its own tradition requires it.

14. Hick's Christology is examined in the next chapter.

15. See *The Quest of the Historical Jesus*, p. 3, in which Schweitzer argues that the sublimation of the historical Jesus into the supramundane idea had been the habitual assumption of the tradition, exacerbated at Chalcedon with the two natures doctrine to the point that the historical Jesus could not be recovered without abandoning traditional Christology. By engaging in the quest of the historical Jesus, therefore, the questers fought against the two natures doctrine, because only under its rejection could the humanity of Jesus be retrieved. It is unclear to what extent Schweitzer's nineteenth-century forebears in the quest would have agreed with this characterization. The same argument appears in various ways at other places in Schweitzer's introduction, and throughout the book.

16. It is illuminating to pursue Schweitzer another step, for it is easy to get

the impression that he overreacted in this argument. After all, surely the idea of incarnation is not especially problematic in itself, if framed modestly enough for his tastes—perhaps defined as Schleiermacher's God-consciousness, for example, present to some degree in all human beings. Indeed, he seems to have held something very much like this point of view himself. The teeth of Schweitzer's argument are sharpest, it seems, when the idea of incarnation is interpreted in the light of the absolutist principle. Arguably, therefore, it is the absolutist principle's vision of incarnation he was railing against, rather than the "truly God, truly human" formula itself.

17. There are a number of significant twentieth-century attempts to treat Christology primarily in terms of the potential of authentic humanity. This is a slightly more general view than the one just described because it focuses less decisively on the human species in its historical actuality. Accordingly, Immanuel Kant rather than Schelling is the enlightenment forefather of such an archetypal reading of the significance of the symbol of Jesus Christ (see Kant, *Religion within the Limits of Reason Alone*). Karl Rahner's well-known (but not modest) Christology has elements of this view, for instance. However, owing more to Hegel than to Kant in this respect, Rahner always keeps Jesus Christ squarely and classically in view as the actual, historical exhibition of this archetypal human potential.

18. Strauss, *The Life of Jesus Critically Examined*, p. 780. The four editions of *Life of Jesus* show a considerable amount of revision in which Strauss's indecision about whether and how to make this point is evident. Whether the indecision at this level corresponds to indecision about the point itself is debatable.

19. Panikkar in *The Unknown Christ of Hinduism* (2nd ed.) is prone to overstating the conceptual continuities based on continuities of language in just this way, though there are certain rhetorical considerations about the book (mentioned in its preface) that make it unclear how precise Panikkar might be if he felt free to be more candid. John Macquarrie's reconstruction of the classical tradition in *Jesus Christ in Modern Thought*—by which he hopes to warrant his claim that his modest Christology is "classical"—tends to understate the vast differences between his Christology and traditional Christological reflection, in favor of drawing out the continuities. This, of course, is a problematic observation for modest Christologies since Macquarrie's is the finest attempt to date to claim classical status for a modest Christology.

20. This judgment about scope sometimes is accompanied by a shift from claiming the *qualitative* uniqueness of Jesus Christ to affirming his *quantitative* uniqueness instead, though this distinction occasionally has been argued to be unintelligible.

21. Ogden says, for example, that "My conviction, obviously, is that such alternative answers [as I will be investigating] are indeed possible and that, taken together, they provide a way of talking about the point of Christology that is fully

consistent with revisionary aims, even while being considerably more adequate in our situation today than the way in which most of the Christologies pursuing these aims have talked about it" (*The Point of Christology*), p. 18.

Chapter 5

1. See Hick, "An Inspiration Christology for a Religiously Plural World"; references to this essay are from Hick, *Disputed Questions*. See also "The Non-Absoluteness of Christianity," pp. 16–36, especially pp. 30–33.

2. See Hick, *The Metaphor of God Incarnate*.

3. Hick, "Jesus and the World Religions," p. 168.

4. Ibid., p. 176.

5. Ibid., p. 170.

6. Ibid., p. 171.

7. Ibid., p. 176.

8. See Goulder, "Jesus, the Man of Universal Destiny" and "The Two Roots of the Christian Myth," and Young, "A Cloud of Witnesses" and "Two Roots or a Tangled Mass."

9. Hick, "Jesus and the World Religions," p. 177.

10. Ibid., pp. 177–78.

11. Ibid., p. 178.

12. Ibid.

13. Ibid., pp. 178–79.

14. See Schleiermacher, *The Christian Faith*, §§96–99; the quote is the "theorem" at the head of §96.

15. See Harnack, *History of Dogma*, especially vol. 4, p. 106.

16. Pannenberg, *Jesus—God and Man*, Robinson, *The Human Face of God*, and Ottati, *Jesus Christ and Christian Vision*.

17. Ogden, *The Point of Christology*, especially pp. 8–9.

18. Hick, "Jesus and the World Religions," p. 179.

19. Ibid.

20. Emerson, "Self-Reliance," p. 44.

21. In chs. 3 and 4 of Hick, *The Metaphor of God Incarnate*, Hick traces in rough outline the development of ecclesial structure and belief from the original inspirational effect of encountering Jesus. Hick makes a great deal of the substantial consensus among New Testament scholars that Jesus did not think of himself as an object of worship. This is one of the strongest arguments that the emergence of belief in Jesus' deity depended not so much on the details of Jesus' inspirational character as on a generalized impression preserved in the churches' cultic

(and later scriptural) memories and enhanced by imaginative and powerful preachers and evangelists.

22. See Hick, *The Metaphor of God Incarnate*, pp. 17–18, for example.

23 Hick, "An Inspiration Christology for a Religiously Plural World," p. 36.

24. Hick, *The Metaphor of God Incarnate*, p. 26.

25. Hick, "Jesus and the World Religions," pp. 172.

26. Hick, "An Inspiration Christology for a Religiously Plural World," p. 37.

27. Ibid., p. 38.

28. Ibid., pp. 36–37.

29. Hick, "Jesus and the World Religions," p. 173.

30. Ibid., pp. 171–172.

31. See Küng, *On Being a Christian*, Moltmann, *The Way of Jesus Christ*, Pannenberg, *Jesus—God and Man*, and Schilebeeckx, *Jesus and Christ*.

32. Hick, "The Non-Absoluteness of Christianity," p. 32. See also *The Metaphor of God Incarnate*, pp. 105ff.

33. See Hick, *An Interpretation of Religion*, pp. 3–6, where Hick introduces religion as a family resemblance concept. He goes on to say: "Given this family-resemblance understanding of the concept [of religion], different scholars and communities of scholarship are free to focus their attention upon the features that specially interest them. Thus sociologists of religion legitimately focus upon one set of features, ethnologists upon another, psychologists upon another. The feature upon which I shall primarily focus in this book is belief in the transcendent. Although this is not of the essence of religion—for, as I have suggested, there is no such essence—nevertheless most forms of religion have affirmed a salvific reality that transcends (whilst also usually being thought of as immanent within) human beings and the world, this reality being variously conceived as a personal God or non-personal Absolute, or as the cosmic structure or process or ground of the universe" (pp. 5–6). Note that many of the central themes of *An Interpretation of Religion* are already explored in other of Hick's writings, especially *God Has Many Names*.

34. Hick, *An Interpretation of Religion*, p. 243.

35. Ibid., p. 244. The culture-relative and mutable nature of categorial schemes is developed with great precision in Körner, *Categorial Frameworks*, though Körner is not especially attentive to religious experience as such.

36. See Schleiermacher, *The Christian Faith*, especially pp. 371–524, Baillie, *God Was In Christ*, and Lampe, *God As Spirit*.

37. Hick, "The Non-Absoluteness of Christianity," p. 35 n. 21.

38. See Hick's discussions of Baillie and Lampe in *The Metaphor of God Incarnate*, pp. 109–10, and at greater length in "An Inspiration Christology for a Religiously Plural World," pp. 51–56.

39. Hick, "The Non-Absoluteness of Christianity," p. 32. Presumably such in-

formation would have to be possessed about those with whom Jesus was hypothetically being compared, as well! In any event, not having such information is
more than merely a matter of historiographical bad luck. It is clearly impossible
that much of the relevant information could be transferred historically. Moreover,
even were such information in our possession about Jesus and a figure comparable in stature to him within another tradition, it is unclear how such information
could be meaningfully compared, since intratraditional norms would be an in-
alienable part of any judgment of significance.

40. See Hick's reflections on this point in "Jesus and the World Religions,"
pp. 168–70.

41. See Panikkar, *The Unknown Christ of Hinduism* and Samartha, *One
Christ, Many Religions*. This need for, and intelligibility of, this kind of multiple-
incarnations Christology is disputed by Thomas V. Morris in *The Logic of God
Incarnate*. But this approach can be quite subtle, as it is in Raimon Panikkar's
Christology, which is discussed in more detail in a later chapter.

42. Cobb, *Christ in a Pluralistic Age*, p. 19.

43. Ibid.

44. Ibid., pp. 17–23.

45. Ibid., p. 45.

46. Ibid., p. 58.

47. Ibid., p. 62.

48. Ibid., p. 65.

49. Ibid.

50. Ibid., p. 71.

51. Ibid., p. 76.

52. Ibid., p. 77.

53. Ibid., p. 80.

54. Ibid., especially ch. 5, pp. 97–110. Cobb embraces without sufficient
steadiness of criticism the view point of Czech Marxist philosopher Milan Ma-
chovec, who argues for the strength of Jesus' authority and certainty of purpose.
The conclusion is not problematical as such; it is rather the oddly definite tone
with which it is drawn, and subsequently used, that discloses a failure of requisite
historical judiciousness. If there is one project that modern historical criticism has
almost entirely abandoned, it is the kind of speculation about Jesus's internal
states of mind and intentions that is required to determine his "certainty of purpose."

55. Ibid., p. 142. Cobb never allows the examples of Jesus' wavering of purpose in the temptation and the Garden of Gethsemane to influence his case. He
admits that these stories probably express a conviction that Jesus' disciples recall
their master as having been subject to some uncertainty of purpose at times, but

this admission does not appear to ameliorate the definiteness of his conclusion, which is already problematic for the reasons already stated.

56. Ibid., pp. 130–31.

57. Ibid., pp. 138–40.

58. See Suchocki, *God Christ, Church*, especially Part 3, "God as Presence: God in Christ: A Process Christology," pp. 87–125.

59. Cobb, *Christ in a Pluralistic Age*, p. 141.

60. Ibid., pp. 143–46.

61. Ibid., p. 142.

62. See, for example, Cobb, *Christ in a Pluralistic Age*, p. 132: "In the past, Christians could argue from the saving power of Jesus' field of force to his divinity. Today that is not possible." If the undeniable efficacy of this field of force does not warrant the inference of divine incarnation, then neither does the less reliable knowledge of Jesus' life and work.

63. See D'Costa, ed., *Christian Uniqueness Reconsidered*.

64. Cobb, "Beyond Pluralism," pp. 81–84.

65. Ibid., p. 81.

66. The irony is due to the fact that Cobb in *Christian Uniqueness Reconsidered* explicitly charges Hick and Knitter with holding this essentialist view (pp. 81–84). However, the view Cobb attacks is not Hick's—this is clear because of Hick's espousal of religion as a family resemblance concept in *An Interpretation of Religion* and his disavowal of there being an essence to religion—and it is certainly not Knitter's, neither in *No Other Name?* nor in his more recent work. In fact, both Knitter's *No Other Name?* and Hick's *An Interpretation of Religion* espouse much the same nonessentialist view of religion as Cobb does. Perhaps Cobb means that they do not take their nonessentialist understanding of religion as seriously as they ought to do. Though there may be some cause for this criticism in Hick's case, it does not apply in Knitter's case. But Cobb does not say this, and interpreting his remark is difficult as a result.

67. Cobb, "Beyond Pluralism," pp. 84, 83.

68. See Smith, *Forgotten Truth*. But even a casual glance through his *The World's Religions*—or its 1958 edition, *The Religions of Man*—shows that Smith is profoundly aware of, and faithful to, the distinctive character of each tradition.

69. Cobb, "Beyond Pluralism," pp. 85–88.

70. Ibid., pp. 86–88.

71. It is possible to pile on other distinctions, but this is not the place to do that. However, it should be noted that the objectivist/pragmatic distinction conveniently conflates two finer distinctions. The first is whether or not there is a place for questions about the superiority and unique value of religious traditions. The second is whether or not such questions can be answered by theoretical criteria.

Now it seems that confusing these two pairs of distinctions is helpfully economical. On the one hand, if questions of the intrinsic superiority and uniqueness of religious traditions can be entertained in a way that exceeds the partly extrinsic issue of their survival capability, then there must be theoretical criteria applicable to the decision that predominate over the pragmatic criteria of actual survival. On the other hand, if a tradition's aptitude for survival is the only kind of superiority that is admitted, then no other criteria except those bearing on the actual survival of religious traditions could be relevant to deciding superiority in this sense. If cross cases are possible between the two pairs of positions, then they do not seem to be important in the literature, so the assimilation of the two distinctions into the objectivist/pragmatic one seems justified.

72. The presentation of Knitter's ethic of dialogue and relational view of truth in a later chapter will show that Knitter thinks there can be no objective, theoretical criterion for assessing the superiority and uniqueness claims of religious traditions apart from their actual testing in history; that is, apart from the actual survival in and through assimilation and dialogue of the fittest, truest, most adaptable traditions. In fact, it appears that Cobb and Knitter are in substantial agreement on their views of religion, religious pluralism, and interreligious dialogue.

73. See Cobb, "Beyond Pluralism," pp. 92–93, where Cobb says this and then goes on to predict that Christianity will prove to be better equipped to handle the adaptation and change that survival in a religiously plural world requires.

74. Ibid., p. 92.

Chapter 6

1. Barth, *The Epistle to the Romans*, p. vii.

2. Ibid., pp. 10–11.

3. See Niebuhr, "Radical Faith" and "The Reconstruction of Faith."

4. See Braun, "The Meaning of New Testament Christology," pp. 89–127. More generally on the theme of Christology, see Braun, *Jesus of Nazareth*.

5. Ogden, *The Point of Christology* (San Francisco: Harper and Row, 1982), p. 82.

6. Ibid.

7. Ibid., pp. 83–84.

8. Ibid., p. 84.

9. Ibid.

10. Ibid., pp. 84–85.

11. Ibid., p. 88.

12. Ibid., p. 87.

13. Borg, *Jesus: A New Vision*, especially ch. 10, pp. 190–200; Crossan, *The Historical Jesus*, especially pp. 417–26; Horsley, *Jesus and the Spiral of Violence* and *Sociology and the Jesus Movement*; Mack, *A Myth of Innocence*; and Fiorenza, *In Memory of Her*. For a compact summary of developments in North American Jesus scholarship, along with some connections to parallel developments in other parts of the world, see Borg, *Jesus in Contemporary Scholarship*.

14. Schweitzer, *The Quest of the Historical Jesus*, pp. 2–3.

15. Mahayana Buddhism is intriguing in this connection. Buddhist piety in many Mahayanist groups is much more unfettered and unsupported by historical actuality than Christian piety toward Jesus. The question is how to interpret this fact sociologically. It may be that Western historical consciousness and Buddhist piety are significantly at odds with each other, in the sense that the institutional viability of Buddhism may be threatened in modern Western contexts. This would be so if (hypothetically) a sociologically significant number of Western Buddhists would have the same need for a feeling of tangible historical connection to Gautama in order to express their love and faithfulness to the Buddha that appears to be necessary in regard to Jesus for Western Christians to maintain their piety and cult. Alternatively, Mahayana Buddhism may potentially be an example of a way to create a stable institution and cult in the absence of critically reliable information—even much of a reliable outline—of the life and teaching of the central cultic figure. The stability of the Mahayanist cult appears to derive primarily from other factors. Whether these factors would be available to the Mahayanists in a modern Western society, or whether they are presently available to Christianity in the post-enlightenment West, or even what precisely they are, is difficult to determine. One thing is certain, however: this sociological experiment is in process as the number of Buddhists in the West increases.

16. Harvey, *The Historian and the Believer*, p. 103.

17. Harnack's view was that the Nicene and Chalcedonian conciliar decisions were taken in spite of the fact that they were narrow interpretations that failed to do justice either to the New Testament scriptures or to the faith of ordinary Christian believers. See *History of Dogma*, especially vol. 4, chs. 1–3.

18. Robinson, *Honest to God*.

19. See *Essays and Reviews*. Hick, ed., *The Myth of God Incarnate* did not stir as much controversy in North America and Germany, partly because British scholars were involved, and partly because scholarship in those places probably had exercised themselves over Bultmann's demythologization program more completely than had scholars in the UK. Pannenberg confirms this in relation to Germany, linking the debate on these matters with Harnack especially and with liberal Protestantism generally. See Pannenberg, "Religious Pluralism and Conflicting Truth Claims," p. 100.

20. An attempt to assess the impact of this disunity is found in John Charlot,

New Testament Disunity. An impression of the consensus on the degree of Christological diversity in the Gospels and Paul's writings can be obtained by consulting almost any group of two or three of the major comprehensive or survey oriented works on New Testament Christology in the twentieth century.

21. See Fredriksen, *From Jesus to Christ.*

22. Ottati, *Jesus Christ and Christian Vision*, p. 46.

23. See van Buren, *Christ in Context*, pp. 233–44.

24. Ibid., p. 234.

25. Ibid., p. 39.

26. Williams, *Arius*, Gregg and Groh, *Early Arianism*, and Gregg, ed., *Arianism*.

27. See, for instance, Hasel, *New Testament Theology*, especially parts II, III and V.

28. While there is a certain kind of tentativity in the theological conclusions of Dunn's works in biblical Christology, the theological conclusions that *are* advanced tend to be hermeneutically absolutist in regard to Christology. See J. D. G. Dunn, *Unity and Diversity in the New Testament* and *Christology in the Making.*

29. Ruether, *Faith and Fratricide*, p. 94.

30. Ibid., p. 248.

31. Ibid., pp. 111–16.

32. Ibid., p. 246.

33. Ibid., p. 111.

34. See especially Ruether, *Faith and Fratricide*, pp. 246–51.

35. Ibid., pp. 249–50.

36. Ibid., p. 250.

37. This viewpoint is expressed with characteristic precision in Rahner, "The Development of Dogma," especially pp. 43–47, and in "Considerations on the Development of Dogma."

38. The title of the pertinent section of Pannenberg, *Jesus—God and Man* is "Jesus' Resurrection as the Ground of His Unity with God." See pp. 53–114. Pannenberg equates unity with God in this special sense with the apprehension of divinity in connection with Jesus' resurrection. For example, "Jesus' resurrection is the basis for the perception of his divinity" (p. 108).

39. Acts 2:14–41.

40. See Pannenberg, *Jesus—God and Man*, pp. 108–14.

41. Ibid., p. 98.

42. Ibid.

43. Ibid.

44. Ibid., pp. 97–98.

45. The absolutist principle can be preserved without the hypothesis of Jesus' resurrection, though this would seem to be a half-hearted move toward

grappling with the challenges of modern historiography. Likewise, modest Christologies of the incarnational type (though not, in almost all cases, the inspirational type) can function *with* this hypothesis. However, just because the bodily resurrection hypothesis, if true, has some tendency to warrant hermeneutically extreme assertions like the absolutist principle, resurrection reports in other religions notwithstanding, modest Christologies even of the incarnational types can be strained by affirming the resurrection, unless a great deal of care is taken to present the systematic context of this affirmation so as to be consistent with rejection of the absolutist principle.

46. See, for example, Starkey, *The Easter Experiences*.

47. See TeSelle, *Christ in Context*, ch. 2, especially pp. 47–113.

48. Ibid., pp. 113–15.

49. Ibid., pp. 114–15.

50. See Pannenberg, *Systematic Theology*, Braaten, *The Future of God*, Braaten and Jenson, *Christian Dogmatics*, and Peters, *God—The World's Future* and *God as Trinity*.

51. TeSelle, *Christ in Context*, p. 115.

52. The debate within cultural anthropology over how culturally independent and culturally variable contributions combine to form human self-understandings is traced in Tambiah, *Magic, Science, and the Scope of Rationality*. See especially chs. 5 and 6.

53. A good example of a balanced critique of the significance of Jesus for the Christian construction of archetypal ideals appears in Kaufman, *In Face of Mystery*, especially ch. 7, pp. 83–93.

Chapter 7

1. See essays in Brown and Bohn, eds., *Christianity, Patriarchy and Abuse*, especially Brock, "And a Little Child Will Lead Us," pp. 42–61; and Brown and Parker, "For God So Loved the World?" pp. 1–30.

2. Van Buren, *A Theology for the Jewish-Christian Reality*. A brief discussion of one aspect of this work appears in the previous chapter.

3. See Gustafson, *Ethics from a Theocentric Perspective*, especially vol. 1, pp. 275–79, and vol. 2, pp. 26–42 on Christology. Gustafson's arguments against anthropocentric ethics, with their powerful Christological connections, are scattered throughout especially the first volume.

4. See Driver, *Christ in a Changing World*.

5. See, for example, Driver, *Christ in a Changing World*, p. 19.

6. Ibid., pp. 50–52.

7. Ibid., p. 39.

8. Ibid., pp. 54–55.

9. Ibid., pp. 55–56.

10. See Driver, *Christ in a Changing World*, chs. 6–8 for the development of this perspective.

11. Driver lists six methodological principles whose conceptual interrelatedness can probably be expressed by grouping them into the three guiding ideas listed here. Ibid., ch. 2.

12. Ibid., p. 5.

13. Ibid., p. 8.

14. See, for example, the case studies on "Information Theory and Revelation" by Puddefoot and Peacocke, and on "Quantum Complementarity and Christology" by MacKinnon, Loder, Neidhart, and Kaiser, in Richardson and Wildman, eds., *Religion and Science*.

15. TeSelle, *Christ in Context*, pp. 130–31.

16. Ibid., p. 131.

17. Ibid., p. 132.

18. Ibid., p. 142.

19. See Whitehead, *Process and Reality* and *Adventures of Ideas*, especially Parts II and III; and Teilhard, *The Phenomenon of Man*, especially Book 4. See TeSelle, *Christ in Context*, especially pp. 133–42, for a discussion of the relevance of Teilhard to this view.

20. TeSelle, *Christ in Context*, pp. 142–43.

21. Ibid., p. 143; the discussion of convergence is in pp. 138–39.

22. This is the perspective of Peacocke, *Theology for a Scientific Age*. His Christological reflections on the assumption that God works to realize the highest potentialities of the world and humanity are developed especially in Part 3.

23. TeSelle, *Christ in Context*, p. 143.

24. Ibid., p. 164: "In the language of traditional Christology, the priority must lie with the divine Word, for this is where the "ideal" for humanity—God's purpose, covenant, call—is conceptualized and developed."

25. Ibid., p. 164.

26. Ibid., p. 146.

27. There are many technical philosophical and scientific problems surrounding the issue of the probability of life elsewhere in the universe and many specific questions remain unanswered. Most important is the estimate of the improbability of development of life on our own planet. For a review of this and other issues, see Davies, *Are We Alone?*

28. See Tillich, *Systematic Theology*, vol. 2, p. 95.

29. See TeSelle, *Christ in Context*, p. 144.

30. This point of view is presented most conveniently in Rahner, *Foundations of Christian Faith*, especially ch. 6.

31. Brian Hebblethwaite is the most prominent current advocate of this point of view, as in the following passage: "If God himself, in one of the modes of his being, has come into our world in person, to make himself vulnerable to the world's evil, in order to win our love and bind us to himself, we cannot suppose that he might have done so more than once. For only one man can actually *be* God to us, if God is one." See "The Uniqueness of the Incarnation," p. 189. Also see similar arguments in Hebblethwaite, *The Incarnation*.

32. Rahner, *Foundations of Christian Faith*, p. 445.

33. Ibid., pp. 445–46.

34. Tillich, *Systematic Theology* 2, p. 95.

35. Ibid., pp. 95–96.

36. See Pauck and Pauck, *Paul Tillich*, pp. 243–45, and Gilkey, "Tillich: The Master of Mediation," pp. 52–53.

37. See Boff, *Jesus Christ Liberator*.

38. Ibid., p. 217.

39. Ibid., p. 216.

40. Rahner, *Foundations of Christian Faith*, p. 57.

41. Ibid., p. 54.

42. Ibid., p. 98.

43. Ibid., p. 94.

44. Ibid., pp. 104–5.

45. Ibid., p. 106.

46. Rahner, "Christology Within an Evolutionary View of the World," p. 173.

47. Ibid., pp. 176 ff.

48. See Rahner, *Foundations of Christian Faith*, ch. 6, especially pp. 188–202.

49. Rahner, "Christology Within an Evolutionary View of the World," p. 173.

50. "Christ" is etymologically rendered "the anointed one" or "messiah." However, in a natural extension of this lexical usage, "Christ" in isolation from the proper name "Jesus" is frequently used to designate either the principle of incarnation, as distinct from its actualization in Jesus, or the second person of the immanent Trinity, conceived of as in principle independent of divine self-revelation in creation and redemption.

51. Knitter, *No Other Name?*, p. 157.

52. See Panikkar, *The Unknown Christ of Hinduism*.

53. Knitter, *No Other Name?* p. 171.

54. Ibid., pp. 186–88, 190–92.

55. Ibid., pp. 189–92.

56. It may be that Knitter should have omitted Cobb from this list. As we saw in chapter 6, Cobb in *Christ in a Pluralistic Age* takes a complex stance on the uniqueness question, saying that there is no reason to think of Jesus as a unique instantiation of incarnation, while overconfidently claiming that there no other significant potential candidates for description under that category. The principal Christological works of the scholars Knitter mentions are Cobb, *Christ in a Pluralistic Age*, "A Whiteheadian Christology," and "The Finality of Christ"; Griffin, *A Process Christology*; Ford, "The Power of God and the Christ"; Mellert, *What Is Process Theology?*; Pittenger, *Christology Reconsidered*, *Christ and Christian Faith*, and *The Word Incarnate*.

57. This is the title of Knitter, *No Other Name?* ch. 10.

58. Ibid., p. 205.

59. Ibid., pp. 171–72.

60. Ibid., p. 219.

61. Ibid., pp. 219–20.

62. Panikkar remarks, "At present the writer would be much more radical in his approach, but to preserve intermediate steps in respect for the rhythm of the cosmos and of history is, as always, an indispensable condition for safeguarding the possibility of further progress" (*The Unknown Christ of Hinduism*, p. 30).

63. When he wishes to draw out the cosmic significance of this theandric principle, Panikkar will typically use the word "cosmotheandric." See, for example, *The Unknown Christ of Hinduism*, p. 29.

64. Panikkar, *The Unknown Christ of Hinduism*, p. 27.

65. Ibid., pp. 48–49.

66. Ibid., p. 28.

67. Ibid., p. 29.

68. Ibid., p. 23.

69. Ibid., p. 24–25.

70. Ibid., p. 23.

71. Ibid., p. 24.

72. Ibid., p. 25.

73. Ibid.

74. Ibid., p. 35.

75. Ibid., p. 51.

76. Ibid., p. 52.

77. Ibid., p. 29.

Conclusion

1. This essentially expresses H. Richard Niebuhr's view of the matter in *Faith on Earth*, especially the chapter on "Reconstruction," pp. 83–101. But it is important to note that there are also contemporary theologians who abandon this approach as seriously wrong-headed. Carter Heyward in *Speaking of Christ* offers a striking illustration—though by no means an isolated one—of the rejection of a range of traditional Christological loci and methods on the basis of a distinctive perspective. In the first essay, the only "explicitly Christological exploration" (p. 10) of the book, she states her thesis that "the historical doctrinal pull between Jesus of Nazareth and Jesus Christ, the human Jesus and his divine meaning, is no longer, if it ever was, a place of creative Christological inquiry. Worse, it is a distraction from the daily praxis of liberation, which is the root and purpose of Christian faith" (p. 13). Again, "classical Christology, as an arena of constructive work, is dead. Its symbolic universe belongs to the history of Christian thought which, when studied honestly, reveals the history of Christian power relations. By that, I mean the history of how the church, in its doctrine, discipline, and worship, has legitimated the use of ecclesial, civil, and social power either to exercise coercive control or to elicit voluntary cooperation" (p. 14). There is no shortage of other examples and other perspectives, though in many cases the rejection of the categories in which the Christological problem often has been posed is expressed in a more or less indifferent or restless acceptance of the classical Christological doctrines in order to pass onto more important matters. For more systematic examples of Heyward's thought, see *Redemption of God*, as well as *Touching Our Strength*.

2. See, for example, Murphy, *Theology in the Age of Scientific Reasoning* and Clayton, *Explanation from Physics to Theology*. The language derives from Imre Lakatos's philosophy of science, which elaborates the methodology of research programs. Insofar as there is relevance in these ideas for theology, however, they need to be traced further back, to the American pragmatist tradition, and especially to Charles Sanders Peirce and John Dewey. That is the birthplace of systematic antifoundationalism with regard to epistemology (before Quine), a social orientation to inquiry (before Kuhn), the importance of knowledge through traditions (before MacIntyre), and the principle of the hypothetico-corrective method which places such a premium on conversation in as broad an intersubjective field as possible (before Gadamer and Habermas). Still, the language of research programs offers some advantages.

3. The basic positions in this debate are laid out in Lakatos, *The Methodology of Scientific Research Programmes*, and Feyerabend, *Against Method*.

4. Works of Søren Kierkegaard referred to in this discussion are all trans-

lated in the Princeton University Press series of *Kierkegaard's Writings*: *Either/Or*, *Fear and Trembling*, and *Concluding Unscientific Postscript*.

5. See, for instance, Hick, "The Non-Absoluteness of Christianity," p. 30: "The conclusion to be drawn seems to be that each tradition has constituted its own unique mixture of good and evil. . . . It is of course possible that, to the eye of omniscience, one tradition is in fact, on balance, superior to the rest. But to our partial and fallible human view they constitute different ways of being human in relation to the Eternal, each with both its cultural glories and its episodes of violent destructiveness, each raising vast populations to a higher moral and spiritual level and yet each at times functioning as a vehicle of human chauvinism, cupidity, and sadism. We may well judge that in some respects, or in some periods or regions, the fruits of one tradition are better than, whereas in other respects or periods or regions inferior to, those of another. But as vast complex totalities, the world traditions seem to be more or less on a par with each other. None can be singled out as manifestly superior." Hick's whole argument in this essay can be understood as an attempt to establish this result, which is an important aspect of his view of religion.

6. The recognition of this situation is one of the strengths of Lindbeck's proposal in *The Nature of Doctrine*, which decisively opts for orienting Christian theology and practice within this plural, critical situation by means of reliance on the steadying effects of the Christian tradition thought of somehow by means of its classical texts and motifs as more or less univocal. Though by itself this seems to me impossible, its other main weakness is illuminating for my purposes: Lindbeck's proposal fails to register the importance of seeking correction of theological doctrines and proposals in as wide an intersubjective sphere of inquiry as possible. As such, it represents ultimately a betrayal of the ideal of fidelity by isolating it from its proper companion, the ideal of plausibility.

7.   See especially Nietzsche, *Thus Spoke Zarathustra*.

Bibliography of Works Cited

Baillie, D.M. *God was In Christ: An Essay on Incarnation and Atonement*. London: Faber, 1948. 2nd ed., 1956. 1st Faber paperback ed., 1961.

Barth, Karl. *Church Dogmatics*. Ed. by G. W. Bromily; T. F. Torrance. 14 vols. Edinburgh: T. & T. Clark, 1951–1963. Tr. of *Die Kirchliche Dogmatik* (Zürich: Evangelischer Verlag, 1932–1952).

———. *The Epistle to the Romans*. New York and London: Oxford University Press, 1933. 1st Oxford University Press paperback ed., 1968. Tr. of the 6th German ed.,1928, by Sir Edwyn C. Hoskyns.

———. "Evangelical Theology in the Nineteenth Century" (a 1957 address) in Barth, *The Humanity of God*.

———. *The Humanity of God*. Richmond, Virginia: John Knox Press, 1960. Tr. of a series of 3 separate monographs in *Theologische Studien* (Zollikon-Zurich: Evangelischer Verlag A.G., 1953–1956) by Thomas Wieser and John Newton Thomas.

———. *Protestant Thought: From Rousseau to Ritschl*. New York: Harper & Row, 1959. Tr. of eleven chapters of *Die Protestantische Theologie im 19. Jahrhundert* (Zürich: Evangelischer Verlag, 1952) by Brian Cozens.

Bettenson, Henry, ed. *Documents of the Christian Church*. London: Oxford University Press, 1943. 2nd ed., 1963. 1st Oxford paperback ed., 1967.

Blondel, Maurice. *The Letter on Apologetics and History and Dogma*. New York,

1964. Tr. of "Historie et dogma: Les Lacunes philosophiques de l'exégèse moderne," *La Quinzaine* (1904), pp. 145–67, 349–73, 433–58.

Boff, Leonardo. *Jesus Christ Liberator: A Critical Christology for Our Time*. Trans. Patrick Hughes. Maryknoll: Orbis, tr. 1978. Tr. of *Jesus Cristo Libertador* (1972).

Borg, Marcus J. *Jesus: A New Vision: Spirit, Culture and the Life of Discipleship*. San Francisco: Harper & Row, 1987.

———. *Jesus in Contemporary Scholarship*. Valley Forge: Trinity, 1994.

———. "An Orthodoxy Reconsidered: The 'End of the World Jesus'," in Hurst and Wright, eds., *The Glory of Christ in the New Testament*, pp. 207–17.

———. "A Temperate Case for a Non-Eschatological Jesus," in *Society of Biblical Literature: 1986 Seminar Papers*, pp. 521–35. Atlanta: Scholar's Press, 1986. Also in *Foundations and Facets Forum*, vol. 2, no. 3 (September, 1986), pp. 81–102.

Bornkamm, Günther. *Jesus of Nazareth*. New York: Harper & Row, 1960. Tr. of 1956 German original ed.

Braaten, Carl E. *The Future of God: The Revolutionary Dynamics of Hope*. New York: Harper & Row, 1969.

———; Roy A. Harrisville, trs. and eds. *Kerygma and History: A Symposium on the Theology of Rudolf Bultmann*. Nashville: Abingdon, 1962.

———; Robert W. Jenson. *Christian Dogmatics*. Philadelphia: Fortress Press, 1984.

Braun, Herbert, ed. *God and Christ: Existence and Province*. New York: Harper & Row, 1968. *Journal for Theology and the Church*, vol. 5.

———. *Jesus of Nazareth: The Man and His Time*. Philadelphia: Fortress, 1979. Tr. by Everett R. Kalin of *Jesus* (Kreuz Verlag, Stuttgart, 1969).

———. "The Meaning of New Testament Christology," in Braun, ed., *God and Christ*, pp. 89–127.

Briggs, Sheila; Richard P.Busse, eds. *Papers of the Nineteenth Century Working Group*, American Academy of Religion, 1989 Annual Meeting.

Brock, Rita Nakashima. "And a Little Child Will Lead Us: Christology and Child Abuse," in Brown and Bohn, eds., *Christianity, Patriarchy and Abuse*, pp. 42–61.

Bromley, David G.; Hammond, Phillip E., eds. *The Future of New Religious Movements*. Macon: Mercer University, 1987.

Brown, Delwin; Ralph E. James, Jr.; Gene Reeves, eds. *Process Philosophy and Christian Thought*. Indianapolis: Bobbs-Merrill, 1971.

Brown, Joanne Carlson; Carole R. Bohn, eds. *Christianity, Patriarchy and Abuse: A Feminist Critique*. Cleveland: Pilgrim, 1989.

———; Rebecca Parker. "For God So Loved the World?" in Brown and Bohn, eds. *Christianity, Patriarchy and Abuse*, pp. 1–30.

Bultmann, Rudolf. *Theology of the New Testament*, 2 vols. New York: Charles Scribner's Sons, 1951–1955. Tr. of *Theologie des Neuen Testaments*, 2 vols. (Tübingen: J.C.B. Mohr, 1948–1952).

Buri, Fritz. "Albert Schweitzer," in Martin E. Marty; Dean G. Peerman, eds., *A Handbook of Christian Theologians*. Nashville: Abingdon, 1984. Enlarged ed.

Cadbury, H.J. *The Peril of Modernizing Jesus.* New York: Macmillan, 1937.

Cargas, Harry James; Bernard Lee, eds., *Religious Experience and Process Theology*. New York: Paulist, 1976.

Chadwick, Owen. *From Bossuet to Newman: The Idea of Doctrinal Development*. 2nd ed. Cambridge: Cambridge University, 1957.

Channing, William Ellery. *The Works of William Ellery Channing*, 5 vols. Boston: American Unitarian Association, 1903.

Charlot, John. *New Testament Disunity: Its Significance for Christianity Today*. New York: E.P. Dutton, 1970.

Chilton, Bruce. *The Kingdom of God in the Teaching of Jesus*. Philadelphia: Fortress, 1984.

Clayton, John Powell, ed. *Ernst Troeltsch and the Future of Theology*. New York: Cambridge University, 1976.

Clayton, Philip. *Explanation from Physics to Theology: An Essay in Rationality and Religion*. New Haven: Yale, 1989.

Clooney, Francis X. *Theology After Vedanta: An Experiment in Comparative Theology*. Albany: State University of New York, 1993.

Coakley, Sarah. *Christ Without Absolutes: A Study in the Christology of Ernst Troeltsch*. Oxford: Oxford University, 1988.

Cobb, John B. *Beyond Dialogue: Toward a Mutual Transformation of Christianity and Buddhism*. Philadelphia: Fortress Press, 1982.

———. "Beyond Pluralism," in D'Costa, *Christian Uniqueness Reconsidered*, pp. 81–95.

———. *Christ in a Pluralistic Age*. Philadelphia: Westminster, 1975.

———. "The Finality of Christ in a Whiteheadian Perspective," in Kirkpatrick, ed., *The Finality of Christ*.

———. "A Whiteheadian Christology," in Brown, ed., *Process Philosophy*.

———; Christopher Ives, eds. *The Emptying God: A Buddhist-Jewish-Christian Conversation*. Faith Meets Faith series. Maryknoll, N.Y.: Orbis Books, 1990.

Collins, Anthony. *A Discourse of Freethinking*. 1713.

———. *Discourse of the Grounds and Reasons of the Christian Religion*. 1724.

Crossan, John Dominic. *The Historical Jesus: The Life of a Mediterranean Jewish Peasant*. San Francisco: Harper & Row, 1991.

Dahl, Nils Alstrup. "The Problem of the Historical Jesus," in Braaten and Harrisville, eds. *Kerygma and History*, pp. 138–71.

Davies, Paul. *Are We Alone? Philosophical Implications of the Discovery of Extraterrestrial Life*. New York: Basic Books, 1995.

Davis, Stephen, ed. *Encountering Jesus*. Philadelphia: Fortress, 1988.

D'Costa, Gavin, ed., *Christian Uniqueness Reconsidered: The Myth of a Pluralistic Theology of Religions*. Maryknoll: Orbis, 1990.

Dorner, J.A. *History of the Development of the Doctrine of The Person of Christ*. 5 vols. Clark's Foreign Theological Library, third series, vol. XVIII. Edinburgh: T. & T. Clark, 1863. Tr. by D.W. Simon.

Drews, A. *Die Christusmythe*. Jena, 1909.

Driver, Tom. *Christ in a Changing World: Toward an Ethical Christology*. New York: Crossroad, 1981.

Dunn, James D.G. *Unity and Diversity in the New Testament*. 2nd ed. London: SCM, 1990. 1st ed., 1977.

———. *Christology in the Making: A New Testament Inquiry into the Origins of the Doctrine of the Incarnation*. 2nd ed. Philadelphia: Westminster, 1989. 1st ed., 1980.

Dupuis, Jacques. *Jesus Christ at the Encounter of World Religions*. Maryknoll, N.Y.: Orbis, 1991.

Emerson, Ralph Waldo. "Self-Reliance," in *Emerson's Essays*, First and Second Series complete in one volume with an introd. by Irwin Edman. New York: Harper & Row, 1926. Reprint ed.

Essays and Reviews. London: John W. Parker, 1860. Essays by Frederick Temple, R. Williams, B. Powell, H. B. Wilson, C. W. Goodwin, M. Pattisohn, and B. Jowett.

Feyerabend, Paul K. *Against Method*. London: Verso, 1978.

Fiorenza, Elizabeth Schüssler. *In Memory of Her: A Feminist Theological Reconstruction of Christian Origins*. New York: Crossroad, 1985.

Ford, Lewis. "The Power of God and the Christ," in Cargas and Lee, eds., *Religious Experience and Process Theology*.

Fredriksen, Paula. *From Jesus to Christ: The Origins of the New Testament Images of Jesus*. New Haven, Yale University, 1988.

Frei, Hans. *The Eclipse of Biblical Narrative: A Study in Eighteenth and Nineteenth Century Hermeneutics*. New Haven: Yale University, 1974.

Gilkey, Langdon. "Tillich: The Master of Mediation," in Kegley, ed., *The Theology of Paul Tillich*.

Gilovich, Thomas. *How We Know What Isn't So: The Fallibility of Human Reason in Everyday Life*. New York: The Free Press, 1991.

Goulder, Michael, ed. *Incarnation and Myth: The Debate Continued*. Grand Rapids: Eerdmans, 1979.

———. "Jesus, the Man of Universal Destiny," in Hick, ed., *The Myth of God Incarnate*.

————. "The Two Roots of the Christian Myth," in Hick, ed., *The Myth of God Incarnate*.

Gregg, Robert C., ed. *Arianism: Historical and Theological Reassessments*. Philadelphia: Philadelphia Patristics Foundation, 1985.

————; Dennis E. Groh. *Early Arianism: A View of Salvation*. Philadelphia: Westminster, 1981.

Griffin, David Ray. *A Process Christology*. Philadelphia: Westminster, 1973.

Gustafson, James M. *Ethics from a Theocentric Perspective*. 2 vols. Chicago: University of Chicago, 1981, 1984.

Hammond, Phillip E.; Benton Johnson, eds. *American Mosaic: Social Patterns of Religion in the United States*. New York: Random House, 1970.

Harnack, Adolf von. *History of Dogma*, 7 vols. bound in 4. New York: Dover, 1971. Tr. of the 3rd German ed. of 1900 by Neil Buchanan.

————. *What is Christianity? Sixteen Lectures delivered in the University of Berlin during the Winter-term 1899–1900*. Introd. to the 50th anniversary German edition (Ehrenfried Klotz, 1950) by Rudolf Bultmann, tr. by Salvator Attanasio and Ephraim Fischoff. New York: Harper and Brothers, 1957. Fortress Texts in Modern Theology. 1st Fortress Press ed., 1986. 1st English ed. in 1901, tr. by Thomas Bailey Saunders from the original German ed., *Das Wesen des Christentums*, 1900.

Harvey, Van Austin. *The Historian and the Believer: The Morality of Historical Knowledge and Christian Belief*. New York: Macmillan, 1966.

Hasel, Gerhard. *New Testament Theology: Issues in the Current Debate*. Grand Rapids, Michigan: Eerdmans, 1978.

Hebblethwaite, Brian. *The Incarnation: Collected Essays in Christology*. Cambridge: Cambridge University, 1987.

————. "The Uniqueness of the Incarnation," in Goulder, ed. *Incarnation and Myth*.

Hegel, George W.F. *Lectures on the Philosophy of Religion*. Peter C. Hodgson, ed. Berkeley: University of California, 1988. 1 vol. abridged ed. of the 3 vols. published 1983, 1984, 1985. Tr. from Walter Jaeschke, ed., *Vorlesungen über die Philosophie der Religion* (the lectures of 1827) by R.F. Brown, Peter C. Hodgson, J.M. Stewart, and H.S. Harris.

————. *The Phenomenology of Mind*. Introd. to Torchbook ed. by George Lichtheim. London: Macmillan, 1910. 2nd revised ed., 1931. 1st Harper Torchbook ed., 1967. Tr. with introd. and notes by J.B. Baillie.

Heim, S. Mark. *Salvations: Truth and Difference in Religion*. Maryknoll, N.Y.: Orbis, 1995.

Herrmann, Wilhelm. *The Communion of the Christian with God (described on the basis of Luther's statements)*. Philadelphia: Fortress, 1971. A revision by R.W. Stewart of the 1st ed. of the tr. in 1896 by J. Sandys Stanyon of the 4th ed. of *Der Verkehr des Christen mit Gott* (Stuttgart: Cotta, 1886, 2nd ed.; 1st ed. 1886, 3rd ed. 1896, 4th ed. 1903, 5th and 6th eds. 1908; 7th ed. 1921 with J.C.B. Mohr in Tübingen).

———. "Der geschichtliche Christus der Grund unseres Glaubens," *Zeitschrift für Theologie und Kirche* 2:3 (1892), pp. 232–73.

———. *Schriften zur Grundlegung der Theologie*, vol. 1. Munich, 1966.

Heyward, Carter. *Redemption of God: A Theology of Mutual Relation*. Washington D.C.: University Press of America, 1982.

———. *Speaking of Christ: A Lesbian Feminist Voice*. New York: Pilgrim, 1989.

———. *Touching Our Strength: The Erotic as Power and the Love of God*. San Francisco: Harper & Row, 1989.

Hick, John. *Disputed Questions in Theology and the Philosophy of Religion*. New Haven: Yale University, 1993.

———. *God Has Many Names*. Philadelphia: Westminster, 1980.

———. "An Inspiration Christology for a Religiously Plural World," in Davis, ed., *Encountering Jesus*. Reprinted in Hick, *Disputed Questions*.

———. *An Interpretation of Religion: Human Responses to the Transcendent*. New Haven: Yale University, 1989.

———. "Jesus and the World Religions," in Hick, ed. *The Myth of God Incarnate*.

———. *The Metaphor of God Incarnate: Christology in a Pluralistic Age*. Louisville: Westminster/John Knox, 1993.

———, ed. *The Myth of God Incarnate*. Philadelphia: Westminster, 1977.

———. "The Non-Absoluteness of Christianity," in Hick and Knitter, *The Myth of Christian Uniqueness*.

———; Paul F. Knitter, eds. *The Myth of Christian Uniqueness: Toward a Pluralistic Theology of Religions*. Faith Meets Faith Series. Gen. Ed.: Paul Knitter. Maryknoll, N.Y.: Orbis, 1987.

Hodgson, Peter. *God in History: Shapes of Freedom*. Nashville: Abingdon, 1989.

Hoge, Dean R. *Converts, Dropouts, Returnees: A Study of Religious Change Among Catholics*. New York: Pilgrim, 1981.

———; Benton Johnson; Donald A Luidens. *Vanishing Boundaries: The Religion of Mainline Protestant Baby Boomers*. Louisville: Westminster/John Knox, 1994.

Horsley, Richard. *Jesus and the Spiral of Violence*. San Francisco: Harper & Row, 1987.

———. *Sociology and the Jesus Movement*. New York: Crossroad, 1989.

Hume, David. *An Inquiry Concerning Human Understanding*. 1748.

Hurst, L.D.; and N.T. Wright, eds. *The Glory of Christ in the New Testament: Studies in Christology in Memory of George Bradford Caird*. Oxford: Oxford University, 1987.

Kähler, Martin. *The So-called Historical Jesus and the Historic Biblical Christ.* Philadelphia: Fortress, 1964. Tr. of the first two essays in the 2nd ed. of *Der sogenannte historische Jesus und der geschichtliche, biblische Christus* (Leipzig, 1892) by Carl E. Braaten; 2nd ed., 1896. Note: the second, enlarged ed. of 1896 includes an essay in reply to Herrmann. The tr. includes parts of the 2nd ed., but not Kähler's reply to Herrmann. Herrmann's response to Kähler's book was published as "Der geschichtliche Christus der Grund unseres Glaubens," and reprinted in Herrmann, *Schriften zur Grundlegung der Theologie*, vol. 1, pp. 149–85.

Kant, Immanuel. *Religion within the Limits of Reason Alone.* New York: Harper & Row, 1960. Tr. from the second German ed. of 1794 (1st ed., 1793) with introd. and notes by Theodore M. Greene and Hoyt H. Hudson. Corrected and revised from the 1st English tr. of 1934.

———. *Allgemeine Naturgeschichte und Theorie des Himmels [Universal natural history and theory of the heavens].* Published anonymously, 1755.

Kattenbusch, Ferdinand. "In Sachen der Ritschlschen Theologie," *Die Christliche Welt* 12 (1898).

Kaufman, Gordon D. *God, Mystery, Diversity: Christian Theology in a Pluralistic World.* Minneapolis: Fortress Press, 1996.

———. *In Face of Mystery: A Constructive Theology.* Cambridge: Harvard University, 1993.

Kegley, Charles W., ed. *The Theology of Paul Tillich.* 2nd ed. New York: Pilgrim Press, 1982. Updated from original ed. (Macmillan, 1952) by Charles W. Kegley and Robert W. Bretall.

Kierkegaard, Søren. *Concluding Unscientific Postscript*, tr. David F. Swenson and Walter Lowrie (1991), in *Kierkegaard's Writings.*

———. *Either/Or*, tr. Walter Lowrie, 2 vols. (1987), in *Kierkegaard's Writings.*

———. *Fear and Trembling*, tr. Howard V. Hong and Edna H. Hong (1983), in *Kierkegaard's Writings.*

———. *Kierkegaard's Writings.* Princeton: Princeton University, 1978–. Gen. Ed. Howard V. Hong.

Kirkpatrick, Dow, ed. *The Finality of Christ.* Nashville: Abingdon, 1966.

Knitter, Paul F., Gen. Ed. Faith Meets Faith Series, Maryknoll, N.Y.: Orbis Books.

———. *No Other Name? A Critical Survey of Christian Attitudes Toward the World Religions.* American Society of Missiology Series, 7. Maryknoll, N.Y.: Orbis Books, 1985.

———. *One Earth, Many Religions: Multifaith Dialogue and Global Responsibility.* Maryknoll, N.Y.: Orbis Books, 1995.

———. "Theocentric Christology," *Theology Today* 40 (1983), pp. 130–49.

Körner, Stephan. *Categorial Frameworks.* Oxford: Basil Blackwell, 1974.

412   Bibliography

Küng, Hans. *Christianity and the World Religions: Paths of Dialogue with Islam, Hinduism, and Buddhism*. Garden City, N.Y.: Doubleday, 1986. 2nd ed., 1993.

————. *On Being a Christian*. Garden City, New York: Doubleday, 1984. Tr. of *Christ Sein* (Munich: R. Piper and Co., 1974) by Edward Quinn.

————. "Towards an Ecumenical Theology of Religions: Some Theses for Clarification." *Concilium* 183, pp. 119–25.

Lakatos, Imre. *The Methodology of Scientific Research Programmes*. John Worral, Gregory Currie, eds. Cambridge: Cambridge University, 1978.

————; Alan Musgrave, eds. *Criticism and the Growth of Knowledge: Proceedings of the International Colloquium in the Philosophy of Science*, London, 1965. New York: Cambridge University Press, 1970. Reprinted with corrections, 1974.

Lampe, G.W.H. *God As Spirit*. Oxford: Oxford University, 1977. The Bampton Lectures for 1976.

Lindbeck, George. *The Nature of Doctrine: Religion and Theology in a Postliberal Age*. Philadelphia: Westminster, 1984.

Livingston, James C. *Modern Christian Thought: From the Enlightenment to Vatican II*. New York: Macmillan, and London: Collier Macmillan, 1971.

Loisy, Alfred Firmin. *The Gospel and the Church*. Philadelphia: Fortress, 1976. 1st ed., 1903. Tr. by Christopher Home of *L'évangile et l'Eglise* (Paris, 1902).

Mack, Burton. *A Myth of Innocence: Mark and Christian Origins*. Philadelphia: Fortress, 1988.

MacKinnon, Edward; James E. Loder; W. Jim Neidhart; Christopher B. Kaiser. "Case Study on Quantum Complementarity and Christology," in Richardson and Wildman, eds., *Religion and Science*.

Macquarrie, John. *Jesus Christ in Modern Thought*. Philadelphia: Trinity, 1990.

Mandelbaum, Maurice. "Subjective, Objective, and Conceptual Relativisms." *The Monist* 62:4 (1979), pp. 403–23.

Meiland, Jack W.; Michael Krausz, eds. *Relativism: Cognitive and Moral*. Notre Dame: University of Notre Dame, 1982.

Mellert, Robert B. *What is Process Theology?* New York: Paulist, 1975.

Moltmann, Jürgen. *The Way of Jesus Christ: Christology in Messianic Dimensions*. San Francisco: HarperCollins, 1990. Tr. of *Weg Jesu Christi*.

Morris, Thomas V. *The Logic of God Incarnate*. Ithaca and London: Cornell University, 1986.

Murphy, Nancey. *Theology in the Age of Scientific Reasoning*. Ithaca and London: Cornell University, 1989.

Neville, Robert Cummings. *Behind the Masks of God: An Essay toward Comparative Theology*. Albany: State University of New York Press, 1991.

————. *A Theology Primer*. Albany: State University of New York, 1991.

————. *The Truth of Broken Symbols*. SUNY series in Religious Studies. Albany: State University of New York Press, 1996.

Newman, John Henry. *An Essay on the Development of Christian Doctrine*. Notre Dame, University of Notre Dame, 1989. Notre Dame Series in the Great Books.

Niebuhr, H. Richard. *Faith on Earth: An Inquiry into the Structure of Human Faith*. Richard R. Niebuhr, ed. New Haven: Yale University, 1989.

————. "Radical Faith—Incarnate and Revealed in History," in Niebuhr, *Radical Monotheism and Western Culture*.

————. *Radical Monotheism and Western Culture: With Supplementary Essays*. New York: Harper & Row, 1943.

————. "The Reconstruction of Faith," in *Faith on Earth*.

Nietzsche, Friedrich. *Thus Spoke Zarathustra*. Ed. and tr. by Walter Kaufmann in *The Portable Nietzsche*. New York: Penguin, 1954.

Ogden, Schubert M. *The Point of Christology*. San Francisco: Harper & Row, 1982.

Ottati, Douglas F. *Jesus Christ and Christian Vision*. Minneapolis: Fortress, 1989.

Panikkar, Raimon. *The Cosmotheandric Experience: Emerging Religious Consciousness*. Maryknoll, N.Y.: Orbis Books, 1993.

————. *The Unknown Christ of Hinduism: Towards an Ecumenical Christophany*. Revised and enlarged ed. Maryknoll, NY: Orbis, 1981. 1st ed., 1964.

Pannenberg, Wolfhart. *Jesus—God and Man*. Second ed. Philadelphia: Westminster Press, 1977. 1st ed., 1968. Tr. of *Grundzüge der Christologie* (Gütersloh: Gütersloher Verlagshaus Gerd Mohn, 1964) by Lewis L. Wilkins and Duane A. Priebe. "Afterword" tr. by Duane A. Priebe from the fifth German ed., 1976.

————. "Religious Pluralism and Conflicting Truth Claims: The Problem of a Theology of World Religions," in D'Costa, ed., *Christian Uniqueness Reconsidered*.

————. *Systematic Theology*, vol. 1. Grand Rapids: William B. Eerdmans, 1991. Tr. from *Systematische Theologie*, band 1 (Göttingen: Vandenhoek & Ruprecht, 1988) by Geoffrey W. Bromiley.

Pauck, Wilhelm; Marion Pauck. *Paul Tillich: His Life and Thought*. San Francisco: Harper & Row, 1989.

Peacocke, Arthur. *Theology for a Scientific Age: Being and Becoming—Natural, Divine, and Human*. Enlarged ed. Philadelphia: Fortress, 1993.

Pelikan, Jaroslav. *Development of Christian Doctrine: Some Historical Prolegomena*. New Haven and London: Yale University, 1969.

————. *Jesus Through the Centuries: His Place in the History of Culture*. New Haven: Yale University, 1985.

Peters, Ted. *God as Trinity: Relationality and Temporality in the Divine Life*. Louisville: Westminster/John Knox Press, 1993.

———. *God—The World's Future: Systematic Theology for a Postmodern Era*. Minneapolis: Fortress Press, 1992.

Pittenger, W. Norman. *Christ and Christian Faith: Some Presuppositions and Implications of the Incarnation*. New York, Round Table, 1941.

———. *Christology Reconsidered*. London: SCM, 1970.

———. *The Word Incarnate: A Study of the Doctrine of the Person of Christ*. New York, Harper, 1959.

Puddefoot, John C.; Arthur Peacocke. "Case Study on Information Theory and Revelation," in Richardson and Wildman, eds. *Religion and Science*.

Rahner, Karl. "Christology within an Evolutionary View of the World," in *Theological Investigations*, vol. V, pp. 157–92.

———. "Considerations on the Development of Dogma," in *Theological Investigations*, vol. IV, pp. 3–35.

———. "The Development of Dogma," in *Theological Investigations*, vol. I, pp. 39–77.

———. *Foundations of Christian Faith: An Introduction to the Idea of Christianity*. New York: Crossroad, 1987. Tr. in 1978 from *Grundkurs des Glaubens: Einführung in den Begriff des Christentums* (Herder Freiburg im Breisgau, 1976) by William V. Dych.

———. *Theological Investigations*. New York: Seabury, 1974–1981.

Richardson, W. Mark; Wesley J. Wildman, eds. *Religion and Science: History, Method, Dialogue*. New York: Routledge, 1996.

Robinson, John A.T. *Honest to God*. London: SCM, 1963.

———. *The Human Face of God*. London: SCM, 1973.

Ruether, Rosemary Radford. *Faith and Fratricide: The Theological Roots of Anti-Semitism*. New York: Seabury, 1974.

Samartha, Stanley J. *One Christ, Many Religions: Toward a Revised Christology*. Maryknoll, N.Y.: Orbis Books, 1991.

Schillebeeckx, Edward. *Christ: The Experience of Jesus as Lord*. New York: Seabury Press, 1980. Tr. of *Gerechtigheid en liefde*.

———. *Jesus: An Experiment in Christology*. New York: Seabury Press, 1979. Tr. of *Jezus*.

Schleiermacher, Friedrich D.E. *The Christian Faith*. Ed. by H.R. Mackintosh; J.S. Stewart. Edinburgh: T. & T. Clark, 1928. Tr. of the 2nd German ed. of *Der Christliche Glaube*, 1830–31; 1st German ed., 1821–22.

———. *On Religion: Speeches to its Cultured Despisers*. Cambridge: Cambridge University, 1988. Tr. with introd. and notes by Richard Crouter from the final 1831 ed. (1st ed., 1799).

Schweitzer, Albert. *The Mysticism of Paul the Apostle*. London, 1931. Tr. by W. Montgomery.

————. *The Quest of the Historical Jesus*. 1926. Tr. of *Geschichte der Leben-Jesu-Forschung*. 1st German ed., 1906 (as *Von Reimarus zu Wrede*); 6th ed., 1950.

Smart, Ninian; Steven Konstantine. *Christian Systematic Theology in a World Context*. World Christian Theology Series. Minneapolis: Fortress, 1991.

Smith, Huston. *Forgotten Truth: The Primordial Tradition*. New York: Harper & Row, 1976.

————. *The World's Religions*. New York: HarperCollins, 1991.

Spinoza, Baruch. *Tractatus theologico-politicus*. 1670.

Starkey, John. *The Easter Experiences*. Boston: Boston University, forthcoming doctoral dissertation, 1998.

Strauss, David Friedrich. *The Life of Jesus Critically Examined*. Philadelphia: Fortress Press, 1972. Ed. by Peter C. Hodgson. Tr. from the 1840 4th German ed. of *Das Leben-Jesu kritisch bearbeitet* by George Eliot. 1st German ed., 1835.

Suchocki, Marjorie Hewitt. *God, Christ, Church: A Practical Guide to Process Theology*. Revised ed. New York: Crossroad, 1989. 1st ed., 1982.

Swidler, Leonard. *After the Absolute: The Dialogical Future of Religious Reflection*. Minneapolis: Agusburg Fortress, 1990.

Swoyer, Chris. "True For," in Meiland and Krausz, *Relativism*.

Sykes, S.W. "Ernst Troeltsch and Christianity's Essence," in Clayton, *Ernst Troeltsch and the Future of Theology*, pp. 139–71.

————. "Note" on "What Does 'Essence of Christianity' Mean?" in Troeltsch, *Ernst Troeltsch*, pp. 180–81.

Tambiah, Stanley Jeyaraja. *Magic, Science, Religion, and the Scope of Rationality*. Cambridge: Cambridge University, 1990. The Lewis Henry Morgan Lectures for 1984.

Teilhard, Pierre de Chardin. *The Phenomenon of Man*. New York: Harper, 1959. Tr. of *Le Phenomène Humain*, Editions du Seuil, 1955.

Tertullian (c.160–c.225). *De carne Christi*.

TeSelle, Eugene. *Christ in Context: Divine Purpose and Human Possibility*. Philadelphia: Fortress, 1975.

Thangaraj, M. Thomas, ed. *The Crucified Guru: An Experiment in Cross-Cultural Christology*. Nashville: Abingdon Press, 1994.

Tillich, Paul. *Systematic Theology*, 3 vols. Chicago: University of Chicago, 1951, 1957, 1963. Phoenix paperback ed., 1976.

Troeltsch, Ernst. *The Absoluteness of Christianity and the History of Religions*. Atlanta: John Knox, 1971. Tr. of *Die Absolutheit des Christentums und die Re-*

ligionsgeschichte (Tübingen: 1st ed., 1902; 2nd ed., 1912; 3rd ed., 1929; Hamburg and Munich, 1969: new ed. of 1929).

————. "Aus der religiösen Bewegung der Gegenwart," *Die neue Rundschau* (1910), pp. 1169–1185.

————. *The Christian Faith*. Minneapolis: Fortress Press, 1991. Ed. by Gertrud von le Fort, with a Foreword by Marta Troeltsch. Fortress Texts in Modern Theology, Brian A. Gerrish, General Ed. Tr. with an introd. by Garret E. Paul from *Glaubenslehre*, a series of lectures delivered at the University of Heidelberg, 1912–13 (Berlin: Duncker und Humblot, 1925).

————. *Christian Thought: Its History and Application*. Ed. with an introd. and index by Baron F. von Hügel. New York: Meridian Books, 1957.

————. "Christianity and the History of Religion" (1897), in Troeltsch, *Religion in History*.

————. "The Dogmatics of the History-of-Religions School" (1913), in Troeltsch, *Religion in History*, pp. 87–108. New ed. of "The Dogmatics of the Religionsgeschichtliche Schule," *American Journal of Theology* 17/1 (January, 1913), pp. 1–21, in the light of Troeltsch's later additions in *Gesammelte Schriften* 2, pp. 500–24, tr. by Walter E. Wyman, Jr.

————. *Ernst Troeltsch: Writings on Theology and Religion*. Ed. and tr. by Robert Morgan and Michael Pye. Atlanta: John Knox, 1977.

————. "The Essence of the Modern Spirit" (1907), in Troeltsch, *Religion in History*.

————. "Faith and History" (1910), in Troeltsch, *Religion in History*.

————. *Gesammelte Schriften*. 4 vols. Tübingen, 1912–1925.

————. "Half a Century of Theology: A Review" (1908), in *Ernst Troeltsch: Writings on Theology and Religion*.

————. "Historical and Dogmatic Method in Theology" (1898), in Troeltsch, *Religion in History*.

————. *Der Historismus und seine Probleme*, vol. I: *Das logische Problem der Geschichtsphilosophie* (1922), published as *Gesammelte Schriften* III.

————. "Meine Bücher" (1922), in *Gesammelte Schriften* IV.

————. "Modern Philosophy of History" (1904), in Troeltsch, *Religion in History*. Tr. from the revised edition in *Gesammelte Schriften* II, pp. 673–728, by James Luther Adams.

————. "On the Possibility of a Liberal Christianity" (1910), in Troeltsch, *Religion in History*.

————. "On the Question of the Religious A Priori" (1909), in Troeltsch, *Religion in History*.

————. "The Place of Christianity among the World Religions" (1923), in Troeltsch, *Christian Thought*.

————. "Religion and the Science of Religion" (1906), in *Ernst Troeltsch: Writings on Theology and Religion*.

————. *Religion in History*. Minneapolis: Fortress, 1991. Ed. and tr. by James Luther Adams and Walter F. Bense with an introd. by James Luther Adams.

————. "The Significance of the Historical Existence of Jesus for Faith." Tr. by Robert Morgan from *Die Bedeutung der Geschichtlichkeit Jesu für den Glauben* (Tübingen, 1911), in *Ernst Troeltsch: Writings on Theology and Religion*.

————. "The Social Philosophy of Christianity" (1922), in Troeltsch, *Religion in History*.

————. *The Social Teaching of the Christian Churches*. 2 vols. London, 1931. Tr. of *Die Soziallehren der christlichen Kirchen und Gruppen*. Tübingen: J.C.B. Mohr, 1912.

————. "What Does 'Essence of Christianity' Mean?" (1st ed., 1903; 2nd ed., 1913), in *Ernst Troeltsch: Writings on Theology and Religion*.

————. *Ernst Troeltsch: Writings on Theology and Religion*. Ed. and tr. by Robert Morgan and Michael Pye. Atlanta: John Knox, 1977.

Tyrrell, George. *Christianity at the Cross-Roads*. London: Allen and Unwin, 1963. 1st ed, Longmans, Green and Company, 1909.

Van Buren, Paul M. *Christ in Context*. Vol. 3 of A *Theology of the Jewish-Christian Reality*. 3 vols. San Francisco: Harper & Row, 1980, 1983, 1988.

Ward, Keith. *Religion and Creation*. Oxford: Oxford University, 1996.

————. *Religion and Revelation: A Theology of Revelation in the World's Religions*. Oxford: Oxford University, 1994.

Weber, Max. *The Protestant Ethic and the Spirit of Capitalism*. London: Allen & Unwin, 1930.

Weinberg, Steven. *The First Three Minutes: A Modern View of the Origin of the Universe*. 2nd ed. London and New York: HarperCollins, 1993.

Weiss, Johannes. *Jesus' Proclamation of the Kingdom of God*. Philadelphia: Fortress, 1971. ET of 1st ed. of *Die Predigt Jesu vom Reiche Gottes* (Göttingen: Vandenhoek & Ruprecht, 1892, 1st ed.; 2nd and greatly expanded ed., 1900). Tr. with an introd. by Richard H. Hiers and D. Larrimore Holland.

Welch, Claude. *Protestant Thought in the Nineteenth Century*. 2 vols. New Haven: Yale University, 1972, 1985.

Whitehead, Alfred North. *Adventures of Ideas*. New York: Macmillan, 1933.

————. *Process and Reality*. New York: Macmillan, 1929. Corrected ed., 1978.

Williams, Rowan D. *Arius*. London: Darton, Longman, and Todd, 1987.

Wyman, Walter E., Jr., *The Concept of Glaubenslehre: Ernst Troeltsch and the Theological Heritage of Schleiermacher*. Chico: Scholars Press, 1983.

————. "Theology After Ritschl: The Case of Troeltsch," in Sheila Briggs and

Richard P. Busse, eds. *Papers of the Nineteenth Century Working Group*, American Academy of Religion, 1989 Annual Meeting.

Yasukata, Toshimasa. *Ernst Troeltsch: Systematic Theologian of Radical Historicality*. Atlanta: Scholars Press, 1986. AAR Academy Series, 55.

Young, Frances. "A Cloud of Witnesses," in Hick, ed., *The Myth of God Incarnate*.

———. "Two Roots or a Tangled Mass," in Hick, ed., *The Myth of God Incarnate*.

Index